THE GRANGER MOVEMENT

THE
GRANGER MOVEMENT

A STUDY OF AGRICULTURAL
ORGANIZATION AND ITS POLITICAL, ECONOMIC
AND SOCIAL MANIFESTATIONS

1870—1880

SOLON JUSTUS BUCK

UNIVERSITY OF NEBRASKA PRESS · Lincoln

First Bison Book printing April, 1963
Second Bison Book printing October, 1965

Bison Book edition reprinted by arrangement with the Harvard University Press.

PREFACE

SOCIAL unrest has been one of the most marked characteristics of the last half-century in the United States. During this period the country, and especially the western part of it, has been transformed from a comparatively simple agricultural community into a complex modern industrial state; and in the process of adjustment the agricultural class of the population, among others, has been inclined to feel aggrieved. The result has been a series of radical agitations on the part of the farmers for the improvement, by organized effort, of their relative condition. Of this general " farmers' movement," the first wave, which is the subject of this study, began with the establishment of the order of Patrons of Husbandry in 1867, slowly gathered headway for a few years, and then suddenly culminated in a series of startling manifestations, political and economic, during the years from 1873 to 1875. From then on to the end of the decade, this " Granger movement " gradually subsided, although many of its features were embodied in the programs of the more radical agricultural movements which took their rise in the early eighties.

It may be well to explain at the outset that this is not intended to be a history of the " Grange," as the order of Patrons of Husbandry is frequently called. The term " Granger movement," nevertheless, is used advisedly: in the first place, because the phrase has the sanction of considerable usage, both contemporary and later, in the sense in which it is here applied; and secondly, because the movement did seize upon the order of Patrons of Husbandry as an efficient means of organization and a convenient rallying point. The contentions of members of the order that it should not be held responsible for many of the features of the movement are doubtless sound, and it should be understood that the term "Granger" is here frequently used in the derived sense as applying to the general agrarian movement which centered around the secret and professedly non-partisan order of Patrons of Husbandry.

The first chapter, which is introductory to the rest of the book and is intended to bring out the causes of the movement, is concerned with the condition of the farmers in the different sections of the country during the decade 1870–80 and their relations to the various economic and political problems of the day. Chapter II tells the story of the Grange and the other organizations by which the farmers proposed to effect their regeneration; and Chapter III is devoted to the political aspects of the movement — the independent parties which grew out of it and the attempts of the farmers to use their organizations for influencing legislation. The three following chapters deal with the first serious attempt to subject railways to effective regulation by the state, an attempt which, though independent in its origins, became so closely interwoven with the movement for agricultural organization as to be essentially a part of it. In Chapter VII the efforts of the farmers to render themselves independent of middlemen and manufacturers by the establishment of coöperative enterprises are treated, while Chapter VIII sets forth the influence of the movement on social and economic conditions. The last chapter attempts to trace the connection of the movement with later organizations of farmers and working-men and to indicate its relation to the general field of American history.

My obligations to library officials, secretaries of state granges, and others who have assisted me in the collection of material or the preparation of the manuscript are too numerous to permit of individual mention. To Professor F. J. Turner of Harvard University and Professor C. W. Alvord of the University of Illinois, who have read the entire manuscript, I am indebted for valuable criticisms and suggestions. I am also under obligations to Professors A. B. Hart and E. F. Gay of Harvard, and Professor B. H. Meyer of the Interstate Commerce Commission for critical reading of several chapters. To the Carnegie

Institution of Washington acknowledgments are due for an appropriation which has enabled me to make a much more thorough study of the subject than would otherwise have been possible.

S. J. B.

The University of Illinois,
Urbana–Champaign.

CONTENTS

CHAPTER I

FUNDAMENTAL CONDITIONS

CHAPTER II

ORGANIZATION

CHAPTER III

THE GRANGER MOVEMENT AS A POLITICAL FORCE

CHAPTER IV

GRANGER RAILWAY LEGISLATION (ILLINOIS)

CHAPTER V

GRANGER RAILWAY LEGISLATION (CONTINUED)

CHAPTER VI

GRANGER RAILWAY LEGISLATION (CONTINUED)

CHAPTER VII

BUSINESS COÖPERATION

CHAPTER VIII

SOCIAL AND EDUCATIONAL FEATURES

CHAPTER IX
CONCLUSION

BIBLIOGRAPHY

ILLUSTRATIONS

THE GRANGER MOVEMENT

CHAPTER I

FUNDAMENTAL CONDITIONS

PERIODS of agrarian discontent have been of frequent occurrence in the world's history and it has generally been assumed that they were preceded or caused by depressions in the condition of the agricultural population. Recent investigations into the causes of the English peasants' revolt of 1381 and the Peasants' War in Germany in 1524–25 have suggested that the contrary may be the case: the status of the peasant seems in both instances to have been one of gradual improvement, and the risings, attempts to hasten the amelioration. Similarly it would be untrue to say that the condition of the American farmers was retrograding in the decade following the Civil War. Nevertheless, the farmers believed that they were not advancing so rapidly as the other classes of American society, and it was useless to point out to them that they lived much better and enjoyed far more comforts than their grandfathers had, or to tell them that their financial embarrassments were due to extravagent desires.[1] The fact was, their standard of living was advancing nearly, if not quite, as rapidly as that of other ranks of society, while their incomes were not increasing in the same proportion. The causes of this situation, and of the Granger movement, are to be sought primarily in economic conditions, and to a less extent in political, social, and intellectual conditions, as they affected the American farmer.

THE AGRICULTURAL SITUATION

Although the Granger movement was national in its scope and some of the conditions which it sought to remedy were

[1] *Nation*, xvii. 68 (July 31, 1873).

prevalent throughout the country, still the characteristics of the movement differed in the various sections and were conditioned in part on differences in the agricultural situation.

The northeastern part of the United States, including New England and the Atlantic coastal plain stretching as far south as Chesapeake Bay, was primarily a region of diversified farming. The presence of numerous large centers of population made dairying and market gardening profitable employments; while in New England large crops of hay and potatoes were produced and further south the raising of fruit for canning was becoming an extensive industry. The production of cereals in this region was small in proportion to the population and a large part of the food supply had to be shipped in from the West.[1] The pressure of competition due to the great increase in agricultural production in the more undeveloped parts of the country and the cheapening of through transportation was beginning to manifest itself in a decline in value of eastern farm lands, which was to become far more serious in a later period.[2] During the seventies, however, the agriculturists of this section were still fairly prosperous because of personal thrift, a diversified production, and convenient markets.

A somewhat similar situation prevailed in western New York and Pennsylvania and eastern Ohio. This region had been the granary of the continent shortly before the war and it was still largely engaged in the production of cereals in 1870; but the stress of western competition and the ravages of insect pests were leading farmers to turn their energies more and more to diversified agriculture and particularly to dairy farming. The dairy interests of this section grew with great rapidity during the decade from 1860 to 1870 and at the latter date New York, Pennsylvania, and Ohio led all the states in the production of butter and cheese. Although the farm property

---

[1] Charles Seymour, " A Western View of Interstate Transportation," in *Atlantic Monthly*, xxx. 347 (September, 1873).

[2] C. F. Emerick, " An Analysis of the Agricultural Discontent in the United States," in *Political Science Quarterly*, xi. 452–463 (September, 1896); A. H. Peters, " The Depreciation of Farming Land," in *Quarterly Journal of Economics*, iv. 18–33 (October, 1889); J. R. Elliot, *American Farms*, bk. ii. ch. iii.

in this region also was already beginning to depreciate in value, there seems to have been little discontent.[1] While the absence of any considerable discontent among the farmers in this section, and in the northeastern section as well, may have been due in part to diversified farming and a fair amount of prosperity, still it seems that the process of natural selection which resulted from the westward movement of population had something to do with it. The great flood of migration to the Middle West during the first half of the century drained off the elements which were disadvantageously situated or were inclined to be discontented with their lot, while those who resisted the attractions of the West were generally of the more prosperous and conservative class.

The southern states of the Union remained, agriculturally, as they had been before the war, producers of staples. Cotton, rice, sugar, and tobacco were the principal crops in different sections, but corn and some other grains were also produced largely, though not in sufficient quantities to supply the demand for home consumption.[2] The South was left by the war in a state of complete exhaustion in which agriculture shared to the fullest extent: farms had been devastated or neglected, often the owners had been killed in battle or rendered incapable of work, and worst of all the complete change in the industrial system made a return to normal agricultural conditions extremely slow. Most of the large land-owners among the whites had been unaccustomed to personal manual labor in the conduct of their plantations, while the blacks were altogether untrained in the management of agricultural operations and unused to labor except under supervision. The available capital of the section had been largely drained out by the exigencies of the war. This fact made more difficult the development of any wage labor system.[3] Nor did the political conditions of the South in the reconstruction period conduce to the welfare of

[1] *United States Census*, 1870, volume on *Agriculture;* Emerick, in *Political Science Quarterly*, xi. 454 (September, 1896).

[2] *United States Census*, 1870, volume on *Agriculture.*

[3] W. L. Fleming, *Civil War and Reconstruction in Alabama*, 251–283, 710–733; C. H. Otken, *The Ills of the South*, ch. i.

agriculture. The overwhelming extravagance and corruption, ignorance and bad management of the negro, " carpet-bag," and " scalawag " governments greatly increased the rate of taxation, and the inefficiency of local government resulted in perpetual disorder and disregard for the rights of property.[1]

Two undesirable features of the agricultural situation in the South were inherited from ante-bellum times: the credit system based upon crop mortgages; and the excessive attention devoted to the production of great staples, especially cotton. Although the credit system was in existence even in colonial times, it received a new lease of life as a result of the general poverty of the agricultural class, both black and white, at the close of the war. Under this system the impecunious farmer purchased all his supplies during a year on credit from a merchant who relied on the sale of the forthcoming crop for payment. Though apparently a plan to help the farmer tide over the hard times, it was really an injury to him in several ways. It put him in the power of the merchant, and thus eliminated all competition in the sale of commodities, the result of which and of the natural risks and inconveniences of the system was a raising of prices far above the normal cash scale;[2] and it led inevitably to carelessness, waste, and extravagance. As a result when the farmer came to balance up at the end of the year he frequently found himself still in debt to the merchant, after the disposal of his crop. In many cases the annual residue of debt increased year by year until finally crops, stock, farm, and all were absorbed by the ruinous system.[3]

The over-production of cotton, also, was partially a result of the credit system, although the roots went back to the beginning of agriculture in the South. The indebted farmer naturally wanted to devote most of his energies to the one crop which

[1] Fleming, *Civil War and Reconstruction in Alabama*, 571–607, 733–771; J. W. Garner, *Reconstruction in Mississippi;* C. W. Howard, " Condition of Agriculture in the Cotton States," in United States Commissioner of Agriculture, *Reports*, 1874, pp. 215–238; J. T. Trowbridge, *The South*.

[2] It has been estimated that prices were fully twenty-five per cent higher because of the prevailing credit system. Otken, *Ills of the South*, ch. ii.

[3] M. B. Hammond, *The Cotton Industry in the United States*, ch. v.

brought in money, and in addition the influence of the merchant to whom he was indebted was usually exerted to induce him to produce as much cotton as possible with which to pay off the accumulated debt and purchase new supplies. As a result of this and other factors, there was an over-production of cotton, which led to a rapid decline in prices, and often the value of a farmer's crop grew less and less in spite of its increase in quantity. This devotion to cotton meant also a neglect of corn and meat raising and a consequent necessity for the purchase of additional supplies through the medium of the merchant and the omnivorous credit system.[1] From all these causes southern agriculture was far from flourishing in the reconstruction period.

The great prairie states of the upper Mississippi Valley, stretching from Ohio to the edge of settlement in Kansas and Nebraska, were also producers of staples, but here the staples were the cereal crops of wheat and corn. This section was the center of agricultural discontent during the period with which we are dealing, and it was here that the protective movement among the farmers manifested itself most vigorously. The farmers in this area were from the first handicapped by the notion that they were to make their fortunes by raising wheat, and for a long time were unable to grasp the fact that conditions of soil, climate, and market facilities demanded a change from the shiftless and ruinous one-crop method to a more intensive and diversified agriculture. The states of the upper Mississippi Valley were experiencing the same conditions which had been faced in western New York a generation or so earlier; but here the farmers seemed determined to resist the westward tendency of the wheat industry, and for a long time refused to turn their attention to the now more profitable stock raising and dairy farming.[2]

Even as early as the fifties the farmers of Illinois and Wisconsin were feeling the depression in the wheat industry and

[1] M. B. Hammond, "The Southern Farmer and the Cotton Question," in *Political Science Quarterly*, xi. 450–475; Otken, *Ills of the South*, chs. iv, vii; National Grange, *Proceedings*, ix. 60–63 (November, 1875).

[2] See B. H. Hibbard, *The History of Agriculture in Dane County, Wisconsin*, 121–134, for an excellent account of the one-crop period and its results.

some of the more progressive were thinking of turning their attention to other lines, but the transition was delayed by the remarkable rise in the price of wheat in 1854-55, usually attributed to the Crimean War, and again by the prevailing high prices of the Civil War period. During the latter part of the sixties, and the early seventies, depressed conditions returned and the competition from the virgin wheat fields of the farther West finally forced the long delayed transition to a more diversified and soil-saving agriculture. Meanwhile the farmers of Illinois, Wisconsin, and parts of Iowa and Minnesota, burdened with debt and almost despairing, but unable to see that their own inertia and lack of progressiveness were partly at fault, began to look about them for the causes of their misfortune. They fastened the blame upon the bankers, the railways, the legislatures, the tariff, and monopolies, and their grievances along these lines were legion and some of them well founded. These are matters, however, of a national rather than sectional character, and will be treated later on.

Agriculture on a large scale was a new industry in California, for it was not until the gold fever began to die down that people realized that the soil of the state was laden with other than mineral wealth. Oregon, on the other hand, had been from the first an agricultural state and had helped to furnish California with her supply of cereals, a large part of which also came from the prairie states and Chile. In 1862 California first produced enough wheat for her own consumption and from that time on the increase in cereal production was rapid, until by 1880 the total crop in the state had reached forty-five million bushels. The rise of a great staple wheat crop in California involved the farmers in a peculiar problem of distribution. Because of the geographical position of the state, seven-eighths of the surplus was shipped directly to Liverpool and the price was supposed to be regulated by the Liverpool quotation and the cost of shipment. The business of shipping this grain was not in the hands of the farmers but of commission merchants who bought up the crop, stored it in their warehouses, and shipped it to Liverpool. It was not long before the farmers reached the conclusion that a monopoly had developed among these commission men or middlemen, as they were called, and that the price which they received for their grain was no longer controlled by the Liverpool market but by a grain ring which went so far as to juggle the Liverpool quotations in order to deceive them. This situation was the immediate cause of the farmers' movement in that state.[1]

FARMERS AND RAILROADS

The farmer's prosperity depended as much on his ability to send the crop to the consumer cheaply and get back in return the variety of articles which he required for his consumption, as it did on his ability to produce those crops. To help in the solution of this problem of distribution, two things were desired by the farmers: a cheapening of transportation and a reduction of the cost of handling commodities by the middlemen who stood between producer and consumer. It was in connection with these two aspects of the problem of distribution that the work of the Granger movement was most significant.

At the time with which we are concerned the problem of transportation in the United States had come to be, in the main, a railroad problem; and other means of transportation were of subsidiary importance only. The period of active railroad construction in the fifties had been checked by the panic of 1857, and there was no opportunity for a revival until the close of the war. But from the end of the war to the panic of 1873 the amount of railroad construction increased by leaps and bounds. The great western plains were then first bridged by a railroad to the Pacific; the upper Mississippi Valley was covered with a network of roads; and in the South the railway system, shattered by the war, was repaired, reorganized and extended.[2]

The mania for railroad construction which developed out of the real need for transportation facilities very soon outran

[1] Ezra Carr, *The Patrons of Husbandry on the Pacific Coast*, 65–87.
[2] C. F. Adams, Jr., "The Granger Movement," in *North American Review*, cxx. 397 (April, 1875).

the limits of ordinary conservative capital and a new class of promoters was developed — men who were able to build roads without capital of their own and at the expense of the people.[1] The desire for greater transportation facilities led towns, counties, states, and the federal government to furnish a large part of the means of construction in the shape of loans or donations of bonds, purchases of stock, and grants of land.[2] Not satisfied with public charity, the promoters appealed to private individuals along the right of way, and more particularly to farmers who would be benefited by the new road. A great many shares were thus disposed of to the unsuspecting farmers, who frequently paid for them by giving mortgages on their farms, and who expected to get good returns on the stock and at the same time to assist in the creation of a highway which would enable them to market their products more readily.[3]

The farmer was doomed to disappointment in both of his expectations. The dividends on stock did not materialize, and the new transportation was not cheap enough to offset the increased competition. As a result of the operations of construction rings and unscrupulous directors many of these roads went through receiverships and reorganizations in the course of which the stock purchased by the farmers and municipalities was not seldom wiped out.[4] The farmer who had invested with a view to the development of the country thus found himself with a mortgage on his land, his railway stock worthless, and

[1] *Nation*, xx. 148 (March 4, 1875).

[2] E. R. Johnson, *American Railway Transportation*, ch. xxii; W. W. Cook, *The Corporation Problem*, 96–99; J. B. Sanborn, *Congressional Grants of Land in Aid of Railways;* J. W. Million, *State Aid to Railways in Missouri;* C. W. Pierson, " The Rise of the Granger Movement," in *Popular Science Monthly*, xxxii. 202 (December, 1887); F. A. Cleveland and F. W. Powell, *Railroad Promotion and Capitalization*, chs. xii–xiv.

[3] Johnson, *American Railway Transportation*, 320; Cook, *Corporation Problem*, 28; J. W. Cary, *Organization and History of the Chicago, Milwaukee, and St. Paul Railway Company;* J. G. Thompson, *The Rise and Decline of the Wheat Growing Industry in Wisconsin*, ch. ix. An investigation into the records of eight counties in Wisconsin disclosed about thirteen hundred of these mortgages amounting to more than a million and a half dollars. R. E. Smith, *The Wisconsin Granger Movement* (Ms.).

[4] *Nation*, xx. 148 (March 4, 1875).

the expected advantages from the road a chimera. His taxes, moreover, were increased by the investment or donation which his town or county had made for the same purpose. This was one of the principal causes which operated to produce a somewhat blind antagonism among the agricultural population towards railroads and everything connected with them. The farmers felt that, having furnished, either in their private or public capacity, a large share of the funds for the construction of the roads, they were entitled to more advantages therefrom. A result of this feeling was a sporadic movement which might be termed a forerunner of the Granger movement and had for its object the repudiation of the county and municipal railway bonds. An attempt was made to have them declared illegal, because issued for the benefit of private corporations; but when a case finally reached the Supreme Court of the United States, their legality was upheld as well as the public character of the railway companies, a decision which was later to be of importance in the contest over state control.[1]

Previous to about 1870 there was little thought of public control of railways: they were looked upon as blessings to the country, the extension of which should be encouraged, rather than checked by subjecting them to any interference. It was generally supposed that competition would prove an efficient regulator, and so the demand was for more railroads and hence more competition rather than for governmental regulation.[2] During the period of railway expansion that followed the war, however, it began to be evident that competition was not going

[1] C. F. Adams, Jr., "The Granger Movement," in *North American Review*, cxx. 410 (April, 1875); *Nation*, xvii. 140 (August 28, 1873), xxi. 18 (July 8, 1875), xxv. 166 (September 13, 1877); D. C. Cloud, *Monopolies and the People*, 114–124; M. H. Carpenter, *Speech on the Power of the Legislature to Govern Corporations* (pamphlet, 1874), 16–18; Case of Olcott *v.* The Supervisors, 16 *Wallace*, 678. See below, p. 209.

[2] C. F. Adams, Jr., *Railroads, their Origin and Problems*, 118–120; E. R. A. Seligman, "Railway Tariffs and the Interstate Commerce Commission," in *Political Science Quarterly*, ii. 408 (September, 1887); W. Larrabee, *The Railroad Question*, 129; Windom Committee, *Report of the Select Committee on Transportation Routes to the Seaboard*, 1874, i. 242; National Grange, *Proceedings*, ix. 11 (November, 1875).

to curb the power of the railroad corporations because of the ease with which consolidations were effected. Agreements between the various trunk lines for the maintenance of rates, made necessary by the ruinous rate wars, were also frequent during this period, and nothing could serve better to arouse the anger of the farmers and rural politicians than the thought of two or three railroad magnates meeting together and agreeing to maintain a certain rate or, as they put it, to impose an additional tax on the products of agricultural labor.[1] It was evident, moreover, that the very nature of the case precluded competition at the vast majority of intermediate stations, and that these might suffer because of increased competition at the junction points.[2]

There were many things in the management of railroads in the early seventies which tended to arouse antagonism on the part not only of the farmers but of the public in general. Prominent among those was the uncompromising attitude assumed by the railroad authorities. Shielding themselves behind the Dartmouth College decision and asserting their private character so far as the management of the business was concerned, they denied the right of the public, the states, or the nation to regulate or in any way interfere with their operations.[3] There seems to have been, also, a general disregard of the convenience of customers on the part of railway officials and employees. Travelers and shippers are said to have been subjected to all sorts of discourtesies and even injuries and any attempt to secure justice was apt to result in persecutions by the powerful corporation.[4] The feeling was quite general in the West that

---

[1] *Nation*, xvii. 289 (October 30, 1873), xix. 326 (November 19, 1874); Speech of Horace Greeley at Minneapolis in 1871, quoted in National Grange, *Proceedings*, xiv. 29 (1880).

[2] Johnson, *American Railway Transportation*, 213–227; Cook, *Corporation Problem*, 18, 166–181; A. B. Stickney, *The Railway Problem*, 224–226; Windom Committee, *Report*, i. 115–122, app., 219.

[3] Adams, *Railroads*, 127; Seligman, in *Political Science Quarterly*, ii. 408 (September, 1887); Wisconsin Railroad Commission, *Reports*, 1874, p. 62.

[4] J. A. Coleman, "The Fight of a Man with a Railroad," and "My Railroad Fight in and out of Court," in *Atlantic*, xxx. 641–653, xxxi. 610–618 (December, 1872; May, 1873). See also *Nation*, xix. 36 (July 16, 1875); *Atlantic*, xxxi. 380–

many of these abuses were due to the fact that the railroads were owned and controlled by men who lived in the East or in Europe. "Absentee ownership" was the term used and it was maintained that the stockholders and directors were far less amenable to public opinion than would have been the case had they been residents of the affected districts.[1]

Complaint was also made of the influence which was exercised by the railroad corporations over legislators and public officials. The most generally prevalent form of this influence was the free pass system, by which all public officials from the highest judges to the local selectmen received free transportation for themselves and their families over the lines of interested railroads. To say that no return was expected from this munificence is absurd. Even if direct services were not desired, it was intended that a frame of mind should be created which would prevent unfavorable treatment by the public officials. But the corporations did not stop with passes, and bribery appears to have flourished in more subtle forms, such as the transfer of valuable stock to legislators at a price much below the market value, and that to be paid out of the dividends. This is said to have been the case in the famous *Crédit Mobilier* scandal in Congress, an investigation of which revealed the purpose of preventing any unfriendly legislation, by distributing stock among members of Congress.[2]

It was in the shape of rates or tariffs, however, that the railroad problem was most closely brought home to the farmer. The charges preferred were that railroad rates in general were

384, xxxii. 509–512 (March, October, 1873); Adams, in *North American Review*, cxx. 402–404 (April, 1875); Martin, *Grange Movement*, ch. iv; Paine, *Granger Movement in Illinois*, 18; S. L. Clemens and C. D. Warner, *The Gilded Age* (Hartford, 1874), 264–269.

[1] Illinois Railroad Commission, *Reports*, 1874, p. 17; Adams, in *North American Review*, cxx. 398–402 (April, 1875); Cook, *Corporation Problem*, 16; Paine, *Granger Movement in Illinois*, 17.

[2] J. F. Rhodes, *History of the United States since the Compromise of 1850*, vii. 1–19; *Nation*, xix. 36 (July 16, 1875); Illinois State Grange, *Proceedings*, iv. 103 (1875); *House Reports*, 42 Cong., 3 sess., no. 77; W. A. Dunning, *Reconstruction, Political and Economic*, 231–233; Larrabee, *Railroad Question*, 205–230; Martin, *Grange Movement*, chs. vii, viii.

too high and that gross discrimination was practised in fixing them. When the Iowa farmer was burning corn for fuel, because at fifteen cents a bushel it was cheaper than coal, while at the same time it was selling for a dollar in the East, he felt that there was something wrong and quite naturally accused the railroads of extortion.[1] Furthermore he looked upon the various discriminations in rates, justifiable or otherwise, as evidence of extortion; for if the railroad could afford to make one rate in one instance why could it not in all? The railroads and their apologists, in answer to this charge of extortionate rates, pointed to the small average dividends which were paid and maintained that the rates were not high enough to give a reasonable return on the investment,[2] but the extensive over-capitalization of railway values weakened the force of this argument. It is probably true, as the railroad men claimed, that the maximum rates were fixed, not by the profit desired but by what the traffic would bear, but it is also true that the existence of a large capitalization and the desire to pay dividends thereon sometimes prevented reductions which would otherwise have been forced by public opinion.[3]

There were many forms of discrimination in railroad rates but those complained of at this time were principally of two sorts: discrimination between places, or charging higher rates at intermediate points than at points where competition in the shape of other roads or water routes prevailed; and discrimination between persons, or giving better terms to certain favored individuals or firms than were enjoyed by the general public.

---

[1] Illinois State Grange, *Proceedings*, iv. 102 (1875); W. C. Flagg (President, Illinois State Farmers' Association), in *American Social Science Journal*, vi. 109 (July, 1874); Campaign speech by Senator Sherman at Alliance, Ohio, in *Cincinnati Semi-Weekly Gazette*, September 26, 1876, p. 5; Martin, *Grange Movement*, ch. v.

[2] *Nation*, xxi. 1 (July 1, 1876).

[3] Windom Committee, *Report*, 72–76; Hepburn Committee (N. Y.), *Report*, 18; Interstate Commerce Commission, *Reports*, ii. 63; Wisconsin Railroad Commission, *Reports*, i. 62 (1874); C. F. Adams, Jr., "Railroad Inflation," in *North American Review*, cviii. 130–164 (January, 1869); E. Stanwood, "Farmers and Railroads," in *Old and New*, viii. 335–342 (September, 1873); Larrabee, *Railroad Question*, 163–188; Cook, *Corporation Problem*, 11–34; Martin, *Grange Movement*, ch. iii; Paine, *Granger Movement in Illinois*, 16.

The claims of the farmers that rates were raised at intermediate points to make up for losses at competitive points are probably not true but there was, nevertheless, a distinct injury to the unfavored places in the advantages given to their better situated rivals.[1] Of discrimination between persons, there can be no justification. It appeared in the passenger service mainly in the shape of free passes, the political aspects of which were more important than the economic. In the freight service this sort of discrimination was usually accomplished by secret rates and rebates and was almost always in favor of the large and powerful shipper. It should be borne in mind, however, that most of this discrimination, instead of being freely granted by the railroads, was rather extorted from them by large shippers, who were often able to force a rebate by threats of transferring their business to a rival road.[2]

It is quite evident then that the farmers had a number of real grievances against the railroads, although they did not always clearly understand the situation or realize just where the trouble lay. The power of railway corporations was growing and was being used to influence public officials; the system of construction was wasteful and corrupt; the stocks and bonds were badly watered; and in some instances the rates were undoubtedly higher than was necessary for a fair return on the physical value of the road. There were also gross and often totally unjustifiable discriminations which injured both shippers and consumers and indirectly added to another cause of complaint by fostering monopolies.

[1] Adams, *Railroads*, 123–125; Hepburn Commission, *Report*, 48–71, and testimony; Interstate Commerce Commission, *Reports*, i. 7; Larrabee, *Railroad Question*, 143–163; J. F. Hudson, *The Railways and the Republic*, 25–55; E. P. Alexander, *Railway Practice*, 5–23; W. D. Dabney, *The Public Regulation of Railways*, 67–174; Paine, *Granger Movement in Illinois*, 16.

[2] Hepburn Commission, *Report*, 40–70, and testimony; Larrabee, *Railroad Question*, 136–143; Hudson, *Railways and the Republic*, 55–66; Cook, *Corporation Problem*, 34–40; I. M. Tarbell, *History of Standard Oil*.

FARMERS, MERCHANTS, AND MANUFACTURERS

Among the economic doctrines propounded by the agricultural agitators of the seventies, none was more frequently heard or appears to have been more popular with the farmers than one which bears a resemblance to some of the ideas of the physiocratic philosophers of pre-revolutionary France. Like the physiocrats, the farmers were wont to look upon agriculture and land as the source of all wealth [1] and to divide society into the two classes of producers and non-producers, including in the latter all those engaged in the distribution of the products of the former. Although the indispensableness of the non-productive class to society was often admitted, that class was nevertheless looked upon distinctly as a necessary evil, which ought to be restricted to the smallest possible dimensions; and it was always stated that the proportion of the returns received by the distributing factors was altogether too large, and, conversely, that received by the producers was too small.[2] Next in importance to transportation among these factors were the middlemen who served as agents for the distribution of commodities between producer and consumer: and it was against the exactions of these middlemen that much of the wrath of the farmers was directed. From the standpoint of the farmer the middlemen were of two principal classes: the commission merchants and produce buyers through whom he disposed of his products, and the numerous agents and retail dealers through whom he purchased his supplies.[3]

When the farmer carried the product of his summer's work to market and found himself practically obliged to dispose of

[1] For example, the *Prairie Farmer*, the leading agricultural paper of the Northwest, offered in 1869, as a premium for subscriptions, an allegorical picture depicting the relation of the farmer to the " so-called professions and business occupations " in which the farmer was represented as saying, " I pay for all." See *Prairie Farmer*, xl. 364 (November 6, 1869).

[2] For a sample of this sort of economic reasoning, see R. H. Furgeson, " Coöperation," an address in Illinois State Grange, *Proceedings*, iv. 91–96 (1875). See also Carr, *Patrons of Husbandry*, 131–140.

[3] On this subject generally, see F. A. Fetter, " The Theory of the Middleman " and P. M. Kieley, " The Middleman in Practice," both in L. H. Bailey, ed., *Cyclopedia of American Agriculture*, iv. 239–243.

it to commission men at quite unremunerative prices,[1] it was but natural for him to look upon these dealers as his enemies and to feel that they controlled the situation and fixed such prices as they chose, and indeed it seems to be true that the returns to the farmer were often smaller and the share retained by the commission man larger than would have been the case had there been more competition among the merchants and more organization among the farmers. In a small place there was frequently but one produce buyer and where there were more the number was so small that combination was easy for the purpose of eliminating competition and maintaining prices. The produce buyers were in a position to watch the markets and their facilities for storage were such that they could take advantage of fluctuations; while the farmers, usually ignorant of the state of the market and with no facilities for holding their crops, often brought about a glut and reduced prices by throwing large quantities of produce on the market at once. The charges of the farmers were that the commission men exacted too high rates for their services in getting the crops to market and that the products of agriculture were obliged to pass through too many toll-taking hands before they reached the consumer. This latter evil they proposed to remedy, as will appear later, by eliminating the commission merchant or buyer at the local center and shipping directly to the merchant at the large central market.[2]

---

[1] For an instance, see Illinois State Grange, *Proceedings*, iv. 92 (1875). Stories of this sort are quite common. One, which was frequently used by the agitators, told of a farmer carrying a load of grain to market and returning with a pair of shoes for his boy — the sole purchase which he was able to make with the returns from the sale of his grain.

[2] United States Industrial Commission, *Report*, vi. 6, 36–143, 235–268; Illinois State Grange, *Proceedings*, iv. 42–46 (1875); National Grange, *Proceedings*, vii. 13, 57, 79 (1874); Carr, *Patrons of Husbandry*, 75–103; J. R. Dodge, " The Discontent of the Farmer," in *Century*, xxi. 447–456 (January, 1892); W. A. Peffer, " The Farmers' Defensive Movement," in *Forum*, viii. 464–473 (December, 1889). The tendency to monopoly in the commission business was sometimes fostered by the railroads. Because of convenience or on account of business relations, they are said to have favored the established elevators at the expense of would-be competitors. See letter from Winona County, Minnesota, in *Farmers' Union*, January 18, 1873.

Just as the price which the farmer received for the commodities
he sold seemed to him to be fixed by those to whom he sold, so
also, he felt that the price of his supplies was fixed by those from
whom he bought.[1] The retail dealers, like the commission men,
were comparatively few in number and usually able to prevent
serious competition among themselves. Then in many parts
of the country and especially in the newly settled areas of the
western states there prevailed a credit system somewhat similar
to that already described in connection with the southern states.
The feature of crop mortgages was usually absent in the West
but otherwise the system was very much the same; the farmer
lacked ready money and was forced to buy on credit, and an
account having been begun, he was practically placed at the
mercy of the dealer until he could square himself on the books.
A large part of the farmers' supplies were purchased, however,
not from retail dealers, but from agents who handled the articles
on a commission for the manufacturer; this was particularly
true of all sorts of farm machinery, of sewing machines, and other
patented devices. The complaints against these agents were
that their large commissions unduly increased prices, that they
frequently persuaded farmers to purchase machinery which
they did not need or could not afford, and that they sold on credit
and in addition charged exorbitant rates of interest.[2]

The principal complaints in regard to these supplies were
directed, however, not against the middlemen, but against the
manufacturers themselves. In the general attack upon monop-
olists — a term which was applied to practically everyone except farmers and day-laborers — the manufacturing establishments operating under the protection of patents for inventions
came in for their full share of denunciation. That there were
many abuses of the privileges of patent rights is indubitable:
in case of meritorious inventions, the profits obtained by the
inventor or his assigns were often enormous; patents which
were about to expire were renewed and extended by means of
so-called improvements or through the help of political influence;

---

[1] *Prairie Farmer*, xliii. 369, xliv. 1 (November 23, 1872, January 4, 1873).

[2] Martin, *Grange Movement*, ch. xviii.

but worst of all, the patent office failed to make sufficiently thorough investigations to prevent the occasional issuance of patents on articles or principles which were in no sense inventions but had long been in common use. This seems to have been the case, for example, with the Teal patent on a sliding gate which was successfully fought in the courts by the Patrons of Husbandry of Michigan, though not until after considerable money had been collected from the farmers in the shape of royalty.[1] That the monopoly based on patent rights, combined with the expensive agency and commission system of selling, resulted in exorbitant prices for farm machinery is readily seen when we note that many of these protected machines were shipped to Europe by the manufacturer and there sold at considerably less than the retail price in the United States.[2] The great reductions in prices which the Grangers were able to bring about when they got their business departments into working order also throws some light on preëxisting conditions.

FARMERS AND FINANCE

The prevalence of a system of buying on credit among the agricultural population has already been noted. Another result of the general poverty, or at least of the lack of ready money, among the farmers, was a widespread indebtedness as represented by the growing burden of mortgages upon rural property. That some of these mortgages represented enterprise and the improvement or extension of a farmer's operations is probably true, but it is also true that many of them indicated straitened financial circumstances. The worst part of the situation was the excessive rate of interest, running as high as fifteen or twenty per cent, which was often exacted for these loans. The West was infested with loan agents to whom the

---

[1] *American Agriculturist*, xxxviii. 493, 521 (December, 1879); *Prairie Farmer*, xli. 185, 349, xliii. 132, 161, 252, 292, xlv. 89, 91, 129 (1870–74); National Grange, *Proceedings*, xii. 68, xiv. 107 (1878, 1880); Michigan State Grange, *Proceedings*, vi. 60–62 (1878).

[2] Cloud, *Monopolies and the People*, 248–254; National Grange, *Proceedings*, vii. 13, viii. 62 (1874, 1875); Flagg, in *American Social Science Journal*, vi. 110 (July, 1874).

farmer who had met with reverses or who wished to make improvements or purchase additional land was obliged to apply for loans. The agent did not furnish the money himself but procured it from eastern capitalists and loaned it to the farmer on a mortgage at usurious rates of interest, after charging a commission at both ends of the deal.[1]

That the disturbed state of the currency, due to inflation during the war, was a cause of financial depression among the agricultural classes and especially of the high rates of interest, seems probable; however that may have been, it is evident that the currency situation was detrimental to the welfare of the farmer in various ways. The agricultural products of the country, always in excess of home consumption, were obliged to seek markets abroad, and this sale of the surplus in the world market also fixed prices at home; but these sales abroad had to be made in the standard gold and silver currency of the world, while all purchases of supplies were made in a depreciated paper currency, and there was sure to be more or less leakage in the process of changing from one to the other.[2] The farmer also suffered from the fluctuations resulting from the unstable condition of the currency and the accompanying speculation, but the most serious injury came from the rise in value of the currency, as measured in gold, during the period from 1865 to the resumption of specie payments in 1879. As has already been noted, a large part of the agricultural population was in debt from one cause or another and most of these debts, contracted in greatly depreciated currency, had to be paid with money worth from fifteen to twenty per cent more than the actual value of that which had been borrowed.[3] These financial burdens were little noticed during the six or seven years of prosperity immediately following the war, but the panic of

---

[1] *Nation*, xxv. 282 (November 8, 1877); W. A. Peffer, *The Farmer's Side*, 34–42, 68–86; J. R. Elliot, *American Farms*, 45–52.

[2] Flagg, in *American Social Science Journal*, vi. 114 (July, 1874).

[3] *Nation*, xvi. 381 (June 5, 1873); Peffer, *The Farmer's Side*, 67–115; Carr, *Patrons of Husbandry*, 392–428; Flagg, in *American Social Science Journal*, vi. 111–113 (July, 1874); Rhodes, *History of the United States*, vii. 53–73; D. R. Dewey, *Financial History of the United States*, 292–298, 342, 344–352, 357.

1873 had a disastrous effect on agriculture and aggravated the evils. The farming class, which had begun to feel the pinch some time before the crash came, suffered in common with others during the protracted depression which followed. Business was stagnant, money scarce, and prices low, and the farmers frequently found it difficult to dispose of their crops at anywhere near remunerative prices.[1]

Another result of the Civil War which worked to the disadvantage of the agricultural class was the high customs tariff, adopted during the war primarily for the purpose of raising revenue but continued as a measure of protection to American manufacturers. The urgent need of revenues occasioned by the war, the greed of manufacturers, the necessity of off-setting the new internal revenue duties, and the lack of any systematic study of the subject resulted in an illogical and unsystematic aggregation of tariff rates which were often so high as to reduce the national revenue by restricting importation. As a war measure, emanating from a Congress too much occupied by more vital problems to devote itself to a study of the tariff, this might be excusable, but there can be no justification for its continuance in practically the same form after the war was over. The efforts of the interested manufacturers, however, were successful in preventing any serious alteration.[2] This tariff, as all high protective tariffs in a country whose production exceeds the demand for home consumption, bore with especial severity on the farmers, particularly in the staple producing regions of the South and West. The price which the farmer received for his cotton and his grain was fixed by the sale of the surplus in the unprotected markets of the world, while the cost of nearly everything he consumed, whether imported or of domestic production, was vastly enhanced for the benefit of the manufacturers. Even the home market idea proved a

[1] Rhodes, *History of the United States*, vii. 36–53.
[2] Dewey, *Financial History*, 299–305, 396–398; C. B. Spahr, *An Essay on the Present Distribution of Wealth in the United States*, 346; Elliot, *American Farms*, 187–205.

delusion when the agricultural production was continually in excess of the needs of that market.[1]

Upon the subject of taxation the farmers made many complaints, and some of these were well founded.[2] The American people were undoubtedly carrying a very large burden of taxation in the period following the war, the causes of which are to be sought in the great public debts incurred for the conduct of the war and for the assistance of railroads and other internal improvements,[3] and in the carelessness, extravagance, and corruption of public administration. Not only was the aggregate *per capita* taxation, national, state, and local, unusually high, but its incidence was far from being arranged in proportion to the ability to pay. In regard to the national taxation, which was almost wholly indirect, this was particularly true because so much of the revenue was derived from articles of common consumption by the mass of the people. For example, practically one-half of the customs revenue was levied on the importation of sugar, molasses, and woolen and cotton goods, which are consumed by everyone in very similar proportions. In like manner the internal revenue duties on tobacco and liquors bore with greatest severity on the cheaper grades of the product. Thus an undue share of the taxes for the support of the national government and the payment of its enormous war debt was

[1] Peffer, *The Farmer's Side*, 129–147; Cloud, *Monopolies and the People*, 239–247; Carr, *Patrons of Husbandry*, 392–412; Elliot, *American Farms*, 90–109, 119–131, 138; Flagg, in *American Social Science Journal*, vi. 110 (July, 1874).

[2] Flagg, "Revenue," an address in Illinois State Grange, *Proceedings*, iv. 60–74 (1875); Carr, *Patrons of Husbandry*, 411; Spahr, *Distribution of Wealth*, 346; Elliot, *American Farms*, 141–144; A. H. Peters, "The Depreciation of Farming Land," in *Quarterly Journal of Economics*, iv. 22 (October, 1889); *Nation*, xvi. 381 (June 5, 1873); New York Commission to revise the laws for the assessment and collection of taxes, *Report*, 1871; D. A. Wells, *Rational Principles of Taxation*, in American Social Science Association, *Transactions*, 1874; *Patron's Bulletin* (Kentucky), December, 1876 (Master's address to the state grange).

[3] As an indication of the part played by the railway in the increase of public indebtedness, it might be noted that in Illinois in 1869, the state auditor reported an aggregate local debt, — county, city, town, and township, — of thirty-nine million dollars, forty-eight per cent of which consisted of railroad obligations. Illinois State Auditor, *Reports*, 1869, pp. 93–98; Flagg, in Illinois State Grange, *Proceedings*, iv. 69 (1875).

borne by the people of small means, among whom we must certainly class the agricultural population.[1]

In the raising of state and local revenue, the farmer fared somewhat better, for here practically the whole reliance was placed on direct taxation, mainly in the form of a tax on the valuation of real and personal property. The complaints of the farmers in regard to state and local taxation were that their property, being principally in real estate and other readily discoverable forms, was sure to be assessed and usually at its full value; while other property, particularly that of dwellers in urban communities and of corporations, being largely personal and difficult to get at, often escaped taxation altogether.[2] The farmers also maintained that their real property was assessed higher in proportion than that of the other classes, and particularly was there complaint about the assessment of uncultivated land or land held for speculative purposes at a lower rate than that of equal quality which was under cultivation.[3] In some parts of the country there was also considerable outcry against the assessment of growing crops, which the farmers preferred to look upon as prospective property only.[4]

It is evident then that the financial condition of the country at this time as it affected the agricultural population was far from satisfactory: many farmers were burdened with large private debts, on which they were paying high rates of interest; the condition of the currency, because of its depreciation, of its fluctuation, and especially of its subsequent contraction, affected them adversely, in common with many other classes; and the system of protection to American manufacturers also operated to their disadvantage. The enormous

---

[1] Spahr, *Distribution of Wealth*, 133–146; Elliot, *American Farms*, 156–162; Peters, in *Quarterly Journal of Economics*, iv. 23 (October, 1889); Flagg, in Illinois State Grange, *Proceedings*, iv. 64, 67–70 (1875); and in *American Social Science Journal*, vi. 111 (July, 1874).

[2] Cloud, *Monopolies and the People*, 149–153; Flagg, in Illinois State Grange, *Proceedings*, iv. 64, 67–70 (1875); Peters, in *Quarterly Journal of Economics*, iv. 22 (October, 1889); Resolution of Bethel Grange, in *Prairie Farmer*, xliv. 187 (June 14, 1873); United States Industrial Commission, *Reports*, xix.

[3] Elliot, *American Farms*, 163–169.

[4] *California Patron*, July 11, 1877, p. 5.

public debts also imposed a considerable burden of taxation
on the people and the methods by which the taxes were collected
forced the farmers and other people of small means to bear an
undue proportion of the burden.

Agricultural Products and Prices

In considering the various causes which made agriculture
largely unremunerative in the seventies, it is difficult to assign
to each its relative importance, but if any one thing can be said
to be the primary cause of that situation, it is the great extension
or even inflation of agricultural operations in the decade following the war; an inflation which was shared by many other
industries and which presents many of the features of a speculative boom. The prevailing high prices just at the close of the
war, the inflated condition of the currency, and the spirit of
restlessness and enterprise developed by the war, all contributed
to produce a feverish industrial condition and turned men's
minds to the development of the great unsettled areas of the
West, as a new field for exploitation.[1] The railroads, aided by
subsidies, pushed rapidly out, population followed, and the two
reacting on each other quickly advanced the frontier another
step across the continent.[2]

When the war closed in 1865, there were but twelve thousand
miles of railroad in all the states and territories of the Northwest. This amount was almost doubled by 1870 and a decade
later the mileage was over forty-three thousand. Taking the
territory west of the Mississippi only, there were less than
four thousand miles of railroad in operation in 1867, an amount
which was increased by 1877 to sixteen thousand, or considerably more than the mileage of the whole Northwest at the
close of the war.[3] The accompanying movement of population
can be seen by tracing the frontier line of settlement, which
in 1860 ran east and west across central Wisconsin, took in

---

[1] *Nation*, xvii. 68, xix. 36 (July 31, 1873, July 16, 1874); *Atlantic*, xxxii. 508–512
(October, 1873); Pierson, in *Popular Science Monthly*, xxxii. 202 (December, 1887);
Adams, in *North American Review*, cxx. 421–424 (April, 1874).

[2] Peffer, in *Forum*, viii. 464–466 (December, 1889).

[3] Porter, *The West*, 47; E. E. Sparks, *National Development*, ch. iv.

the southeastern part of Minnesota, the eastern fringe of Nebraska and Kansas, and continued down through western Arkansas and Texas. By 1880 this line had advanced in the Northwest to include the Dakotas and nearly all of Nebraska and Kansas, while the partially settled areas of Minnesota and Iowa were filled out and extended. In the Southwest, the Texan frontier was advanced and the density of settlement in Arkansas and eastern Texas considerably increased.[1]

A comparison of the population statistics of 1860, 1870, and 1880 shows a remarkable growth in the whole western area. The population of the prairie states—the North Central division according to the census—increased from nine million in 1860 to thirteen million in 1870 and seventeen million in 1880 an increase during the twenty years of ninety-one per cent. The four frontier states and territories of this section, Minnesota, Dakota, Kansas, and Nebraska, increased from three hundred thousand in 1860 to nearly a million in 1870 and to nearly two and a half million in 1880. The Southwest had not recovered sufficiently from the war to expand much by 1870 but the population of Texas and Arkansas leaped from a million three hundred thousand in 1870 to nearly two and a half million in 1880. In the states of the Pacific slope, the first rush of settlement was over, but a gradual increase was kept up and many of the settlers were drawn from mining to agricultural pursuits.

That the greater part of this new population of the West devoted itself to agriculture can be seen by examining the statistics of improved farm lands as given in the table[2] on the following page.

Two factors made possible this great agricultural expansion: the land was more accessible and more easily obtained than ever before; and there was a surplus of industrial population ready to take possession. In 1862, Congress adopted a new principle in the disposition of the public lands by enacting the

[1] See maps illustrating density of population in *United States Census*, 1890, *Population*, pt. 1; Sparks, *National Development*, ch. ii.

[2] Arranged from tables in *United States Census*, 1880, volume on *Agriculture*, xviii. See also United States Commissioner of Agriculture, *Reports*, 1869, p. 17, on westward progress of wheat-growing.

homestead law, which made it possible for each head of a family to obtain a free homestead on the public domain. In the very next year a million acres of government land were thus occupied and by 1880 over fifty-five million had been filed on

	Acreage of improved land			Percentage of increase	
	1860	1870	1880	1860–70	1870–80
United States	163,110,720	188,921,099	284,771,042	15.8	50.7
N. Atlan. Div. ...	38,981,911	41,117,185	46,385,632	5.5	12.8
S. Atlan. Div.	71,619,829	60,010,064	65,249,232	13.5[1]	19.8
N. Cent. Div.	52,308,699	78,409,509	136,842,319	49.9	74.5
S. Cent. Div.	33,232,226	31,088,775	49,806,771	6.4[1]	60.2
Western Div.	3,689,942	8,102,639	15,565,989	119.8	92.1

under this law. Under the somewhat similar provisions of the timber-culture act of 1873, nine million more acres were occupied, and the grant by Congress in 1862 of nearly ten million acres of land to the states for agricultural colleges operated in the same direction, for much of this land passed into private possession at merely nominal prices.[2] The enormous grants to railway companies during this period also helped to make land available to settlers.[3] The corporations were eager to dispose of their land at low prices in order to attract settlers; and they were enabled to build railroads which made accessible, not only their own lands, but the reserved alternate sections of the government as well. They served as an intermediary between the people and the desired land, bringing the one to the other and making profitable the cultivation of the land by furnishing a comparatively cheap means of transportation to the distant markets.

The causes which led to the existence of a surplus industrial population were various. Probably the most effective was the

[1] Decrease.

[2] Donaldson, *The Public Domain*, 351–355, 360; A. B. Hart, " The Disposition of Our Public Lands," in *Quarterly Journal of Economics,* i. 176 (January, 1887); E. D. Fite, *Social and Industrial Conditions in the North during the Civil War*, 11.

[3] Hart, in *Quarterly Journal of Economics*, i. 179; W. G. Moody, *Land and Labor in the United States*, 88–111.

disbanding of the armies at the close of the war. Not only were a million and a half men, who had for several years been employed by the government, now thrown upon their own resources, but the cessation of those industries which were dependent on the war added many more to the numbers of the unemployed. One writer has estimated that, in 1865, one-fifth of the able-bodied men of the country were in army service, with another fifth employed in furnishing them material and sustenance, and that four million men were thrown out of employment by the ending of the war.[1] Many of these men found their former niche in the industrial world filled by others and went west to make a new start on the frontier; or, if they returned to their old occupations, some one else was displaced who might take up the westward march.

Immigration, too, which had been checked at first by the war, contributed its share to the peopling of the new regions in the West. The number of imigrants had fallen in 1862 to less than ninety thousand, but from that time on it rose steadily until in 1873 it amounted to four hundred and fifty-nine thousand, the highest point reached up to that time. The hard times brought a reaction and the number sank to one hundred and thirty-eight thousand in 1878, only to rise again rapidly to the astounding figure of seven hundred and eighty-eight thousand in 1882.[2] That a large number of these immigrants went into the agricultural states of the West can be seen by examining the census statistics of birth and parentage. In 1880 the percentage of persons of foreign parentage in Wisconsin was seventy-three; in Minnesota, seventy-one; in Dakota, sixty-six; in Nebraska, forty-four; and in California, fifty-nine.

Another factor which helped along the great agricultural expansion in this period was the technical advance, particularly in the line of invention and extended use of agricultural machinery. This development had taken place to a certain extent, in the older settled parts of the country, during the war, partly

---

[1] Moody, *Land and Labor*, 149–163.

[2] Emerick, in *Political Science Quarterly*, xi. 640–643 (September, 1896); Sparks, *National Development*, ch. ii; Industrial Commission, *Reports*, xix. 958.

as a result of the scarcity of labor and the need of something to take the place of the men who were in the army.[1] The machines enabled one man to do the work which had formerly been done by many and thus helped to increase the surplus population after the war closed. They made possible the cultivation of the staple crops on a large scale in the new western lands, the result being a thin settlement spread over an extensive area but producing large crops *per capita*.[2] This tendency was carried to an extreme in the so-called bonanza farms, against which there was bitter complaint. Large tracts of land were obtained by capitalists and converted into industrial plants for the production of wheat and corn. By means of machinery, operated by gangs of hired labor, and with large-scale production, great crops were produced at a minimum of cost; and when, as is said to have been the case in some instances, special favors were received from the railroads in transportation, it is easily seen that this competition was a real injury to the individual farmer producing crops on a small scale.[3] There was also technical advance in agricultural science in other ways, as is illustrated by the increasing application of commercial fertilizers to the cotton fields of the South, which made possible a considerable expansion of the area of the cotton belt in the older states at the same time that new cotton lands were being developed in Texas.[4]

The effect of all these combined causes in producing a great increase in agricultural operations in the staple crops, together with a corresponding decrease in prices, can be seen from the following tables which show the acreage, production, total value, and average annual price of the corn, wheat, and cotton crops in the United States from 1866 to 1880 inclusive.[5]

[1] Fite, *Social and Industrial Conditions in the North during the Civil War*, 6–9.

[2] H. W. Quaintance, *The Influence of Farm Machinery on Production and Labor;* Moody, *Land and Labor*, 9–30.

[3] *Ibid.* 31–87; Elliot, *American Farms*, 33–57, 78–89.

[4] M. B. Hammond, *The Cotton Industry*, 123.

[5] The statistics of acreage, production, and value given in these tables are taken from United States Department of Agriculture, *Yearbook*, 1897, pp. 710, 712. The price figures are computed from the total production and value. The values

CORN

Year	Acreage	Prod. in bushels	Value	Price per bushel
1866	34,306,538	867,946,295	$411,450,830	$.47
1867	32,520,349	768,320,000	437,769,763	.57
1868	34,887,246	906,527,000	424,056,649	.47
1869	37,103,245	874,320,000	522,550,509	.60
1870	38,649,977	1,094,255,000	540,520,456	.54
1871	34,091,137	991,898,000	430,355,510	.43
1872	35,526,836	1,092,719,000	385,736,210	.35
1873	39,197,148	932,274,000	411,961,151	.44
1874	41,036,918	850,148,500	496,271,255	.58
1875	44,841,371	1,321,069,000	484,674,804	.37
1876	49,033,364	1,283,827,500	436,108,521	.34
1877	50,369,113	1,342,558,000	467,635,230	.35
1878	51,585,000	1,388,218,750	440,280,517	.32
1879	53,085,450	1,547,901,790	580,486,217	.37
1880	62,317,842	1,717,434,543	679,714,499	.40

WHEAT

Year	Acreage	Prod. in bushels	Value	Price per bushel
1866	15,424,496	151,999,906	$232,109,630	$1.52
1867	18,321,561	212,441,400	308,387,146	1.45
1868	18,460,132	224,036,600	243,032,746	1.08
1869	19,181,004	260,146,900	199,024,996	.77
1870	18,992,591	235,884,700	222,766,969	.94
1871	19,943,893	230,722,400	264,075,851	1.14
1872	20,858,359	249,997,100	278,522,068	1.11
1873	22,171,676	281,254,700	300,669,533	1.07
1874	24,967,027	308,102,700	265,881,167	.86
1875	26,381,512	292,136,000	261,396,926	.89
1876	27,627,021	289,356,500	278,697,238	.96
1877	26,277,546	346,194,146	385,089,444	1.06
1878	32,108,560	420,122,400	325,814,119	.78
1879	32,545,950	448,756,630	497,030,142	1.11
1880	37,986,717	498,549,868	474,201,850	.95

and consequently the prices here given are in gold so that the effect of currency inflation is largely eliminated. If currency prices were taken the apparent decline would be much greater in each instance.

COTTON

Year	Acreage	Prod. in bales	Value	Price per bale
1866	....	2,097,254	$204,561,896	$97.54
1867	....	2,519,554	199,583,510	79.21
1868	....	2,366,467	226,794,168	95.74
1869	7,933,000	3,122,551	261,067,037	83.61
1870	9,985,000	4,352,317	292,703,086	67.25
1871	8,911,000	2,974,351	242,672,804	81.44
1872	9,560,000	3,930,508	280,532,629	71.38
1873	10,816,000	4,170,388	289,853,486	69.50
1874	10,982,000	3,832,991	228,113,080	59.51
1875	11,635,000	4,632,313	233,109,945	50.53
1876	11,500,000	4,474,069	211,655,041	47.31
1877	11,825,000	4,773,865	235,721,194	49.38
1878	12,266,800	4,694,942	193,467,706	41.40
1879	12,595,500	4,735,082	242,140,987	51.14
1880	15,475,300	5,708,942	280,266,242	49.09

It will be seen from these tables and the accompanying chart (I) that the increase in acreage devoted to these crops was rapid

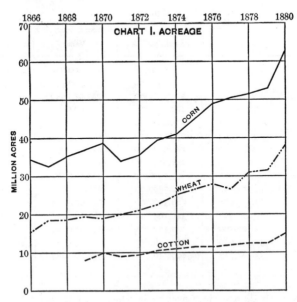

and almost unbroken throughout the period, amounting, for corn, to 81 per cent; for wheat, to 146 per cent; and for cotton,

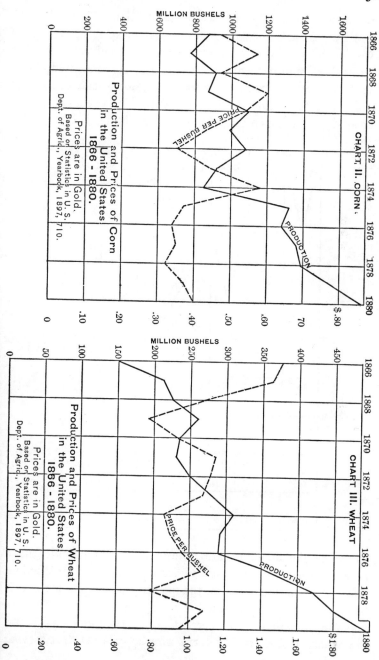

to 94 per cent. The increase in production (Charts II, III, and IV), though not so regular as that of acreage, because of varying harvest, was, on the whole, considerably greater, thus indicating improvement in technique. It amounted, from 1866 to 1880, for corn, to 98 per cent; for wheat, to 221 per cent; and for cotton, to 172 per cent. The effect of this increased production on the price is seen on Charts II, III, and IV,

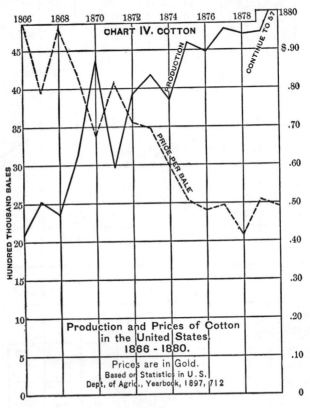

on which the lines indicating the average annual price have been superimposed on those indicating the total production. As a rule each fluctuation in the quantity of the product is met by a fluctuation in the price of nearly equal ratio and in the opposite direction. The percentage of decline in price for the whole period is for corn, fifteen; wheat, thirty-seven;

and cotton, forty-nine; but if the last two years, which were years of recovery from the previous depression, are stricken out and the period from 1866 to 1878 inclusive is taken, the decline amounts to thirty-two, forty-nine, and fifty-eight per cent, respectively.

As a result of these off-setting fluctuations of price, the value of the total annual crop (Chart V) shows less fluctuation and less increase during the period than does the quantity, the

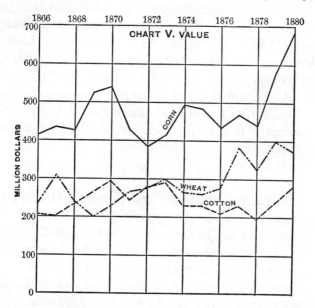

increase from 1866 to 1880 amounting to only sixty-five per cent for corn, one hundred and five per cent for wheat, and thirty-seven per cent for cotton; and substituting for 1880 the last year of the depression, 1878, the increase amounts to only seven per cent for corn, and forty per cent for wheat, while the total value of the cotton crop shows a decrease of five per cent. Thus, although the number of men engaged in agriculture and the amount of capital invested in improved land and machinery was constantly and rapidly increasing, the resulting increased production brought in little or no more revenue than had the smaller crops of fifteen or twenty years before.

The effect of this situation upon the agricultural population was undoubtedly severe, and particularly so on those who, lured by the high prices just after the war and the inducements held out by the advancing railroads, had sought a field for more extended operations in the new West, but had been barely able to get under way when the depression began. Many others, also, who had assumed a burden of debt in order to purchase additional land and machinery, found themselves with an increased investment, on part of which they were paying exorbitant interest, while the returns remained stationary or declined. Adding to this the other factors which have been considered — the treatment the farmers received at the hands of the railway corporations, the large proportion of profits consumed by the middlemen, an unjust protective tariff and a depreciated currency, and finally an overgrown burden of debt and taxation — it is readily seen that the Granger movement was not without economic foundation.

FARMERS AND POLITICS

The relative political power and position of those engaged in agricultural pursuits was a much discussed subject during the Granger period. In the early days of the republic, farming was looked upon as the most suitable occupation for gentlemen, and a large proportion of the positions of high political preferment were filled by men from the ranks of the agriculturists; planters or farmers were to be found in considerable numbers, serving as legislators, as executive officials, or in judicial positions; and the interests of agriculture were sure of adequate consideration. Just previous to the Civil War the controlling influence in national affairs had been for some time in the hands of the planter element of the South, whose interests, apart from the question of slavery, generally coincided with those of agriculturists throughout the country. The commercial and manufacturing classes, however, were rapidly forging to the front, particularly in the North and East, and the Civil War marks their definite triumph in national affairs over the agricultural interests of the country as represented by the southern planters. From that time on, the needs and interests of the more or less organized mercantile and manufacturing classes received primary consideration and the positions of political power were occupied more and more by representatives from these classes or by lawyers who took substantially the same point of view.[1]

The Forty-third Congress of the United States, in session from 1873 to 1875, will furnish an example of this lack of representation in the councils of the nation, of which the farmers complained. Sixty-one per cent of the members of this Congress were lawyers, sixteen per cent were engaged in commercial or manufacturing pursuits, and only seven per cent professed the occupation of farming. Yet the census of 1870 shows that forty-seven per cent of the working population of the country was still engaged in farming while commerce and manufacturing could claim only thirty-one per cent. That this situation was not confined to national politics can be seen from the statistics of the legislature of Illinois in 1874. This included but eight farmers among fifty-one senators and forty farmers among the one hundred fifty-three members of the lower house, in spite of the fact that over half of the population of the state was agricultural.[2]

Not only did the farmers feel that as a class they failed to receive adequate direct representation in the government of the country, but there was also a belief that their interests were not given due consideration by those who were supposed to represent them. Ignorant often of what their true interests were, scattered broadcast over the country, without either time or opportunity to make their wants known, and often following blindly in the wake of the political party to which they had been attached by issues now dead and gone, the farmers were looked upon by the political leaders as a stable element whose

[1] Flagg, in *American Social Science Journal*, vi. 108 (July, 1874); Elliot, *American Farms*, 175–186; Alpha Messer, *Benefits of the Grange* (pamphlet, 2d ed.), 5.

[2] Flagg, in *American Social Science Journal*, vi. 108 (July, 1874). Similarly, a constitutional convention in Ohio in 1873 contained sixty-two lawyers and sixteen farmers out of a total of one hundred and two members. *American Annual Cyclopedia*, 1873, p. 607.

vote could be depended upon for the party. Hence their interests received little consideration in the drawing up of party platforms or the framing of legislation.[1]

Many of the farmers were wont to look upon this loss of political power as the fundamental cause of the relative decline of agriculture, laying at its door all or nearly all of the economic evils which have been considered.[2] The transportation problem was looked upon as a result of governmental favors to the railway companies, while its cure was prevented by the grip of the railway interests upon Congress and the legislatures. In the same way it was believed that patent rights, the currency problem, banking legislation, and the tariff were manipulated by the opposing interests to the detriment of the agricultural population.

How far the farmers were justified in this belief, it is impossible to say. Certainly many of the economic evils under which they suffered could not have been entirely remedied by the wisest of legislation. It is equally true, on the other hand, that the political conditions in the period immediately following the war were anything but pure. The political influence exerted by the railways and the *Crédit Mobilier* scandal have already been mentioned, and in general this seems to have been a period of exceptional corruption and inefficiency, in state as well as in national government. Some of the southern states were in the grip of notoriously corrupt reconstruction governments which squandered their resources; and in the North several of the state legislatures were found to be largely subservient to the transportation and commercial interests.[3] Such being the situation, the farmers were well justified in seeking the cure for their material ills, in part at least, through increased political power.

[1] *California Patron*, November 14, 1874, p. 2; C. S. Walker, " The Farmer's Alliance," in *Andover Review*, xiv. 132–140 (August, 1890); Elliot, *American Farms*, 187–205.

[2] See the address by W. C. Flagg (President of the Illinois State Farmers' Association), in *American Social Science Journal*, vi. 100–115 (July, 1874).

[3] Dunning, *Reconstruction, Political and Economic*, chs. xiii, xiv, xviii; *Nation*, xix. 36 (July 16, 1874); National Grange, *Proceedings*, xix. 20 (1885).

Social and Intellectual Conditions

A somewhat similar condition of affairs prevailed with reference to the social and intellectual position of the farmers. Just as they had lost political power, so their relative social position had been lowered until the tilling of the soil, formerly considered one of the highest of occupations, had come to be looked upon as a pursuit suitable only to those who were not equipped for anything else. This was due not so much to a positive decline in status on the part of the farmers as to the rapid increase in the social and educational advantages of those who were engaged in occupations which permitted their lives to be spent in the cities. The farmers, living in their scattered homesteads and often forced by the pinch of adversity to devote their whole time to their calling in order to provide for the mere material wants of themselves and their families, were not in a position to keep pace with the dwellers in urban centers who had all the advantages which go with density of population; [1] for it must be remembered that this was before the day of interurban trolleys, farm telephones, and rural free delivery of mail — the three great factors which help to ameliorate the position of the farmers today. That they keenly realized their disadvantages is seen in the fact that so many of them made every effort to have their children equipped for some other occupation which might give them an opportunity to rise in the world.

Agriculture, like other industries, demands the application of knowledge and skill as well as mere physical labor for its highest development, but the only teacher which the farmer had was experience, and there was no means by which he might equip himself with the accumulated experience of his fellows.[2] The agricultural colleges of the country were then in their infancy, and insistent complaint was heard that the gifts made by Congress for agricultural education had been misapplied

[1] *Nation*, xix. 36 (July 16, 1874); Peters, in *Quarterly Journal of Economics*, iv. 25–30 (October, 1889); National Grange, *Proceedings*, xix. 17 (1885); Messer, *The Grange* (pamphlet); D. Kinley, "The Movement of Population from Country to City," in Bailey, *Cyclopedia of Agriculture*, iv. 117.

[2] Messer, *The Grange*, 9.

to the so-called classical institutions.[1] So also, the agricultural press, which has since become an important educational factor, was then weak, impractical, and little patronized. Not only were the farmers deficient in technical education, but as a class they lacked that knowledge of a more general nature which the best interest of their business demanded. They knew little of the conditions and prospects of the various crops throughout the country, and the probable future condition of the markets; they were ignorant of many of the usages of business; and the lack of knowledge of simple economic principles and their application to the politico-economic problems of the day made it difficult for them to reason intelligently in matters in which their own interests were at stake.[2] Thus what little political influence or power they did possess was largely nullified by their lack of knowledge as to the true interests of agriculture.[3]

Such, then, was the situation as it presented itself to the farmers of the country in the decade of the seventies; and in casting about for a remedy it was but natural that they should look for examples to those other classes of society which had been forging so rapidly ahead. The one thing which presented itself again and again in almost every other industry, but which appeared to be lamentably lacking in agriculture, was organization — the organization and coöperation, for their mutual advantage, of those whose interests coincided. The manufacturers were united into stock companies and more or less vague associations; the merchants had their commercial organizations; the bankers and brokers, their stock-exchanges and clearing houses; and even the laboring men were beginning to find and assert their common interests in trade-unions; but for the farmer there was nothing of the sort. Each individual went his own way unmindful of his neighbor or of the interests of his class as a whole, which in the long run meant his own interests.[4]

[1] National Grange, *Proceedings*, xix. 17 (1885); Messer, *The Grange*, 16.

[2] *Ibid.* 11; Elliot, *American Farms*, 211–220.

[3] Messer, *Benefits of the Grange* (pamphlet, 2d ed.), 3.

[4] *Nation*, xviii. 55; *Prairie Farmer*, xliii. 369, xliv. 1 (November 23, 1872, January 4, 1873).

The idea of some form of association among the farmers for coöperation in the improvement of their condition, materially, socially, and intellectually, appealed to them in many ways. If they lacked opportunities for social intercourse and enjoyment, how better could these be furnished than in the weekly or bi-weekly meetings of a local association of farmers ? If they lacked a knowledge of public problems and of their own interest, or the ability to reason logically about them and to present their ideas to others, how better could they gain these things than by discussions in these same meetings ? If their political power and prestige were waning, how could these better be rehabilitated than by a grand national union of branch associations of farmers, which would display their overwhelming strength as a united class ? If they were being worsted in the struggle with the organized mercantile and manufacturing classes with whom they had to deal, how better could they equip themselves than by extensive counter-organization ? [1] An agricultural organization including a great part of the farmers of the nation would be able to demand fairer treatment from the railway corporations and to enforce it with the help of the state; it could use its immense influence to secure more favorable legislation on such matters as the tariff, currency, and taxation; by means of a widespread local organization it could gather and disseminate useful information concerning the crops and the markets; and in general it could foster a beneficent spirit of coöperation and mutual assistance among its members. In this way alone can a satisfactory explanation be found for the widespread and phenomenal movement for organization which appeared among the farmers in the decade of the seventies.

[1] *Farmers' Union*, January 18, 1873.

CHAPTER II

ORGANIZATION

Origin of the Patrons of Husbandry

Ever since the latter part of the eighteenth century agricultural associations, both state and local, have existed in different parts of the United States; but their influence was slight previous to the Civil War and was confined principally to such aristocratic gentlemen farmers as the large planters of the southern states. After the close of the war the idea of organization took a firm hold on the farming classes, and the country witnessed the rise, rapid development — and often equally rapid decline — of a number of great agricultural orders, some of which have exerted considerable influence on the progress of the farming population and on the economic and social development of the country as a whole.

The first of these orders to be organized was the Patrons of Husbandry, or Grange, as it is commonly called, which came into existence in 1867.[1] Although the phenomenal growth of this order was due principally to the economic and political causes set forth in the preceding chapter, its immediate conception came from the fertile brain of Oliver Hudson Kelley,[2] a clerk in the government service at Washington. Kelley was

---

[1] The material for the ensuing account of the origin and early years of the Patrons of Husbandry to the permanent organization in 1873 is contained mainly in Kelley, *The Patrons of Husbandry.* Short accounts covering the field are to be found in Carr, *Patrons of Husbandry,* ch. x; Paine, *Granger Movement in Illinois,* 3–15; C. W. Pierson, " Rise of the Granger Movement," in *Popular Science Monthly,* xxxii. 199–208 (December, 1887); J. W. Darrow, *Origin and Early History of the Order of Patrons of Husbandry;* D. W. Aiken, *The Grange, its Origin, Progress, and Educational Purposes* (United States Department of Agriculture, *Special Report,* No. 55); N. A. Dunning, *Farmers' Alliance History,* 232–236; Martin, *The Grange Movement,* 407–411.

[2] Father Kelley, as he has long been known to the members of the order, died at his home in Washington, D.C., January 20, 1913, while these pages were going through the press.

a New Englander who had settled on a farm near Itasca, Minnesota. In 1864 he secured a position as clerk in the agricultural bureau and in January, 1866, he was appointed to travel through the southern states in order to gather information for the department.[1] On his trip through the South, which lasted three months, Kelley was struck by the lack of progressive spirit among the agricultural classes. A Mason, and appreciative of the benefits of fraternity, he came to the conclusion that a national secret order of farmers was needed for the furthering of the industrial reconstruction of the South and the advancement of the agricultural class throughout the country. On returning, Kelley went to Boston, where he discussed the idea with his niece Miss Carrie Hall, to whom is given the credit for first suggesting the admission of women to full membership in the order. The following summer Kelley spent on his farm in Minnesota, but in June, 1867, he received a clerkship in the post-office department at Washington and set about developing his plans.

W. M. Ireland, another clerk in the post-office department, was interested in Kelley's ideas and the two began planning a ritual for the order. Later in the year they enlisted William Saunders, a clerk in the agricultural bureau, into the ranks of the " founders," and as he was about to attend a meeting of the United States Pomological Society at St. Louis in August, Kelley gave him a written outline of the proposed order to circulate among the farmers with whom he might come in contact. This circular [2] set forth the deficiencies of existing agricultural societies and county fairs, and proposed the establishment of a secret order of farmers, modeled on the Masonic order, with the usual equipment of degrees, signs, and passwords, the object being to advance agriculture and bind the farmers together. Women were to be admitted to the order with separate degrees and the dues were to be as low as one dollar for each degree. This outline was circulated by Saunders while

[1] See Kelley, " Origin of the Order," in *The Connecticut Granges*, 1–7, for a somewhat humorous account of the way in which this appointment was secured.

[2] Printed in full in Kelley, *Patrons of Husbandry*, 17–20.

on his trip, with the result that several people wrote to Kelley and manifested an interest in his scheme.

The work of getting the order under way and preparing an elaborate ritual was now taken up in earnest by a number of government clerks in Washington and outsiders with whom they kept up a correspondence. Kelley, however, seems to have been the moving spirit throughout, although he delegated the composition of several parts of the ritual to others. In November, 1867, three hundred printed circulars[1] were sent to farmers whose addresses had been obtained, the result being much additional correspondence concerning the order with interested farmers.

Seven men are usually recognized by the Grange as the "founders" of the order. These were, as a writer in the *Popular Science Monthly* rather sarcastically puts it,[2] "one fruit-grower and six government clerks, equally distributed among the Post-Office, Treasury, and Agricultural Departments." All but one of them, however — so a Grange circular asserts — were born upon farms.[3] They were O. H. Kelley and W. M. Ireland of the post-office department, William Saunders and Rev. A. B. Grosh of the agricultural bureau, Rev. John Trimble and J. R. Thompson of the treasury department, and F. M. McDowell, a pomologist of Wayne, New York. These men, having worked out a ritual for the order, framed a constitution, and adopted a motto — *Esto perpetua* — met on December 4, 1867, constituted themselves the National Grange of the Patrons of Husbandry, and elected officers. Saunders was given the office of "Master" because of his position in the agricultural bureau; Thompson took the office of "Lecturer"; Ireland, that of treasurer; and Kelley became secretary of the incipient order. Neither Grosh nor McDowell was present at this meeting, but a little later the former was made chaplain. McDowell arrived in Washington on the eighth of January, 1868, and

[1] Reprinted in Kelley, *Patrons of Husbandry*, 38–40.

[2] Pierson, in *Popular Science Monthly*, xxxii. 199 (December, 1887).

[3] *Origin of the Grange*, a leaflet, issued by authority of the National Grange (*ca.* 1899).

immediately suggested changes which resulted in a complete reorganization of the upper frame-work of the order.

The arrangement then adopted, which has remained substantially in force ever since, embraced seven degrees, four to be conferred by the subordinate grange, one by the state grange, and the two highest by the National Grange. The four subordinate degrees for men were entitled; Laborer, Cultivator, Harvester, and Husbandman; and the corresponding degrees for women were; Maid, Shepherdess, Gleaner, and Matron. The state grange was to confer the fifth degree, Pomona (Hope), on masters and past-masters of subordinate granges, and their wives if Matrons. The National Grange would confer the sixth degree, Flora (Charity), on masters and past-masters of state granges and their wives who had taken the fifth degree. Members of the sixth degree would constitute the National Council and after serving one year therein might take the seventh degree and become members of the Senate, which body had control of the secret work of the order. This degree, Demeter or Ceres (Faith), embraced a number of new features introduced by McDowell and was put forward as " a continuation of an ancient Association once so flourishing in the East." [1] McDowell accepted the position of supreme head of this degree with the title of High Priest. Although there was considerable agitation for the abolition of the higher degrees among the rank and file of the Grangers when the organization was at the height of its prosperity in the seventies,[2] all that was accomplished was a series of changes which rendered these degrees accessible to all Patrons in regular order; while the control of the order was kept in the hands of representative delegate bodies.

Immediately after the establishment of the National Grange, the founders proceeded to organize a subordinate grange (Potomac No. 1) in Washington as a school of instruction. Its membership was made up mainly of clerks in the post-office department and their wives, but it served as a test of the ritual

---

[1] Kelley, *Patrons of Husbandry*, 64.

[2] Wisconsin State Grange, *Bulletin*, June, 1875; *California Patron*, November 15, 1876, p. 4.

and familiarized the organizers with its workings. Another circular setting forth the plan and aims of the order was now printed,[1] and in February, Kelley resigned his position in the post-office department and determined to devote his whole energies to the order. The work of drilling in Potomac Grange went on during February and March; parts of the ritual and constitution were printed; and a beginning was made in the work of advertising the order by means of letters to the newspapers. New ways were constantly suggesting themselves in which the order might make itself useful to the farmers, such as the protection of members from frauds and impositions, and the collection of reliable crop statistics. Finally Kelley determined that everything was ripe for the introduction of the order among the farmers, and decided to start for Minnesota, organizing granges on the way. The National Grange held a meeting, supplied him with a letter authorizing him to establish subordinate granges, and voted him a salary of two thousand dollars a year and traveling expenses, to be collected, however, from the receipts from subordinate granges which he should establish. Thus equipped, Kelley bought a ticket for Harrisburg, and, with two and a half dollars in his pocket, started out to work his way to Minnesota by organizing granges.

Early Years of the Grange

The center of interest now shifts to the Northwest, which was particularly ripe for the introduction of such an order because of discontent among the agricultural classes and a growing desire for some means of joint action against oppressive railroads and monopolies. Still it took several years of vigorous work on the part of Kelley and his associates to start the ball rolling. When, however, the order had been sufficiently advertised by the use of circular letters, personal correspondence, and above all by the coöperation of a number of agricultural papers and by judicious advertisement in local papers, it soon became evident that the farmers had here the weapon which they had

[1] Reprinted in Kelley, *Patrons of Husbandry*, 67-71, and in part in National Grange, *Proceedings*, xiv. 10 (1880).

been looking for, ready fashioned for their hands; and as a consequence the new order swept over the states of the Northwest like a prairie fire.

Kelley, on his trip to Minnesota, succeeded in disposing of four dispensations for the establishment of subordinate granges at the regular fixed price of fifteen dollars each, but only one of these resulted in a permanent grange. He had been corresponding for some time with A. S. Moss of Fredonia, New York, and with his help succeeded in establishing in that place the first regular, active, and permanent grange. Two of the dispensations, those for Harrisburg, Pennsylvania, and Columbus, Ohio, were paid for by men who agreed to work up a grange in these places, but nothing came of their efforts. The fourth dispensation was issued to a grange gathered together by H. D. Emery, editor of the *Prairie Farmer*, in Chicago, which, however, failed to develop. Kelley had already borrowed fifty dollars from McDowell at Wayne, New York, and now, after another unsuccessful attempt to establish a grange at Madison, Wisconsin, he was obliged to borrow fifteen dollars from the master of the Masonic lodge there in order to get to his home at Itasca, Minnesota. He seems to have made the mistake of attempting to introduce an agricultural order by working in the large cities instead of getting out among the real tillers of the soil; and it was not until after he returned to his farm in Minnesota and began to work among fellow farmers that any real success attended his efforts.

Fortunately perhaps for Kelley, though he complained about it at the time, the members of the so-called National Grange at Washington began to lose interest in the work and left him pretty much to his own devices, with the exception of calling on him occasionally for money with which to pay printing bills long past due in Washington. Kelley, thus thrown on his own resources, soon found himself so embarrassed that at times he could not even buy stamps for his correspondence; but he never lost faith in the order and continued to keep up the delusion of a great national organization at Washington by circulating photographs of the founders and issuing grandiloquent circulars.

His correspondence with A. Failor, of Newton, Iowa, resulted in the formation of a grange in that place, the first in the state, and on May 2, 1868, the fifteen dollars for its dispensation was received. At intervals in his farm work, Kelley endeavored to keep the order before the public during the summer by letters in leading agricultural papers such as the *Prairie Farmer* of Chicago, the *Farmers' Union* of Minneapolis, and the *Rural World* of St. Louis. He also induced various papers to print the constitution of the order and such notices concerning it as he was able to manufacture.

Finally in August, 1868, Colonel D. A. Robertson of St. Paul was enlisted in the work, and on September 2, North Star Grange, the first permanent grange in Minnesota, was organized at St. Paul with his assistance. Robertson and the other members of this grange took an immediate and active interest in the propagation of the order. The circulars were revised [1] and emphasis was laid upon such features as protection against corporations, the advantages of crop and market statistics, depots for the sale of produce, and concerted action in the purchase of stock and the testing of new farm implements. The new energy thus manifested in the work soon brought results and two more active granges were organized before the end of the year. These were followed by three more in January, 1869, and three in February; and on February 23, representatives of these subordinate granges met in St. Paul and organized the Minnesota State Grange. [2] Within two months after its organization, the Minnesota State Grange, without the sanction of the National Grange, appointed a state purchasing agent for the coöperative purchase of supplies and agricultural implements for Patrons; thus taking the first step in what was to become one of the most important activities of the order. This seems to have had much influence on the movement in Minnesota, and by the close of the year 1869 there were thirty-seven active granges in the

[1] This revised circular is reprinted in Kelley, *Patrons of Husbandry*, 125–130; extracts in *Minnesota Monthly*, i. 255 (August, 1869) and National Grange, *Proceedings*, xiv. 11 (1880).

[2] *Minnesota Monthly*, i. 97 (March, 1869).

state.[1] Some of the new granges were organized by Kelley and others by deputies appointed by the master of the state grange.

After getting the Minnesota State Grange on its feet, Kelley, in March, 1869, left Minnesota for a trip to the East. After visiting Fredonia, New York, where he found an active grange with a hundred members, he went on to Washington. In that city, on April 13, 1869, the National Grange convened in its so-called first annual session with six members present; it listened to the report of the secretary on the work accomplished, enacted a few laws for the regulation of the order, and then relapsed into inactivity.[2]

Kelley soon returned to Minnesota. There, with the help of his niece, Miss Hall, who acted as his assistant, he continued his active work of organization, and, by an extensive correspondence, laid the foundations for the order in other states. Late in October he made a trip to northern Iowa, where the second grange in that state was organized at Pottsville. This trip also resulted soon after in the formation of Waukon Grange, Iowa, which was said in 1875 to have held more meetings than any other grange in the United States. Dudley W. Adams, first master of the Iowa State Grange and later master of the National Grange, came into the work as secretary of Waukon Grange. Kelley followed up this trip by another into Illinois and Indiana, lasting from November, 1869, to January, 1870, which resulted in the permanent introduction of the order in each of those states, by the establishment of granges in Illinois at Nunda (Eureka Grange) and Henry, and in Indiana at Honey Creek, Terre Haute, and Indianapolis (Capital Grange).[3] Kelley then proceeded to Washington to join with the other " founders " in a meeting of the National Grange, and on his way back organized the first grange in Ohio at East Cleveland, March 2, 1870. He then hurried on to his Minnesota home, where he found a batch of letters containing inquiries concerning the

[1] Compiled from table in Kelley, *Patrons of Husbandry*, 216.

[2] *Ibid.* 174–179.

[3] *Prairie Farmer*, xl. 372 (November 13, 1869) announced this trip of Kelley's and recommended both him and the order to the editorial fraternity.

Patrons of Husbandry or requests for deputies to organize, and in general showing a growing interest in the order in all parts of the country.

The plan of work during the next few years was to get a few active subordinate granges started, and out of them to organize a temporary state grange, the master of which would appoint deputies to carry on the work of organizing subordinate granges in the different parts of the state. Charters were issued for subordinate granges only when at least nine men and four women were pledged as members, and the number of charter members was limited to thirty, of whom ten must be women. The initiation fee was usually three dollars for men and fifty cents for women, but this varied somewhat from time to time. Of the money thus collected, fifteen dollars went to the National Grange to pay for the dispensation, and sums ranging from five to fifteen dollars and expenses were received by the deputies for organizing the grange. In some states the state grange also took a small fee from each grange organized, and whatever remained went into the treasury of the subordinate grange.

During the remainder of the year 1870, the work of organization progressed but slowly. In Illinois, the feeling of antagonism to railroads had led to the calling of a Producers' Convention which met at Bloomington, April 20, and appointed a committee to take measures for the establishment of town and county transportation leagues. Efforts were made by Kelley and W. W. Corbett, the editor of the *Prairie Farmer*, to capture this movement for the Patrons of Husbandry; and in June, 1870, they revived Garden City Grange, which had been organized by Kelley on his trip to the West in 1868, and then proceeded to organize a temporary state grange made up largely of deputies, but with H. C. Wheeler, a member of the committee on organization appointed by the Bloomington convention, as its secretary. This move proved abortive, and but one new grange was organized in Illinois in 1870.[1]

[1] Kelley, *Patrons of Husbandry*, 245, 269–272, 285, 289, 295; *Prairie Farmer,* xli. 89, 130 (March 26, April 30, 1870). For a fuller account of this Producers' Convention, see below, p. 127.

In April, 1870, a correspondence concerning the establishment of the order in Missouri was opened with Norman J. Coleman, editor of the *Rural World* of St. Louis; and in August, Kelley spent two weeks in St. Louis and vicinity, organizing two subordinate granges and a temporary state grange. No further granges were organized in Missouri during the year; but Kelley's trip brought Thomas Allen and William Muir into the ranks, and their efforts later resulted in the rapid spread of the order in that state.[1] On his way back to Minnesota, Secretary Kelley met General William Duane Wilson, editor of the *Iowa Homestead and Farm Journal*, who had been appointed general deputy of the order in Iowa, and together they organized two granges in the neighborhood of Des Moines [2] By October, 1870, Kelley came to the conclusion that the transfer of his headquarters to Washington would be an advantageous step. A circular was sent to every grange and to every person who had inquired concerning the order, announcing the permanent location of the secretary's office in Washington. This circular also stated that the order was working in fifteen states and rapidly increasing, that a plan had been adopted for organizing by letter, and that necessary documents would be sent to anyone desiring to take an active part in the work.[3]

The labors of the secretary and the deputies during the year 1870 gave to the order nineteen new granges in Minnesota, making forty-seven in all, and nine in Iowa, established mainly through the efforts of General Wilson, which, added to the two previously organized, gave that state eleven granges. Indiana, Illinois, and New York, each added one new grange during the year, making their totals three, three, and two respectively; and the order was newly introduced into Missouri — two granges — and Ohio, Tennessee, and California — one grange each. The organizations in Tennessee and California were made by letter as a result of correspondence with interested parties, and similar correspondence was under way with parties in Vermont, Massachusetts, New Jersey, South Carolina, Georgia,

---

[1] Kelley, *Patrons of Husbandry*, 250, 273–275, 281, 289, 295.
[2] *Ibid.* 283.   [3] *Ibid.* 285, 289.

Kentucky, and Kansas.[1] Thus it will be seen that on January 1, 1871, the order was in actual operation in nine states — instead of fifteen as stated in Kelley's circular — and that in Minnesota and Iowa alone had it shown any signs of the rapid growth which it was soon to experience. As yet Minnesota had the only active state grange, though temporary organizations had been established in Illinois and Missouri.

During the year 1871, the order continued to flourish with the most vigor in the states of the North Central division;[2] especially in Iowa, where a state grange was organized on January 12, 1871, with representatives present from eleven subordinate granges in six different counties of eastern and central Iowa. Dudley W. Adams — later master of the National Grange when at the height of its prosperity — was elected master of the new state grange and General Wilson became its secretary. The work of organization was now taken over by the state grange, several local deputies were appointed, and by April 22, 1871, the number of granges in the state had risen to thirty-seven. On September 14, 1871, the state grange held its first regular session, which was a marked success, and at the end of the year the state headed the list with one hundred and two granges.[3] In Minnesota the order did not fare so well; the state grange met for its annual session in February, but not more than six or seven new granges were organized during the year.[4]

Wisconsin, Indiana, and Illinois were coming to the front, however. In Wisconsin, the first grange was organized in Adams County on January 1, 1871, by Deputy Burnham, and was followed by nineteen more in Adams, Sauk, and Waushara counties. On June 12, 1871, the state grange was organized at Plainfield. This fair prospect was blighted by dissensions between the deputy and the officers of the state grange, with

---

[1] Kelley, *Patrons of Husbandry*, 209, 243, 254, 261, 273, 278–282, 286, 291, 293–296.

[2] The expressions " North Central," " North Atlantic," " South Central," etc., are used in this book in the same sense as in the reports of the United States census bureau, to cover certain defined groups of states.

[3] Kelley, *Patrons of Husbandry*, 294–296, 305, 310, 314, 323, 326, 333, 338, 341; *Prairie Farmer*, xliii. 124 (April 22, 1871), xliv. 44 (February 8, 1873).

[4] Kelley, *Patrons of Husbandry*, 317.

the result that most of the granges had ceased operations by the end of the year.[1] In March, 1871, active work was begun in the four northwestern counties of Indiana by Oscar Dinwiddie, which proved to be the real starting point of the order in that state; and the operations of J. Wilkinson, one of the successful Iowa deputies, in northwestern Illinois resulted in the establishment of five granges there in the latter half of 1871. The only other grange established in this group of states in 1871 was one organized by letter in Ohio in February; but active correspondence had led to the appointment of deputies in Kansas, Nebraska, and Missouri.[2]

In the southern states the spread of the order began about the same time in South Carolina and Mississippi. On the recommendation of Colonel Jacques, editor of the *Rural Carolinian* of Charleston, William E. Simmons, Jr. was appointed a special deputy; and on May 25, 1871, Ashley Grange No. 1 was organized at Charleston. In Mississippi, the first two granges were organized, June 3, at Rienzi, by W. L. Williams, and June 17, at Columbus, by R. D. Powell, as a result of correspondence with Secretary Kelley. Powell also organized another grange at Aberdeen, December 15. One was started at Allenville, Kentucky, by W. S. Reeves, August 10, 1871. These five, with the one at Stockton, Tennessee, organized in 1870, were all the granges in the South at the end of the year 1871.[3]

In the East, the order did not progress any more rapidly. A grange was organized at Clinton, Pennsylvania, by Luke Eger, on February 22, 1871; one at St. Johnsbury, Vermont, by Jonathan Lawrence, July 4; and another in New Jersey by Secretary Kelley, December 26, 1871. Both Kelley and J. R. Thompson of the National Grange spent some time in Vermont in the latter part of the year, but they failed to get any more granges established; Kelley also failed in an attempt to organize

[1] Kelley, *Patrons of Husbandry*, 302, 305, 310, 334, 374, 382, 388; E. M. Maynard, *Patrons of Husbandry in Wisconsin* (Ms.), ch. ii; R. E. Smith, *Wisconsin Granger Movement* (Ms.), ch. ii.

[2] Kelley, *Patrons of Husbandry*, 210, 316, 319, 333, 339, 342, 354, 356, 359; *Prairie Farmer*, xliii. 4 (January 6, 1872); Paine, *Granger Movement in Illinois*, 10.

[3] Kelley, *Patrons of Husbandry*, 310, 318, 320, 327–332, 345, 349, 354.

a grange in Boston with the assistance of George Noyes of the *Massachusetts Ploughman*, who had shown himself favorable to the order.[1]

Thus the year 1871 saw the introduction of the order into seven additional states: Wisconsin, Pennsylvania, South Carolina, Mississippi, Vermont, Kentucky, and New Jersey, making a total of sixteen in which the order was at work; also the organization of two state granges, in Iowa and Wisconsin, although the latter had to be reorganized in the following year.

RAPID GROWTH OF THE GRANGE, 1872–73

Before taking up the work of organization of the year 1872, it will be well to notice some features which were being introduced into the order that tended to increase its popularity and led to its rapid spread during the next three years. Although the original idea of the founders appears to have been that the benefits of the order to its members would be primarily social and intellectual, it very soon became apparent that the desire for financial advantages would prove a far greater incentive to induce the farmers to join. This early led to two forms of activity which left an indelible stamp upon the order, and gave it, in large part, its importance in the history of the period: first, the efforts to secure cheaper transportation; and, secondly, the introduction of all sorts of schemes for coöperation in the purchase of supplies, the marketing of farm products, insurance, and even in the manufacture of agricultural implements.

The desire for cheaper transportation assumed the form of a somewhat vague antagonism to railroad corporations and agitation for government regulation of freight and passenger rates. This matter will be taken up more fully in connection with the Granger railroad legislation, and is merely mentioned here in order to bring out the fact that this agitation came into the order prior to its remarkable expansion in 1873–74 and was in fact one of the causes of that expansion. The attempt in 1870 of Secretary Kelley and Editor Corbett of the *Prairie Farmer*

---

[1] Kelley, *Patrons of Husbandry*, 313, 325–327, 337, 341, 350, 355.

to turn the anti-railroad sentiment of Illinois to the benefit of the order has been noted. In May of the same year, (1870) Corbett wrote a strong letter in which he asserted that " Railroad, Insurance Companies, Warehouse and Telegraph Companies, are crushing the life out of the producing classes," and advocated action on the part of the Patrons of Husbandry to protect the people from these evils, even to the extent of forming a third party to hold the balance of power and secure the election of candidates to office pledged to carry out the reforms demanded.[1] This letter was read before the state grange of Minnesota and then printed for circulation, and early in the following year Kelley followed it up by securing reprints of articles by Rufus Hatch published in the New York *Independent* upon stock-watering and other railroad abuses. These, he says, " proved excellent ' fuel ' for deputies to circulate." [2]

By April, 1871, according to Kelley, " ' Coöperation ' and ' Down with monopolies ' were proving popular watchwords." [3] The early activity of the Minnesota State Grange in the direction of coöperation has been alluded to. The first efforts of the National Grange along that line were not particularly successful,[4] but by the latter part of 1872, the business agent appointed by the Iowa State Grange was showing the possibilities of coöperative buying and selling as a means of reducing prices and commissions.[5] From this time on coöperation was a recognized part of the work of every state grange as soon as organized, and in many states, county councils, afterwards officially recognized as Pomona granges, were formed to further the business features of the order.

Largely as a result of the emphasis thus laid upon its pecuniary advantages, the order began to grow vigorously in 1872, especially in the North Central group of states and in some parts of the South. 1150 granges were organized during the year, as

---

[1] Reprinted in Kelley, *Patrons of Husbandry*, 256–259.

[2] *Ibid.* 256, 315, 320.

[3] *Ibid.* 322.

[4] *Ibid.* 302–305, 385; *Rural Carolinian*, iv. 36 (October, 1872). See also below, p. 256.

[5] Kelley, *Patrons of Husbandry*, 409.

compared with 132 the previous year. Of these, 652, or over half, were in the state of Iowa.[1] In Minnesota the lethargy of the previous year was shaken off and some forty-six new granges organized,[2] and in Illinois the work of Wilkinson resulted in enough granges to enable Kelley to reorganize the state grange on a permanent basis at Dixon, March 5, 1872. Considerable activity ensued and sixty-five granges were organized in the state during the year making a total of seventy-two or seventy-three active granges.[3] In Indiana, Kelley organized a state grange about the same time, February 22, 1872, at Terre Haute, but the order did not take hold so vigorously there at the start as in some of the more western states, and only thirty-eight granges were established during the year.[4]

Six granges were organized in Ohio in 1872, and S. H. Ellis, who was to make the order a success in that state, was enlisted in the work. In Wisconsin the order was in bad repute, as has been noted, and early in the year, Burnham, the offending deputy, was removed and J. C. Abbot of Iowa sent into the state to carry on the work. He transferred the field of operations to the more fertile counties in the southeastern part of the state, organized sixteen granges in five months, and on October 2, 1872, reorganized the state grange at Portage with all the new and seven of the old granges represented. Six more granges were organized in the state during the year. In Michigan, the first grange was organized January 10, 1872, by E. M. Jones, a special deputy, and when Abbot had completed the revival of the movement in Wisconsin, he was sent to Michigan, where he organized seven granges before the end of the year. Nebraska came into the field with two granges organized by correspondence in January and February, 1872.

[1] National Grange, *Proceedings*, vi. 6, 8 (1873).

[2] *Ibid.* 8.

[3] Kelley, *Patrons of Husbandry*, 359, 368, 374; National Grange, *Proceedings*, vi. 8 (1873); *Prairie Farmer*, xliii. 100, 153, 273, 284, 292, 356, 388, 401, 404 (March–December, 1872); Paine, *Granger Movement in Illinois*, 10.

[4] Kelley, *Patrons of Husbandry*, 359, 374, 388; Indiana State Grange, *Proceedings*, xxxvi. 96 (Appendix); *Prairie Farmer*, xliii. 20, 105, 273 (January–August, 1872); National Grange, *Proceedings*, vi. 8 (1873).

Others followed rapidly during the summer, and on August 2, General Wilson of Iowa organized the Nebraska State Grange with sixteen subordinate granges represented. Before the year closed there were forty-nine granges in the state. In Kansas, the movement got under way about the same time; the state grange was organized by General Wilson in December, 1872; and there were twelve granges in the state at the end of the year. Missouri also began to take new interest in the movement, and General Deputy Thomas Allen went actively to work during the latter part of 1872, with the result that fourteen new subordinate granges were organized.[1]

In the South considerable opposition to the spread of the Patrons of Husbandry was encountered from commission men and local merchants, and it was stated that mortgages held against planters were sometimes foreclosed as a penalty for joining the order.[2] There was also a natural tendency to look with suspicion on anything of northern origin " with a great *central* head at Washington City," [3] but in spite of these obstacles, the work progressed rapidly in South Carolina under the leadership of Colonel D. Wyatt Aiken of Cokesbury. He was appointed deputy at large for the southern states in January, 1872, organized ten granges in April, and by the ninth of October there were seventy-six granges in South Carolina. On that date the state grange was organized by Kelley at Columbia with seventy-two subordinate granges represented, and by the end of the year the state ranked next to Iowa in number of granges, having 101 on its roll. In Mississippi, the work, which was begun by W. L. Williams at Rienzi, was kept up by him and county deputies under his direction, and on the fifteenth of March the state grange was organized by Kelley. Subsequent

---

[1] Kelley, *Patrons of Husbandry*, 367–413; National Grange, *Proceedings*, vi. 8 (1873). On Ohio, see also Ellis, in *Ohio Farmer*, c. 147 (August 29, 1901); on Wisconsin, Maynard, *Patrons of Husbandry in Wisconsin* (Ms.), ch. iii; Smith, *Wisconsin Granger Movement* (Ms.), ch. ii; Wisconsin State Grange, *Proceedings*, ii (January, 1874); on Kansas, J. K. Hudson, *Patron's Handbook*, 8; on Missouri, *Prairie Farmer*, xliv. 3 (January 4, 1873).

[2] *Prairie Farmer*, xliii. 356 (November 9, 1872).

[3] *Southern Cultivator* (Athens, Georgia), xxx. 76 (February, 1872).

meetings of the state grange occurred on July 2, and December 10, 1872, and fifty-five granges were organized in the state during the year. Kentucky added one new grange in 1872 and in Tennessee four were organized, mainly through the efforts of General A. J. Vaughn, master of the Mississippi State Grange. In five other southern states, the first granges were organized in 1872: Virginia, February 16; Louisiana, March 15; Alabama, July 15; Arkansas, August 3; and Georgia, October 2. Before the year closed, seven more granges were organized in Alabama, two in Louisiana, and one in Georgia.[1]

In the eastern states, the only active work in 1872, besides the organization of one additional grange in New Jersey, was done in Vermont, where Deputy Eben Thompson began work in January and by the twenty-second of February had organized nine granges. The state grange was established by Kelley on the fourth of July, in connection with a Patrons' celebration at St. Johnsbury, there being thirteen granges in the state, but no more appear to have been organized during the year. The year 1872 also saw the organization of the first grange in Oregon, January 6, and the introduction of the order into Canada, where Eben Thompson organized the first grange August 16, and two more before the close of the year.[2]

To summarize the advance of the order in 1872: state granges were organized in six states — Indiana, Vermont, South Carolina, Nebraska, Mississippi, and Kansas — and reorganized in Illinois and Wisconsin, thus making, in all, ten state granges in operation. In nine states — Nebraska, Oregon, Michigan, Virginia, Louisiana, Kansas, Alabama, Arkansas, and Georgia — the order found lodgment during 1872, so that, at the close of the year, twenty-five states had active subordinate granges within their limits. Although the strength of the order was, at this

---

[1] Kelley, *Patrons of Husbandry*, 354–403; *Rural Carolinian*, iii. 1, 70–72, 217, iv. 37, 39, 88–93, 213 (October, 1871–January, 1873); National Grange, *Proceedings*, vi. 8 (1873); South Carolina State Grange, *Minute Book* (Ms.), 1–6, 18; Mississippi State Grange, *Proceedings*, iii. 9 (1875).

[2] Kelley, *Patrons of Husbandry*, 359, 370, 390–393, 398; National Grange, *Proceedings*, vi. 8 (1873). On Vermont, see also *Bryan Fund Publication*, no. 4 (Grange circular); Vermont State Grange, *Proceedings*, i–iii. 3, 8, 37 (1872–74).

time, concentrated mainly in Iowa and Minnesota in the North-west and South Carolina and Mississippi in the South, still its spread was so general and its centers so far apart, that it must be looked upon even thus early as distinctly national in character. In the North Central group, every state had now been entered, and the territory of Dakota alone remained un-touched by the order; while of the southern states, all had granges except Delaware, Maryland, West Virginia, Florida, and Texas. In the eastern or North Atlantic states, little progress had been made except in Vermont, while on the Pacific coast, the order had been introduced into both California and Oregon, though as yet these states had but one grange apiece.

In the fall of 1872, Secretary Kelley sent letters to all the masters of state granges, general deputies, the "founders," and a few others who had taken an active part in the building of the order, inviting them to attend the sixth annual session of the National Grange, and on January 8, 1873, twenty-three men and four women, including six of the "founders," six masters of state granges, and a number of deputies, representing in all eleven different states, assembled in Georgetown, D. C. It was now a little over five years since the organization of a temporary National Grange by a little band of government clerks in Wash-ington, and the active workers had been looking forward eagerly to the time when that body could be reorganized on a permanent basis. This was now accomplished, and the control of the great and rapidly growing agricultural order of the Patrons of Husbandry passed into the hands of actual farmers.[1]

The principal business of this session was the revision of the constitution and by-laws, the election of a new set of officers, and the incorporation of the National Grange under an act of Congress providing for the creation of corporations in the District of Columbia.[2] Among the articles of the constitution

---

[1] National Grange, *Proceedings*, vi (1873); Kelley, *Patrons of Husbandry*, 414–421; Darrow, *Patrons of Husbandry*, 38–40; Messer, *The Grange*, 5; Dunning, *Farmer's Alliance History*, 235; Pierson, in *Popular Science Monthly*, xxxii. 199–208; Aiken, *The Grange*, 7.

[2] The certificate of incorporation, dated January 10, 1873, is in National Grange, *Proceedings*, vi. 33–34 (1873).

are two that call for special mention because of their bearing on the future development of the order. These are: Article V, which provided for the admission into the order of "any person interested in agricultural pursuits"; and Article XII, which prohibited the discussion of political or religious questions in the work of the order or the application of political or religious tests for membership therein. The proper interpretation of these two articles was to be a vexing question for the leaders of the order for many years to come. In the election of officers, the position of master went to Dudley W. Adams of Iowa, Kelley retained the secretaryship, and an executive committee was elected consisting of William Saunders of the District of Columbia, D. Wyatt Aiken of South Carolina, and E. R. Shankland of Iowa.[1] On these men devolved the difficult duty of guiding the order during the years of its greatest activity.

The expansion of the order of Patrons of Husbandry during 1873 and 1874 and the beginnings of its decline in the two following years can best be followed in connection with the accompanying table of statistics showing the number of granges and their proportion to the agricultural population in each state and territory at different times during the four years. The accompanying series of four maps, based upon these statistics, will also be of assistance in comparing the movement in different parts of the country.[2]

The rapid expansion of the order during 1873, especially in the North Central group of states, is shown by the statistics of its condition on May 19, August 2 (Map I), and October 18. Iowa was strongly in the lead at the start with 1507 granges, or 631 per hundred thousand of agricultural population. This lead in number of granges was kept up throughout the year, but the rate of increase was naturally not so rapid as in some of the other states where the movement got under way a little later. Thus Kansas and Nebraska forged rapidly to the front, until, by October 18, Kansas almost and Nebraska quite equaled

---

[1] National Grange, *Proceedings*, vi. 15, 18, 24; Kelley, *Patrons of Husbandry*, 421; Darrow, *Patrons of Husbandry*, 39.

[2] The maps will be found facing pages 61, 65, 67, and 69.

State	May 19, 1873		August 2, 1873		October 18, 1873		March 1, 1874		Se
	No. of granges	No. per 100,000 agr. pop.	No. of granges	No. per 100,000 agr. pop.	No. of granges	No. per 100,000 agr. pop.	No. of granges	No. per 100,000 agr. pop.	g
Maine	....	....	....	....	....	....	3	4	
New Hampshire	....	....	....	....	6	13	20	44	
Vermont	22	38	24	42	27	47	83	146	
Massachusetts	....	....	1	1	6	9	36	52	
Connecticut	....	....	....	....	....	....	1	2	
New York	(6)	(2)	8	2	12	3	115	31	
New Jersey	(2)	(3)	3	5	12	19	68	110	
Pennsylvania	(7)	(3)	9	3	29	11	132	48	
North Atlantic Div.	(37)	(4)	45	4	92	9	458	45	
Delaware	....	....	....	....	....	....	1	6	
Maryland	....	....	....	....	3	4	43	51	
Virginia	(2)	(1)	3	1	5	2	44	18	
West Virginia	....	....	2	2	18	21	31	35	
North Carolina	(20)	(6)	30	10	110	37	243	79	
South Carolina	118	51	131	56	171	73	249	103	
Georgia	16	4	73	20	257	70	551	148	
Florida	....	....	....	....	14	30	31	63	
South Atlantic Div.	(156)	(11)	239	17	578	42	1,193	85	
Ohio	47	12	80	20	163	41	594	149	
Indiana	142	50	266	93	467	163	1,502	513	
Illinois	431	109	562	142	676	171	1,148	284	
Michigan	24	12	40	20	91	45	284	136	
Wisconsin	140	82	189	111	222	130	410	235	
Minnesota	219	238	327	355	362	394	467	478	
Iowa	1,507	631	1,763	741	1,818	763	1,918	775	
Missouri	245	84	483	166	920	315	1,807	603	
Dakota	(8)	(78)	11	107	25	242	47	364	
Nebraska	100	231	300	694	331	763	504	1,010	
Kansas	128	113	399	353	596	526	1,073	847	
North Central Div.	(2,991)	(134)	4,420	197	5,671	253	9,754	422	
Kentucky	1	.4	1	.4	27	10	567	199	
Tennessee	13	5	60	22	183	66	548	196	
Alabama	9	3	21	7	127	40	471	144	
Mississippi	112	40	189	67	392	138	560	192	
Louisiana	(9)	(6)	11	7	26	16	79	47	
Texas	....	....	1	4	25	11	151	62	
Indian Territory	....	....	....	....	....	....	....	....	
Arkansas	15	11	26	18	69	49	244	160	
South Central Div.	(159)	(10)	309	18	849	50	2,620	150	
Montana	....	....	....	....	....	....	6	195	
Colorado	....	....	2	23	2	23	45	483	
Arizona	....	....	....	....	....	....	....	....	
Nevada	....	....	....	....	....	....	....	....	
Idaho	....	....	....	....	....	....	2	83	
Washington	....	....	....	....	5	77	19	258	
Oregon	(9)	(52)	12	69	37	213	112	595	
California	8	14	35	61	91	159	156	258	
Western Division	(17)	(13)	49	38	135	106	340	250	
United States	(3,360)	(52)	5,062	78	7,325	114	14,365	217	
Canada	(6)	...•.	8	....	8	....	....	....	

[1] The statistics of granges in this table have been obtained from the following sources: for May 19, from the *Vermont Record and Farmer*, June 13, 1873, p. 3; for August 2, 1873, from the *Prairie Farmer* 260; for October 18, 1873, from *ibid.* 355; for March 1, 1874, from National Grange, *Secretary's Report*, (circular); for September 1, 1874, from National Grange, *Monthly Bulletin*, September 1, 1874 (circular) January 1, 1875, from National Grange, *Secretary's Report*, 1875 (circular); for October 1, 1875, from Na Grange, *Proceedings*, ix. 190; for July 1, 1876, from *ibid.* x. 179.

In some cases, where statistics of granges for particular states at the given date are lacking, these been supplied by careful estimates based on statements for the nearest dates for which they were obtai

	January 1, 1875			October 1, 1875			July 1, 1876		
	No. of granges	No. per 100,000 agr. pop.	No. per 10,000 sq. m.	No. of members	No. of granges	No. per 100,000 agr. pop.	No. of members	No. of granges	No. per 100,000 agr. pop.
	75	91	23	8,247	180	230	11,773	218	265
	42	92	45	2,528	69	152	3,947	77	170
	159	281	166	10,193	198	350	10,908	208	369
	66	96	79	3,825	98	142	3,776	86	126
	4	9	8	480	16	36	328	13	30
	276	73	56	11,723	275	73	16,184	320	85
	83	136	106	4,495	94	154	4,923	99	163
	428	152	95	22,471	536	191	28,174	626	220
	1,133	110	67	63,961	1,475	144	80,013	1,647	160
	16	95	78	503	23	136	969	25	146
	126	147	103	5,635	153	179	5,859	148	171
	449	180	106	13,885	663	266	16,041	479	191
	157	173	63	5,990	280	309	9,376	295	313
	477	151	91	10,166	342	109	7,562	240	74
	314	125	103	10,922	342	136	8,440	232	89
	683	178	115	17,826	545	142	10,161	277	70
	127	251	28	3,804	83	164	2,894	94	180
	2,349	163	86	68,731	2,431	168	61,302	1,790	121
	1,102	278	268	53,327	879	221	53,977	1,214	306
	2,000	667	550	60,298	1,485	498	48,959	1,145	375
	1,533	377	271	29,063	789	194	12,639	646	157
	551	258	97	33,196	605	283	29,901	593	271
	505	284	90	17,226	446	251	12,385	294	162
	506	490	61	16,617	456	441	9,330	295	271
	1,891	735	338	51,332	1,164	452	32,019	1,018	382
	2,009	649	291	80,059	1,901	613	42,529	974	305
	56	361	4	1,178	53	341	697	26	143
	592	1,042	76	8,177	289	508	9,867	361	568
	1,332	952	162	40,261	409	293	24,658	874	571
	12,077	508	157	390,734	8,485	357	276,961	7,440	304
	1,493	513	370	52,463	1,549	535	35,933	1,003	338
	1,042	372	248	37,581	1,092	389	19,411	492	174
	650	183	124	17,440	531	158	11,200	(287)	(83)
	630	210	135	30,797	645	216	20,606	449	146
	237	137	49	10,078	315	182	9,750	264	147
	916	348	35	37,619	1,203	457	38,149	902	319
	10	....	1	450	15	....	231	8	....
	567	348	105	20,471	631	388	11,344	321	185
	5,545	307	91	206,899	5,981	331	146,624	(3,726)	(200)
	24	725	2	946	26	787	888	25	704
	67	671	6	2,098	63	629	1,653	43	402
	....	....	....	....	....	....	20	(1)	(39)
	7	224	1	378	15	481	214	9	270
	15	565	2	390	16	602	378	(15)	(518)
	63	763	9	2,169	66	800	1,963	68	741
	177	877	18	8,233	186	926	8,544	(190)	(885)
	240	377	15	14,228	263	413	9,965	173	259
	593	413	5	28,442	635	442	23,625	(524)	(348)
	21,697	320	71	758,767	19,007	279	588,525	(15,127)	(217)
	....	....	....	450	27	....	....	....	....

...e table for July 1, 1876, in National Grange, *Proceedings*, the numbers of granges are omitted for some
...e western states. These are supplied by estimates based on the number of members of the order in
...states. All such cases, in which the exact number of granges has not been obtained, are indicated in
...able by the use of parentheses.

...ne statistics of the proportion of granges to agricultural population are based on the United States census
...as of population engaged in agriculture in the census years 1870 and 1880, with estimated correction for
...ntervening years.

Iowa in relative proportion of granges to agricultural population; a result which the comparative sparsity of population made possible with a considerably smaller number of granges. Missouri also experienced a phenomenal growth during the period, while Minnesota continued to advance slowly, though it fell back in relative rank from second to fourth place; but the Territory of Dakota, with only twenty-five granges, surpassed, on October 18, all the states east of the Mississippi in relative proportion of granges to agricultural population. In the old Northwest Territory, the order advanced rapidly in Indiana and Illinois and made considerable gains in Wisconsin, while in Ohio and Michigan it obtained a secure foothold during the year.

Turning to the South, a much smaller development of the order than in the North Central division is seen, especially as regards proportion of granges to agricultural population, but here it is necessary to take into consideration the fact that the census figures of agricultural population, on which the statistics are based, include large numbers of negroes who were not admitted into the ranks of the Patrons of Husbandry. In view of this condition, it is probable that a given ratio in the South represents as extensive participation by the white farmers in the work of the order, as would a ratio nearly twice as large in the Northwest. On May 19, 1873, South Carolina ranked first among the southern states both in actual number of granges and in relative proportions, but the rapid development of the order in Mississippi soon carried that state to the front, and by October 18 there were 392 granges within its borders. In Georgia, Tennessee, Alabama, and North Carolina, the order was also making rapid strides; Kentucky, Virginia, Arkansas, and Louisiana showed a healthy growth; and in Maryland, West Virginia, Florida, and Texas, the first granges were organized during the year. Thus by October 18, 1873, every southern state except Delaware had been entered by the order.

Little progress was made by the Patrons of Husbandry on the Pacific coast previous to 1873; and, indeed, the first move toward effective agricultural organization in that district came in the form of independent clubs. The extortions of various rings of middlemen and shippers, the high rates of interest charged upon money loaned in the country, and, above all, the monopoly of the carrying trade enjoyed by the Central Pacific railroad and its subsidiary lines led in 1871 and 1872 to an agitation among the farmers of California in favor of protective and coöperative organization. The first manifestation of this movement was the establishment of a farmers' club at Sacramento in December, 1871, followed rapidly by others in the vicinity, and in September, 1872, delegates from eleven of these clubs met at Sacramento and organized the California Farmers' Union. This body at once began to make plans for the establishment of extensive business enterprises on a coöperative basis, its first efforts being an attempt to secure grain sacks for the farmers at reduced rates; and the failure of this project, due to the inability of the farmers to keep their arrangements secret, exposed the need of a closer and more secret form of organization. An opening was thus made for the Patrons of Husbandry, and W. H. Baxter, who had been appointed general deputy for the order in 1871, appeared before the Farmers' Union convention at San Francisco in April, 1873, and so successfully set forth the advantages of the order that the work of agricultural organization was formally turned over to the Grange and the Farmers' Union went out of existence.[1]

The officers of the National Grange at once sent N. W. Garretson of Iowa as a special deputy to the Pacific coast and the organization of granges went on apace, thirty-five being formed by the fifteenth of July, on which date representatives of these granges met at Napa City and organized the state grange of California.[2] Having started the order on its way in California, Garretson proceeded to Oregon where the antagonism of the farmers of the Columbia River Valley to the monopoly of the Oregon Steam Navigation Company made it easy for him to organize twenty granges in a short time.[3] In both of these states the growth of the order was rapid during the remainder

---

[1] Carr, *Patrons of Husbandry*, 75–103.

[2] California State Grange, *Proceedings at Organization* (1873); Carr, *Patrons of Husbandry*, 131–135.

[3] Carr, *Patrons of Husbandry*, 142.

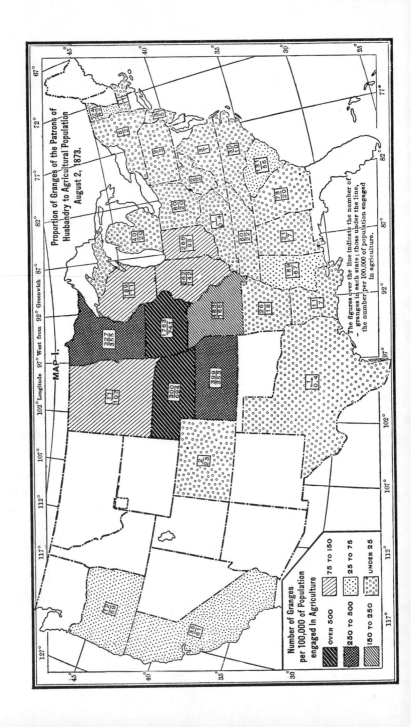

MAP-I.

Proportion of Granges of the Patrons of
Husbandry to Agricultural Population
August 2, 1873.

The figures over the line indicate the number of
granges in each state; those under the line,
the number per 100,000 of population engaged
in agriculture.

Number of Granges
per 100,000 of Population
engaged in Agriculture

OVER 500

250 TO 500

150 TO 250

75 TO 150

25 TO 75

UNDER 25

of the year, in view of the comparative sparseness of the population; and by October 18, 1873, California had ninety-one, and Oregon, thirty-seven granges, which was at the rate of 159 and 213 per hundred thousand of agricultural population, respectively. Two other states of the Western division, Colorado and Washington, were added to the roll of the order during this period, the former having two and the latter five granges on the eighteenth of October.

In the North Atlantic division the order made little progress in 1873, there being but ninety-two granges in the whole division on October 18, half of which were in the two states of Vermont and Pennsylvania. First granges were organized in New Hampshire and Massachusetts, but Maine, Connecticut, and Rhode Island remained untouched by the movement.

There are a number of things which help to explain the comparatively slow growth of the Patrons of Husbandry in the North Atlantic division during this and subsequent years; but perhaps the most important of these was the fact that the eastern farmers were, in the nature of things, largely out of sympathy with what at that time appeared to be the principal aim of the order in the North Central states — the reduction in the cost of transportation of farm products from the West to the markets of the Atlantic seaboard. The way in which eastern farmers were suffering from competition with the virgin soil of the West has been pointed out in the preceding chapter, and it will readily be seen that any reduction in transportation charges would only heighten this competition and make it still more difficult for the eastern farmers to make a living. So it was not until some years later, when the increase of dairy-farming and market-gardening relieved the eastern farmers to a considerable extent from the pressure of western competition, and when the order began once more to place the leading emphasis on its social and educational features, that the Patrons of Husbandry obtained any considerable sway in the states of the North Atlantic division.

Another matter which undoubtedly served to retard the growth of the order in the East, and to some extent throughout the country, was the organization of granges in Boston and New York City composed almost entirely of grain-dealers and commission men. The Boston Grange was organized by J. C. Abbot of Iowa in August, 1873, and immediately drew forth a storm of remonstrances from all parts of the country. Secretary Kelley defended the organization at first, but Master Adams, on request of the executive committee, decided to revoke the dispensation because of the ineligibility of most of its members. The Boston Grange took no notice of this action, and the Massachusetts State Grange, which had just been organized, sustained it in its position of insubordination. The matter was thoroughly investigated by a committee at the seventh session of the National Grange in February, 1874, the state grange was censured for its action, and the Boston Grange declared no longer connected with the Patrons of Husbandry.[1] A year later the charter of Manhattan Grange in New York City was similarly revoked by the National Grange for ineligibility of members and attempts to involve the order in partisan politics.[2]

By October 18, 1873, there were granges in every state in the Union but five — Maine, Connecticut, Rhode Island, Delaware, and Nevada — and also in the territories of Dakota, Colorado, and Washington. Before the end of the year, a grange was organized in Maine and one in the territory of Montana, making in all thirty-three states and four territories in which the order had gained a foothold. At the beginning of the year 1873, 1362 granges had been established and at its close the number had reached 10,029, being an increase of 8667 or over six hundred per cent during the year. For the accomplishment of this work of organization, in addition to the lecturer and general deputies of the National Grange, 1294 state deputies were supplied with outfits during the year. The number of state granges was ten at the beginning of the year, but before its close twenty-two additional state and territorial granges

[1] National Grange, *Proceedings*, vii. 20, 33, 73–76 (1874); *Chicago Tribune*, August 29, 1873, p. 1; August 22, 1873, p. 4; *Cincinnati Semi-Weekly Gazette*, September 26, 1873, p. 1; *Prairie Farmer*, xliv. 339, 371 (October 25, November 22, 1873), xlv. 83 (March 14, 1874); Darrow, *Patrons of Husbandry*, 45.

[2] National Grange, *Proceedings*, viii. 104 (February, 1875).

had been organized: five in the North Atlantic division — New Hampshire, Massachusetts, New York, New Jersey, and Pennsylvania; five in the South Atlantic division — Virginia, West Virginia, North Carolina, Georgia, and Florida; four in the North Central division — Michigan, Ohio, Missouri, and Dakota; six in the South Central division — Kentucky, Tennessee, Alabama, Louisiana, Texas, and Arkansas; and two in the Western division — Oregon and California.[1]

THE ST. LOUIS SESSION AND THE CULMINATION OF THE ORDER, 1874

Such, then, was the scope of the order of Patrons of Husbandry at the beginning of 1874, when everybody was looking forward with interest to the approaching session of the National Grange. This meeting, distinguished as the seventh annual session, was held in St. Louis from February 4 to 12, 1874, and was the most representative gathering of farmers which had ever taken place in the United States. It was, moreover, the most important and harmonious of all the meetings of the National Grange, during the decade. The body of members present at this meeting and entitled to vote was not large — forty-five in all, including twelve women — but these members represented thirty-two state and territorial granges, having jurisdiction over more than ten thousand subordinate granges and somewhere in the neighborhood of half a million members.[2] With such a backing it was but natural that considerable interest should attach itself to the action of the leaders, who were expected at this time to formulate the purposes and principles of the movement.

This they did in a fairly sane and conservative though badly arranged document, which has stood from that time to this as the avowed platform of the order, and the principles of which have been largely incorporated into the platforms of every

---

[1] Kelley, *Patrons of Husbandry*, 422; National Grange, *Proceedings*, vii. 21 (1874); National Grange, *Monthly Bulletin*, September 1, 1874.

[2] National Grange, *Proceedings*, vii. 8–10 (1874); Darrow, *Patrons of Husbandry*, 41.

subsequent agricultural organization in the United States. The
" Declaration of Purposes of the National Grange " was written
by Deputy J. W. A. Wright of California under the supervision
of a committee composed of the masters of the state granges
of Florida, California, Tennessee, Arkansas, and New York.[1]
It declared the general objects of the Patrons of Husbandry to
be " to labor for the good of our Order, our country, and mankind " and endorsed the motto: " In essentials, unity; in non-
essentials, liberty; in all things, charity." This was followed
by a list of specific objects, including enhancement of the comforts and attractions of the homes, maintenance of the laws,
reduction of expenses, diversification of crops, systematization of
work, coöperation in buying and selling, avoidance of litigation,
the suppression of personal, local, sectional, and national prejudices, and the discountenancing of " the credit system, the
fashion system, and every other system tending to prodigality
and bankruptcy."

As to business relations, the declaration stated that the Patrons
waged " no aggressive warfare against any other interest,"
but it also asserted an intention to dispense with a surplus of
middlemen; they (the Patrons) were not enemies to capital
but were opposed to the tyranny of monopolies, high rates of
interest, and exorbitant per cent profits in trade. On the
question of transportation, it was declared that the order was
not inimical to railroads, but held that transportation companies
of all kinds were necessary to the success of the farmer and
advocated the increase in every practical way of facilities for
cheap transportation to the seaboard. As regards politics,
the declaration emphatically asserted that the Grange was not
a political or party organization; but at the same time the
political rights and duties of the members as individual American
citizens were proclaimed. The advance of the cause of education, especially along agricultural and industrial lines, was also
put forward as one of the important objects of the order.

[1] National Grange, *Proceedings*, vii. 44 (1874); Darrow, *Patrons of Husbandry*,
17, 43. The declaration is given in National Grange, *Proceedings*, vii. 56–60 (1874);
Carr, *Patrons of Husbandry*, 108–110; Messer, *The Grange*, 32–36; and many other
Grange circulars and publications.

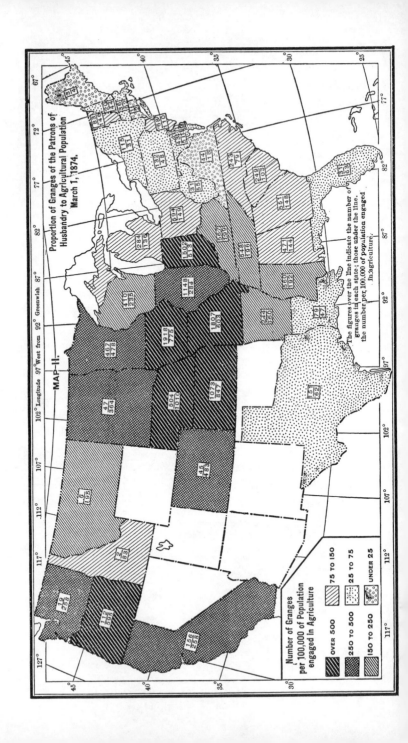

Proportion of Granges of the Patrons of Husbandry to Agricultural Population March 1, 1874.

MAP-II.

The figures over the line indicate the number of granges in each state; those under the line, the number per 100,000 of population engaged in agriculture.

Number of Granges per 100,000 of Population engaged in Agriculture

OVER 500
250 TO 500
150 TO 250
75 TO 150
25 TO 75
UNDER 25

Such, in brief, together with considerable vague generalization and many repetitions, was the platform of the Patrons of
Husbandry as promulgated by its leaders in the National Grange.
Had the order held strictly, during the years of its greatest
popularity, to the principles here enunciated, it probably would
have been spared a part, at least, of the notable loss in membership and prestige during the latter years of the decade.

At this session it was again necessary to revise the constitution, to make it better applicable to the new conditions resulting
from the great extension of the order, and more consonant with
the ideas of the rank and file of the membership.[1] Provision
was made for the reduction of representation in the state granges,
some of which had become of unwieldy proportions, and for the
establishment of district or county (Pomona) granges in the
fifth degree, to have charge of the educational and business
interests of the order. Other amendments made the state and
national granges more strictly delegate bodies, changed the time
of meeting of the National Grange from February to November,[2]
reduced the dues paid by the state granges to the National
Grange from ten to five cents per member, and changed the
article on membership to read: " Any person engaged in agricultural pursuits and having no interest in conflict with our
purposes, of the age of sixteen years . . . is entitled to
membership." These amendments did not become part of
the constitution until they were accepted by three-fourths
of the state granges, while four other amendments passed at
this session never received the consent of a sufficient number
of these bodies and hence were of no effect.[3]

The month of February, 1874, in which occurred the session
of the National Grange which has just been considered, saw

[1] The revised constitution is given in Carr, *Patrons of Husbandry*, 110–113; the
amendments can be found in National Grange, *Proceedings*, vii. 67–72 (1874).

[2] This did not go into effect until after the next annual meeting and resulted in
two sessions in 1875.

[3] These provided life membership in the National Grange for the seven " founders " and for past-masters of the National Grange; additional proportionate
representation in the National Grange for states having over thirty thousand
members; and an increase in the membership fee for charter members.

the organization of 2239 new granges, an average of eighty per day throughout the month. This was the largest number ever organized in one month, though January and March of the same year were not far behind with 2119 and 2024 new granges, respectively. From then on, however, the number declined rapidly and during the last six months of the year the average number of new granges formed was only about four hundred.[1] This check in the rate of increase was, in the main, merely a result of the fact that all available territory was now pretty thoroughly organized, but its suddenness would also lead to the conclusion that the popularity of the order was already somewhat on the wane in those parts of the country where it had aroused the greatest enthusiasm.

Two of the maps, numbers II and III, fall within the period between the seventh and eighth annual sessions of the National Grange, and portray the condition of the order on March 1, 1874, and January 1, 1875. The first of these shows a very considerable advance in all parts of the country. Since October 18, 1873, first granges had been organized in Maine, Delaware, Montana, and Idaho, bringing into the ranks all of the states except Rhode Island, which did not find room for a grange within her borders until the next decade, and Nevada, in which, however, seven granges were organized before the end of the year. The map for January 1, 1875, marks the culmination of the order of Patrons of Husbandry, with 21,697 granges in the

---

[1] The following table shows the number of new granges organized monthly from January, 1873, to September, 1876, inclusive. It is based on data in Kelley, *Patrons of Husbandry*, 422, and National Grange, *Proceedings*, ix. 189 (November, 1875), x. 178 (1876).

	1873	1874	1875	1876
January	158	2119	306	109
February	338	2239	286	108
March	666	2024	361	117
April	571	1487	309	88
May	696	937	242	58
June	623	752	170	45
July	611	419	125	32
August	829	396	125	21
September	917	412	89	12
October	1050	410	92	
November	974	363	103	
December	1235	383	100	

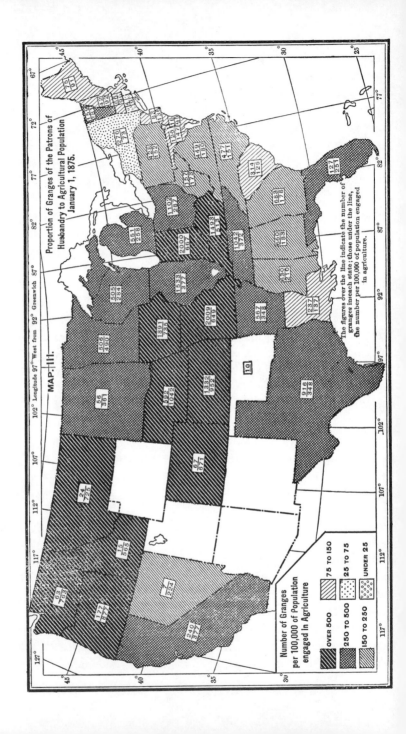

MAP. III.

Proportion of the Patrons of
Husbandry to Agricultural Population
January 1, 1875.

The figures over the line indicate the number of
granges in each state; those under the line,
the number per 100,000 of population engaged
in agriculture.

Number of Granges
per 100,000 of Population
engaged in Agriculture

OVER 500   75 TO 150
250 TO 500   25 TO 75
150 TO 250   UNDER 25

United States. In many of the states of the Northwest, however, the decline had already begun by the close of the year 1874, and the division as a whole showed an increase between September 1 and January 1 of but fifty-eight granges, which scarcely kept pace with the increase in population. Minnesota, Iowa, Nebraska, and Kansas experienced an actual decrease in granges during the four months and only Ohio and Michigan of the other states of the division were able to show any considerable advance.

Such a result was quite the natural one in view of the extent to which this section was now crowded with granges.[1] Three of the states, Indiana, Iowa, and Missouri, reached the two thousand mark in numbers of subordinate organizations, which gave them from six to nine hundred granges per hundred thousand of agricultural population; but in Kansas and Nebraska with their sparser settlement, the ratio reached 1190 and 1064 respectively. This means that in Kansas there was a grange for every eighty-four persons engaged in agricultural occupations, the conclusion from which would be that at least three-fourths of all who were eligible were members of the order in this state. Indiana, on the other hand, had the greatest number of granges in proportion to size, the ratio being one for every eighteen square miles, or an average of two for every township in the state. That such a situation could be permanent was not to be expected, and the inevitable result, as soon as the first enthusiasm began to cool, was a decrease in the number of granges, by the consolidation of some, the disbanding of others, and the revocation of charters because of delinquency in dues to the state grange.

During the years 1874 and 1875 the great size of the order of Patrons of Husbandry gave it prestige and influence throughout the land, and the vastness of its projects excited universal astonishment. The treasury of the National Grange was plethoric with the receipts from dues and the sale of dispensations; the officers and members of the executive committee drew salaries ranging from a thousand to twenty-five hundred dollars

[1] See statistics of the density of granges, January 1, 1875, in table following p. 58.

per year and traveling expenses; the members received five dollars per day and a five cent mileage for attendance at the St. Louis session; and at the eighth session in Charleston, February, 1875, the per diem was increased to six dollars.[1] In spite of these and other somewhat lavish expenditures, the surplus in the treasury of the National Grange, which was about fifty thousand dollars on January 1, 1874, had doubled at the beginning of 1875.[2] The accumulation of such a large amount of money excited feelings of distrust among many members of the order, who feared that it would be squandered or misappropriated and could see no reason why they should be compelled to pay dues to increase the funds under the control of an exclusive body, the members of which held superior degrees to which the great mass could never hope to rise. This feeling was inflamed by many newspaper articles, probably inspired by opponents of the order, which hinted at the misuse of funds and denounced the exclusiveness and extravagance of the National Grange. The result was a widespread agitation for the reduction of dues, the division of the surplus among the state granges, and the reformation of the National Grange on more democratic lines.[3]

Many of the state granges, on the other hand, having embarked upon elaborate coöperative projects, found the means at their disposal entirely too meager for the successful development of their plans. This, combined with the distrust of the National Grange, led that body, at the Charleston session in February, 1875, to vote a loan of over fifty thousand dollars of its accumulated funds to the state granges on the basis of $2.50 for every subordinate grange of good standing within the jurisdiction. By the next session, it was evident that these loans would never

---

[1] National Grange, *Proceedings*, vii. 54, 64 (1874), viii. 49, 59 (February, 1875); Aiken, *The Grange*, 9–11.

[2] National Grange, *Proceedings*, vii. 82–84 (1874), viii. 127 (February, 1875).

[3] Iowa State Grange, *Proceedings*, iv. 7, 9, 48 (1873), v. 47 (1874); Michigan State Grange, *Proceedings*, i. 12 (1874); Kansas State Grange, *Proceedings*, iii. 26 (1875); *Western Rural*, xiii. 188, 196 (June, 1874); *Prairie Farmer*, xlvi. 371 (November 20, 1875); *Maryland Farmer*, xiii. 20 (January, 1876); Aiken, *The Grange*, 11–13.

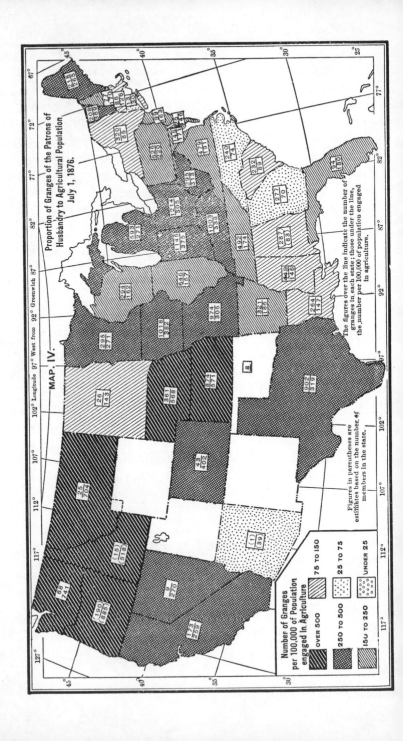

MAP. IV.

Proportion of Granges of the Patrons of Husbandry to Agricultural Population
July 1, 1876.

The figures over the line indicate the number of granges in each state; those under the line, the number per 100,000 of population engaged in agriculture.

Figures in parentheses are estimates based on the number of members in the state.

Number of Granges per 100,000 of Population engaged in Agriculture.

OVER 500

250 TO 500

150 TO 250

75 TO 150

25 TO 75

UNDER 25

be repaid and they were accordingly changed into donations.[1]
The results of this policy were disastrous. It led the state
granges into business schemes which, in nearly every instance,
brought financial loss and discredit on the order; while it left
the National Grange financially embarrassed during the remainder of the decade, since the revenue from the sale of dispensations had almost entirely ceased, and that from dues was very
materially reduced by the shrinkage of membership.

DECLINE OF THE GRANGE, 1875–80

Tables giving the number of granges in the different states
are available for only two dates during the period of the decline
of the order — from 1875 to 1880 inclusive. These are found in
the reports of the secretary at the ninth and tenth annual sessions of the National Grange, which display the state of the
order about October 1, 1875, and July 1, 1876, respectively.[2]
From January to October, 1875, the number of granges
increased somewhat in each of the five census areas, with the
exception of the North Central division, but the decline there
was so great — over thirty per cent — that the gains in the
other sections were overbalanced, and the total number of
granges in the United States fell from 21,697 to 19,007, or from
320 to 279 per hundred thousand of agricultural population.
Every state in the North Central division, Michigan alone
excepted, experienced a decline during the period, while in the
South Atlantic division the order was almost stationary, with
a falling off in North Carolina, Georgia, and Florida, and but
slight advances in the other states. In the other divisions,
however, a healthy growth was still maintained, though the
rate of increase was somewhat diminished.

From October, 1875, to July, 1876 (see Map IV), the
decline was not quite so rapid in the North Central division,
but it continued, and was joined by a corresponding decline in

[1] National Grange, *Proceedings*, viii. 55, 65 (February, 1875), ix. 84 (November, 1875).

[2] The only complete statistics of actual membership in the order are given in these two reports. See table following p. 58.

all of the other census divisions except the North Atlantic, so that the total number of granges in the United States fell to about fifteen thousand. Two states of the North Atlantic division, Massachusetts and Connecticut, dropped off in number of granges, and in Connecticut a recently organized state grange was unable to keep up its existence. The increase of the order in that section as a whole, however, was maintained at about the same moderate rate which it had experienced since it first got under way there in 1873.

After 1876, the officials of the National Grange appear to have come to the conclusion that it would be the part of wisdom to refrain from publishing the story of the decline of the order. Consequently no further tables of granges in the different states are available, but it is possible to follow the decrease in actual membership in the country as a whole by means of a never failing index — the annual dues paid to the National Grange. In 1875, these amounted to almost forty-three thousand dollars. By 1880, they had fallen to but little over six thousand, representing probably about four thousand subordinate granges and perhaps a hundred and fifty thousand members all told. This marked the lowest point in the position of the order. From 1881 on it has increased slowly, with some fluctuation, until now it claims a total membership about equal to what it had in 1874, though quite differently distributed, for the states of the North Atlantic division have a much larger proportion of the granges now than they had in the early days of the order.[1]

Some of the causes of this falling off in size and influence of the order of Patrons of Husbandry during the latter part of the decade 1870–80 have already been indicated and others will be more fully developed in the following chapters, but it may be well to summarize these causes here in order to complete the survey of the order during the decade. Undoubtedly the decline was in large part merely a reaction from the excessive growth in the years 1873 and 1874. The system of organization by deputies, the popularity and novelty of the movement, and often the hopes of political and financial regeneration led many

[1] Darrow, *Patrons of Husbandry*, 44.

into the order who had no permanent interest in its real aims and who began to drop out as soon as the excitement of organization was over and it was seen that the order would not prove a cure-all for the troubles of the farmers.[1] The laxness of organizers, moreover, permitted many to creep into the ranks who were not only not engaged in agricultural pursuits, but whose interests were directly opposed to those of the farmers.[2] The granges of commission men in some of the eastern cities have been noted, but this feature was not confined to these places; throughout the country disgruntled politicians, business and professional men sought entrance into the order during the days of its prosperity, purely as a means of personal advancement; and when the influence of the Grange began to wane, partly as a result of the discredit which they brought upon it in the eyes of many observing farmers, they hastened to sever their connections with the order.[3]

The rapidity of organization resulted in an unwieldy and undisciplined mass of members, whom the leaders were unable to control, and dissensions soon arose within the ranks. The successful agitation for the distribution of the funds of the National Grange at the Charleston meeting in 1875 is an illustration of this situation. The jealousy of those in control, thus manifested, was kept up throughout the decade and resulted in continual agitation against the higher or " fancy " degrees, as they were called, and demands for a revision of the constitution to transform the National Grange into a mere convention of

[1] Wisconsin State Grange, *Proceedings*, iv. 6 (1876); *Patrons' Bulletin* (Kentucky), November, 1876; *California Patron*, June 13, 1877, p. 5; *Bulletin* (Wisconsin), February, 1877, May, 1878; Pierson, "Outcome of the Granger Movement," in *Popular Science Monthly*, xxxii. 371-373 (January, 1888); National Grange, *Proceedings*, x. 38 (1876).

[2] " Everybody wanted to join the Grange then; lawyers, to get clients; doctors, to get patients; merchants, to get customers; Shylocks, to get their pound of flesh; and sharpers, to catch the babes in the woods." Aitken, *The Grange*, 11-13.

[3] *Farmers' Union*, June 14, 1873, p. 188; June 28, 1873, p. 205; *Patrons' Bulletin* (Kentucky), December, 1876; *California Patron*, October 17, 1877, p. 2; *American Farmer*, January, 1881, p. 9; Pierson, in *Popular Science Monthly*, xxxii. 371-373 (January, 1888); Aiken, *The Grange*, 11-13; Paine, *Granger Movement in Illinois*, 10; Small, *Joining the Grangers or Trying to be a Patron of Husbandry* (pamphlet).

delegates from the state granges. Some even went so far as to favor the abolition of the national body and the reduction of the powers of the state granges to the lowest possible limits. This agitation led to an almost continuous tinkering with the constitution, which, while failing to satisfy the demands of the discontented, helped to weaken the influence of the order.[1]

The connection of the Grange with a number of political movements of the time contributed in large measure to its decline. In spite of constitutional provisions against political discussions and the efforts of a number of leaders to keep the movement clear from partisan politics at least, it proved to be impossible to prevent subordinate granges in a number of states and in some cases even the state granges from taking an active part in the work of the various Independent, Farmers', and Anti-Monopoly parties which flourished at the time.[2] The general public classed all these phenomena together under the designation of the " Granger movement " ; and, indeed, they were all component parts of the same general movement for protective and coöperative organization of the agricultural class. Thus when these political movements came to naught, or discredited themselves by their extreme radicalism, the order of Patrons of Husbandry had to suffer along with the rest.[3]

Similarly in the matter of railroad regulation, the order was compelled to suffer in part for the sins of others. The impression seems to have been quite prevalent that the main purpose of the order was to " fight railroads," and large numbers of farmers undoubtedly joined it with this object in view. Consequently, in spite of the conservative position assumed in the " Declaration of Purposes," the order in a number of states became involved in efforts to secure railway legislation of the most radical sort. The failure of this legislation to accomplish its purpose, and the

---

[1] *Bulletin* (Wisconsin), June, 1875; *Prairie Farmer*, xlvi. 371 (November 30, 1875); *California Patron*, November 15, 1876, p. 4; Pierson, in *Popular Science Monthly*, xxxii. 371–373 (January, 1888).

[2] See below, pp. 80–102.

[3] *Patrons' Bulletin* (Kentucky), December, 1876; *Southern Farmers' Monthly*, iii. 60 (February, 1880); Paine, *Granger Movement in Illinois*, 8.

sentiment which the railroads were able to work up against it were potent causes for the rapid decline of the order in a number of northwestern states.[1]

The one feature which probably had more influence than any other in building up the great membership of the order was the idea of coöperative business, and this feature also contributed more than anything else to the almost total collapse of the Grange throughout the West. One by one, the extensive coöperative enterprises established by the western state granges went to pieces, leaving behind a burden of discredit and indebtedness which almost destroyed the order. Some state granges, notably those of Nebraska and Arkansas, were unable to weather the storm and surrendered their organizations; while district and subordinate granges disbanded for fear of being held responsible for the debts of the state granges. In other states — Iowa, for example — a few of the faithful kept up the state grange and strove to reinvigorate the order· but even to the present day it has been impossible to make the Grange flourish in those states where it suffered the severest financial disasters.[2]

OTHER AGRICULTURAL ORGANIZATIONS

The order of Patrons of Husbandry was the largest, most comprehensive, and most thoroughly organized of the agencies which the farmers used in their efforts to improve their position materially, politically, socially, and intellectually, through organized coöperation. It was not, however, the only agency which this movement called into existence or adapted to its purposes. For many years isolated farmers' clubs had existed in numerous localities throughout the United States, usually in or near some of the large cities; but their attention had been confined almost wholly to topics of practical agriculture. Early in the seventies this germ was taken up by a large number of farmers imbued with the rising spirit of organized effort, and the result

[1] Aiken, *The Grange*, 14, 29.
[2] *Nation*, xix. 358 (December 3, 1874); *California Patron*, June 13, 1877, p. 5; Pierson, in *Popular Science Monthly*, xxxii. 368–371 (January, 1888); Paine, *Granger Movement in Illinois*, 8, 43.

was the development of a series of more or less independent clubs, usually avowedly political, and always devoted to the project of advancing the interests of the agricultural class in every possible way. To many farmers the secret features of the Grange were objectionable, while others disapproved of its non-partisan attitude; and for these the farmers' club presented the most satisfactory solution of the problem of agricultural organization.[1] Fostered by the same influences which led to the great multiplication of granges, the number of these farmers' clubs increased rapidly in many of the southern and western states during the first half of the decade 1870–80. It quickly became evident that some sort of machinery must be developed whereby these clubs could work together for the common purpose, if they were to hold their place against the Patrons of Husbandry and accomplish anything for the elevation of the agricultural class.

The first state in which the open farmers' clubs succeeded in uniting, and the only state in which their organization had any considerable importance, was Illinois. Even before the Civil War some dissatisfaction with economic conditions made its appearance among the farmers of this state, and on September 15, 1858, a convention of farmers met at Centralia, set forth their grievances against the " non-producers " and proposed the formation of farmers' clubs which should " produce concert of action on all matters connected with their interests." [2] During the

---

[1] It appears that a considerable number of Roman Catholic farmers did join the Grange, especially in Minnesota, in spite of its secret features. See *Prairie Farmer*, xliv. 315 (October 4, 1873), xlv. 107 (April 4, 1874); *Richmond Whig and Advertiser* (semi-weekly), July 3, 1874, p. 3. In the South the question of organization for the negro farmers received some attention. Occasionally northern Grangers, ignorant of conditions in the South, advised their southern brethren to admit the negroes into their granges, and the master of the Missouri State Grange declared his intention to organize separate granges for them, but there is no evidence that any negroes ever became members of the order. There were some efforts to establish an independent secret order of negro farmers similar to the Patrons of Husbandry, but these seem to have had no results. See *Prairie Farmer*, xliv. 275 (August 30, 1873); *Industrial Age*, September 27, 1873, p. 5; *Western Rural*, xiii. 143 (May 8, 1875); *Farmers' Home Journal*, November 13, 1875, p. 364.

[2] The only reference to this convention which has been found is in Jonathan

war the attention of the farmers was diverted by more pressing issues and by the prevailing high prices of agricultural products,[1] but unrest began to manifest itself again in the later sixties, a number of local clubs were formed, and in 1870, a Producers' Convention, made up largely of farmers, met in Bloomington to consider the transportation question.[2] Finally, in the fall of 1872, a call was issued by the Union Farmers' Club of Avon for delegates to meet at Kewanee, October 16, for the purpose of forming a permanent state organization. By this time the order of Patrons of Husbandry had made its appearance in the state, and it was planned to include both the clubs and the granges in the proposed central union. The Kewanee convention was attended by delegates from only thirteen clubs and granges, but it got the movement under way by appointing a state central committee on organization. Willard C. Flagg of Moro, a member of the state senate and a prominent horticulturist, was the chairman of this committee. On November 16, 1872, he published in the *Prairie Farmer* a request for all clubs, granges, horticultural and agricultural associations in the state to send him the names of their officers and other information. Following this up, the committee issued a call on January 11, 1873, for a meeting of delegates from all such local bodies at Bloomington, January 15 and 16. At this convention, 275 regularly appointed delegates from clubs and granges organized themselves as the Illinois State Farmers' Association; adopted a constitution in which the object of the organization was said to be the promotion of the moral, intellectual, social, and material welfare of the farmers; and elected as officers Hon. W. C. Flagg, president; S. M. Smith, secretary; Duncan Mackay, treasurer; and one vice-president for each congressional district.[3]

Periam, *The Groundswell*, 204–206. The state fair was being held in Centralia at this time. See *Illinois State Journal*, September 15, 22, 1858.

[1] See Periam, *The Groundswell*, 222.

[2] See below, p. 127.

[3] Testimony of W. C. Flagg, in Windom Committee, *Report on Transportation Routes to the Seaboard*, ii. 646; *Prairie Farmer*, xliii. 316, 364 (October 5, 26, November 16, 1872), xliv. 9, 12, 25 (January 11, 25, 1873); Periam, *The Groundswell*, chs. xix–xx.

The work of local organization went on rapidly after the Bloomington convention, and many county organizations of clubs and granges were also formed throughout the state. On July 4, the farmers of Illinois took advantage of the occasion to hold picnics and celebrations at which inflammatory political speeches, filled with denunciations of railroads and monopolies, were the rule. Mass-meetings and farmers' conventions, mainly of a political nature, were frequent throughout the summer of 1873; and in the fall, many of the county associations assumed the functions of a political party and nominated candidates for office. All this excitement helped on the movement for organization, and on December 15, when the state association convened at Decatur for its second annual session, the secretary was able to announce 830 clubs in the eighty counties from which he had reports.[1] After this meeting the State Farmers' Association drifted rapidly into an Anti-Monopoly party, and this seems to have injured its prestige, for the third annual session, held at Springfield, January 19, 1875, was attended by delegates from but twenty-one counties, although the secretary estimated the number of clubs in the state at sixteen hundred. Accepting this estimate as approximately correct, there were, including the granges, some three thousand local farmers' organizations with a membership of at least one hundred and fifty thousand in a state in which about four hundred thousand people were engaged in agriculture.[2]

Although many delegates from the subordinate granges helped to form the Illinois State Farmers' Association and took part in its earlier meetings, there was, nevertheless, a continual rivalry and even hostility between the two forms of organization from the beginning. The officers of the State Farmers' Association attempted to keep them in harmony, but the leaders of the Patrons of Husbandry in the state looked upon the clubs

---

[1] *Prairie Farmer*, xliv. 36, 59, 100, 217, 220, 225, 409 (February–December, 1873); *Chicago Tribune*, 1873, March 12, p. 2, March 22, p. 4, May 10, p. 2; *American Annual Cyclopedia*, 1873, pp. 367–369; Illinois State Farmers' Association, *Proceedings*, ii; Flagg, in *American Social Science Journal*, vi. 105 (July, 1874).

[2] *Prairie Farmer*, xlv. 27, 129, 155, 161, 195, 275, 403 (1874), xlvi. 35 (January 5, 1875); *Appleton's Annual Cyclopedia*, 1875, p. 393.

as preliminary steps in the formation of granges, and their proselyting zeal caused considerable friction. The local granges soon found their double allegiance bringing them into difficulties, for the state grange would not look with favor upon the payment of dues by the subordinate granges to the State Farmers' Association. The order of Patrons of Husbandry, moreover, avowed itself to be a non-political organization, and its officers, although they encouraged the members to take part in politics as individuals, condemned their participation as official delegates of granges in the partisan politics into which the State Farmers' Association was rapidly drifting. Although the inability of the two systems to pull together undoubtedly weakened their effectiveness and hastened the rapid collapse of the whole movement, they should, nevertheless, be looked upon as merely two phases of the same general "farmers' movement" or "Granger movement" for protective and coöperative organization.[1]

During the early part of 1873, open clubs and local and county coöperative associations were springing up in a number of the other western states. Kansas was the first state to follow the example of Illinois and organize these into a state association. On March 26, 1873, a state farmers' convention was held at Topeka pursuant to a call issued by the state board of agriculture. About 250 delegates of clubs and granges attended this meeting and organized the Farmers' Coöperative Association of the State of Kansas, some of the declared objects of which were coöperative buying, control of prices of agricultural products, reduction and regulation of freight rates, reform of taxation, and independent political action.[2]

Both mass and delegate conventions of farmers were of frequent occurrence in a number of states during these years.

[1] Illinois State Farmers' Association, *Proceedings*, ii (December, 1873); Paine, *Granger Movement in Illinois*, 12–14; *Prairie Farmer*, xliv. 401–403, xlv. 131, xlvi. 27 (December, 1873–January, 1875).

[2] *Prairie Farmer*, xliv. 91, 139, 155, 187 (March–June, 1873); *Chicago Tribune*, June 10, 1873, p. 2, January 12, 1874, p. 8; *American Annual Cyclopedia*, 1873, p. 396; *History of Kansas* (published by Andreas), 263; Periam, *The Groundswell*, 271–279.

The Missouri farmers had one in Jefferson City, October 1, 1873;[1] there was one in Maryland, April 8, 1874;[2] and in Wisconsin an agricultural convention was held at Madison in February of each year throughout the decade, under the auspices of the State Agricultural Society.[3] In most cases these conventions got no further than discussion and resolutions and no permanent organization was attempted, but in a few instances state organizations were established in imitation of the Illinois State Farmers' Association. Thus the Tennessee State Farmers' Association was formed by a convention which met at Nashville, September 16, 1873,[4] and Indiana fell into line June 10, 1874, with the Indiana State Farmers' Association.[5] None of these institutions appear to have been very long-lived or to have exerted any considerable influence; but they indicate the general trend toward agricultural organization.

Early in the decade efforts were made to establish some sort of a national association of agriculturists. In October, 1870, an Agricultural Congress of the southern states was formed at Augusta, Georgia, and in October, 1871, a National Agricultural Association was organized at Nashville, Tennessee. In May of the following year, these two bodies held a joint meeting at St. Louis and merged under the name of the National Agricultural Congress. In February, 1873, the secretary of the congress issued a call for a meeting in Indianapolis in May, in which he stated that the congress assumed to occupy the same relative position to the farmers' clubs as the National Grange did to the subordinate granges. This meeting was attended by about two hundred delegates, representing twenty-five states. Questions of organization, transportation, agricultural colleges, and public lands were discussed, and made the subjects of resolutions.

[1] *Prairie Farmer*, xliv. 121, 187 (April, June, 1873); *Industrial Age*, September 6, 1873, p. 5.

[2] *Maryland Farmer*, xi. 149 (May, 1874).

[3] *Prairie Farmer*, xliii. 20, xliv. 4, 404 (1872–73); Wisconsin State Agricultural Society, *Transactions*, 1872–80.

[4] *Industrial Age*, September 6, 1873, p. 5; *Chicago Tribune*, September 17, 1873, p. 8; *American Annual Cyclopedia*, 1873, p. 728; Periam, *The Groundswell*, 100–103.

[5] *Industrial Age*, June 18, 1874, p. 5; *Chicago Tribune*, June 11, 1873, p. 12.

Annual meetings of a similar nature were held throughout the decade; but the National Agricultural Congress appears to have been too loosely organized to exert any considerable influence, or to serve the purpose of the general farmers' movement.[1]

Such were the agencies which the farmers developed or adapted to their purposes in the movement for the elevation of the agricultural class. The most effective of these were the order of Patrons of Husbandry, the Illinois State Farmers' Association, and the local open farmers' clubs.

[1] *Rural Carolinian*, i. 776 (September, 1870); *Prairie Farmer*, xlii. 260, xliii. 113, 172, 177, xliv. 35, xlv. 116, 163, xlvi. 276 (1871–75); *Maryland Farmer*, ix. 120, xiii. 332, 389, xiv. 292, xv. 85, 152, 332 (1872–78); *American Annual Cyclopedia*, 1873, p. 376; Periam, *The Groundswell*, chs. xvii, xxviii; National Agricultural Congress, *Proceedings*, v (1876).

CHAPTER III

THE GRANGER MOVEMENT AS A POLITICAL FORCE

INDEPENDENT PARTIES

IT has been a peculiarity of American politics since the Civil War that the two principal parties have been controlled, in the main, either by men of a conservative type who are naturally opposed to taking up any new or radical issues, or by professional politicians who find it to their interests to keep in the foreground the old familiar questions on which parties have been divided in the past, and thus to draw away attention from new issues which are likely to disrupt party lines.[1] Consequently almost the only method by which the advocates of new measures have been able to get them before the public has been the formation of third parties. Though these parties have seldom had any considerable or lasting success as parties, they have frequently accomplished their purpose by forcing the adoption of their platforms on one or the other of the old parties, and this it is which gives to third parties their importance in American political history.

The close of the Civil War in 1865 left the Republican party[2] in control in every state of the Northwest from Ohio to the Pacific coast. In Ohio and Indiana on the east, in Missouri on the south, and in California and Oregon on the west, the Democratic party remained a factor to be reckoned with, but in the rest of this section — in Illinois, Michigan, Wisconsin, Minnesota, Iowa, Kansas, and Nebraska — the great majority of the voters looked upon the term " Democrat " as practically

---

[1] Cf. Bryce, *American Commonwealth*, ii. chs. liii–lvi, and Ostrogorski, *Democracy and the Organization of Political Parties*, ii.

[2] The party called itself " Union " at that time, but in 1868 it adopted the name of " National Republican." In an article in the *American Historical Review* for October, 1910, Professor W. A. Dunning points out that this party was distinct in purpose, in personnel, and in name, from the Republican party which elected Lincoln to the presidency in 1860.

synonymous with " rebel " or " Copperhead," and the party which was thus handicapped could not be expected to make much headway for many years to come. There was, however, considerable opposition to the dominant Republicans in this section during the decade of the seventies, and almost of necessity much of this opposition took the form of third parties. The first movement in this direction was the organization of the Liberal Republican party, which won some victories in Missouri, but the presidential election of 1872 demonstrated that this was a party of leaders rather than of the people. Following closely on the heels of the failure of this movement, there appeared a series of " Independent " parties which were distinctly popular in their origin, and were able to make a considerable showing in the elections, though they received little support from prominent politicians of the old school.[1]

These Independent parties have received very little consideration from historical writers, and there has been a tendency to look upon them as merely preliminaries leading up to the organization of the National Greenback party. This tendency is a natural one in view of the fact that in one or two states the Independent organization did affiliate with the Greenback party. In other states, however, the platforms of the Independent parties specifically rejected the Greenback policy, and an examination of the movement in all the states in which it appeared makes it clear that its causes are to be sought primarily, not in the desire for fiat currency, but in two other factors which had no connection with the old issues of war time. The first of these factors was the growing demand for the regulation of railway charges by the state, a demand which the dominant Republican party was not inclined to heed, and closely related to this was the second — the rapid organization of the agricultural population of the West into clubs and granges.

[1] That this movement attracted considerable attention among the politicians of the country is evident from President Grant's fifth annual message to Congress, dated December 1, 1873, which contains the statement that " political partisanship has almost ceased to exist, especially in the agricultural regions." Just what meaning the president intended to convey by these words and whether or no he looked upon the situation as one to be deplored, is difficult to determine.

The order of Patrons of Husbandry was professedly non-political in character, but that profession did not prevent it from taking a decided stand on questions of public policy, and especially upon the railroad question, while in some states the local granges took part in the organization of new political parties.[1] On the whole, however, the leaders of the order were able to keep it from participating directly in partisan politics, but the large number of non-secret and more or less independent farmers' clubs which were growing up side by side with the granges were usually avowedly political in character,[2] and the union of these local clubs into state farmers' associations paved the way for the establishment of the Independent parties in a number of states.   This was particularly the case in Illinois, where the movement for a new political party, with railroad regulation as its principal plank, first came to a head. There the agitation for restrictive railroad laws had been going on with more or less intensity ever since 1865, and finally in 1870 its advocates succeeded in incorporating mandatory provisions in the new constitution, which directed the legislature to enact laws to prevent extortion and unjust discrimination in railway charges.   The general assembly of 1871 responded with a series of so-called " Granger laws," one of which was declared contrary to the constitution by the state supreme court in January, 1873, because it prohibited not merely unjust discrimination, but all discrimination in railway charges.[3]

In the same month in which this decision was handed down by Chief-Justice Lawrence, the State Farmers' Association of Illinois was organized. It immediately adopted a series of

[1] The " Declaration of Purposes " adopted by the National Grange in February, 1874, asserted " that the Grange . . . is not a political or party organization. No Grange, if true to its obligations, can discuss political or religious questions, nor call political conventions, nor nominate candidates, nor even discuss their merits in its meetings."   National Grange, *Proceedings*, vii. 58.

[2] This is illustrated by the preamble to the constitution of the Central Farmers' Association of Centralia, Illinois, which declared the object of the association to be " to advance the interest of agriculture in every way possible; especially to influence the Legislature and courts in behalf of the farmers' interests of the country."   *Prairie Farmer*, xliv. 4 (January 4, 1873).

[3] This subject is more fully developed in the following chapter.

radical resolutions on the transportation question, and asserted " that the power of this and all local organizations should be wielded at the ballot-box, by the election of such, and only such, persons as sympathize with us in this movement." [1] The legislature was in session at this time, and was considering a revision of the railroad laws to overcome the objections of the supreme court.[2] In order to insure the enactment of effective laws on this subject, the executive committee of the newly organized State Farmers' Association issued a call for a State Farmers' Convention, to be held at Springfield, the capital city, April 2, 1873, " for the purpose of attending to our interests in the Legislature, and of giving that body and the Governor to understand that we mean business and are no longer to be trifled with; and that while we have no disposition to infringe upon the rights of others, we demand that protection at their hands from the intolerable wrongs now inflicted upon us by the railroads which they have a constitutional right to give us." [3]

The principal work of this convention, which was opened with speeches by Governor Beveridge and ex-Governor Palmer, was the adoption of a series of resolutions setting forth its ideas concerning railroad legislation, but these were followed by other resolutions relating to competition in lake transportation and the protective tariff, which furnish the first important indication that the movement was to spread out from an agitation for railroad regulation into a full-fledged political party, with views to express on a variety of questions. These resolutions, which were said to be the result of efforts of Democratic politicians to capture the movement and of railroad men to nullify it by throwing the blame for high charges upon the policy of

[1] *Prairie Farmer*, xliii. 316, 364, xliv. 9, 12, 25 (October, 1872–January, 1873); *Chicago Tribune*, 1873, January 16, p. 4, January 17, p. 8, January 18, p. 2; Periam, *The Groundswell*, 232–262.

[2] Illinois, *Senate* and *House Journals*, 1873. The pages of the *Chicago Tribune* and the *Prairie Farmer* at this time are filled with resolutions of farmers' meetings on the railroad question. For example, see resolutions of a Livingston County convention of farmers, in *Chicago Tribune*, January 10, 1873, p. 5.

[3] *Prairie Farmer*, xliv. 100 (March 29, 1873); *Chicago Tribune*, March 21, 1873, p. 2.

protection, met with considerable opposition in the convention on the ground that the farmers should concentrate their efforts upon the question of railroad regulation; and the next day a rump composed of about one hundred of the delegates to the convention held a meeting, at which the resolutions in question were reconsidered and laid on the table.[1] Despite this split in the ranks, the work of this convention on the railroad problem and the sustained agitation on the part of the farmers finally bore fruit in the passage by the legislature, May 2, 1873, of a new act for the regulation of railroads, more radical and more effective than the laws of 1871.

The first attempt of the farmers of Illinois to take part as an organized body in the election of public officers appears to have been a result of the decision of Chief-Justice Lawrence on the constitutionality of the railroad law of 1871. The idea was gaining ground that the farmers must control the courts as well as the legislature if they were to secure any solid results, and the judicial elections of June, 1873, seemed to them a good opportunity for making a beginning in that direction. Particularly was that the case in the fifth district, where the term of the chief-justice himself was about to expire. Lawrence was renominated by means of a petition widely signed by the lawyers of the district, but the farmers, who felt that he was not in sympathy with their interests, held a convention at Princeton in April and nominated Hon. Alfred M. Craig for the position. No pledges were exacted of the nominee, but he had shown himself favorable to the regulation of corporations by his action in the constitutional convention of 1869–70. The convention which nominated him also adopted a series of resolutions demanding such action by the legislature and the courts as would make effective the railroad provisions of the constitution, declaring an intention to support no one whose sentiments were not in accord with the farmers' in these matters, and recommending to the " anti-monopolists " of the state the nomina-

[1] *Prairie Farmer*, xliv. 114, 123 (April, 1873); *Chicago Tribune*, 1873, April 2, p. 8, April 4, p. 8; *American Annual Cyclopedia*, 1873, p. 367; Periam, *The Groundswell*, 280–291.

tion of candidates for the judicial positions in the various districts.[1]

This advice was followed by the farmers of the second district, the only other one in which a supreme court vacancy occurred at this time, and in eight or nine of the twenty-six circuits of the state, in each of which a judge was to be elected; while in many of the other districts one or more of the candidates openly declared themselves in sympathy with the farmers' views.[2] The election which followed first displayed to the astonished politicians of the country the political possibilities of the movement; for in nearly every instance the candidate nominated or favored by the farmers was elected, even Chief-Justice Lawrence being defeated by a large majority in spite of a vigorous campaign waged in his behalf.) These victories provoked a storm of criticism from the conservative press, especially in the East, and the movement was denounced as an attempt to pack the judiciary in the interests of a class.[3] Given an elective judiciary, however, it is difficult to see how the voters can justly be blamed for casting their ballots for candidates who were expected to uphold what they believed to be their rights.[4]

Greatly encouraged by the success which had been won and nothing daunted by the adverse criticism incurred, the farmers of Illinois threw themselves with vigor into the campaign for the election of county officers in the fall. Even before the judicial elections had taken place, a movement was started in Livingston County to put a farmers' ticket in the field for the

---

[1] *Prairie Farmer*, xliv. 153 (May 17, 1873); Periam, *The Groundswell*, 312–316. Many of the local clubs and granges ratified the nomination of Craig, but in one or two cases they indorsed Lawrence. See *Prairie Farmer*, xliv. 266 (May 31, 1873); *Chicago Tribune*, May 15, 1873, p. 1; Paine, *Granger Movement in Illinois*, 35, note.

[2] *Prairie Farmer*, xliv. 153 (May 17, 1873); *Chicago Tribune*, May, 1873, *passim;* Periam, *The Groundswell*, 312–316.

[3] *Nation*, xvi. 393, 397 (June 12, 1873); *Prairie Farmer*, xliv. 185 (June 14, 1873); *Chicago Tribune*, 1873, June 6, p. 4, June 21, p. 8; Periam, *The Groundswell*, 312–316.

[4] Lawrence was later attorney for the Chicago and Northwestern Railroad in litigation over the Granger law of Wisconsin. *Industrial Age* (Chicago), June 6, 1875, p. 4.

fall elections. May 31, 1873, the committee-men, representing the different townships in the county farmers' association, adopted a platform or declaration of principles which so well expressed the sentiments of farmers throughout the state that it was adopted or indorsed by farmers' meetings in many other counties. The preamble to this document asserted the failure of the old parties, declared in favor of a new political organization, and invited the coöperation of all other classes in carrying out the declaration of principles. The platform which followed expressed opposition to " railroad steals, tariff steals, salary-grab steals," approved the control by law of railway corporations, denounced taxation for the benefit of special classes, favored equal privileges for all in the banking system, " so that supply and demand shall regulate our money market," opposed further grants of public lands to corporations, and favored " a true system of civil service reform " and the application of the principle " that the office should seek the man and not the man the office." [1]

The adoption of this declaration was followed by the appointment of a committee to call a convention of farmers and all others in sympathy with them to nominate candidates for county officers. This action received the approval of Secretary Smith of the State Farmers' Association and similar steps were taken in other counties.[2] A great impetus was given to the movement by the celebrations, on Independence Day, of what was widely known as the " Farmers' Fourth of July." At the suggestion of the executive committee of the State Farmers' Association this day was made the occasion of numerous and well attended gatherings of farmers in nearly every county in the state. At most of these meetings an important part of the program was the reading of the new " Farmers' Declaration of Independence," which was circulated by the association. This document was a skilful parody on the original Declaration

---

[1] *Prairie Farmer*, xliv. 187 (June 14, 1873); *Chicago Tribune*, June 3, 1873, pp. 2, 4; *Industrial Age*, August 20, 1873, p. 7. For indorsements of the declaration, see *Chicago Tribune*, June–August, 1873, *passim*.

[2] *Chicago Tribune*, June, 1873, *passim; Industrial Age*, August 20, 1873, pp. 4, 7.

of Independence, and set forth at great length the conditions which had led to the uprising of the agricultural class. It concluded by declaring the farmers absolutely independent of all past political connections, and by pledging them to give their suffrage to such men only as would use their best endeavors to promote the desired ends.[1] This declaration was solemnly read at hundreds of gatherings in Illinois and in some of the neighboring states, and the customary spread-eagle oratory by local politicans gave way to earnest discussions of political topics by the farmers themselves, and fiery addresses by leaders of the movement, such as that by Hon. S. M. Smith, the secretary of the State Farmers' Association, at Pontiac in Livingston County.[2]

Thus the enthusiasm of the farmers for their cause was wrought up, and numerous picnics and harvest festivals,[3] together with

[1] *Prairie Farmer*, xliv. 196 (June 21, 1873); *Chicago Tribune*, June 16, 1873, p. 1. The declaration is printed in full in *Prairie Farmer*, xliv. 217 (July 12, 1873), and in *Chicago Tribune*, June 17, 1873, p. 2. Some extracts from this curious document may not be out of place: —

" When in the course of human events it becomes necessary for a class of the people, suffering from long continued systems of oppression and abuse, to rouse themselves from an apathetic indifference to their own interests, which has become habitual . . . a decent respect for the opinions of mankind requires that they should declare the causes that impel them to a course so necessary to their own protection."

Then follows a statement of " self-evident truths " and a catalogue of the sins committed by the railroads, together with a denunciation of railroads and Congresses for not having redressed these evils. The document concludes: —

" We, therefore, the producers of the state in our several counties assembled . . . do solemnly declare that we will use all lawful and peaceable means to free ourselves from the tyranny of monopoly, and that we will never cease our efforts for reform until every department of our government gives token that the reign of licentious extravagance is over, and something of the purity, honesty, and frugality with which our fathers inaugurated it, has taken its place.

" That to this end we hereby declare ourselves absolutely free and independent of all past political connections, and that we will give our suffrage only to such men for office, as we have good reason to believe will use their best endeavors to the promotion of these ends; and for the support of this declaration, with a firm reliance on divine Providence, we mutually pledge to each other our lives, our fortunes, and our sacred honor."

[2] *Prairie Farmer*, xliv. 217, 220, 225 (July 12, 19, 1873); *Chicago Tribune*, July, 1873, *passim*.

[3] *Prairie Farmer*, xliv. 224 (August 2, 1873); *Chicago Tribune*, 1873, August 7, pp. 1, 2, 4, August 22, p. 1.

the many regular meetings of local clubs and granges, kept it at fever heat throughout the summer; the political results being seen when county after county fell into line, held conventions, and nominated farmers' tickets for the fall elections. The procedure in organizing the new party in most of the counties was similar to that in Livingston, already described,[1] and the platforms adopted were generally similar to the Livingston County declaration of principles, though in some instances they contained more outspoken denunciation of the protective tariff. The completeness with which old party lines were broken up by this movement is seen in the fact that in some counties one party and in others the opposite party, either openly joined the " Reformers " or refrained from making separate nominations.[2]

Of the one hundred and two counties of the state, independent nominations were made by the new party in sixty-six, while in many of the other counties the candidates of one or the other of the old parties were acceptable to the farmers. The returns of the elections, which took place early in November, showed the farmers' or " Anti-Monopoly " tickets victorious in fifty-three of the sixty-six counties in which they were in the field, while Republican candidates were elected in sixteen, Democratic in twenty, and independents in thirteen of the remaining counties of the state.[3] The total vote in the sixty-six counties contested by the new party was 176,263, of which the Reform candidates received 94,188, leaving 82,075 to all the other candidates; and it was calculated that the same ratio carried throughout the state would have given the party a majority in a state election of twenty-two thousand over all.[4] In esti-

---

[1] For examples, see *Chicago Tribune*, 1873, June 25, p. 1, August 2, p. 1.

[2] This was generally, but not always, the party which had previously been in a minority in the county. See *Chicago Tribune*, August, 1873, *passim*.

[3] These figures are based on votes for county treasurers, who appear to have been the most important officials elected in the several counties.

[4] For returns and classification of counties, see *Industrial Age*, 1873, November 8, pp. 4, 5, November 15, pp. 3, 6; *Chicago Tribune*, 1873, October 20, p. 4, November 6, p. 1, November 10, p. 5, November 19, p. 4; *Prairie Farmer*, xliv. 361, 363, 371, 379 (November, 1873); *American Annual Cyclopedia*, 1873, p. 368; *World Almanac*, 1874, p. 23.

mating this election, the results of which were more favorable to the new party than any other in which it took part, the fact must be taken into consideration that it was for local officers, and that, in general, party politics play a less important part in local than in state elections. The Reformers were to find their party unable to retain these handsome majorities when it entered the broader field of state politics, because many voters, while willing to cast their ballots for neighbors running on an Anti-Monopoly ticket, were likely, when it was a question of unknown candidates for offices, to return to their old party allegiance.

Meanwhile similar movements were getting under way in Iowa, Minnesota, and Wisconsin, which resulted in state Anti-Monopoly or Reform parties in the general elections in the fall of 1873. The political situations in these three states were strikingly similar. In each the Republican party was in complete control; in each a growing demand for railroad regulation was being reflected in messages and addresses of the governor, and in numerous bills before the legislature and in each the farmers were being rapidly organized into granges of the Patrons of Husbandry. The outcome was the organization of new parties which took the name of Reform in Wisconsin, and Anti-Monopoly in Iowa and Minnesota; and in each case the Democratic party either fused with or accepted the candidates of the new party. The method of getting the movement under way was about the same in the three states: the farmers and Grangers in the different counties got together during the summer in meetings "outside the gate" and nominated candidates for county and legislative offices; after which calls were issued, either by one of these local meetings, or by self-constituted leaders of the movement, for state conventions, which were held in Iowa at Des Moines, August 13, in Minnesota at Owatonna, September 2, and in Wisconsin at Milwaukee, September 23.[1]

[1] The summary in this and the following paragraphs is based on a study of legislative journals, governors' messages, party platforms, and the files of the *Chicago Tribune*, *Prairie Farmer*, and local papers. Information concerning parties and elections, including the platforms in full, can usually be found in the *American*

In Iowa the state central committee of the Democratic party decided to hold no convention, and issued an address advising Democrats to support the Anti-Monopoly ticket.[1] In Minnesota the Democratic convention was held and adopted a platform, but indorsed the nominees of the new party.[2] In Wisconsin the Democratic convention met in Milwaukee the day after the Reformers came together, and the two conventions agreed upon a fusion ticket and adopted a joint platform.[3] All three of the platforms adopted by these new parties declared for the regulation of railroads or, putting it more generally, for the subjection of corporations to the authority of the state. Reduction of the tariff to a revenue basis, lower salaries for public officials, and a more economical administration of the government, were also demanded by each platform. In no case did these platforms contain planks favorable to the Greenback idea, while the Wisconsin platform contained a declaration that the public debt should be honestly paid, and in Minnesota the platform adopted by the Democratic convention which indorsed the Anti-Monopoly nominees, declared for a speedy return to specie payment. It early became evident that large numbers of Republicans were going into the new party movement in these states, and the Republican politicians made frantic efforts to counteract it. Fortunately for them, the Republican governors in each state had advocated railroad regulation, and these governors were all renominated on platforms which expressed great concern for the welfare of the farmers, and which contained planks favoring the regulation of railroads by the state.

The campaigns which followed were spirited, and the new parties achieved some surprising results. In Iowa the Anti-Monopoly committee suffered from a lack of campaign funds, and the Republican state ticket was elected, but its majority,

(after 1874, *Appleton's*) *Annual Cyclopedia* under the name of the state. The Owatonna platform of the Minnesota Anti-Monopolists, which is not given in the *Cyclopedia*, is in Martin, *Grange Movement*, 510–513.

[1] *Chicago Tribune*, September 2, 1873, p. 1.

[2] *American Annual Cyclopedia*, 1873, p. 511.

[3] *Chicago Tribune*, August–September, 1873, *passim; Industrial Age*, September 6, 1873, p. 5.

which had been sixty thousand the year before, was cut down to about twenty thousand, and it was claimed that the facts that Governor Carpenter was himself a prominent Patron, and that he had pledged himself to favor the farmers' policy, were all that prevented an Anti-Monopoly victory. The district elections resulted in a legislature composed of thirty-four Republican and sixteen opposition senators, with fifty of each party in the lower house.[1] As a result of this tie, a long struggle ensued over the organization of the House of Representatives, in the course of which, the seventy members who were also Patrons held a meeting and tried to unite on a Grange candidate for speaker, but found that they too were equally divided into Republicans and opposition. This shows clearly that a large proportion of the Grange element had not gone definitely into the Anti-Monopoly party. The deadlock was finally broken after 140 ballots by a compromise, according to which the Republicans got the speakership and the opposition the other officers, and the control of a number of committees.[2]

In Minnesota the outcome was somewhat the same. The Republican majority for the head of the ticket was reduced from the usual fifteen or twenty thousand to about five thousand, and the Anti-Monopoly candidates for secretary of state and treasurer were elected, while the Republican majority in the lower house of the legislature was reduced to two. A considerable number, moreover, of the members of the legislature elected as Republicans were also Grangers, and in favor of state regulation of railroads.[3]

---

[1] *Chicago Tribune*, November 8, 1873, p. 2; *Industrial Age*, 1873, October 18, p. 4, November 8, p. 6, November 15, p. 5; *American Agriculturist* (New York), xxxii. 439 (November, 1873).

[2] Iowa, *House Journal*, 1874, pp. 3–48; *Chicago Tribune*, January, 1874, *passim; Industrial Age*, 1874, January 24, p. 3, February 7, p. 6.

[3] *Chicago Tribune*, May, 1873–January, 1874, *passim; Industrial Age*, September 6, 1873, p. 4; *Prairie Farmer*, xliv. 291 (September 13, 1873); Martin, *Grange Movement*, 510–513; Stephe Smith, *Grains for the Grangers*, 233–236; E. D. Neill, *History of Minnesota* (4th ed.), 760–763; *American Annual Cyclopedia*, 1873, pp. 510–513. For the attitude of the Patrons of Husbandry toward this political movement in Minnesota, see the *Farmers' Union* (Minneapolis), 1873, pp. 172, 194, 197, 218, 243, 261, 269, 276, 279, 285, 356 (May–November, 1873).

It was in Wisconsin, however, that the most startling results were achieved. The campaign in that state developed a peculiar alignment of interests. Governor Washburn, who was renominated by the Republicans, had frequently recommended legislation for the regulation of railroads, and in other ways incurred the enmity of the railroad interests. As a consequence much of the railroad influence was exerted in favor of Taylor, the Reform candidate, whose principles were not so well known as those of Washburn, apparently with the idea of putting him under obligation to these interests. Another factor in the election was the Graham liquor law, passed by a Republican legislature, which imposed serious restrictions on the liquor traffic, and resulted in turning the powerful brewery interests of the state, as well as a large part of the foreign vote, to the new Reform party. Then, of course, the order of Patrons of Husbandry was a factor in the election, and it seems probable that the major part, though by no means all, of the " Granger vote " was cast for the Democratic-Reform ticket. Although Wisconsin was normally Republican by large majorities, this "unholy alliance" of the railroad interests and the liquor interests with the Granger movement was sufficient to turn the scale and bring about the election of Taylor and the whole fusion ticket of state officers. The Democrats and Reformers also secured a majority of twenty in the lower house of the legislature, though the Republicans retained a majority of one in the Senate.[1]

In Kansas and Nebraska there were no state elections in 1873, but Independent or farmers' tickets were put in the field in a number of counties. In Kansas the result was the election of a sufficient number of Independents or Reformers to give the opposition to the Republican party a majority of about twenty in the lower house of the legislature. This was sufficient

[1] *Prairie Farmer*, xliv. 379 (November 29, 1873); *Chicago Tribune*, October, 1873–January, 1874, *passim; Industrial Age*, November, 1873, *passim;* Wisconsin, *Legislative Manual*, 1874, pp. 325, 348; *American Annual Cyclopedia*, 1873, pp. 774–776; C. W. Lea, *Granger Movement in Wisconsin* (Ms.), 20; C. R. Tuttle, *Illustrated History of the state of Wisconsin*, 642; G. W. Peck, editor, *Wisconsin in Cyclopedic Form*, 183.

to overbalance the strongly Republican hold-over Senate, and made possible the election of ex-Governor Harvey, a farmer and a Reformer, to the United States Senate.[1] In California also, the new party movement made its appearance in a struggle to control the legislature elected in 1873. The Republican party there was believed by many to be under the influence of the Central Pacific railroad, and a large number of Republicans, led by Governor Newton Booth, broke away from the party organization and supported Anti-Monopoly or Reform tickets in the various districts. The result of the election was a legislature composed of thirty-seven Republicans, forty-two Democrats and forty-one Reformers, but many members elected as Republicans or Democrats were opposed to the railroad monopoly. The principal business of this legislature was the election of two United States senators, and a long struggle finally terminated in the election of Governor Booth for the long term, and of John S. Hager, an " anti-railroad Democrat," for the short term.[2]

During the year 1874 state Reform or Anti-Monopoly parties were organized in all these states, and in some other states as well. Even in Ohio there were a few local efforts in the fall of 1873 looking toward the organization of farmers' or workingmen's parties,[3] but these came to naught, probably owing to a vigorous revival which took place in the Democratic party in the state at that time. In Indiana, on the other hand, similar local meetings in the fall of 1873, at which former party bonds were declared to be severed, finally led up to the calling of a state convention of Independents, which met at Indianapolis, June 10, 1874, and nominated candidates for state offices. The platform here adopted differed from those of the Reform parties

---

[1] *Chicago Tribune*, June, 1873–February, 1874, *passim; Industrial Age*, 1873, November 8, p. 4, November 15, p. 5; *History of the State of Kansas* (published by Andreas), 264.

[2] *Chicago Tribune*, December 22, 1873, p. 4, January 23, 1874, p. 3; *Industrial Age*, 1873, October 18, p. 4, December 27, p. 4; California State Grange, *Proceedings at Organization* (July, 1873); Carr, *Patrons of Husbandry on the Pacific Coast*, 75–103, 131–153; *American Annual Cyclopedia*, 1873, p. 83.

[3] *Chicago Tribune*, 1873, June 9, p. 1, June 18, p. 5.

in the other states in that its principal plank was a demand, not for railroad regulation, but for the issue of greenbacks interchangeable with government bonds and the payment of the government debt in legal tender. Two of the nominees of this convention refused the honor and another convention, held in August, not only filled their places, but also nominated new candidates in the places of two others who had accepted Democratic nominations for the same offices. In the election the new party cast about sixteen thousand votes, the Democratic candidates for state offices being victorious. The Independents secured five senators and eight representatives in the legislature, which gave them the balance of power in the Senate, but the Democrats controlled the House.[1]

In Michigan an attempt was made to break the Republican dominance by the organization of a " National Reform " party, which held conventions in August and September, 1874. The principal planks in its platform were civil service reform, state rights, tariff for revenue only, and a speedy return to " hard money." Some of the Reform nominees were accepted by the Democratic convention, but the Republicans were victorious, though by greatly reduced majorities. The vote for Reform candidates on which there was no fusion ran from two to seven thousand.[2]

In Illinois the movement which had been so successful in local elections in 1873 speedily developed into a state party in 1874. The resolutions adopted at the meeting of the State Farmers' Association in December, 1873, furnished the basis for the organization of the new party. These declared that the old parties had forfeited the respect and confidence of the people and demanded a reduction of the salaries of public officials, civil service reform, and the enforcement of the railroad laws.

---

[1] On the Independent party movement in Indiana, see *Chicago Tribune*, 1873, June 18, p. 5, August 23, p. 1, June 11, pp. 1, 12, August 13, p. 7; *Industrial Age*, 1874, April 18, p. 4, June 13, p. 5, June 27, p. 4, September 5, p. 5, October 17, p. 4; *American Annual Cyclopedia*, 1874, pp. 412–415.

[2] *Chicago Tribune*, 1874, February 12, p. 8, June 18, p. 3, August 7, p. 1; *Industrial Age*, February 28, 1874, p. 4; *American Annual Cyclopedia*, 1874, pp. 557–559.

The resolutions on tariff and currency were somewhat ambiguous, but the latter seems to have definitely committed the association to the Greenback policy.[1] In May, 1874, the advisory board of the State Farmers' Association issued a call to " the farmers, mechanics, and other laboring men, as well as all other citizens of Illinois who believed as declared by this Association at Decatur, December 18, 1873," to send delegates to a state convention at Springfield, June 10.[2] This convention chose " Independent Reform " as a name for the new party; nominated candidates for treasurer and superintendent of public instruction — the only state officers to be elected — and adopted the resolutions of the State Farmers' Association as a platform, with almost no changes, although a vigorous minority, led by the Hon. Willard C. Flagg, president of the association, strove for the adoption of a resolution " uncompromisingly opposing any further inflation." [3]

The Democratic convention, which met in August, took issue with the Independents by demanding the resumption of specie payments as soon as practicable, and nominated a separate candidate for treasurer, but accepted the Independent nominee for superintendent.[4] In the election which ensued, the fusion candidate for superintendent of public instruction received a majority of about thirty thousand votes, but the Republican candidate for treasurer was elected with a plurality of thirty-five thousand, while the Independent nominee received about

[1] Illinois State Farmers' Association, *Proceedings*, ii. 98–109. The resolutions and reports of this meeting are also to be found in *Prairie Farmer*, xliv. 409, xlv. 1 (December 27, 1873, January 3, 1874); *Industrial Age*, December, 1873–January, 1874, *passim; American Annual Cyclopedia*, 1873, p. 368.

[2] *Prairie Farmer*, xlv. 155 (May 16, 1874); *Chicago Tribune*, 1874, May 6, pp. 1, 5, May 11, p. 2.

[3] For the platform and reports of this convention, see *Prairie Farmer*, xlv. 195 (June 20, 1874); *Chicago Tribune*, June 11, 1874, p. 1; *Industrial Age*, June 13, 1874, p. 5; *American Annual Cyclopedia*, 1874, p. 402; John Moses, *Illinois, Historical and Statistical*, ii. 824–826. On the campaign and local conventions, see *Industrial Age*, 1874, September 19, p. 4, October 10, p. 4; *Prairie Farmer*, xlv. 275 (August 29, 1874). Thirty-three papers which supported the Independent party in the campaign are listed in the *Chicago Tribune*, June 22, 1874, p. 7.

[4] *American Annual Cyclopedia*, 1874, p. 403; Moses, *Illinois*, ii. 827; Gustav Koerner, *Memoirs*, ii. 583.

seventy-five thousand votes out of a total of nearly three hundred and seventy thousand. In the congressional elections the opposition fared somewhat better, regular Republican candidates being elected in but seven of the nineteen districts, while the remainder were classified: eight as Democrats, three as Independent Reformers, and one as an independent Republican. In the state legislature also, the Republicans lost their majority through this election, while the Independents secured the balance between the two other parties with three senators and twenty-seven representatives.[1]

In Wisconsin, Iowa, and Minnesota there were enough representatives of the new party in the legislatures of 1874 to secure the enactment, with some assistance from anti-railroad Republicans, of the Granger railroad laws of those states.[2] Although the railroad companies denied the validity of these laws and endeavored to have them set aside by the courts, they entered at the same time upon a campaign to secure their repeal. In the legislative elections of 1874 the railroad forces generally supported the Republican candidates, and the Republicans secured a majority over the combined Democratic and Reform opposition in both houses of all three of the legislatures.[3] In Minnesota the result was the immediate repeal of the Granger railroad law enacted the year before, but in Wisconsin and Iowa, enough of the Republican legislators were " anti-railroad " to prevent the repeal of the Granger laws in those states at this time.

[1] Election returns can be found in *Industrial Age*, 1874, November 7, p. 4, November 14, p. 5; *American Annual Cyclopedia*, 1874, p. 404; *Tribune Almanac*, 1875, pp. 47, 80–82; *World Almanac*, 1875, p. 24; Moses, *Illinois*, ii. 827.

[2] The history of this legislation and of the struggle over its enforcement is dealt with in chapter v below.

[3] On the campaigns of 1874 in these states, see *Chicago Tribune*, January–July, 1874, *passim;* *Industrial Age*, February–November, 1874, *passim;* *American Annual Cyclopedia*, 1874, pp. 418, 564, 810; Tuttle, *Wisconsin*, 649.

In Wisconsin the officers of the state grange took part in this campaign, first by calling upon all Patrons to vote for candidates who would support the Granger railroad law, and then by circulating a list of questions calculated to be submitted to candidates and to force them to declare their positions on the question of railroad regulation. Wisconsin State Grange, *Proceedings*, ii (1874), especially the appendix, pp. 3–12; M. E. Maynard, *Patrons of Husbandry in Wisconsin* (Ms.), 57.

The various local farmers' and Reform parties were also drawn together into state parties in Missouri, Kansas, and Nebraska in 1874. In Missouri the new party was one of opposition to the Democrats who were then in control and received the support of the Republicans;[1] in Kansas, on the other hand, all the elements of opposition to the dominant Republican party were joined under the " Independent Reform " banner;[2] and in Nebraska candidates were put in the field by all three of the parties.[3] The new party movement does not seem to have made much of an impression upon the political situation in these states, for the Democrats won in Missouri with nearly forty thousand majority, and the Republicans in Kansas with about twenty thousand, while in Nebraska the vote cast by the third party was inconsiderable.

In Oregon an Independent party made its appearance in the spring of 1874 with candidates for the June election and an anti-monopoly platform. The two old parties were very closely balanced in this state, and are said to have formed a coalition in some districts to defeat the new movement. The Independents had the support of a considerable portion of the press and probably of most of the Grangers, who at this time numbered nearly all the farmers of the state in their ranks, and they displayed considerable strength in the election, the votes on state officers and congressman being about ninety-seven hundred for the Democrats, ninety-two hundred for the Republicans, and sixty-five hundred for the Independents. In the legislative elections the new party fared even better, securing twenty-nine members of the lower house to twenty-eight Republicans and twenty Democrats, while in the Senate six Independents held the balance of power between the two

---

[1] *Chicago Tribune*, 1874, January 10, p. 2, January 12, p. 8, February 21, p. 8, June 11, p. 1; *Industrial Age*, 1874, May 16, p. 5, May 30, p. 5, June 13, p. 4, July 25, p. 6, September 5, p. 4; *Prairie Farmer*, xlv. 75 (March 7, 1874); *American Annual Cyclopedia*, 1874, pp. 576–579.

[2] *Chicago Tribune*, February 21, 1874, p. 8; *Industrial Age*, 1874, July 25, p. 5, September 26, p. 4; *American Annual Cyclopedia*, 1874, pp. 435–437; D. W. Wilder, *Annals of Kansas*, 643–646, 655, 658; Andreas, *Kansas*, 218, 264.

[3] *American Annual Cyclopedia*, 1874, p. 586.

old parties. Two supreme court judges and many county officials were also elected by the Independents.[1]

The " People's Independent " party of California, which had been fairly successful in the legislative elections of 1873, did not have an opportunity to take part in a state election until 1875. In that year candidates were put in the field by all three of the parties, the outcome being the election of the Democratic ticket with about sixty-two thousand votes, the Republican vote being thirty-one thousand and the Independent, thirty thousand.[2]

Although some striking results were achieved by these Independent parties in 1873 and 1874, and in a few states in 1875, their careers were all brief. In Michigan, Missouri, Kansas, and Nebraska, where the movement met with little success, nothing further was heard of it after 1874. The Independent Reform parties of Indiana and Illinois took part in the formation and became component parts of the National Greenback party in 1875 and 1876;[3] and as such cast considerably smaller votes than they had in 1874, although enough Independents and Greenbackers were elected to the legislature in Illinois to hold the balance between the two old parties and bring about the election of Judge David Davis as an Independent to the United States Senate.[4] In Wisconsin and Iowa, the fusion of

[1] *Chicago Tribune*, 1874, April 16, p. 8, April 17, p. 5, May 6, p. 4, June 3, p. 5, June 4, p. 5, June 26, p. 2; *American Annual Cyclopedia*, 1874, pp. 671–674.

[2] W. J. Davis, *History of Political Conventions in California*, 331–333; T. H. Hittell, *History of California*, iv; *Appleton's Annual Cyclopedia*, 1875, pp. 98–101.

[3] The State Farmers' Association of Illinois was represented by delegates in the conventions at Cleveland and Philadelphia, in 1875, which made arrangements for the national " Independent " or Greenback convention in Indianapolis, May 17, 1876. See the proceedings at the third annual session of the association in *Prairie Farmer*, xlv. 403, xlvi. 35, 38 (December 19, 1874, January 30, 1875). On the last stages of the Independent Reform party in Illinois and its transition to the Greenback party, see *ibid*. xliv. 163, 196 (May 22, June 19, 1875); *Western Rural* (Chicago), xiii. 196 (June 19, 1875); *Appleton's Annual Cyclopedia*, 1875, p. 393, 1876, p. 392; Moses, *Illinois*, ii. 834, 839, 848–850. The fourth and fifth, which were probably the last, annual sessions of the State Farmers' Association, were held in January, 1876, and January, 1877. *Industrial Age*, 1876, February 5, March 25; Illinois State Farmers' Association, *Proceedings*, v (1877).

[4] Judge Davis had been agreed upon as the independent member of the electoral commission to decide the Hayes-Tilden contest, but his election to the Senate at

Democrats and Reformers or Anti-Monopolists was tried again in 1875, and with some success in Wisconsin, where the fusion candidates for state officers, with the exception of governor, were elected, though by very small majorities. The Republicans regained complete control of the legislature, however, in both states and repealed the Granger railroad law of Wisconsin in 1876, the Iowa Granger law meeting the same fate two years later. The presidential campaign of 1876 put an end to the Independent movement in both of these states.[1] In Minnesota a " Reform" party, which seems to have had no direct connection with the Anti-Monopoly party of 1873, although probably composed of about the same men, put a ticket in the field in 1875 against both Republicans and Democrats, but secured less than two thousand votes, and did not appear again.[2]

There was an election for congressman in Oregon in 1875 and the Independent party again had a candidate in the field, but he received only about eight hundred votes. In the legislature which was elected in June, 1876, there were also a few Independents in both houses, but the presidential election in the fall probably put an end to the movement there also.[3] Nor does the People's Independent party of California appear to have kept up its organization after 1875, although many of the Grangers and others who belonged to it cast in their lot with the "Workingmen's party," which was organized by the followers of Dennis Kearney in 1877 and played a considerable part in California politics until 1880.[4]

this time necessitated the choice of another. If the Independents had not held the balance of power in this Illinois legislature, it is probable that Tilden instead of Hayes would have become president of the United States. See John T. Campbell, *The Hayes-Tilden Contest*, in Illinois State Historical Society, *Transactions*, 1909, pp. 184–189 for an account of the election of Davis and its connection with the presidential controversy.

[1] *Wisconsin Statesman* (Madison), 1875, September 18, p. 3, November 13, p. 2, 1876, March 11, p. 1, March 25, p. 1; *Appleton's Annual Cyclopedia*, 1875, pp. 402, 763, 1876, pp. 413–415, 806–808.

[2] *Appleton's Annual Cyclopedia*, 1875, pp. 509–511.

[3] *Ibid.* 609; *Wisconsin Statesman*, July 10, 1875, p. 3.

[4] Bryce, *American Commonwealth*, ii. ch. xc; E. Benjamin Andrews, *The Last Quarter Century*, i. ch. xiii; Bancroft, *California*, vii. 335–412; Lucile Eaves, *History of California Labor Legislation* (Berkeley, 1910).

As a result of this survey of western state and local politics from 1873 to 1876, it appears that Independent, Reform, or Anti-Monopoly parties were organized in eleven states — Indiana, Illinois, Michigan, Wisconsin, Minnesota, Iowa, Missouri, Kansas, Nebraska, California, and Oregon. In some of these states, as in Wisconsin and Iowa, the new parties secured victories, including the election of the state ticket in Wisconsin, by coalescing with the Democrats and forming a new party of opposition to the dominant Republicans. In other states, as in Oregon and in part in Illinois, they maintained their independence of the old parties and secured local victories over both of them, and in three states — Illinois, Kansas, and California — they secured the election of " Reformers " to the United States Senate.[1]

The purpose and character of this Independent movement can best be determined by an examination of the platforms adopted. In all of the states, except Indiana and Michigan, these contained planks demanding the subjection of corporations, and especially of railroad corporations, to the control of the state, and in several states regulation of all monopolies was demanded. It was thus an " anti-monopoly " movement, and in this direction the Granger laws were its principal achievement. But it was more than an " anti-monopoly " movement — it was also a " reform " movement. Every platform adopted by the new parties in all of the states denounced corruption in government and demanded reform, economy, and reduction of taxation, and several of the platforms contained specific demands for " civil service reform." In this direction the movement seems to have been a result of the unusually large amount of corruption which prevailed in both national and state governments during the first half of the decade of the seventies.[2]

These, then, were the two principal and distinguishing characteristics of the new parties — they were anti-monopoly (or

---

[1] The *Biographical Congressional Directory* lists Harvey of Kansas as a Republican, but Booth of California is described as an " Anti-monopolist " and Hager of the same state as an " Anti-monopoly Democrat," while Davis of Illinois is listed as " elected . . . by the votes of Independents and Democrats."

[2] See W. A. Dunning, *Reconstruction, Political and Economic*, chs. xiv, xviii.

anti-railroad) and reform movements. Their platforms contained many other planks, but some had reference to local matters only, while others, such as a demand for the reduction of the tariff to a revenue basis,[1] were borrowed from the Democrats. On the currency question the platforms were somewhat varied, but the majority took definite stand in favor of a return to specie payment as soon as practicable. In some cases the currency planks appear to have been attempts to straddle the issue, but in only two states — Indiana and Illinois — is it possible to trace a direct connection between the Independent movement and the Greenback parties which followed it.

There are a number of reasons which help to explain the shortness of the lives of these Independent parties. While the issue of reform is a good one upon which to arouse temporary enthusiasm, it is hardly a satisfactory basis for the organization of a new party — if the reform is accomplished the *raison d'être* of the party is gone, and if it is not accomplished the party is a failure. It might seem that the issue of railroad regulation would furnish a basis upon which a more permanent political party might be built up. In this direction, however, the movement suffered from the fact that the Granger laws for which it was held responsible did not work well, partly because of their crudeness, partly because of the determination of the railroads to make them appear injurious to everybody, but most of all because of the financial depression which followed the panic of 1873. In many parts of the West, moreover, the people still desired the construction of more railroad lines, and there was a feeling that this would be checked by restrictive legislation.

Again, it seems to be true, on the whole, that no political party can survive a presidential campaign without a national organization. The appearance of the National Greenback party and its absorption of the Independent Reform organization in Illinois, where the movement had been most promising,

---

[1] The objection to the protective tariff seems to have been based upon the feeling that it was class legislation — that it taxed the farmer for the benefit of the manufacturer — rather than upon the more recent argument that it fosters monopolies. See above, p. 21.

practically barred the way to the organization of a National Reform party for the campaign of 1876. Large numbers of the Independents, not only in the states where the parties had declared for sound money but in Illinois and Indiana as well, could not reconcile themselves to the Greenback doctrine and as a result most of the wandering sheep returned to the Democratic or Republican folds. The fundamental cause for the failure of the movement, however, seems to have been the same as that which has caused the failure of every third-party movement in the United States since the Civil War — the innate political conservatism of the bulk of the American people. Although recognizing that the issues which originally divided the old parties have largely passed away, they have preferred, even though it be a somewhat slower process, to bring forward the new issues and to work out the desired reforms in the established parties rather than to attempt to displace them with new organizations.[1]

The Grange and State Legislation

The formation of Independent parties was not the only way in which law-making was affected by the Granger movement. The order of Patrons of Husbandry, and to a less extent the other farmers' organizations, exerted considerable direct influence upon legislative activity in the different states of the Union. This was usually by means of resolutions or petitions requesting the enactment of desired legislation, in some cases particular bills before the state legislatures being specified; and in most states the politicians had such a wholesome respect for the strength of the order that these petitions were likely to be granted unless there were some other powerful interest opposed to them. This was especially true with regard to legislation on more or less technical agricultural subjects, such as the establishment and regulation of state boards of agriculture, the collection of agricultural statistics, the taxation of dogs for the protection of the sheep industry, the establishment of public weighers of grain, and the regulation of fences. Upon such

[1] This paragraph was written before the campaign of 1912.

matters as these, it was generally felt that the desires of the farming class should prevail, and since the Patrons of Husbandry were looked upon as representing that class, their petitions for legislation along these lines were likely to receive favorable consideration.

When it was a question of legislation upon subjects of more general interest, such as the regulation of corporations, taxation, education, and the rate of interest, the Patrons often found their resolutions and petitions productive of no results, and sometimes adopted more effective ways of making their influence felt. One of these methods was the holding of a Grange meeting at the state capital while the legislature was in session, in order that the presence of a large number of constituents might exert an influence on the legislators. This plan was followed in Iowa during the struggle for legislation to regulate railroads.[1] Another favorite method of attempting to influence legislation was that of interrogating candidates for office regarding their position on certain proposed legislative measures.[2] This plan was made use of by the order in Wisconsin and Illinois and was at times effective in forcing candidates to declare themselves in favor of the desired legislation in order to insure their election.

Among the subjects upon which the Patrons of Husbandry attempted to secure legislation, first place was occupied during this period by the question of regulating railroad corporations. This subject will be taken up more fully in subsequent chapters, so it will be unnecessary to go into it here, further than to state that the different granges were practically unanimous in demanding some measure of regulation of railroads by the state, and the enactment of " anti-pass " legislation.

Another subject upon which many of the state granges frequently requested legislation was that of education.[3] In general

[1] See below, p. 169.

[2] See Wisconsin State Grange, *Proceedings*, iii, appendix (January, 1875), for a list of questions used in a campaign in Wisconsin during the struggle over the Potter law.

[3] See especially state grange proceedings: Alabama, iii; Indiana, iv; Iowa, iv; Michigan, ii, iii, vi; Missouri, iii; New Hampshire, i, iv, vii; Maine, vi; North Carolina, iii; Vermont, iv; Wisconsin, iii–vii. See also below, pp. 290–293.

it may be said that the Patrons desired liberal appropriations for agricultural colleges, demanded that these be kept separate from the so-called " literary institutions," and favored the introduction of agricultural subjects into the curriculum of the public schools. They did not, however, confine their interest to agricultural education; on the contrary, the benefits of general education, to the state as well as to the individual, and the duty of the state to provide it were usually recognized, while the Wisconsin State Grange in 1875 and the National Grange in 1879 even went so far as to advocate compulsory education.[1] One example, however, of a somewhat reactionary spirit should be noted; in 1873, the Indiana State Grange passed a resolution opposing grants of state funds to aid colleges " as being a great injustice to a large portion of the children of the state and a detriment to the interests of institutions of learning run by private enterprise." [2]

The matter of text-books also engaged the attention of the granges and in a number of states, notably Maine, Michigan, and Wisconsin, resolutions were passed for the adoption of uniform text-books, to be furnished to the children at cost.[3] How far any of these resolutions were of influence in determining the course of legislation on the subject is difficult to determine. It might be noted, however, that in Wisconsin, it was claimed that a bill providing for uniform text-books was only prevented from passage by offers of the book publishers to reduce greatly the prices of their books. At its next session, the state grange complained that the quality had been reduced as well as the price, and demanded the adoption of a uniform set of books to be published within the state.[4]

A reflection of the prevailing indebtedness among farmers in this period is seen in the many resolutions and petitions of

---

[1] Wisconsin State Grange, *Proceedings*, iii. 91 (1875); National Grange, *Proceedings*, xiii. 99, 111 (1879).

[2] *Prairie Farmer*, xliv. 403 (December 20, 1873).

[3] Michigan State Grange, *Proceedings*, iii. 74 (1875); Maine State Grange, *Proceedings*, vi (1879); Wisconsin State Grange, *Proceedings*, v. 69 (1877), vi. 65 (1878), vii. 65 (1879).

[4] Wisconsin State Grange, *Proceedings*, vii. 65 (1879).

state granges on the subjects of taxation, interest rate, and exemption laws. As concerns taxation, resolutions can be found in the proceedings of nearly all the state granges demanding reduction and equalization, for it was felt that the farmers were bearing an undue proportion of the heavy burden of taxation.[1] Often specific measures were proposed for accomplishing these objects, as in California, where the taxation of uncultivated land, held for speculation, at an equal rate with cultivated land was demanded.[2] Exemption of railroad property from taxation was condemned by the granges of Ohio and Wisconsin. The Ohio State Grange even demanded the taxation of church property. The most general proposition on this subject, however, was that of taxing mortgages and relieving the mortgaged property from a proportionate amount of the burden. Various ingenious schemes were proposed for accomplishing this purpose; but the order was not unanimous in the matter, for the California State Grange opposed taxation of mortgages or other credits, as well as of growing crops.[3] Here again the results of the efforts of the order are difficult to measure, and the most that can be said is that changes were made during the decade in the revenue systems of a number of states, in the direction of a more equal distribution of the burden of taxation between urban and rural property, between personal property and real estate, and between the property of individuals and that of corporations. In bringing about these reforms there were other influences at work besides the Grange, but its work was undoubtedly a factor in the movement.[4]

In several of the states of the North Central group, where the prevailing interest rate was high, attempts were made by the state granges to secure legislation reducing the legal rate of interest.[5] The Wisconsin State Grange, for example, adopted resolutions along this line in 1874, 1875, 1876, 1879, and 1880 and

[1] See above, pp. 21–23.
[2] *California Patron*, July 18, 1877, p. 5.
[3] Carr, *Patrons of Husbandry*, 99.
[4] Messer, *The Grange*, 18.
[5] State grange proceedings: Michigan, vi; Indiana, iv; Wisconsin, ii–iv, vii, viii.

went even so far as to advocate the regulation of the interest rate by federal legislation. The Wisconsin legislature passed a law in 1878 reducing the legal rate in the state from ten to seven per cent. This was probably a result, in part, of the Grange agitation, although it is impossible to show any direct connection, and the Grange continued to pass resolutions on the subject. Another indication that farmers in general belonged to the debtor class at this time is seen in the resolution of the Nebraska State Grange, opposing any change in the stay or exemption laws or the laws relating to foreclosure of mortgages and collection of debts as likely to " do great injury to the debtor class." [1] On the other hand, resolutions of the Iowa and New Hampshire State Granges looking to the safeguarding of deposits in state banks [2] would indicate that some farmers, at least, were not in debt.

One practically universal demand of the Patrons was that of reform and retrenchment in the administration of government, state and local as well as national. In state affairs this took the form mainly of a demand for a reduction of salaries and fees of state and local officials, and resolutions embodying this demand or protesting against proposed increases can be found in the proceedings of nearly every state grange from New Hampshire to California.[3] The general argument was that, since the income from all other occupations had decreased and since all commodities were at bottom prices, it was but fair that salaries of public officials should be reduced to a corresponding basis. It is probable that this attitude of the granges, together with the general sensitiveness on the subject resulting from the so-called " salary grab " in Congress,[4] was effective in keeping down the compensation of public officials in a number of states. Thus in Illinois a movement to increase the salaries of supreme court

---

[1] Nebraska State Grange, *Proceedings*, iv. 33 (1874).

[2] Iowa State Grange, *Proceedings*, vi (1875); New Hampshire State Grange, *Proceedings*, iv (1877).

[3] For good examples see state grange proceedings: Indiana, iv; Michigan, i; New York, ii; Ohio, iii; Wisconsin, vi.

[4] Dunning, *Reconstruction, Political and Economic* (*American Nation*, xxii), 233–235.

judges was frustrated,[1] and in Ohio a law fixing the salaries of county officials was passed in 1875, against the proposed repeal of which the state grange protested vigorously in 1876.[2] In addition, the general watchfulness and suspicion of public officials which was inculcated by the granges undoubtedly served to check to some extent the corruption and extravagance which permeated the government of many states during the decade following the Civil War.[3]

Numerous other legislative projects, mainly of local interest, attracted the attention of different state granges. Thus in California, a committee of the state grange circulated a petition asking the legislature to establish a general system of irrigation under the control of the state. Some of the granges, located in parts of the state where the direct advantages of the proposed system would not be felt, refused their support to the measure; but a bill embodying the features of the proposed system was presented to the Assembly in January, 1874, by a Granger member from Los Angeles. This bill, known by the name of its introducer as Venable's bill, passed the Assembly by a majority of thirty votes, but was defeated in the Senate, through the influence, it was claimed, of the San Joaquin and King's River Canal Company, a corporation which controlled a considerable part of the private irrigation business of the state. The Grange committee in its report to the state grange, made in the fall of 1874, intimated strongly that money was used with the senators to defeat this measure.[4]

In the proceedings of a number of southern granges, resolutions are to be found which reflect the conditions prevailing in that part of the country during the era of reconstruction. Thus the South Carolina Grange, at its fourth annual session in 1875, asked for legislation to prohibit the traffic in produce at night,[5] and in Mississippi in the same year, the state grange demanded

---

[1] Paine, *Granger Movement in Illinois*, 32.

[2] Ohio State Grange, *Proceedings*, iii. 85 (1876).

[3] Dunning, *Reconstruction*, ch. xiv.

[4] California State Grange, *Declaration of Purposes;* Carr, *Patrons of Husbandry*, 146–148, 183–185.

[5] South Carolina State Grange, *Proceedings*, iv (1875).

the enactment of more stringent laws for the enforcement of
contracts to labor.[1]   In Alabama the influence of the Grange,
as exerted by agitation and memorials to the legislature, appears
to have been a factor in securing the repeal of the personal
recognisance law and the enactment of many laws in the interests
of the white farmers; including a high license law, a law to
restrict the sale of liquor by druggists, and more stringent laws
to prevent trespass, burning of woodlands, and stealing of
agricultural products.[2]

Such were the main lines along which the order of Patrons
of Husbandry sought to influence the course of legislation in
the different states, and in general it would seem that the results
of this influence were salutary; certainly that was the case in
so far as it served to check the tendency toward extravagance
and corruption on the part of public officials.   True, the amount
of legislation which can be pointed to as a direct result of Grange
influence, aside from the Granger railroad laws, is slight, but
the work of agitation performed by the order served at least
to inculcate an interest and a watchfulness in legislative matters
on the part of the farmers, the indirect influence of which was
probably quite extensive.

The Grange and National Legislation

The constitution of the order of Patrons of Husbandry expressly declared that political questions would not be tolerated
as subjects of discussion,[3] and the founders repeatedly asserted
that the order was not a political organization.   Nevertheless,
the phenomenal increase in the membership of the order during
1873 and 1874 awakened the liveliest interest, and sometimes
apprehension, among politicians throughout the Union.   Thus
the *New York Tribune*, referring to the Grange, declared that

[1] Mississippi State Grange, *Proceedings*, v (1875).

[2] Hawkins, " The Grange in the South," in Allen, *Labor and Capital*, ch. xx.
Mr. Hawkins also declares that the Grange was a considerable factor in uniting
the farmers and white men in general in preparation for the reëstablishment of
white supremacy in Alabama in 1874.

[3] See Article XII of the constitution in National Grange, *Proceedings*, vi. 18
(1873), and many other places.

" within a few weeks it has menaced the political equilibrium of the most steadfast states. It has upset the calculations of veteran campaigners, and put professional office-seekers to more embarrassment than even the Back Pay." [1] There was considerable justification for this conception of the Grange in the fact that large numbers undoubtedly did join it in the years of its prestige with the idea of using the order for political ends; but the principal reason for this misapprehension of the real purposes of the order was probably the failure of a considerable part of the press throughout the country, particularly in the East, to distinguish clearly between the order of Patrons of Husbandry and the openly political aspects of the general farmers' movement, such as the farmers' clubs and the Independent political parties of the western states.

Despite considerable internal pressure to the contrary and some transgression on the part of local granges, the National Grange succeeded in maintaining the non-political position of the order; and the " Declaration of Purposes " adopted at the seventh annual session [2] in February, 1874, emphasized the position of the order on this subject by the following assertion: [3] " We emphatically and sincerely assert the oft-repeated truth taught in our organic law, that the Grange, National, State, or Subordinate, is not a political or party organization. No Grange, if true to its obligations, can discuss political or religious questions, nor call political conventions, nor nominate candidates, nor even discuss their merits in its meetings."

The idea of a secret society of farmers with political objects, which the organization of the Grange had suggested, appears to have been too enticing to let slip, and this declaration of the Patrons was followed almost immediately by the organization in New York of the " Order of Independent Grangers." [4] A few years later, O. H. Kelley, the " Father of the Grange " evolved

[1] Quoted in Martin, *Granger Movement*, 415–418.

[2] This was the second session of the National Grange as a delegate body. The first five sessions were merely meetings of the founders. See above, pp. 63–65.

[3] National Grange, *Proceedings*, vii. 56–60 (1874).

[4] *Rural Carolinian*, v. 372 (April, 1874); *American Agriculturist*, xxxiii. 125 (April, 1874).

the idea of the " Degree of the Golden Sheaf," which was apparently intended as a sort of secret inner circle within the Grange with the object of securing concert of action at the ballot box.[1] For some reason, secret political associations have never flourished in the United States, and both of these movements appear to have been fiascos. In general the farmers preferred to keep the secret feature out of their political organizations, as witness the open farmers' clubs of the western states.

At first there seemed to be a tendency on the part of some of the leaders of the Grange to interpret the political restriction of the constitution in such a way as to prohibit the discussion of politico-economic questions, and the agitation for legislation in the interest of farmers. Thus, the National Grange, when confronted, at its seventh session, with a resolution for memorializing Congress on the subject of national finance and the bonded debt, decided that it would be injudicious to take any action in the matter.[2] These scruples were soon wiped away, however, and the " Declaration of Purposes," adopted at the same session, plainly exhibits an intention to agitate for legislation along a number of lines.[3] By the tenth session of the National Grange, in November, 1876, this work had become one of the most prominent functions of the order, and a general plan of action was adopted for securing the desired legislation.[4] According to this plan the master of the National Grange was to draw up forms of a petition to Congress on the subjects decided upon; these were to be sent to the state masters, who would circulate

[1] All the evidence that has been secured relating to the "Degree of the Golden Sheaf " is comprised in a number of circulars in the library of the Wisconsin Historical Society. These are signed by Kelley as " actuary," and one of them, dated April 12, 1886, declares that the association was organized in 1875. One is tempted to wonder if the fee, of at least five dollars, which was to be paid to the National Branch by each subordinate branch established, was not the real *raison d'être* for the degree. In 1877 the National Grange adopted a resolution denouncing as conspirators any members of the order " found engaged in organizing a secret society within our order, or consisting in part or the whole of members of our Order." National Grange, *Proceedings*, xi. 136 (1877).

[2] National Grange, *Proceedings*, vii. 41 (1874).

[3] *Ibid.* 56 (1874).

[4] *Ibid.* x. 159 (1876).

them among the subordinate granges, and then return them to the national master for presentation to Congress. In addition, the national master was to draw up a form for a circular letter to the individual congressmen, requesting reports on the progress of the desired legislation and urging the necessity for action, copies of which should be sent by the master of each state grange to every senator and representative from his state. In this way the demands of the farmers were to be brought to the attention of all the congressmen at the same time; for the date upon which the letters were to be mailed was to be fixed by the master of the National Grange. This procedure, or some modification of it, and the appointment of special committees to lobby for its measures, were the principal methods by which the order attempted to influence the course of national legislation; although it also took advantage of the election, in the latter part of the decade, of several of the members of the National Grange to seats in Congress, to press through them for the desired legislation.[1]

Among the objects of the Patrons of Husbandry and the other farmers' organizations, none was more prominent in the early seventies than that of securing reduction in the cost of transportation. For furthering this object two general lines of procedure presented themselves to the farmers, regulation of the existing means of transportation by the government, national or state and increase in the facilities for transportation. The efforts of the farmers for the regulation of railways will be treated in subsequent chapters, but the agitation for internal improvements can best be considered here in connection with the general legislative activity of the Grange.

Almost as soon as they were organized, the different state granges, especially those of the Mississippi Valley, began to agitate for the construction of canals, and the improvement of the river channels in which they were severally interested.[2] These propositions varied according to the location of the grange, but there was one scheme which received the general approval

---

[1] *Ibid.* xii. 88 (1878), xiv. 99, 151 (1880).

[2] For examples see state grange proceedings: Indiana, iv (1874); Missouri, iii (1874); Vermont, special (May, 1874), iv (1875); Wisconsin, ii (1874).

of the order — the establishment of a workable water route from the Great Lakes to the Gulf of Mexico by improvement of the Fox, Wisconsin, and Mississippi rivers. In order to bring the influence of the Grange to bear more effectively for securing federal aid for this project, the executive committees of the various Mississippi Valley granges held a meeting at Keokuk, Iowa, October 6, 1873, at which arrangements were made for carrying on a correspondence with the congressmen from each state on the subject.[1] Shortly after this a Northwestern Farmers' Convention, which met at Chicago, took up this and other schemes for internal improvement, and the officers of this convention were given an opportunity to present the views of the farmers on the subject before the Windom committee on transportation of the United States Senate.[2] The National Grange, in the "Declaration of Purposes" adopted at its next meeting, February, 1874, declared that the order would advocate the increase of facilities for cheap transportation in every practicable way.[3] Resolutions were also adopted at this and at subsequent meetings favoring specific projects. Meanwhile the various state granges continued to pass resolutions on the subject, and it seems probable that this agitation had considerable influence in inducing Congress to appropriate over fifty-eight million dollars for river and harbor improvement in the decade from 1870 to 1880, a sum more than four times as great as the appropriations for similar purposes in any preceding decade. Of this money, a considerable part was used on the Mississippi, Wisconsin, and Fox rivers, but this general project of a Lakes to Gulf waterway has never been successfully carried out, because of a number of weak links in the chain which do not seem to be susceptible of improvement.

---

[1] The resolution embodying the proceedings of the Keokuk meeting is to be found in Wisconsin State Grange, *Proceedings*, ii. 31 (1874); Iowa State Grange, *Proceedings*, iv (1873); and also printed separately in the form of a circular, a copy of which is in the library of the Wisconsin Historical Society.

[2] Windom Committee, *Report*, ii. 646–688. The proceedings of the Northwestern Farmers' Convention are here given in full together with testimony of the officers before the committee.

[3] National Grange, *Proceedings*, vii. 58 (1874).

Another scheme for increasing the transportation facilities of the country, which was extremely popular with the granges of the interior, was the construction, preferably by the federal government, of a double-track freight railroad from some point in the Mississippi Valley to the Atlantic Ocean.[1] The attitude of antagonism to railroad corporations, which had been assumed by the order in the Northwest, led the granges in that section of the country to oppose strongly any further grants of public lands to aid private companies in the construction of new lines;[2] and in general their schemes for increasing transportation facilities looked toward direct participation on the part of the government. In the South, on the other hand, where the need of more railroads was greatest and the abuses of railroad management had been least felt, the granges were inclined to favor the continuance of the system of federal aid for the construction of lines by private companies. Thus the Texas State Grange adopted a resolution asking Congress to extend aid to the Texas and Pacific railroad, and the matter was brought before the National Grange at its eighth session, with the result that that body also adopted a resolution favoring federal aid for the project, but under such restrictions as would guarantee the government against loss, and protect the agricultural interests against unjust discriminations.[3] This session of the National Grange was held at Charleston, and appears to have been somewhat under the influence of the southern wing of the order, for several other projects for legislation to encourage the construction of railroads by private companies received its approval. These measures were opposed by most of the delegates from the northwestern states,[4] in a number of which, state and local granges afterwards

---

[1] National Grange, *Proceedings*, vii. 85 (1874); Iowa State Grange, *Proceedings*, iv (1873); Wisconsin State Grange, *Proceedings*, ii. 25 (1874), iii. 59 (1875).

[2] State grange proceedings: Indiana, iv (1874); Michigan, i (1874), iii (December, 1875); Ohio, ii (1875).

[3] *Resolutions of Legislatures, Boards of Trade, State Granges, etc., favoring Government Aid to the Texas and Pacific Railway* (pamphlet, Philadelphia, 1874), 35–38; National Grange, *Proceedings*, viii. 85–88 (February, 1875).

[4] Ohio State Grange, *Proceedings*, ii (1875); *Prairie Farmer*, xlvi. 84, 99, 107 (March 13, 27, April 3, 1875).

adopted resolutions condemning the action of the National Grange in this particular.

The interest of the farmers in problems of currency and banking was early reflected in resolutions of a number of state granges calling for increase in the amount of currency, the substitution of legal tender notes for national bank notes, the repeal of the tax on state bank notes, or the payment of customs dues in currency.[1] The National Grange at first took the stand that these were questions of a political nature, and twice refused to consider resolutions relating to the currency problem.[2] In the latter part of the decade, however, when the state granges began to pass resolutions for " the issue of money directly by the government for the benefit of the whole people," and when the Illinois State Farmers' Association and similar bodies in other states made the expansion of the currency one of their cardinal issues,[3] the National Grange reconsidered its position. At its eleventh session in November, 1877, it adopted a resolution for the repeal of the law demonetizing silver and the law fixing a date for the resumption of specie payments.[4] There seems, however, to have been some difference of opinion in the order upon the merits of the question, as well as upon the advisability of considering it,[5] for the New Hampshire State Grange in December, 1877, resolved: " That a dollar should be a full dollar, and all debts honestly paid according to the contract." [6] This might be considered as a mild expression of disapproval of the stand taken by the National Grange. In committing itself on this subject, which had been made the principal issue of the National Greenback party, the Grange undoubtedly laid itself open to the charge of partisanship, and this probably helped to

[1] State grange proceedings: Indiana, iv (1874); Wisconsin, ii (1874), iv (1876); North Carolina, ii (1875); Michigan, iii (December, 1875).

[2] National Grange, *Proceedings*, vii. 41 (1874), ix. 175–177 (November, 1875).

[3] Wisconsin State Grange, *Proceedings*, v. 27 (1877); Illinois State Farmers' Association, *Proceedings*, v (1877).

[4] National Grange, *Proceedings*, xi. 69, 82–85 (1877).

[5] The Grange divided 18 to 30 on the question of the indefinite postponement of the resolution; 34 to 9 on the repeal of the demonetization law; and 30 to 14 on the repeal of the resumption law.

[6] New Hampshire State Grange, *Proceedings*, iv (1877).

weaken its hold on the farming population of the country in the latter part of the decade.

The tariff question, which, as has been seen, nearly caused a split in the ranks of the reforming farmers of Illinois as early as April, 1873, also proved to be an apple of discord for the Patrons of Husbandry. The different state granges often had decided views on the question, but these views were so divergent that all attempts to reconcile them in the meetings of the National Grange proved futile. The granges of the northern states, in general, seemed to be more interested in preventing the removal of duties on agricultural products than in securing the reduction of the duties on other articles, although there was a tendency to oppose an increase in the tax on such articles of common consumption as tea and coffee.[1] This was a time when there was considerable agitation for a reciprocity treaty with Canada; but the farmers were unwilling to meet the competition of Canadian products, and the state granges of Indiana and New York adopted resolutions condemning the proposition and urging the senators from those states to oppose the confirmation of such a treaty.[2] One duty particularly cherished by the northern farmers was that on wool. This was reduced in 1872. It is probable that the activity of the Grange in Michigan and a number of other wool-growing states was largely instrumental in securing its restoration in 1874, and in preventing subsequent reduction during the decade.[3]

The California State Grange, on the other hand, advocated a reduction of the duty on grain sacks, while granges in the South naturally inclined toward free trade or a tariff for revenue only. Thus the Texas State Grange sent a request to the National Grange at its ninth session in November, 1875, that it adopt measures to influence Congress to abolish all protective duties. The committee to which this was referred opposed its consideration as savoring of a political nature, but the subject was again

[1] Iowa State Grange, *Proceedings*, iv (1873).

[2] Indiana State Grange, *Proceedings*, iv (1874); New York State Grange, *Proceedings*, ii (1875).

[3] Michigan State Grange, *Proceedings*, vi. 10 (1878), viii. 16 (1880); Wisconsin State Grange, *Proceedings*, vi. 77 (1878), vii. 18 (1879).

brought up by the Texas delegate and a discussion ensued in which the delegates from Ohio, Michigan, and Missouri opposed the proposition. A motion was then carried to postpone its further consideration and there is no record of any attempt to bring it up again.[1]

Another branch of federal taxation which interested the Patrons of Husbandry was the internal revenue duty on tobacco. This was a matter which vitally concerned the pocket-books of many farmers in Maryland, Virginia, Kentucky, and neighboring states, and the granges in these states early began an agitation for the removal or reduction of this duty. The question was brought up at the eighth session of the National Grange in February, 1875 (the Charleston session), by the delegate from Kentucky, and a resolution was adopted, apparently with little opposition, requesting Congress to repeal all laws levying taxes on tobacco, and to endeavor to secure the reduction of duties imposed by foreign countries on the importation of this product. A resolution in almost the same terms was adopted in the tenth session in 1876, but some opposition developed in the eleventh session, and it was found advisable to change the proposed resolution to a mere request that the revenue laws relating to tobacco be revised. At the next session, the twelfth, the executive committee was directed to prepare a memorial to Congress on the subject, and a year later, November, 1879, the master reported that a reduction had been secured which " had benefited this year the farmers of the State of Kentucky alone to the amount of over three million dollars."[2] This work of the National Grange did not meet with the approval of all parts of the order, however, for the New Hampshire State Grange, in December, 1878, adopted a resolution expressing regret at the position of the National Grange on the subject and taking the stand that Congress should lay heavy taxes on tobacco and liquor, " and thus leave the necessaries of life as free from the burden

---

[1] National Grange, *Proceedings*, ix. 46, 72, 152 (November, 1875). At the eleventh session, resolutions were introduced by the delegate from Pennsylvania in favor of maintaining a high duty on hides, wool, and linseed, but the Grange refused to consider them. *Ibid.* xi. 119, 133 (1877).

[2] *Ibid.* viii. 91.

of taxation as the necessities of the State and Nation will permit." [1]

Numerous other resolutions on federal taxation might be mentioned, such as one adopted by the Ohio State Grange in 1873 in favor of an income tax, a subject which was taken up by the National Grange at the very end of the decade; [2] and one by the Alabama State Grange, requesting the return of the cotton tax collected during the years 1865–67; [3] but enough examples have been given to show that the deciding factor in determining the action of a grange in such matters was generally the financial interests of the individual Grangers, and when these differed, as they were almost sure to in the National Grange, made up of delegates from all parts of the country, it was impossible to bring any effective influence to bear upon Congress. May not the diversity of interests within the class, due in the main to the great extent of the country, be rightly considered as the principal cause for the failure of all attempts, not only on the part of the agricultural class but of other classes as well, to become effectively united forces in national politics?

There were, however, a number of propositions for national legislation on subjects pertaining more directly to agriculture toward which the attitude of the Patrons of Husbandry was more nearly unanimous and their influence correspondingly greater. One of the most important of these was the project for the advancement of the federal bureau of agriculture to the rank of a regular department of the government, presided over by a member of the president's cabinet. This subject was first brought forward in a series of resolutions adopted by the National Grange at its tenth session in November, 1876, and steps were taken to enlist the assistance, not only of all state and local granges, but of unaffiliated farmers and planters as well, in a campaign for the proposition. From this time forth not a session of the National Grange passed by without the adoption

---

[1] New Hampshire State Grange, *Proceedings*, v (1878).

[2] Iowa State Grange, *Proceedings*, iv (1873); National Grange, *Proceedings*, xiv. 91 (1880).

[3] Alabama State Grange, *Proceedings*, ii (1874).

of resolutions demanding the advancement of the bureau of agriculture and more liberal appropriations for its use, while many of the state granges, notably those of the New England states, adopted similar resolutions and took steps to induce the congressmen from their states to support the project.[1] In Congress the measure met the opposition of the chairman of the committee on agriculture of the House, but it was taken in hand by D. Wyatt Aiken, a prominent Patron and congressman from South Carolina, and by him pressed to a vote in February, 1881. The debate developed considerable opposition on the ground that the measure was class legislation, and the bill failed by two votes of the two-thirds necessary for the suspension of the rules. In the next Congress, the forty-seventh, the bill was again brought forward, and was passed in the House on May 10, 1882, by the overwhelming vote of 183 to 7; but it was not until February, 1887, that the bill finally passed the Senate, with amendments, and not until 1889 did the two houses succeed in agreeing on the provisions of the measure and permit it to become a law.[2] While the Grange was, of course, not the only force which exerted an influence in favor of this measure, it seems clear that it was one of the most important factors in securing the establishment and liberal support of the department of agriculture, an institution which has been of great service to the farmers of the country and to the nation in general.[3]

Another proposition for national legislation which received considerable attention from the Patrons of Husbandry was that of reform of the patent laws. The greater part of the machinery and many implements and devices used by the farmers were patented, and it was felt that these laws and the administration

---

[1] National Grange, *Proceedings*, x. 23, 116, 159 (1876), xi. 105 (1877), xii. 64 (1878), xiii. 40, 94, 124, 127 (1879), xiv. 69, 79, 90 (1880); New Hampshire State Grange, *Proceedings*, iv (1877), vii (1880); Maine State Grange, *Proceedings*, vi (1879).

[2] National Grange, *Proceedings*, xv. 15–18 (1881), xvi. 10 (1882); Darrow, *Patrons of Husbandry*, 45–50; *Congressional Record*, xi. 709, 1317–1320, xiii. 3706, 3727, 3753–3776, 3794–3796, 4284, xiv. 1154–1159, 1176–1179, xx. 1399.

[3] Darrow, *Patrons of Husbandry*, 50; Messer, *The Grange*, 17; C. H. Greathouse, *Historical Sketch of the Department of Agriculture* (rev. ed.), 20.

of the patent bureau in general was too favorable to patentees and manufacturers, and bore too heavily on the consumers. The reforms proposed were mainly of three sorts: the limitation of the life of patents and the prevention of their extension by renewals; the establishment of a fixed royalty with permission to anyone to manufacture patented articles upon the payment of such royalty; and finally, the protection of the " innocent purchaser or user of a patented article," making the manufacturer or vendor alone responsible for violations of the law. Resolutions along these lines appear in the proceedings of the National Grange and of the state granges of Iowa and Wisconsin as early as 1874, and the usual method of bombarding Congress with memorials and petitions was followed throughout the decade, though without any considerable results.[1] The National Grange seems to have concentrated its forces on the third of the desired reforms, and a bill purporting to grant protection to innocent users of patented articles, but declared by the master of the National Grange to be worthless, passed the House in 1880 and was allowed to expire in the Senate.[2] Again in 1882 another bill, more satisfactory to the Grangers, was passed by the House, but this was held up by amendments in the Senate.[3] Although the attempt to secure general reform of the patent laws thus came to naught, the Patrons appear to have been more successful in dealing with individual cases, and the claim is made that the influence of the Grange prevented the extension of patents on sewing-machines.[4] In various parts of the country, moreover, and particularly in Michigan, the Patrons made use of their organization to fight successfully the various swindles, such as the patenting and collection of royalty

[1] National Grange, *Proceedings*, vii. 55, viii. 62, ix. 39, 72, x. 159, xi. 105, xii. 58, xiii. 40, 86, 120, 125, xiv. 69, 79, 91, 107 (1874–80); State grange proceedings: Iowa, v (1874); Michigan, ii (1875); New Hampshire, vii (1880); New York, i (1875); Wisconsin, ii–iv (1874–76); Minnesota State Grange, *Constitution* 1873). See also *Congressional Record*, xiv. 1694, 1759, 1942.

[2] National Grange, *Proceedings*, xiv. 27 (1880); *Congressional Record*, x. 768.

[3] National Grange, *Proceedings*, xvi. 11–13 (1882); *Congressional Record*, xiii. 413, 3945, 3952–3955, xiv. 2263, 3684–3686.

[4] Darrow, *Patrons of Husbandry*, 50; Messer, *The Grange*, 18.

upon articles long in common use, which the laxness of the patent laws or the laxness of their enforcement made possible.[1]

The Grangers were also quite unanimous in demanding greater economy in the conduct of the general government. Just as there was a constant demand for reform and retrenchment in state and local government, so was it also felt that there were many ways in which the national government might be made more efficient and less extravagant and corrupt. The various proceedings of state and national granges are filled with denunciations of such specific examples as the " salary grab " law and the *Crédit Mobilier* affair, and with demands for more economical administration of the national government, lower salaries and fees for officials, and less display and extravagance in the erection of public buildings, while the Michigan State Grange in 1875 went so far as roundly to condemn the contemplated appropriation for the centennial exhibition at Philadelphia.[2]

Among the various other projects for national legislation with which the Patrons of Husbandry were concerned at different times during the decade are to be found propositions for stricter quarantine against yellow fever;[3] for legislation to stamp out pleuro-pneumonia among cattle;[4] for the more merciful treatment of live-stock in transit;[5] for the improvement of the system of levees on the Mississippi River — brought forward by the Louisiana State Grange;[6] for the appointment of a commission to devise means for the extermination of destructive insects;[7] for improvements in the signal service of the United States weather bureau;[8] for the regulation of weights and measures;[9] for changes in the rates of postage;[10]

---

[1] See above, p. 18.
[2] National Grange, *Proceedings*, xiii. 124 (1879); State grange proceedings Michigan, i, ii (1874, 1875); New Hampshire, i, iv, vii (1873, 1877, 1880); New York, ii (1875).
[3] National Grange, *Proceedings*, xii. 65 (1878).
[4] *Ibid*. xiv. 55, 140 (1880).
[5] *Ibid*. xii. 67 (1878).
[6] *Ibid*. viii. 67 (February, 1875).
[7] *Ibid*. ix. 56 (November, 1875).
[8] *Ibid*. 174.   [9] *Ibid*. 43, 107.
[10] Wisconsin State Grange, *Proceedings*, iv (1876).

for greater security of bank deposits; and for commercial treaties to open up the markets of the world, and especially of South America, to the products of American agriculture.[1]

On a number of other subjects of more general interest, the National Grange was somewhat chary of putting itself on record, probably for fear of antagonizing some of the members of the order. Thus, when the proposition for the exclusion of Chinese labor, a subject which was agitating the people of the Pacific coast at this time and upon which resolutions had been passed by the California State Grange, was brought before the National Grange at its eleventh session in 1877, through a resolution presented by a delegate from California, the resolution was rejected without consideration.[2] Women's suffrage was another of these questions, and one in which the order had a particular interest, since its ranks and its dignities were open to women on practically the same footing as to men. Various state granges frequently declared themselves in favor of giving the ballot to women, and the question came before the National Grange at its tenth session in 1876. It was referred to a special committee of five which reported unfavorably. The chairman of the committee, " Sister " Washburn of Colorado, then submitted a minority report in favor of the proposition, but the whole subject was indefinitely postponed by a vote of twenty-four (sixteen men and eight women) to nine (five men and four women).[3] Questions of temperance and prohibition also received occasional attention from the order, and the Ohio State Grange once allowed itself to be drawn into a temperance crusade which was under way at Xenia during its session in that place.[4] Resolutions condemning intemperance, and suggesting that members should not cast their ballots for candidates for public office who made use of intoxicating drinks or were in sympathy with the liquor traffic, were presented to the National Grange at its twelfth session in 1878 by the delegate from Ohio, and were carried by

[1] National Grange, *Proceedings*, xi. 133 (1877), xiii. 124 (1879).

[2] *Ibid.* xi. 108, 132 (1877).

[3] National Grange, *Proceedings*, x. 94, 96, 121, 169–171 (1876).

[4] Ohio State Grange, *Proceedings*, i (1873). See also below, p. 298.

a vote of twenty-seven to eleven; several of those who voted in the negative explaining that they were in sympathy with the purposes of the resolution, but objected to its consideration by the Grange.[1]

It cannot be said, on the whole, that the order of Patrons of Husbandry exercised any considerable direct influence on national legislation during the decade 1870–80. With the possible exceptions of the reduction of the internal revenue duty on tobacco and the restoration of the high tariff on wool, practically all of the demands of the order for national legislation went unheeded by Congress or were in line with laws which would have been enacted even without the support of the Grange. The same probably is true of much of the legislation since 1880 for which the members of the order have been wont to claim the credit. Even the elevation of the bureau of agriculture to a cabinet department would doubtless have taken place in time without the agitation of the Grange, though that agitation probably hastened the step somewhat; and no student of national railway legislation would be willing to accept the claim of many members of the order that it was chiefly instrumental in securing the passage of the interstate commerce act.[2] To understand this failure to exercise effective influence on national legislation, even with regard to questions upon which the order was united, consideration should be given to the facts that the Grange did not attempt to exercise such influence to any considerable extent until 1875 or 1876, by which time it had begun to decline rapidly in numbers and prestige; and that when the order began to revive in the next decade, numerous other and more vigorous agricultural organizations had come to the front, and it could no longer claim to be the principal spokesman of the farming class.

---

[1] National Grange, *Proceedings*, xii. 105 (1878).

[2] Messer, *The Grange*, 17; Darrow, *Patrons of Husbandry*, 50; J. J. Woodman in *American Grange Bulletin*, August 1, 1901.

CHAPTER IV

GRANGER RAILWAY LEGISLATION (ILLINOIS)

OF all the various aspects of the movement for agricultural organization in the seventies, none attracted so much attention at the time, or was so significant in its results, as the attempt to subject railway corporations to the control of the state. Indeed, this phase of the movement has so overshadowed its other manifestations, that to most writers, even of the present day, the term "Granger movement" appears to connote primarily this struggle between the farmers and the railroads, to the exclusion of the social, intellectual, and coöperative features of the movement. Not only does this subject present one of the most important manifestations of the desire of the farming classes to band together for mutual assistance and support, but it is likewise a very significant chapter in the history of railway transportation in America. It marks the final abandonment of the *laissez faire* theory that natural laws alone are sufficient to insure the management of railroads in the interest of the public, and the beginning of definite attempts to solve the railway problem by restrictive legislation. It is the first appearance in the legislative arena, in America, of one of the most vital economic problems which confront American legislatures, state and national, at the present time.

In dealing with this subject, special attention will be given to the movement in the four northwestern states of Illinois, Minnesota, Iowa, and Wisconsin. There were attempts at restrictive legislation in many other states during the decade, and these will be summarized so far as they can be considered parts of the Granger movement, but it was in these four states that the most important laws were enacted; it was in these states that the principal cases leading to important judicial decisions arose; and, finally, in these states the movement for railway legislation was most closely connected with the movement for agricultural organization. But even here the agitation for the regulation of railways began long before the Patrons of Husbandry arose to importance, and, in Illinois, even before the movement for rural organization in open farmers' clubs got under way. Thus it is probable that there would have been legislation on the subject even without the accompanying movement for agricultural organization. On the other hand, there is no doubt that the influence of the organized farmers was the principal force back of these movements for railway regulation, giving to them many of their distinctive aspects; and therefore it is eminently proper that they should find a place in any discussion of the Granger movement.[1]

EARLY AGITATION AND THE LAW OF 1869

In most accounts of railway legislation in the northwestern states the date 1870 is taken as marking the transition between the period of feverish anxiety for the construction of more railroads and the period of agitation for the reduction and equalization of rates.[2] While this is fairly accurate as a generalization, the impossibility of marking off historical development into definite periods with fixed dates is well illustrated by the fact that the first period did not end in the more western states and even in many of the less developed counties of Illinois until long after 1870, while the feeling that legislative curbing of the railroads was necessary began to make its appearance as early as 1850 and became a force to be reckoned with in the decade of the sixties.[3]

In Illinois the first positive movement in the direction of restrictive railway legislation was the passage of a bill by the House of Representatives in 1861 " to prevent and punish any

[1] For an account of the conditions of railway construction and management which led to the Granger legislation, see above, pp. 9–15.

[2] See J. H. Gordon, *Illinois Railway Legislation and Commission Control since 1870*, introduction by M. B. Hammond, for a division of railway legislation in Illinois into periods. See also E. C. Clark, *State Railroad Commissions and How they may be Made Effective*.

[3] F. E. Newton, *Railway Legislation in Illinois from 1828 to 1870* (Ms.), ch. x.

fraudulent discrimination by railroad companies." [1] Two years later a bill for the appointment of railroad commissioners passed the Senate but was not acted upon by the House. [2] In 1865, however, the House passed a bill for the appointment of a railroad commission, by a vote of 62 to 1, and also a bill limiting passenger fares to three cents per mile. The Senate had now become conservative and both of these measures were buried by its committee on railroads. [3] In the next general assembly, which convened in 1867, a large number of bills and resolutions were introduced, and the House finally passed, by a vote of 57 to 24, a bill for " An act to assert the control of the state over railroad corporations, to fix the rates of freight, and to prevent extortion." The Senate at this session went so far as to adopt a resolution declaring that the legislature had full power to limit fares or freights, and that the unreasonable, excessive, and oppressive charges of the corporations made the exercise of that power imperative; but the only railroad measure which got so far as a third reading in that house was defeated by a tie vote. [4]

The demand for the curbing of the power of railway corporations continued to grow throughout the state during the following two years. When the twenty-sixth general assembly convened in January, 1869, it was one of the principal subjects confronting the legislature. [5] A number of restrictive bills were introduced in both houses, but the first one passed — a three cent fare measure — was vetoed by the governor, on the ground that the railroad charters were contracts, and not subject to

[1] Illinois, *Senate Journal*, 1861, p. 583.

[2] *Ibid.*, 1863, pp. 89, 193, 210; *House Journal*, 1863, pp. 117, 503, 681, 723–732.

[3] For legislative activity on the subject of railway regulation at this session, see *House Journal*, 1865, pp. 113, 164, 439, 467, 506, 520, 594, 681, 701, 778, 833, 982; *Senate Journal*, 1865, pp. 548, 560, 675, 683, 711.

[4] *House Journal*, 1867, i. 45, 47, 82, 97, 107, 127, 162, 240, 301, 314, 356, 446, 626, ii. 436, 673; *Senate Journal*, 1867, pp. 93, 95, 134, 171, 173–176, 185, 200, 205, 222, 438, 446, 469, 507–512, 532, 550, 870–875, 1231; John Moses, *Illinois, Historical and Statistical*, ii. 769.

[5] *Ibid.* 777. For a characterization of this general assembly, see Davidson and Stuvé, *History of Illinois*, 933–935. Cf. Gordon, *Illinois Railway Legislation*, 21.

alteration by the legislature.[1] In spite of the fact that the governor's veto at this time was merely suspensive and could be over-ridden by a majority vote of both houses, the legislature docilely laid aside the radical bill and enacted a law which was in accord with suggestions made by the governor.[2] This "Act concerning railroad rates" of 1869,[3] which was the first measure on the statute books of Illinois that attempted to interfere with the right of railway companies to fix the charges for their services, was quite inadequate as a solution of the problem of railway regulation and failed entirely to satisfy the growing demand for effective measures. It contained provisions declaring that railroads should be limited to "just, reasonable, and uniform rates," and that they should receive "a reasonable and uniform toll or compensation, according to the service actually rendered"; but the popular *pro rata* principle was specifically rejected by a section providing that these declarations should not be taken to mean that rates must be the same on all roads, or for different classes of freight, or for shipments in opposite directions. Phrased thus guardedly and with no adequate provision for enforcement, the act became a mere encumbrance on the statute books. There is no evidence that the railroad companies paid any attention to it, or that any attempts were made to enforce it.[4]

THE CONSTITUTION OF 1870

The people of the state, and especially the farmers, were not long in discovering that the legislature had given them a stone when they had asked for bread, and the pages of the *Prairie Farmer* and other newspapers soon contained numerous articles, editorials, and letters discussing railroad abuses and the rail-

[1] *Senate Journal*, 1869, i. 44, 186–192, 208–210, 322, 397, 471–474; *House Journal*, 1869, i. 225, 227, 283, 300, 342–350, 463; Moses, *Illinois*, ii. 778.

[2] *Senate Journal*, 1869, i. 404, 506, 566, 856, ii. 9–14, 97, 406, 446, 644; *House Journal*, 1869, ii. 561, 589, iii. 193, 223, 251.

[3] Illinois, *Public Laws*, 1869, pp. 309–312.

[4] Cf. Hammond, in Gordon, *Illinois Railway Legislation*, 17; Newton, *Railway Legislation in Illinois* (Ms.), 75. During this period some of the agitation for state control found vent in restrictive provisions in charters to new railway companies. *Ibid.* ch. x.

road law and asserting the power of the state to control corporations of its own creation. One correspondent of the *Prairie Farmer* declared in May, 1869, that the legislature should have gone further and fixed the " just and reasonable rates " instead of allowing the corporations to determine what were such; another in August declared the law as passed to be " clumsy and effete " and suggested that bribery was used to prevent the passage of more effective measures.[1] Although frustrated this time, the advocates of state control of railroads did not give up the struggle, and an opportunity to inaugurate a flank movement on the enemy was presented by the fact that a convention was to meet in December, 1869, to revise the state constitution. The contest was at once transferred from the legislative to the constitutional field. From the attitude on the subject of a large majority in the convention, and the results as embodied in the new constitution, it is apparent that the farmers and others desirous of restrictive legislation kept that issue in mind in the elections of delegates to the convention.

Various influences were also brought to bear upon the convention in favor of radical provisions for railway regulation. As might be expected, a considerable number of petitions relating to the subject were received,[2] and local pressure was undoubtedly brought to bear upon the individual members, especially during a recess of the convention.[3] But even more important than these was the movement for protective and coöperative organization which was beginning to take a hold among the farmers of the state. Numerous local meetings for the consideration of problems of transportation and rural organization were held in 1869,[4] and on March 26, 1870, Mr. Henry C. Wheeler, a farmer of Du Page County, Illinois, issued in the *Prairie Farmer* a call for a " Producers' Convention." This call contained a somewhat intemperate discussion of the transportation question, the gist of which was that railroad charges had not been reduced to

---

[1] *Prairie Farmer*, xl. 154, 273 (May 15, August 28, 1869).

[2] Illinois Constitutional Convention, 1870, *Debates*, i. 289, 344, 365, 451, 510, 589.

[3] *Ibid.* ii. 1710.   [4] J. Periam, *The Groundswell*, 224.

correspond with the rapidly declining prices in every other department of trade and commerce. Therefore it was proposed

that the farmers of the great North-west concentrate their efforts, power, and means, as the great transportation companies have done theirs . . . And, to this end, I suggest a convention of those opposed to the present tendency to monopoly and extortionate charges by our transportation companies, to meet at Bloomington, Illinois, on the 20th day of April next. Congress is now in session, and the Constitutional Convention of this State will then again be convened. Farmers, now is the time for action.[1]

This movement received the support of the *Prairie Farmer* and the convention was attended by a considerable number of leading Illinois farmers. Its attempt to bring about the formation of " Town, County, State and National Transportation Leagues " failed from lack of funds, but a string of vigorous resolutions was adopted. These declared railroad companies public corporations, subject to be regulated and controlled by legislation; denounced the practice of railroads of delivering grain to warehouses without the consent of the shipper or owner; condemned the tendency to consolidation, and the corrupt influence of corporations on courts and legislatures; and approved of canals for cheap transportation and to furnish competition for railroads.[2]

The result of this activity is seen in the remarks of some of the delegates in the convention. Thus Mr. Washburne declared: " The people expect that this Convention will inaugurate by this article a contest between the people and the railroads " ;[3] Mr. Ross said: " In my judgment there can be nothing done by this convention that will give so much satisfaction as providing in the organic law that the people shall be protected against the aggressions of these monopolies " ;[4] Mr. Snyder of St. Clair

---

[1] *Prairie Farmer*, xli. 89 (March 26, 1870); Periam, *The Groundswell*, 225–227.

[2] *Ibid.* 227–231; *Prairie Farmer*, xli. 130 (April 30, 1870). Periam gives the date of this convention as 1869, and the error is repeated in the *Documentary History of American Industrial Society* (x. 42–46) and in John L. Coulter, " Organization among the Farmers of the United States," in *Yale Review*, xviii. 279–281 (November, 1909).

[3] *Debates*, ii. 1639.

[4] *Ibid.* 1711.

County: " I say, if there is anything like unanimity in this State upon any one thing, it is upon restricting these railroads." [1] On the other hand, the words of Mr. Parks expressed a sentiment which undoubtedly had considerable weight with the members of the convention and with the people at large: " There is another cry from the people, a cry for more railroads . . . in trying to remedy these evils, we should consider whether we may not run to the other extreme, and prevent the building of any more railroads." [2] One of the delegates went so far as to declare that if the courts had decided that a railroad charter was an irrevocable and inviolable contract, that decision must be overruled. " We must have a new deal and new decisions on this subject, and we in this Convention must take the initiative, and declare what the law should be in this regard." [3] There were not wanting arguments against both the right and expediency of state regulation of railroads, and especially against the inclusion in the constitution of mandatory provisions making it the duty of the legislature to enact certain laws; but the advocates of regulation were in the majority, or the popular pressure was effective, and the railroad sections of the new constitution were adopted in the convention by votes ranging from 46 for and 18 against to 32 for and 27 against.[4]

The railroad provisions of the Illinois constitution of 1870 are to be found in Article XI, headed " Corporations," [5] of which sections 9 to 15 inclusive pertain wholly to railroad corporations. The most important provisions relating to regulation are contained in sections 12 and 15.

Section 12. Railways . . . are hereby declared public highways, and shall be free to all persons for the transportation of their persons and property thereon, under such regulations as may be prescribed by law. And the General Assembly shall, from time to time, pass laws establishing reasonable maximum rates of charges for the transportation of passengers and freight on the different railroads in this state.

---

[1] *Debates*, ii. 1710.   [2] *Ibid.* 1711.   [3] *Ibid.* 1645.

[4] *Ibid.* 1637–1664, 1708–1723.   Cf. Moses, *Illinois*, ii. 788; Gordon, *Illinois Railway Legislation*, 23.

[5] The constitution can be found in Illinois, *Revised Statutes*, 1874, p. 79, in Illinois, *Bluebook*, and in Thorpe, *Constitutions*.

There seemed to be considerable doubt among the members of the convention as to the meaning and probable effect of the first part of this section, and some apparently expected it to force the railroads to open their tracks to anyone who might propose to run trains upon them,[1] a solution of the problem which was frequently proposed.[2] The second part of the section contains one of the famous mandatory provisions of this constitution, for the enforcement of which no other means was provided than the oath of members of the legislature to obey the constitution.

Section 15. The General Assembly shall pass laws to correct abuses and to prevent unjust discrimination and extortion in the rates of freight and passenger tariffs on the different railroads in this state, and enforce such laws by adequate penalties, to the extent, if necessary for that purpose, of forfeiture of their property and franchises.

This section was introduced as an amendment during the debate, and was adopted by the closest vote of any of the railroad sections. It appears to have been designed as something to fall back upon in case the courts should prevent the operation of the last part of section 12.[3]

Another subject upon which advanced ground was taken by the Illinois constitution of 1870 and one which came to be closely connected with the regulation of railroads, was the control to be exercised by the state over public elevators or warehouses for the storage of grain. As far back as 1867, the general assembly had enacted a law regulating warehousemen, which laid down rules for the inspection of grain and provided that all public warehousemen should publish their rates on the second Monday in each year, which rates should not be changed during the year to the injury of any customer. Discrimination in rates between grain received over different railroads was prohibited, and railroad companies were forbidden to deliver grain to any warehouse other than that to which it had been consigned, without the consent of the owner or consignee. By other

[1] *Debates,* ii. 1646, 1715.
[2] By Governor Palmer, for example, in his letter to the Producers' Convention at Bloomington. *Prairie Farmer,* xli. 130 (April 30, 1870).
[3] *Debates,* ii. 1722.

sections of the act all dealing in futures was forbidden, but these sections were repealed by the next general assembly in 1869.[1] The warehouse article of the constitution of 1870[2] defined public warehouses; and made it obligatory on railroad companies to weigh or measure grain at points where shipped, to receipt for it, and to deliver the shipment to the consignee provided his warehouse was connected with the tracks of the railroad company; and all railroad companies were to permit such connections to be made by any warehousemen. This article also contained mandatory sections by which it was made the duty of the legislature to pass laws for the inspection of grain, for the regulation of warehouse receipts, and to give effect to this article; "which shall be liberally construed to protect producers and shippers."

The Illinois constitution of 1870 was submitted to the people for approval as a whole and a number of its sections were submitted for separate vote. The vote on the constitution as a whole was 134,227 for and 35,443 against. Among the sections submitted for separate vote were those relating to railroads, which were approved by vote of 144,750 to 23,525; and those relating to warehouses, which were approved by vote of 143,532 to 22,702. In only three of the one hundred and one counties, namely, Hardin, Jackson, and Union, all in the extreme south, was there a majority against the railroad sections.[3]

THE LEGISLATION OF 1871

The duty of giving effect to the railroad and warehouse provisions of the new constitution fell upon the twenty-seventh general assembly, which convened in January, 1871. This general assembly contained an unusually large number of farmers, who banded themselves together in a "Legislative Farmers' Club" and worked unitedly for railroad and other legislation

---

[1] *Public Laws*, 1867, pp. 177–183; 1869, p. 410. An act regulating the transportation of grain had also been passed in 1865. See *ibid.*, 1865, p. 75.

[2] Article XI.

[3] *Debates*, ii. 1894.

desired by the farming classes.[1] The governor now recommended vigorous measures, including the establishment of a board of commissioners to enforce the railroad and warehouse laws.[2] Indeed, most of the members of the legislature, as well as the governor, seem to have " seen the light," and the various railroad and warehouse bills met with little opposition. The legislation proposed and enacted upon these subjects can readily be divided into six different categories: (1) the regulation of passenger fares on railroads; (2) the regulation of freight charges on railroads; (3) the regulation of warehouses; (4) the regulation of the transportation of grain on railroads; (5) the establishment of a board of railway and warehouse commissioners; and finally, (6) the enactment of a general railway incorporation act. Separate acts were passed at the regular session of the twenty-seventh general assembly dealing with each of the first five of these subjects, while the passage of a general incorporation act was postponed to the adjourned session held in the winter of 1871–72.[3]

The first of these subjects taken up was that of the regulation of passenger fares, and " An act to establish a reasonable maximum rate of charges for the transportation of passengers on railroads in this state " passed the two houses by votes of 38 to 7 and 130 to 10, and received the approval of the governor.[4] This passenger act of 1871 was an improvement upon the measure vetoed in 1869, in that it provided for the division of railroads into classes based upon their gross earnings per mile, and fixed a sliding scale of maxima for the different classes, ranging from two and one-half to five and one-half cents per mile.[5] Still it is

[1] *Prairie Farmer*, xlii. 49, 57 (February 18, 25, 1871); Paine, *Granger Movement in Illinois*, 20.

[2] *Senate Journal*, 1871, i. 19–23.   Cf. Moses, *Illinois*, ii. 801; Gordon, *Illinois Railway Legislation*, 25.

[3] *Public Laws*, 1871–72.   Cf. Gordon, *Illinois Railway Legislation*, 26.

[4] For the legislative history of this measure, see *Senate Journal*, 1871, i. 61, 72, 82, 85, 99, 102, 104, 117, 121, 123, 129, 131, 135, 154 (Senate bill passed), 406, 418, 443, 445, 450, 468 (House bill passed); *House Journal*, 1871, i. 209, 236, 332, 527, 529, 545, 550, 588, 612, 627, 631–636 (House bill passed), 704, 724.

[5] *Public Laws*, 1871–72, p. 640; Gordon, *Illinois Railway Legislation*, 28; Paine, *Granger Movement in Illinois*, 21.

difficult to see how it differed in principle from the measure of 1869, or why the governor's reasons for vetoing that act would not have applied equally well to this.

The " Act to prevent unjust discrimination and extortions in the rates to be charged by the different railroads in this state for the transportation of freight on said roads " was passed by votes of 39 to 2 and 132 to 9, and received the immediate approval of the governor.[1] This act is one of the most important of the railroad laws enacted at this session, and as its terms are somewhat complex and have often been incorrectly stated, it will be well to examine them in some detail.[2] Although the title of the act declared that it was to prevent *unjust* discrimination, section 1 was so phrased as to make any discrimination whatever illegal; in other words it provided for the application of the *pro rata* principle that charges should be based entirely upon distance traversed. The essential part of the section reads as follows:

> No railroad corporation . . . shall charge or collect for the transportation of goods, merchandise or property on its said road, for any distance, the same nor any larger or greater amount as toll or compensation than is at the same time charged or collected for the transportation of similar quantities of the same class of goods, merchandise or property over a greater distance upon the same road.

The scope of this provision will be seen when it is compared with the "long and short haul clause" of the interstate commerce act of 1887.[3] That act made illegal the charging of a greater sum for a shorter than for a longer haul only when the shorter distance was included within the longer and the haul was in the same direction; while the Illinois act of 1871 made it an offense to charge *the same* or a greater sum for a shorter distance than is charged for a longer *anywhere on the same road*.

Section 3 of this act further provided that:

---

[1] *Senate Journal*, 1871, i. 222, 272–276, 290 (passed), 476, 542; *House Journal*, 1871, i. 453, 478, 483, 527, 529, 588, 612, 625, 665, 692, 696 (passed), 781.

[2] The act is in *Public Laws*, 1871–72, p. 635; for analyses of it, see Gordon, *Illinois Railway Legislation*, 27; Paine, *Granger Movement in Illinois*, 21.

[3] United States, *Statutes at Large*, xxiv. 379–387, section 4.

No railroad corporation shall increase its rates of toll or compensation to be charged for the transportation, receipt, handling or delivery of any property from any point on its line of road to any other point on its line of road, by reason of any decrease in its rates which may be required to be made under the first section of this act.

The normal or maximum rates for any day, above which no increase was to be made, were fixed as the rates on the corresponding day of the year 1870. These provisions of the act, all taken together, amount to an attempt to force all rates to the level of the lowest competitive rates as they prevailed in the year 1870, and are based upon the apparently logical reasoning that these competitive rates must be profitable to the railroads or they would not do the business; *ergo*, uniform rates in proportion to these throughout the line would also yield a profit.[1] No allowance was made for the fact that a large proportion of the expense in railroad business is a fixed charge and does not vary in proportion to the amount of business done, nor for the fact that conditions might easily vary so much on different parts of the same road as to make different rates perfectly justifiable. The establishment of the rates of 1870 as maxima was especially unwise, because of the unusually large fluctuations in rates during that year.[2]

The " Act to regulate public warehouses and the warehousing and inspection of grain, and to give effect to article thirteen of the constitution of this state " passed the two houses with little opposition, and was approved by the governor April 25, 1871. It established, as maximum charges for the storage of grain, two cents per bushel for the first thirty days and one-half cent per bushel for each succeeding period of fifteen days or part thereof. In addition, all warehousemen were required to publish their rates for each year during the first week in January, which rates might not be increased during the year, and there could be no discrimination between customers.[3]

---

[1] See remarks of Mr. Pierce in the constitutional convention of 1870, *Debates*, ii. 1645.

[2] Illinois Railroad and Warehouse Commission, *Reports*, 1871, p. 21; Gordon, *Illinois Railway Legislation*, 28.

[3] *Public Laws*, 1871–72, pp. 762–773.

The " Act regulating the receiving, transportation and delivery of grain by railroad corporations " forbade discrimination between shippers and warehouses in the handling of grain.[1]

The most important and far-reaching in its effects of any of these acts of the twenty-seventh general assembly was undoubtedly the " Act to establish a board of railroad and warehouse commissioners, and prescribe their powers and duties." This measure passed the Senate without a dissenting vote, 33 being registered in its favor, while in the House the vote was 103 to 9.[2] It provided for the appointment by the governor of a board of three commissioners, none of whom should be connected with or interested in the stock of any railroad company.[3] The first board was to hold office until the meeting of the next general assembly, and thereafter the term was to be two years from January 1. Section 6 of the act required every railroad company doing business in the state to make an annual report to the board and enumerated forty-one particulars to be embraced in this report, including information with regard to capital stock; assets; liabilities; debt; value of property; amount of business; monthly earnings; expenses of operation, repairs, and improvements; rates and tariffs; relations with express, freight, and transportation companies; and arrangements with other railroad companies. To this list the board might add such other queries as it should see fit and warehousemen were also required to make such statements as the board might call for. The information thus gathered was to be compiled and presented to the governor in the annual report of the board.

The provisions for the enforcement of these various acts differed considerably and were, on the whole, inadequate.[4] The act to prevent unjust discrimination and extortions in freight rates provided for the recovery of a penalty for violation,

---

[1] *Public Laws*, 1871–72, pp. 636–641; Gordon, *Illinois Railway Legislation*, 27.

[2] *Senate Journal*, 1871, i. 184, 187–194, 204 (passed), 545, 561; *House Journal*, 1871, i. 102, 133, 324, 420, 544, 548, 655, 693, 698, 782 (passed), 792, 823.

[3] *Public Laws*, 1871–72, pp. 618–625. The act is analyzed in Gordon, *Illinois Railway Legislation*, 29.

[4] Railroad Commission, *Reports*, 1871, pp. 5, 8, 13–15, 65–69.

not to exceed one thousand dollars, in an action of debt by the party aggrieved, and also for forfeiture of franchises for wilful violation; the corporation to be proceeded against by the state's attorneys in any circuit or county through which the road should run, by writ of *scire facias* or *quo warranto*.[1] The act establishing maximum passenger fares also provided for the recovery of a penalty for violation by the party aggrieved, in this case not to exceed five hundred dollars and costs; but only after final judgment had been recovered a fifth time were the state's attorneys authorized to proceed by *quo warranto* for forfeiture of franchise.[2] The act establishing the board of commissioners made it the duty of the board to enforce the railroad laws of the state, but no definite procedure was laid down except in the case of a company failing to make the report required by the law.[3] The provisions for the enforcement of the act regulating warehouses were also inadequate.

ATTEMPTS TO ENFORCE THE LEGISLATION OF 1871

The first step toward carrying out this elaborate and radical program of railroad control was the appointment by Governor Palmer of the members of the new board of railroad and warehouse commissioners on July 3, 1871. They were Gustav Koerner of St. Clair County, Richard P. Morgan, Jr., of McLean County, and David S. Hammond of Cook County. In the message transmitting these names to the Senate for confirmation, at the adjourned session of the general assembly, the governor stated that the choice of these men had been influenced " by a desire to combine in the board the requisite experience drawn from different pursuits and from different parts of the state." [4] The work of these men, under unusual difficulties, would seem to indicate that they were as competent as any who were available, but there was some dissatisfaction over the appointments among the farmers, if the *Prairie Farmer* can be taken as repre-

---

[1] Section 5.   [2] Sections 5, 6.
[3] Sections 11–16.
[4] *Senate Journal*, 1871, ii. 5; Gordon, *Illinois Railway Legislation*, 30; Moses, *Illinois*, ii. 809, 1059.

sentative of their opinions. It objected particularly to Hammond, who was stigmatized as a pretended representative of the farmer's interests but in reality " a political bummer." [1]

Immediately after it was organized the board issued a call to the railroad companies for reports on gross earnings and mileage, which could be used as a basis for classification under the law regulating passenger fares. Four of the principal companies responded with a joint communication declaring

that while the companies do not recognize the validity of the law under which your Honorable Board was appointed, so far as it attempts to impose upon these companies additional duties and obligations; yet we are willing to furnish such information as the mode of doing our business makes reasonable and practicable.

A hope was also expressed that speedy steps would be taken to test the validity of the new laws in the courts. By October reports were received from all but three of the twenty-one roads of the state, although nearly all of these were prefaced by statements denying the validity of the law and declaring all rights of the companies to be reserved. Using the information contained in these resports, the board proceeded to classify the railroads upon the basis of gross earnings, in accordance with the law. This classification was notified to the companies and was also given publicity through the newspapers.[2]

It is impossible to say just what immediate effects, if any, this classification had upon passenger fares in the state. Certainly the leading roads, which were required by the law to reduce their fares to two and a half and three cents per mile (classes A and B), did not observe the law; but the board reported that complaints about passenger fares were fewer and less intense than formerly, because of a liberal use of commutation and

---

[1] *Prairie Farmer*, xli. 213. Commissioner Morgan declared in March, 1873, that Mr. Koerner, the chairman and legal member of the commission, was early found to be acting in the interests of the railroad companies and a drag upon all efforts of the other members to enforce the law. *Chicago Tribune*, March 15, 1873, p. 3. Morgan seems to have had the support of the farmers. Resolutions recommending his re-appointment were adopted by a Livingston County convention of farmers and by the State Farmers' Association. *Ibid.*, January 10, 1873, p. 5; *Prairie Farmer*, xliv. 26 (January 25, 1873).

[2] Railroad Commission, *Reports*, 1871, pp. 1–6, 55–60, 63, 71–156.

season tickets for those who traveled extensively. This may have been a step on the part of the railroads to strengthen themselves with the traveling public, and thus indirectly a result of the law, but the board condemned it as an injustice to the great mass of travelers.[1]

As has already been shown, the commissioners could take no steps for the enforcement of the maximum passenger fares, other than to advise the aggrieved parties to bring suit for the recovery of five hundred dollars. In most cases the private individuals refused to bring such action. The situation with regard to the law prohibiting unjust discrimination and extortion was somewhat different, the law allowing action to be brought by state's attorneys in this case. Complaints of the violation of the long and short haul clause of this law were numerous and were attested by the very reports of the railroad companies. The complainants, however, steadily refused to bring action for the recovery of the one thousand dollar penalty allowed by the law, the reasons alleged being the power of the railroad companies to retaliate by denying them accommodations when most wanted. Indeed, the board found it extremely difficult to get authentic verified statements from the complainants, but finally sufficient evidence was secured to warrant the initiation of *quo warranto* proceedings against the Chicago and Alton.[2] The first annual report of the commission, which was laid before the legislature in January, 1872,[3] promised that this suit would be " pressed with vigor at the earliest day practicable."

This first report of the Illinois railroad and warehouse commission also contained an illuminating discussion of the whole problem of railway regulation, which shows that the members of the board had been making a thorough study of the subject and were prepared to take up advanced positions. The principal burden of the report, however, was the inadequacy of the provisions for enforcement and the inconsistencies of the laws of 1871.[4] These subjects were also brought forward by the

---

[1] Railroad Commission, *Reports*, 1871, pp. 5, 24.   [2] *Ibid.* 5–7.

[3] *Senate Journal*, 1871, ii. 257; *House Journal*, 1871, ii. 726.

[4] Railroad Commission, *Reports*, 1871, pp. 5–8, 13–15, 18–23, 26.

governor in his message to the adjourned session of the legislature.[1] Two bills by which it was proposed to consolidate and revise all the laws relating to the regulation of railroads and warehouses, were prepared by the commissioners and introduced in the House in January, 1872, but the press of other business prevented action upon them,[2] as also upon another bill which proposed to strengthen the enforcement provisions of the acts of 1871.[3]

In the Senate at this session a bill was introduced by Senator Vaughn for " An act to establish reasonable maximum rates of charges for the transportation of freight on the different railroads in this State." This bill, which proposed to classify the various railroads and establish a fixed schedule of maximum rates for each class, was referred to the railroad commission for an opinion. The commission had already expressed its belief in the inadvisability of an inflexible schedule and reported accordingly, but Senator Vaughn pressed the bill to a vote in the Senate, which resulted in its defeat, 19 to 10.[4] An attempt was also made in the Senate to pass a bill prohibiting members of the general assembly from accepting passes. This was laid on the table by the close vote of 14 to 13.[5] On the other hand, an attempt was made to put a stop altogether to the movement for regulating railroads by legislating the railroad and warehouse commission out of existence. A bill to this effect was introduced by Senator Harlan on February 12, but failed to reach a vote.[6] On March 20, 1872, Mr. Harlan followed up the attack by introducing a resolution which cited the failure of the commissioners to enforce the laws, their expense to the state " without ability to render just compensation," and " respectfully requested " them to

---

[1] *Senate Journal*, 1871, ii. 5.

[2] Railroad Commission, *Reports*, 1871, p. 15, 1872, p. 12; *House Journal*, 1871, ii. 338. The bills are given in full in Railroad Commission, *Reports*, 1872.

[3] *House Journal*, 1871, ii. 637, 674.

[4] *Senate Journal*, 1871, ii. 422, 462, 707, 728, 742, 758, 763–765, 776; Railroad Commission, *Reports*, 1872, pp. 13, 148. A similar bill had been introduced at the first session. See *Senate Journal*, 1871, i. 288, 322; *House Journal*, 1871, i. 272, 276, 393, 579, 619, 621.

[5] *Senate Journal*, 1871, ii. 77.

[6] *Ibid*. 461, 502, 707, 721, 744, 766.

resign. The vote on the adoption of this resolution, which appears to be a test of the strength of the opposition to railway regulation in the Senate, was 13 ayes and 19 noes.[1]

Four suits were brought in the courts of Illinois, involving parts of the railroad and warehouse legislation of 1871, during the interval between the enactment of that legislation and the meeting of the next general assembly in January, 1873. The first of these was brought by S. H. Moore of Kankakee against the Illinois Central railroad to recover the five hundred dollar penalty for an overcharge of the maximum passenger fare allowed by the law. This suit was started in a justice's court as early as August, 1871, and then carried to the circuit court of Kankakee County. The case came to trial in September, 1872, on an admitted statement of fact, and in December, Judge Wood rendered a decision for the defendant on the grounds that its charter was a contract, and that the legislature, having no judicial power and no means of ascertaining what is reasonable, could not, at any time, fix the fare. An appeal was immediately taken to the supreme court where it came up in the September term, 1873. The judgment of the lower court was affirmed but the supreme court based its decision upon the grounds that the alleged overcharge had occurred in July, 1872, some time before the railroads of the state had been classified by the commission, and that no evidence had been presented that the Illinois Central belonged at that time in class B, to which it was later assigned. The court further declared that the constitutionality of the act of 1871 was not involved in this decision and so declined to express any opinion on that question.[2]

---

[1] *Ibid.* 699, 707, 721, 744, 766. The only legislation relative to railroads enacted at this session was a general incorporation law made necessary by a provision of the constitution of 1870 which forbade the creation of corporations by special laws.

[2] 68 *Illinois Reports*, 385. The railroad commission had aided Mr. Moore in the prosecution of this suit and two of the commissioners presented an account and discussion of the case as an " Additional Report " incorporated in the annual report of the board for 1872. This was, of course, before the decision of the supreme court on the appeal. One of the commissioners, Mr. R. P. Morgan, took exception to this action, and declared the account given to be incomplete and imperfect. It is true that the fact that the alleged offense had been committed and the action brought before the classification of the roads by the commission is not brought out

The suit against the Chicago and Alton for violation of the long and short haul clause of the act to prevent extortion and unjust discrimination was brought by the commissioners December 5, 1871, in the circuit court of McLean County. Here again the facts were admitted by the defendants, *i. e.*, charging a higher rate on shipments of lumber from Chicago to Lexington, 110 miles, than the rate from Chicago to Bloomington through Lexington, a distance of 126 miles. The case was argued in July, 1872. The defendant's attorneys, asserting that the act of 1871 was a violation of the constitution of the United States, pleaded the charter of the company as a contract under which it had the right to fix the charges, subject only to the requirement that they be reasonable. It was further alleged that the rate to Lexington was a reasonable one, the rate to Bloomington being fixed unreasonably low in order to compete with the Illinois Central and therefore no criterion of the reasonableness of the former rate. In reply, the counsel for the people declared the question at issue to be the relation of the act of 1871 to the provision of the United States constitution concerning contracts. It was maintained that the legislature could not, by contract, deprive the state of the right to prevent unjust discrimination and extortion, a right which was a valid exercise of the police powers and inherent in the sovereignty of the state. Judge Tipton took the case under advisement and in November, 1872, filed a written opinion for the people in which he took the position that no part of the contract between the state and the company was impaired by the act of 1871, and that the state retained the right, in spite of the charter of the railroad, to prevent unjust discrimination.[1]

in the " Additional Report " and the impression is given that the constitutionality of the law was the only point involved. Railroad Commission, *Reports*, 1872, pp. 21–24.

Inaccurate statements with regard to this case are made in Davidson and Stuvé, *Illinois*, 1028; Gordon, *Illinois Railway Legislation*, 35; Moses, *Illinois*, ii. 1060; Governor Cullom, in Railroad Commission, *Reports*, 1879, p. 266. Most of these assert that no appeal was taken from the decision of the circuit court and give the impression that the validity of the law was involved in the final decision.

[1] Railroad Commission, *Reports*, 1872, p. 8, 1873, p. 16. The briefs of counsel and the decision of Judge Tipton are to be found in *ibid.*, 1872, pp. 46–114. See

This decision was felt to be a great victory for the people in their struggle with the railroads, but the elation did not last long. The case was at once appealed to the supreme court of the state and heard in the January term, 1873. A unanimous decision of the court, written by Chief-Justice Lawrence, reversed the decision of the circuit court, and declared the law of 1871 to be in conflict, not with the constitution of the United States, but with the state constitution, in accordance with the mandatory provisions of which it was supposed to have been adopted. This decision was extremely important in that it laid the basis for the railroad legislation of 1873. Its substance is embraced in the concluding summary:

> The opinion of the court is, that while the Legislature has an unquestioned power to prohibit unjust discrimination in railway freights, no prosecution can be maintained under the existing act until amended, because it does not prohibit unjust discrimination merely, but discrimination of any character, and because it does not allow the companies to explain the reason of the discrimination, but forfeits their franchise upon an arbitrary and conclusive presumption of guilt to be drawn from the proof of an act that might be shown to be perfectly innocent.[1] In these particulars, the existing act violates the spirit of the constitution. The judgment of the circuit court, ousting the appellant of its franchises, must therefore be reversed.

In the course of the opinion, Judge Lawrence took exception to much of the argument of the attorneys for the railway company. He declared that a less charge for a long than for a shorter distance should be *prima facie* but not conclusive evidence of unjust discrimination, and that the existence of competition at one point was not sufficient to justify discrimination. This dictum was an indication of the attitude which the courts would take in the struggle over the law of 1873.[2]

---

also Gordon, *Illinois Railway Legislation*, 36–38; *Prairie Farmer*, xliii. 369, 388 (November 23, December 7, 1872).

[1] This point does not seem to have been touched upon by the attorneys for the railroad company. The arguments on both sides were very similar to those presented to the circuit court.

[2] 67 *Illinois*, 11. The arguments and decision of this case are given in full in Railroad Commission, *Reports*, 1873, pp. 46–159. See also *Chicago Tribune*, 1873, February 24, p. 1, February 25, p. 4; *Prairie Farmer*, xliv. 57, 65 (February 22, March 1, 1873); Gordon, *Illinois Railway Legislation*, 39; Railroad Commission, *Reports*, 1873, p. 17; and Governor Cullom, in *ibid.*, 1879, p. 266.

Two suits were instituted in 1871 and 1872 to test the validity of the warehouse law of 1871. The first of these was brought by the commission against Munn and Scott, a warehouse firm of Chicago, and was in the nature of criminal proceedings for failure to take out licenses required by the law. Proceedings were begun in this case in September, 1871, but the Chicago fire and other causes of delay prevented a final hearing until July, 1872. A verdict of guilty was then returned against the defendant; but the case was appealed to the supreme court of the state, which, after numerous delays, affirmed the judgment of the lower court in September, 1873. The case was then carried to the United States Supreme Court as Munn v. Illinois and a final decision rendered in 1876 in favor of the state. This was the first of the celebrated " Granger cases " to be decided by that body.[1] The other suit under the warehouse law was brought in January, 1872, for charging more than the legal rate for storage as fixed by the law, but the circuit court decided in July, 1872, that there was no public remedy, the law having fixed no penalty.[2]

THE RAILROAD LAW OF 1873

In the interval of two years between the passage of the first " Granger legislation " in Illinois and the session of the twenty-eighth general assembly, a new political and economic force had come to the front in the state, the force of an organized agricultural class.[3] While it is probably true that the Producers' Convention of 1870 exerted an influence on the constitutional convention of that year, and that the Legislative Farmers'

[1] The arguments before the state supreme court and decision are in Railroad Commission, *Reports*, 1874, pp. 46–102. The decision and dissenting opinions are also in 69 *Illinois*, 80; and in *Chicago Tribune*, February 4, 1874, p. 2. For the decision of the United States Supreme Court and dissenting opinions, see 94 *United States Reports*, 113; Illinois Railroad Commission, *Reports*, 1877, pp. 5–20. See also below, pp. 206–214.

[2] Railroad Commission, *Reports*, 1873, p. 12. Before the decision of Munn v. Illinois by the United States Supreme Court, the warehousemen had regulated their charges to conform to the rates fixed by law. These rates were lowered by an act of 1877, and there appears to have been no difficulty over enforcement thereafter. *Ibid.*, 1874, p. 24, 1877, p. xv; *Public Laws*, 1877, p. 169.

[3] See above, pp. 51, 54, 75.

Club was a factor in securing the enactment of the restrictive legislation of 1871, still the marked development of the movement for agricultural organization did not come until after the passage of the first " Granger laws." The rapid organization of farmers' clubs and granges throughout the state during the years 1871 and 1872, together with the establishment of the state grange in March, 1872, and the State Farmers' Association in January, 1873, gave the farmers adequate vehicles for the expression of their opinions on the dominant political and economic question of the period in Illinois, the railroad problem. Nor were they at all backward in giving vent to these opinions.[1] To the farmer, who was inexperienced in politics and unfamiliar with legal procedure, it seemed that the politicians and the courts were combining to prevent any effective regulation of railroads, and the demand came in no uncertain tone for the enforcement of the railroad legislation of 1871 and the enactment of additional and more stringent laws.[2] Some of the farmers, despairing of any enforcement of the laws by the commission or the courts, determined to put them into effect themselves, and the result was a curious episode of riding for " legal fares," in which the victory lay sometimes with the farmers and sometimes with the railroad employees. All this agitation served to keep up the interest in the railroad question and was undoubtedly the chief factor in the rapid development of agricultural organization in 1872 and 1873. In the field of practical politics it led directly to the defeat of Judge Lawrence and the organization of the Independent Reform party, while in the field of legislation, it brought about the enactment of another Granger law, the railway act of 1873.

Just a week after the opening of the twenty-eighth general assembly in January, 1873, some two hundred and seventy-five farmers from all parts of the state, in convention at Bloomington for the purpose of organizing the State Farmers' Association,[3]

---

[1] See the columns of the *Chicago Tribune* and the *Prairie Farmer* for 1872 and 1873, *passim*.

[2] See, for example, resolutions adopted by a Livingston County farmers' convention on January 6, 1873. *Chicago Tribune*, January 10, 1873, p. 5.

[3] See above, p. 75.

adopted a series of resolutions which put the demands of the farmers before the legislature in concrete form. These resolutions called for the enforcement of the railroad law of 1871; declared persons tendering "legal fare" entitled to the civil protection of the state; expressed approval of the decision of the McLean County circuit court; requested the appointment of at least one farmer on the board of railroad commissioners "who shall be recommended by them [the farmers]"; and urged the enactment of an anti-pass law and of a law fixing reasonable maximum rates of freight, similar to the bill introduced by Senator Vaughn in the adjourned session of the previous general assembly.[1]

Apparently as a result of these resolutions, the subject of railroad legislation was opened up in the Senate by the unanimous adoption, January 20, 1873, of a resolution instructing the committee on railroads to investigate cases of ejectment of passengers tendering "legal fare," and "to consider what further legislation is necessary to protect citizens in their person and property from overcharges by railroad officials, and more fully and effectually to carry out the requirements of the Constitution contained in sections 12 and 15 of Article XI."[2] Meanwhile the strength of the Granger element in the legislature was demonstrated by a successful struggle with the governor over the appointment of a new board of railroad commissioners;[3] both Senate and House were deluged with petitions, resolutions,

[1] Periam, *The Groundswell*, 242–262; *Prairie Farmer*, xliv. 26 (January 25, 1873); *Chicago Tribune*, 1873, January 16, p. 4, January 17, p. 8, January 18, p. 2.

[2] *Senate Journal*, 1873, p. 95; *Prairie Farmer*, xliv. 28 (January 25, 1873).

[3] The Legislative Farmers' Club, first organized in the session of 1871 and revived for the session of 1873, disapproved of Governor Beveridge's nominees for the board of railroad commissioners, and its efforts, seconded by a flood of petitions and remonstrances from the various farmers' organizations, ultimately secured the appointment of two farmers on the board. See *Senate Journal*, 1873, pp. 154, 226, 323, 325; *Prairie Farmer*, xliii. 404, xliv. 17, 26, 41, 49, 65 (December, 1872– March, 1873); *Chicago Tribune*, February–March, 1873, *passim*; Periam, *The Groundswell*, 302–311; Moses, *Illinois*, ii. 822; Gordon, *Illinois Railway Legislation*, 42. The board as finally constituted consisted of H. C. Cook, D. A. Brown, and J. M. Pearson. Commissioner Cook died November 9, 1873, and his place was filled by J. Steele. This board was re-appointed in 1875, and in 1877, Governor Cullom appointed W. M. Smith, G. M. Bogue, and J. H. Oberly.

and memorials from farmers' organizations, praying for more effective legislation; [1] and finally, late in February, came the announcement of the decision of the supreme court in the McLean County case, declaring the law of 1871 for the prevention of extortion and unjust discrimination to be contrary to the state constitution. Bills were at once introduced into both houses to obviate the unconstitutional features of this law, [2] but it soon became evident that the Granger element would insist on still more radical legislation.

Some thirty-five railroad bills of all sorts were introduced into the two houses at this session. [3] Among the most significant of these were bills for an anti-pass law; [4] to abolish the railroad commission; to establish a fixed schedule of maximum rates; for the state to defend citizens in suits brought against them by the railroad companies, for riding at "legal fares"; and several bills proposing to empower the railroad commission to establish a schedule of maximum rates which should be *prima facie* evidence of the reasonableness of railroad charges. For a time it looked as if the multiplicity of proposed solutions for the problem might prevent the enactment of any effective legislation, and the farmers determined to bring additional pressure to bear upon the general assembly. The method adopted was the holding of a large convention of representatives of the farmers' organizations of the state. [5] This convention met at the state capital, April 2, 1873, with delegates present from seventy-two of the one hundred and one counties, and resolved " that we regard it as the undoubted power and imperative

---

[1] *Chicago Tribune*, March 29, 1873, p. 1; *House Journal*, 1873, pp. 209, 219, 229, 247, 249, 260, 271, 277, 289, 312, 322, 328, 334, 353, 386, 392, 396, 420, 437, 505, 609; *Senate Journal*, 1873, pp. 132, 182, 221, 230, 232, 248, 257, 262, 273, 287, 321, 334, 364, 418, 445.

[2] *Chicago Tribune*, March 3, 1873, p. 2; *House Journal*, 1873, pp. 276, 340, 391; *Senate Journal*, 1873, p. 336.

[3] See *Senate* and *House Journals*, indexes under " Railroads."

[4] Anti-pass resolutions were adopted at meetings all over the state and representatives were asked in vain to surrender their passes. The bill on this subject was introduced into the lower house and referred to the committee on public charities. Later it was referred to the judiciary committee and appeared no more. *Chicago Tribune*, March 20, 1873, p. 2; *House Journal*, 1873, pp. 157, 380.

[5] See above, p. 83.

duty of the Legislature to pass laws, fixing reasonable rates for freight and passengers without classification of roads." Riding on the railroads at "legal fares" was endorsed by the convention, and it was further declared that, the supreme court having pointed the way by which unjust discrimination might be reached, no reason existed for delay on the part of the legislature.[1] Shortly after the adjournment of this convention, the House passed, by vote of 123 to 10, a bill "to prevent extortion and unjust discrimination in the rates charged for the transportation of passengers and freight on railroads in this state, and to punish the same and to prescribe a mode of procedure and rules of evidence in relation thereto." The Senate amended this before passing it by vote of 36 to 6 but a conference committee quickly effected a compromise and the bill was signed by the governor and became law on May 2, 1873.[2]

The Illinois railroad law of 1873, which repealed and superseded the act of 1871 relating to unjust discrimination and extortion, has remained the basis of railroad control in that state to the present day and has served as a model for legislation in other states, so it will be well to examine its provisions with some care.[3] The first two sections of this act declared that any railroad company charging more than a fair or reasonable rate of toll or compensation should be deemed guilty of extortion, and any railroad company making an unjust discrimination should be deemed guilty of having violated the provisions of the act; in either case, the company should, upon conviction, be dealt with as provided in the act. Section 3 defined discrimination in great detail so as to cover every possible difference in charge between persons and places for the same service *in the same direction*. In this latter particular it differed from the

---

[1] These resolutions are to be found in the *American Annual Cyclopedia*, 1873, p. 367, and in Periam, *The Groundswell*, 286–289.

[2] *House Journal*, 1873, pp. 503, 576, 598, 656, 680, 691, 725; *Senate Journal*, 1873, pp. 336, 353, 359–364, 380, 590, 606–610, 613–616.

[3] The act is in Illinois, *Revised Statutes*, 1874, pp. 816–820 and in Railroad Commission, *Reports*, 1873, pp. 162–167. It was omitted from *Public Laws*, 1873, together with other of the acts of 1873 which were included in the *Revised Statutes* of 1874.

act of 1871, which took no account of direction. It further differed from that act — and this was in line with the dictum of the supreme court in the McLean County case — in providing tnat such discriminating rates should be taken merely as *prima facie* evidence of the unjust discrimination prohibited by the act. This allowed the company to bring forward evidence to show the justness of the discriminating rate, but the section contained an express declaration that the existence of competition at certain points should not be deemed a sufficient justification for discrimination. A proviso at the end of the section permitted the issuing of " commutation, excursion or thousand-mile tickets."

Sections 4 and 5 provided for the enforcement of the law by actions in the name of the state to recover fines ranging from not less than one thousand dollars nor more than five thousand dollars for the first offence to twenty-five thousand dollars for the fourth or subsequent offenses. Section 6 gave action to the aggrieved party also for the recovery of three times the amount of the damages sustained, together with costs and attorney's fees. Section 7 made it the duty of the railroad commission " to personally investigate and ascertain whether the provisions of this act are violated " and " to immediately cause suits to be commenced and prosecuted against any railroad corporation which may violate the provisions of this act." This was important as giving the initiative to the commission and relieving it of dependence upon aggrieved shippers, who might fear retaliation on the part of the railroad company.[1]

By section 8 of this act the commission was directed to prepare a schedule of maximum rates for the transportation of passengers, freight, and cars, upon each railroad; which rates should be taken, after January 15, 1874, as *prima facie* evidence of reasonableness in all suits involving charges of railroad companies. Such schedules were to be revised by the commission from time to time as circumstances might require. Although this solution of the railroad problem was roundly condemned, especially in the eastern states, as an attempt to fix rates by

[1] Railroad Commission, *Reports*, 1873, p. 21.

legislation,[1] it should be kept in mind that the general assembly did not authorize, and did not intend to authorize the commission to arbitrarily determine the rates or even maximum rates of railroad charges, but merely placed the burden of proof of the reasonableness of rates upon the railroad companies, just as in a preceding section it had placed upon them the burden of proof of the justness of discrimination. Since practically all the evidence as to reasonableness of rates or justness of discrimination must, by the nature of the case, be in the possession of the companies, it is difficult to see wherein this is not a fair solution of the problem. It was certainly an improvement upon the solution proposed by State Senator Vaughn, and afterwards adopted in several of the Granger states, of having the schedule of maximum rates enacted by the legislature. The commission was undoubtedly in a better position to draw up an equitable schedule than was the legislature, and a desirable element of flexibility was added by the provision allowing the commission to change or revise the schedules at any time.

THE STRUGGLE OVER THE LAW OF 1873

This railroad law of 1873, with the exception noted above of the schedule of maximum rates, went into force on July 1, 1873. On that day the railroad companies, apparently by a preconcerted arrangement, revised their rates so as to make them conform in general to the provisions of the act relative to discrimination; but they did this, not by lowering the high charges at non-competitive points, as had been intended, but by raising the lower rates, in some instances as much as fifty per cent.[2] In meeting this move of the railroad companies the commission was at a disadvantage, because its schedule of maximum rates

---

[1] See *Nation*, xvi. 249 (April 10, 1873).

[2] Railroad Commission, *Reports*, 1873, p. 19; Governor's message in *Senate Journal*, 1874, p. 5; *House Journal*, 1874, p. 5. See also special report of the railroad commission in *House Journal*, 1874, pp. 79–81. Although the new rates were not maintained for any considerable length of time, there appears to have been little discrimination between persons or places after this. Railroad Commission, *Reports*, 1874, p. 26, 1875, p. 22, 1876, p. 22; Governor's message in *Senate Journal*, 1877, p. 19; *House Journal*, 1877, p. 30.

could not be made use of until January 15, 1874. The outcry was so great, however, that the commission determined to bring suits for extortion, relying upon the rather vague terms of section 1 of the law. Two suits were thus instituted in December, 1873, against the Chicago and Northwestern and the Illinois Central railroads. The latter of these was soon dismissed, the commission preferring to institute other suits against the same company after the schedules went into effect; the former was continued for some time and finally dismissed after a decision of the supreme court in another case,[1] to the effect that the schedules were essential to any prosecution for extortion under the act.[2]

The commissioners, meanwhile, had been at work upon the preparation of the schedules. After extensive investigations, in the course of which careful comparisons of the published tariffs of the railroad companies were made and testimony received from well-informed shippers from all parts of the state, the roads of the state were divided into five classes, and a complete schedule of rates drawn up for the roads in each class. In determining these rates, the commission stated that it had taken into consideration such subjects as the amount of capital invested in the road, the amount of business done, and the proportion of operating expenses to gross earnings.[3] When the day arrived for the schedules to go into effect, no attention appears to have been paid to them by the railroad companies, they having evidently determined to fight the issue to a finish in the courts. As a consequence, ten suits for extortion were brought against four different railroads by the commission during 1874. Two of these suits, both against the Chicago, Burlington, and Quincy, were decided by the circuit courts in September, 1874, and judgments rendered for the people, but the cases were immediately appealed to the supreme court. One of these cases was heard in the January term, 1875, the

---

[1] Chicago, Burlington, and Quincy Railroad Company *v.* The People. 77 *Illinois*, 443.

[2] Railroad Commission, *Reports*, 1873, p. 28, 1874, pp. 8–10, 1875, p. 17.

[3] *Ibid.*, 1873, p. 28. See also *ibid.*, 1874, pp. 21–24, 370–394.

judgment of the lower court reversed, and the case remanded because of an error in pleading. The various decisions and dissenting opinions of the different members of the supreme court upon this case showed clearly that a majority of the court were ready to uphold the constitutionality of the law; but an authoritative and explicit decision on that point was prevented by a technicality. As the pleading had been the same in the other cases pending before the supreme and circuit courts, it was necessary to remand the former and to amend the declarations in the latter.[1]

One of the cases against the Illinois Central railroad involved unjust discrimination in charges for delivering grain upon the track. This case was tried in the Alexander County circuit court in January, 1874, and resulted in a judgment for one thousand dollars and costs against the defendant. The fine was paid and this proceeding practically put an end to the practice, previously in vogue, of charging six dollars more per carload for hauling grain when delivered upon the track than when delivered to the elevators.[2]

Another suit, brought against the Illinois Central in Douglas County for extortion, was based on the charging of a higher rate than that fixed by the schedule prepared by the commission. Judgment was rendered by the circuit court against the company and the case appealed to the supreme court, where it was the first case to bring about an explicit decision upon the constitutionality of the law of 1873. This case was tried in the circuit court in January, 1875, but its decision by the supreme court was delayed year after year to await decisions of the United States Supreme Court, or for other reasons. Finally in June, 1880, a decision was handed down which fully confirmed the constitutionality of the law of 1873, and the right of the state to prevent unjust discrimination and extortion, even when the charter of the railroad company expressly conferred

[1] 77 *Illinois*, 443. Railroad Commission, *Reports*, 1874, pp. 11–13, 1875, pp. 15–18, 40–44. The error in pleading consisted of the plaintiff's failing to aver the establishment of a schedule of maximum rates by the commission.

[2] Railroad Commission, *Reports*, 1875, p. 17.

upon it the right to fix charges.[1] Nearly four years before, the Supreme Court of the United States had sustained similar legislation in the case of Munn *v.* Illinois and several other " Granger cases " from Iowa, Minnesota, and Wisconsin;[2] and two years before the supreme court of the state, in the Neal Ruggles case, had sustained the law of 1871 regulating passenger fares, a law which had been repealed in 1873.[3] The railroad companies, nevertheless, refused to conform their charges entirely to the schedules of the board until after the final decision on the law of 1873 by the state supreme court.[4] In the meantime, the commission declined to institute further proceedings against the companies while the test case was still undecided.[5]

After the decision, there appears to have been no further difficulty over the enforcement of the law;[6] the natural development of business had of itself brought the charges below the maxima in the schedules in most cases, for these schedules were not revised from their promulgation in 1873 until 1881; and the violent agitations and frantic demands for lower rates which had characterized the first half of the decade had now almost entirely disappeared, in large part perhaps because of the gradual revival of prosperity. These conditions made it possible for the railroads and the commissioners to get along peaceably for the most part, after 1880; the board serving to prevent

[1] 95 *Illinois*, 313. See also Railroad Commission, *Reports*, 1875, p. 17, 1876, p. 27, 1877, p. xix, 1878, p. xviii, 1879, p. xxv, 1880, pp. 19, 556.

[2] *Ibid.*, 1877, pp. 6–27; 94 *United States*, 113 *et seq.;* Gordon, *Illinois Railway Legislation*, 54.

[3] 91 *Illinois*, 256; Gordon, *Illinois Railway Legislation*, 36, 54; Railroad Commission, *Reports*, 1879, pp. xxv, 306–312. The law was not specifically repealed until the adoption of the revised statutes in 1874; but it was superseded by the railroad law of 1873. *Revised Statutes*, 1874, p. 1044.

[4] Governor's message in *Senate Journal*, 1877, p. 19; *House Journal*, 1877, p. 30

[5] Railroad Commission, *Reports*, 1876, p. 27.

[6] Although the law was so worded as to apply to interstate as well as intra-state traffic, little attempt was made to enforce it except with regard to business wholly within the state. The United States Supreme Court decisions were ultimately adverse to the right of the state to exercise any control over interstate traffic Railroad Commission, *Reports*, 1875, p. 19; Wabash *v.* Illinois, 118 *United States* 557. See below, p. 212.

any serious abuses in railway charges within the state, but not interfering to any considerable extent with the business of the companies.[1]

The railroads, meanwhile, had not been satisfied with opposing the enforcement of the law in the courts; they had also made every possible effort to secure its repeal or modification. The campaign having this end in view can be considered under two headings; conciliation and " education." Apparently the railroads hoped to disarm public opposition by better treatment, and at the same time to " educate " public opinion to appreciate the disadvantages of the law and the policy it embodied to the country. An instance of the more gracious attitude of the companies is seen in their ready coöperation with the railroad commission in its efforts to settle disputes and adjust grievances by arbitration. During the many years in which the protection of the shippers and the traveling public by the means provided in the law was prevented by the delay of the courts, the railroad commission followed a plan similar to that which had been developed by the Massachusetts commission, of endeavoring to adjust grievances by arbitration. Whenever complaints of overcharge, discrimination, or other unjust treatment were received from shippers, these were carefully investigated by the board and, if found well-grounded, the board acted as an intermediary, in presenting them to the railroads for adjustment. The companies, possibly in the hope of having this kind of regulation substituted for the more burdensome and in the end more effective regulation embodied in the law of 1873, accepted almost invariably the recommendation of the commission with regard to these complaints.[2] It is quite likely that this practice contributed materially to the allaying of that antagonism to

---

[1] Railroad Commission, *Reports*, 1876, p. 22, 1879, pp. v–viii, 269, 1880, p. 18; Governor's message in *Senate Journal*, 1877, p. 19, *House Journal*, 1877, p. 30. The revision of the schedule was undertaken in 1881 in response to a request from the general assembly in the form of a resolution. The new schedules fixed a uniform passenger fare of three cents a mile for all roads, and for freight rates the roads were divided into but two groups. Railroad Commission, *Reports*, 1881, p. 15–20.

[2] *Ibid.*, 1872, p. 10, 1877, p. xx, 1878, p. xvii, 1879, p. 267.

railroads which was so strong in 1873 and 1874, but had practically disappeared by the end of the decade.

The policy upon which the railroad forces relied the most, however, in their campaign for the repeal of the law, was that of making the legislation as unpopular as possible by causing it to appear to be contrary to the best interest of the state. In this work a considerable part of the press of the state was interested, as well as a number of the more influential eastern newspapers. It was asserted from the beginning of the movement that any interference with the railroads would prevent all further construction in the state and thus retard its development; it was asserted that eastern and foreign capitalists would no longer invest money in railroads in a state in which the roads were liable to regulation which practically amounted to confiscation. Just at this time there did come a decided decline in the extension of railroad lines, which, although it is possible to point out many causes for it besides the Granger movement, made the railroad argument seem plausible.[1] Doubtless many people were induced to oppose regulation by this argument, for the desire for more railroads was still considerable in many parts of the state.[2]

The first shot in the campaign for the repeal of the law of 1873 was fired on the very day upon which it became a law, May 2, 1873, when four members of the Senate presented to that body a formal written protest against the measure. In this they admitted the necessity of legislation on the subject, but declared that the measure adopted was unconstitutional, and that it would paralyze the commercial and industrial interests of the state. The second shot came on the day upon which the law (with the exception of the schedule feature) went into effect, when the railroads, apparently by a preconcerted agreement, raised the former competitive rates to the level of the

[1] Railroad Commission, *Reports*, 1876, pp. 18–21; *Nation*, xvi. 384, 397, xvii. 49, 156, 218 (1873).

[2] Threats were made that the quality of the service on the railroads would be lowered, but no evidence of such action has been found. See *Nation*, xvi. 306 (May 8, 1873). This method of making the restrictive laws unpopular was used in some of the other Granger states. See below, p. 163.

non-competitive rates, and asserted that this was the working of the new law.[1] This illustrates what was undoubtedly the favorite method of attack, — to appear to obey the law, but to do it in such a way as to make it as obnoxious as possible. It is said, moreover, to have been the constant policy of railroad officials and employees to explain every inconvenience and to answer every complaint with the assertion that the things complained of were results of the railroad law. These methods were followed in other states at this time with more success than in Illinois.

Not all the forces were arrayed on the side of the railroad companies, however, nor did the interest of the farmers' organizations cease with the passage of the laws of 1873. In September, 1873, the railroad commission held a joint meeting with the executive committee of the State Farmers' Association to consider the railroad law and its enforcement.[2] In October, 1873, a " Northwestern Farmers' Convention," which met at Chicago to consider transportation problems, appointed a committee to investigate the workings of the Illinois law. This committee reported that the effects of the law were not such as had been anticipated because of the failure of the railroads to observe it.[3] Later in the year the state grange and the State Farmers' Association each adopted resolutions demanding the enforcement of the law and opposing its repeal or modification.[4] Year after year these resolutions or similar ones were repeated by the various state and local organizations of the farmers, and often even more stringent legislation was demanded.[5] The different political parties, too, mindful of the votes of the farmers,

[1] That the primary object of this action was to influence public opinion is indicated by the fact that most of the new high rates were soon modified.

[2] *Chicago Tribune*, September 19, 1873, p. 8.

[3] *American Annual Cyclopedia*, 1873, p. 368.

[4] Illinois State Farmers' Association, *Proceedings*, ii. 100–109; *Prairie Farmer*, xliv. 401, 403 (December, 1873).

[5] *Ibid.* xlv. 12, 57, 59, 65, 97, 161, 164, 188, 225, xlvi. 27, 33, 38, 48, 73, 105, 237 (1874–75); *Appleton's Cyclopedia*, 1875, p. 393; Illinois State Farmer's Association, *Proceedings*, v. 13–15, 34–36 (1877); Illinois State Grange, *Proceedings*, v. 36 (1876).

continued to insert planks in their platforms favoring the strict regulation of railroads by the state.[1]

The fight over the railroad law of 1873 was the bitterest in the adjourned session of the same general assembly which passed the law. At this session, which began in January, 1874, the legislature was deluged with petitions and memorials for the repeal or modification of the law because of its failure to produce the benefits expected, among the number being two from local farmers' clubs.[2] Most significant of these was a memorial signed by one hundred and three Chicago mercantile firms, which gives a good idea of the arguments and methods of those who were working for the repeal of the law.[3] This memorial opened with a declaration that the legislature did not understand the effect of the railroad law on the commerce of the state. The merchants then proceeded to enlighten the legislature. They admitted that they had not been satisfied with railroad management prior to the passage of the law, and that they had been subject to discrimination and extortion, but asserted that in the majority of cases they had been able to get redress from the companies. Now, the railroad law had injured their business and customers, increased the cost of shipment to the interior of the state and not lessened the cost of shipment to tide-water; it had impaired the credit of the state, and rendered it almost impossible to borrow money to build competing roads. In fact no benefit had accrued to any citizens unless to the officers whose positions were created by the bill. Therefore the repeal or amendment of the law was requested that the commerce and credit of the state might be maintained and fostered.

Violent attacks were made upon the commission as well as upon the law by various members of the legislature and an attempt was made to abolish it on the popular ground of retrench-

---

[1] See for these platforms *Appleton's Cyclopedia*, articles " Illinois," " Tribune Almanacs," etc.

[2] *House Journal*, 1874, pp. 210, 212, 318, 376, 380, 403, 408, 410, 421, 425, 437, 444, 460, 474; *Senate Journal*, 1874, pp. 138, 254, 322, 347, 356, 371, 379, 386, 396, 432; *Chicago Tribune*, March 14, 1874.

[3] Illinois, *Reports to the General Assembly*, 1873, iv. 971.

ment of expenses.[1] This, however, failed by a large majority, 40 to 91 in the House, and an attempt to strike out section 3 of the law, the section which defined discrimination, was defeated by the still larger majority of 25 to 101.[2] At one time it looked as if an attempt would be made to extend the application of the principle of the law of 1873, for the House adopted a resolution instructing its railroad committee to prepare a bill to prevent discrimination and extortion by the Pullman Palace Car Company and other companies running sleepers, and to fix maximum rates.[3] Nothing further appears to have been done in this direction, and though numerous bills of various sorts had been introduced into both houses[4] the only railroad legislation enacted at this session was a minor amendment of a technical nature to one of the enforcement sections of the railroad act of 1873.[5]

During the session of the twenty-ninth general assembly, which met in 1875, the railroad commission was attacked on the ground that it had instituted suits and used the names of persons as aggrieved parties when the persons concerned had not requested or desired any such action.[6] The commission admitted the truth of the charges but declared that to make the prosecution of suits dependent on the initiative of the aggrieved parties would nullify the law because the " fear of the exercise of the power of corporations to inflict punishment would be sufficient, in most cases, to deter those whose business is dependent upon railway transportation from making public their grievances." [7] In this and in each of the next three general assemblies, which met in 1877, 1879, and 1881, respectively, numerous bills were introduced to change the railroad laws, some in the direction of greater restriction and others for more lenient treatment of the companies, but none of the proposed measures were enacted into law. Gradually it was becoming evident that the state of

---

[1] *Ibid.* 849–851, v. 591–595; *House Journal*, 1874, pp. 31, 33, 56–58, 61, 79–81, 194; *Senate Journal*, pp. 178, 226, 333, 368–371, 396.

[2] *House Journal*, 1874, pp. 63, 194, 265.　　　　[3] *Ibid.* 297.

[4] *Ibid.* 95, 163; *Senate Journal*, 1874, pp. 11, 204.

[5] *Public Laws*, 1874, p. 129.

[6] *House Journal*, 1875, pp. 425, 621–628; *Chicago Tribune*, March 13, 1875.

[7] Railroad Commission, *Reports*, 1875, p. 18.

Illinois was determined to maintain the policy of railroad regulation by a commission with power to establish a schedule of maximum rates, and that it would stand by the law of 1873 as the best embodiment of that policy.

In concluding this survey of restrictive railway legislation in Illinois during the Granger period, it will be well to sum up the part which the farmers of the state played in the movement. It is clear that the demand for such legislation made its appearance before the movement for farmers' organization got under way. This early agitation resulted in the law of 1869, which was totally inefficient as a solution of the problem, and then the farmers began to take hold of the matter. In 1870 their influence was a factor in securing provisions in the constitution which laid the basis for effective legislation, and the Legislative Farmers' Club seems to have had a part in securing the enactment of the legislation of 1871, the most important feature of which was the establishment of the railroad commission. Then came the decision of the supreme court invalidating an essential part of this legislation, and thereafter the farmers, by that time thoroughly organized, played the principal rôle in the movement. Their influence was openly exerted upon the legislature by the Springfield convention of April, 1873, which was followed quickly by the enactment of the railroad law of that year. In the trying years which followed, the farmers' organizations stood back of the efforts of the railroad commission to enforce the law and their opposition was undoubtedly of great influence in preventing the law from being repealed or modified before it could be thoroughly tested, a thing which happened to the Granger laws of several other states. On the whole, if we use the term " Granger " as relating to organized efforts of the farming classes, it must be conceded that the phrase " Granger legislation " is rightly applied to the railway laws enacted in Illinois during this period.

CHAPTER V

GRANGER RAILWAY LEGISLATION (CONTINUED)

MINNESOTA [1]

THE agitation in Illinois for railroad regulation was paralleled by similar movements in several of the neighboring states. Minnesota, however, was the only other state in which a stringent law was enacted as early as 1871. The construction of railroads in this state began in 1862, and they were welcomed with open arms as the most effective agents for the development of its resources. By 1872 nearly two thousand miles were in operation.[2] From the first, however, there seems to have been a premonition of the evils which would result from giving the railroads too free a hand. In the constitution, under which the state was admitted in 1858, section 2 of Article IX forbade the formation of companies under special acts; and section 4 of the same article, in providing for the exercise of the right of eminent domain for the benefit of transportation companies, declared that "all corporations being common carriers, enjoying the right of way in pursuance of this section, shall be bound to carry the mineral, agricultural, and other productions and manufactures on equal and reasonable terms." A section of the general railroad incorporation act passed by the legislature in 1858 limited the charges of companies organized under its provisions to three cents per mile for passengers and five cents per ton mile for freight.[3] The demand for more railroads was so strong during the sixties that any attempt to enforce such a measure would have met with disapproval as tending to interfere with railroad construction and the act was soon superseded by another which required merely that charges should be reasonable.

---

[1] See R. S. Saby, *Railroad Legislation in Minnesota, 1849 to 1875.* This was published too late to be of use in the preparation of this section.

[2] Minnesota Railroad Commissioner, *Reports*, 1871, pp. 5–9; *American Annual Cyclopedia*, 1872, p. 543.

[3] Minnesota, *General Laws*, 1858, p. 170.

Toward the close of the sixties, however, complaints began to be heard that the railroads were oppressing the people by extortionate and discriminating rates; a dispute over the payment of railroad bonds, which had been issued by the state to aid various roads, helped to arouse antagonism toward the companies;[1] and the order of Patrons of Husbandry, which had been developing in the state, began to turn its attention to the transportation problem.[2] Restrictive railroad measures were discussed at the session of the legislature in the spring of 1870, but nothing was done.[3] During the ensuing summer and fall, however, the agitation for the regulation of railroads by the state grew rapidly in volume and intensity. It manifested itself in a transportation convention at Owatonna in November, at which resolutions were adopted citing the exorbitant and ruinously discriminating rates and the operation of the roads in the interest of wheat rings and other monopolies, and demanding legislation to protect the producers of the state.[4] This demand was too insistent to be denied and the legislature of 1871 quickly responded to it by enacting two railroad laws.[5] One of these laws established a fixed schedule of maximum rates for passengers and freights, the passenger maximum being five cents per mile and the freight maxima apparently considerably below the rates then prevailing.[6] The other law provided for a railroad commissioner and empowered him to collect statistics and enforce the railroad laws.[7]

The attitude of the Minnesota railroad companies toward these laws was precisely the same as the attitude of the com-

[1] On this question, see W. A. Scott, *Repudiation of State Debts*, 152–161; *American Annual Cyclopedia*, 1869, p. 448, 1870, p. 507, 1871, p. 516.

[2] *Minnesota Monthly*, i. 249 (July, 1869); Kelley, *Patrons of Husbandry*, 256–259. See also below, pp. 46, 49, 53.

[3] Minnesota, *Executive Documents*, 1869, pp. 6–14, 1870, i. 38–55; *Senate Journal*, 1870, pp. 65, 117, 249, 288.

[4] *American Annual Cyclopedia*, 1870, p. 510.

[5] *Senate Journal*, 1871, pp. 11, 21, 26, 114, 176, 269, 292; Special Joint Railroad Investigating Committee, *Report to the Legislature*, February 15, 1871; Stickney, *The Railway Problem*, ch. x.

[6] *General Laws*, 1871, pp. 61–66; *American Annual Cyclopedia*, 1871, p. 517; Railroad Commissioner, *Reports*, 1871, p. 10.

[7] *General Laws*, 1871, pp. 56–59.

panies of Illinois toward the laws enacted by that state in the same year; they denied their validity and refused to make any attempt to conform to their terms.[1] In order to test the law, a suit was brought by the attorney-general against the Winona and St. Peter Company for violation of the rate law, and at the same time a private suit was instituted against the same company to compel it to give up goods held because the owner refused to pay transportation charges in excess of those fixed by the law. The circuit court decided these cases in favor of the railroad, but they were appealed to the supreme court of the state, and there heard together in May, 1873. In its decision the supreme court admitted that a railroad charter was a contract under which the company was entitled to collect *some* tolls, but at the same time upheld the right of the state to regulate or limit the rate of those tolls. The decisions of the lower courts were therefore reversed.[2] As was to be expected, one of these cases was appealed to the United States Supreme Court, where as Winona and St. Peter Railroad Company *v.* Blake it was decided along with other Granger cases, in the October term, 1876; the decision being in favor of Blake and thus upholding the validity of the law of 1871.[3] Before this decision was reached, however, the legislature had superseded that law by another restrictive act, and then had practically given up the attempt to control railroads.

During the interval of three years in which the law of 1871 was nominally in force but was actually a dead letter, the antagonism toward railroad corporations and the demand for their control by the state continued to grow.[4] The state and local granges kept up a constant agitation of the question [5] and the

---

[1] Railroad Commissioner, *Reports*, 1871, p. 10; *American Annual Cyclopedia*, 1872, p. 543.

[2] 19 *Minnesota*, 418, 434 (Gilfillan ed., 362, 377); Railroad Commissioner, *Reports*, 1871, pp. 11, 17, 1873, pp. 241–247; Attorney-general's reports in *Executive Documents*, 1871, i. 74, 1872, i. 541, 1873, ii. 832–836, Governor's message in *ibid.*, 1872, i. 5–10. See also editorial in *Nation*, xvii. 266 (October 23, 1873).

[3] 94 *United States*, 180.

[4] On the railroad question in the legislature of 1873, see *American Annual Cyclopedia*, 1873, p. 506; *Senate Journal*, 1873, pp. 24, 34, 38, 86.

[5] *Farmers' Union*, 1873, January 18, August 9; *Chicago Tribune*, 1873, May 15,

victory of the Independent party in the election of 1873 [1] placed
the Granger element in control of the legislature and ensured
the enactment of a radical railway law.[2] The Minnesota railway law of 1874, which was modelled on the Illinois law of 1873,
established a board of railway commissioners and directed it
to prepare schedules of maximum rates which should be *prima
facie* evidence of reasonableness. Unjust discrimination was
also defined and prohibited and it was made the duty of the
commissioners to enforce the laws by prosecuting suits against
offending companies whenever required by the public interest.[3]

Thus far Minnesota had followed the precedents set by Illinois
in her attempts to regulate railroads, but the commission soon
found that the preparation of schedules to be applied to the
new roads of a frontier state like Minnesota was a very different
matter from the preparation of schedules which would work in
a comparatively well settled community like the state of Illinois.
Many of the roads of Minnesota had been constructed in advance
of settlement and could not possibly return profit to the owners
for a number of years, at any rate which the traffic would bear.[4]
This fact was recognized by the commissioners in making the
schedules and they soon gave up all attempts to consider the
question of dividends upon capital invested. They relied,
instead, upon the existing rates, with modification when shippers
gave evidence of unreasonableness. Effort was made so to draw
up the schedules as to do away with discrimination, and to effect
reductions in passenger fares, and in the freight rates on such
staples as grain and lumber, which constituted the greater part

p. 1, June 23, p. 3; Minnesota State Grange, *Constitution*, 1873, p. 15 (proceedings
at session of February, 1873).

[1] See above, pp. 89–91.

[2] *American Annual Cyclopedia*, 512; *Chicago Tribune*, November 7, 1873, p. 8,
January 6, 1874, p. 5; *Rural Carolinian*, v. 318 (March, 1874). At a session of
the state grange at Faribault, December, 1873, the master advocated the appointment of a special committee by the grange to attend the legislature and assist
in framing a railroad law. Whether or not this recommendation was followed up
by the grange does not appear. *Industrial Age*, December 27, 1873.

[3] *General Laws*, 1874, pp. 140–156; *American Annual Cyclopedia*, 1874, p. 564.
See also E. D. Neill, *History of Minnesota*, 760–763; W. W. Folwell, *Minnesota;
Chicago Tribune*, 1874, January 11, p. 8, January 19, p. 5.

[4] See Railroad Commissioner, *Reports*, 1872, pp. 50–52.

of the transportation business. The principal difficulties which the commission encountered were due to the great inequality of conditions in different parts of the state. These inequalities made the satisfactory application of the *pro rata* principle, as required by the definition of unjust discrimination in the act of 1874, a practical impossibility. If rates were fixed which would be reasonable in the more thickly settled parts of the state, the roads would be forced to operate their western extensions at a considerable loss; while rates which would be reasonable in the sparsely settled districts would be unreasonably high if not extortionate in the southeastern parts of the state. The commission chose sometimes one and sometimes the other horn of the dilemma, with the result that no one was satisfied: the railroad companies complained that the rates were ruinously low, while the farmers declared that the execution of the law had been made a new source of oppression and complained because they had no representative on the board of railway commissioners.[1]

While the act of 1871 was in effect, the railroads of Minnesota had consistently denied the right of the state to regulate their charges and had refused to conform to the rates prescribed; but the act of 1874 gave them so good an opportunity to teach the people a lesson and to make such legislation odious, that a complete change of front was made. The rates scheduled by the commission were quite generally adopted and the law substantially complied with, though in such ways as to emphasize its disadvantages and to convince the people of the desirability of its repeal. The St. Paul and Sioux City Company, for example, claimed that the law made the operation of its line unprofitable and so reduced the service that the people were led to petition the railroad commission for a restoration of the former rate. Perhaps the most glaring example of the injustice of the *pro rata* principle occurred on the St. Paul and Pacific. This road had maintained a rate of three cents a mile between the cities of St. Paul and Minneapolis and five cents on the rest of

---

[1] Railroad Commission, *Reports*, 1874, pp. 3–9. See address of Master Parsons before the state grange, December, 1874, in *Industrial Age*, December 26, 1874, p. 5.

the line. The board decided that, on the whole, five cents was a fair rate and the company accordingly raised its rate between St. Paul and Minneapolis to protect itself from the *pro rata* clause of the law.[1]

As a result of the unsatisfactory working of the schedule — which seems to have been due in part to the law itself, in part to the attempts of the companies to make it unpopular, and in part perhaps to the inexperience and lack of skill of the commissioners — a considerable number of people were doubtless convinced that the rates fixed worked injustice to the companies,[2] while many others became disgusted with the attempt to regulate railroads by law and began to look to competition and the construction of waterways for relief.[3]

In the elections in the fall of 1874 the railroad forces were particularly active, while the enthusiasm which had been back of the Granger movement was on the wane. As a result the newly elected legislature contained a majority opposed to the policy of radical railroad legislation which the state had been trying to follow for the preceding four years. It was soon evident that the law was doomed, but there was some question as to what should be put in its place, in order to prevent the appearance of a total surrender of the policy of state supervision.[4] The final outcome was the enactment of a law which substituted a single elective commissioner with power to investigate and report merely, for the appointive board of three members which had had power to establish schedules of maximum rates and to enforce their observance.[5] In other words it was a change from a commission of the Illinois type to an advisory commission of the type which prevailed at that time in Ohio and Michigan, and which was also adopted at the end of the Granger period in Iowa and Wisconsin. The law also contained provisions that no railroad company should charge unreasonable rates or should discriminate in charges " for a like service from

---

[1] Railroad Commission, *Reports*, 1874, p. 7; Statement of W. R. Marshall, Minnesota railroad commissioner, in Wisconsin, *Senate Journal*, 1876, p. 340.

[2] *Ibid.*   [3] *Industrial Age*, December 26, 1874, p. 5.

[4] *Executive Documents*, 1874, i. 29–31.

[5] *General Laws*, 1875, pp. 135–138.

the same place, and upon like condition and similar circumstances; and all concessions of rates, drawbacks and contracts for special rates shall be open to all persons, companies, or corporations alike, under similar circumstances." Such guardedly phrased restrictions, accompanied by no provisions for their enforcement, were not expected to and did not interfere with the operations of any railroad in the slightest degree.[1]

It might be expected from the intensity of the agitation for railroad control in 1873 and 1874 that this law would have met with a storm of protest from the agricultural population, but such does not seem to have been the case. The fact was that the Granger element had overshot the mark in 1874 by forcing through a law which was not suited to the existing conditions. The order of Patrons of Husbandry, moreover, which undoubtedly had been largely responsible for the movement in this state, had already entered upon a rapid decline, and this was accompanied by an equally rapid decline in the interest of the people in the railroad problem.[2]

The question naturally arises: Did the Granger movement for railroad regulation in Minnesota have any positive results other than the establishment of the constitutional right of the state to control railway charges? The words of Governor Davis in his last annual message, delivered January 7, 1876, are an answer to this question.

The agitation and discussion of the relative obligations of railroad companies and rights of the people have resulted in a better understanding and in sentiments of concession and conciliation in both parties to the controversy. These sentiments found expression in the act approved March 8, 1875. I feel authorized to state, from the entire absence of complaint, that the act has given satisfaction and that no further legislation will be necessary so long as the present situation remains unchanged.[3]

[1] The *Industrial Age* declared that the Minnesota Legislature virtually sold out to the railroads and repealed all the legislation of 1874. See issue of March 27, 1875, p. 4.

[2] This is evidenced by the fact that the commissioner found it impossible to dispose of two thousand copies of his report, and recommended in 1876 that the edition be reduced to eight hundred. Railroad Commissioner, *Reports*, 1876, p. 613 (in *Executive Documents*).

[3] *Executive Documents*, 1875, i. 7. See also Railroad Commissioner, *Reports*, 1875, p. 5.

While it was perhaps unfortunate that the reaction was so thorough and the principle of effective state control so completely given up by Minnesota in 1875 — for it was found necessary to reassert the principle by another restrictive act in the next decade — still there can be little doubt that the act of 1875 was more suited to the conditions prevailing in the state at that time than were the rigidly restrictive railroad laws of 1871 and 1874.

Iowa

The foundation for the regulation of railroads in Iowa was laid as far back as 1856, when an act was passed by the legislature turning over lands, donated for the purpose by the national government, to four different railroad companies.[1] Section 14 of this act declared that the companies accepting the provisions of the act should at all times be subject to such rules and regulations as might be enacted by the general assembly. Similar provisions were inserted in other land grant acts passed during the next ten years, and acts passed in 1866 and 1868 granting lands or legalizing the consolidation of roads contained even more specific provisions reserving to the legislature the right to regulate freight and passenger rates on the roads concerned.[2] As early as 1864, there were complaints of discrimination and extortion by the railroad companies and propositions for restrictive legislation were brought forward in every session of the legislature from that time on.[3] In 1866 the House passed a rate bill, which was not acted upon by the Senate.[4] In 1870,

---

[1] Iowa, *Laws*, 1856, extra session, ch. i. This and all other acts of the Iowa legislature relating to railroads, up to and including 1878, can be consulted conveniently in Iowa Railroad Commission, *Reports*, i. appendix, parts i, ii (1878).

[2] *Laws*, 1858, ch. xcix. section 5, 1860, ch. lix. section 3, 1864, ch. cviii. section 20, 1866, ch. cxxxiv. section 7, 1868, ch. xiii. section 2, ch. lvii. section 3, ch. lviii. section 1, ch. xxiv. section 7. See also F. H. Dixon, *State Railroad Control, with a History of its Development in Iowa*, 21–23; State Senator McNutt, in Cloud, *Monopolies and the People*, 162–166; Larrabee, *The Railroad Question*, 323, 330.

[3] Iowa, *House Journal*, 1864, p. 102; Dixon, *State Railroad Control*, 23; Larrabee, *Railroad Question*, 328–330; McNutt, in Cloud, *Monopolies and the People*, 162.

[4] Iowa, *Senate Journal*, 1866, pp. 25, 495, 540, 661; *House Journal*, 1866, pp. 159, 184, 235, 252, 290, 356, 438–456, 517, 764. On the railroad question in

three bills, — to establish a tariff of freight rates, to regulate passenger fares, and to create a board of railroad commissioners, — were passed in the House by large majorities; but again all legislation on the subject was blocked in the Senate, though the votes in that body were very close.[1]

By this time the demand for railroad regulation had become so strong that the political parties found it advisable to take cognizance of the question in their bids for votes and the platforms of both Democrats and Republicans in 1870 and 1871 contained planks asserting the right of the state to control railroads and demanding legislation on the subject.[2] The action of the legislature in 1872 was much the same, nevertheless, as that of preceding general assemblies.[3] Among the many railroad measures introduced at this session,[4] the most significant was one known as the O'Donnel bill,[5] fixing freight rates, which passed the House by vote of 82 to 13. In the Senate this bill was amended by adding sections providing for an elective commission with power to alter the schedules established by the act, and then passed, the vote being 26 to 23. The House refused to concur in the amendment; the Senate by close votes refused to recede;[6] three conference committees failed to procure an

the next general assembly, see *Senate Journal,* 1868, pp. 27, 227, 283, 435; *House Journal,* pp. 28, 107, 116, 143, 232, 282, 364, 379, 462, 487, 490, 581–583, 601–609.

[1] *Senate Journal,* 1870, pp. 42, 54, 71, 117, 121, 129, 163, 168–170, 193, 203, 212, 219–221, 224–226, 233, 239, 247, 251, 254, 362, 365, 378, 454, 465, 554; *House, Journal,* 1870, pp. 39, 90, 115, 170, 180, 187, 196, 218, 224, 241, 254, 272, 280, 300, 310, 400, 434, 437, 443, 540–542; McNutt, in Cloud, *Monopolies and the People,* 167; C. R. Tuttle, *Illustrated History of the State of Iowa,* 351.

[2] *American Annual Cyclopedia,* 1870, p. 408, 1871, p. 416.

[3] Both Governor Merrill in his annual message and Governor Carpenter in his inaugural address urged railroad legislation. *House Journal,* 1872, pp. 34, 62–64; Tuttle, *Iowa,* 358.

[4] For titles of bills introduced, see *House Journal,* 1872, pp. 80, 146, 388; *Senate Journal,* 1872, pp. 28, 35, 163, 326, 390.

[5] For the legislative history of the O'Donnel bill, see *House Journal,* 1872, pp. 80, 429, 485–487, 530, 781–783, 825–827, 861; *Senate Journal,* 1872, pp. 413–415, 466–468, 474–476, 478–480, 482, 522, 612–615, 654–656. A Senate bill with a similar title was passed by the Senate by vote of 23 to 22, but was not acted upon by the House. *Ibid.* 326, 357–359.

[6] Senator McNutt makes a statement with reference to the O'Donnel bill which

agreement between the two houses; and the legislature once more adjourned without enacting a railroad law.[1]

While the railroad question was thus agitated in session after session of the legislature, and partly as a result of that agitation, the farmers of Iowa had been banding themselves together in the order of Patrons of Husbandry, which by the opening of the year 1873 had a membership of about fifty thousand in the state.[2] After the failure of the fourteenth general assembly in 1872 to enact a law for railroad regulation, it quickly became evident that the Grange was going to concentrate the influence of the agricultural population in favor of such legislation at the first opportunity. Ordinarily that opportunity would not have come until the meeting of the next general

illustrates one of the railroad abuses and a method which the railroad forces employed to prevent hostile legislation: " Those of us in the Senate who voted for the bill, were remembered by the railroad managers when we met in adjourned session last winter, (January 15th, 1873,) by leaving us out of the list of senators whom they favored with free passes. But they sent passes to all the senators who voted *against* the bill. The passes from the Chicago, Rock Island & Pacific Railroad Company were accompanied with a private note, stating that free passes were not now given generally, ' *but only to their friends.*' " McNutt, in Cloud, *Monopolies and the People*, 163–166.

[1] The railroad lobby at this session of the legislature was said to have been made up of four able lawyers, who posed as farmers and members of the Grange. Near the close of the session, a resolution was adopted in the Senate as follows:

" WHEREAS, There has been constantly in attendance on the Senate and House of this General Assembly, from the commencement of the session to the present time, four gentlemen professing to represent the great agricultural interest of the State of Iowa, known as the Grange; and —

" WHEREAS, These gentlemen appear entirely destitute of any visible means of support; therefore be it —

" *Resolved*, By the Senate, the House concurring, that the janitors permit aforesaid gentlemen to gather up all the waste paper, old newspapers, &c., from under the desks of the members, and they be allowed one postage stamp each, The American Aguriculturist, What Greeley Knows about Farming, and that they be permitted to take with them to their homes, if they have any, all the rejected railroad tariff bills, Beardsley's speech on female suffrage, Claussen's reply, Kasson's speech on barnacles, Blakeley's dog bill, Teale's liquor bill, and be given a pass over the Des Moines Valley railroad, with the earnest hope that they will never return to Des Moines."

The *Chicago Tribune* accepted this at its face value and took the Senators to task for their disrespectful treatment of the Grange. *Senate Journal*, 1872, p. 688; *Chicago Tribune*, 1873, June 28, p. 4, July 5, p. 4, July 7, p. 3.

[2] See above, p. 58.

assembly two years later, but it happened that a special session limited to thirty days, was held in 1873, to consider a revision of the code of laws, which had been drawn up by a special commission.

During the earlier part of this special session, the sentiment of the legislators seemed to be in favor of letting the question rest, except for a resolution requesting Congress to legislate on the subject, but about the first of February, 1873, the state grange held a meeting in Des Moines, the capital city, and gave new life to the issue. This body, composed of over twelve hundred representative farmers from all parts of the state, adopted a memorial setting forth the abuses of railway management and demanding the immediate enactment of a rate law to protect the people from outrageous discrimination and extortionate charges. The individual members of the grange, moreover, undoubtedly exercised considerable influence by means of personal contact with their representatives in the legislature and by threats of united political action in the coming election.[1] Possibly as a result of the pressure thus brought to bear, a section was added to the railroad chapter of the code by which passenger fares were limited to three and one-half cents per mile. Other sections which proposed to incorporate a schedule of freight rates in the code were adopted in the House, but failed of passage in the Senate by a tie vote.[2]

During the summer of 1873, the two interacting forces of the demand for railroad regulation and the desire for agricultural organization and coöperation, working largely through the local granges of the order of Patrons of Husbandry, brought about the formation of an Anti-Monopoly party, with government control of railroads as the main plank in its platform.[3] The

[1] *Senate Journal*, 1873, p. 125; McNutt, in Cloud, *Monopolies and the People*, 168; *Farmers' Union*, March 8, 1873; *Prairie Farmer*, xliv. 44, 51 (February 8, 15, 1873); *Chicago Tribune*, February 11, 1873, p. 2.

[2] *Senate Journal*, 1873, pp. 7, 77, 85, 100, 129, 139, 142, 150, 234, 248, 288, 294-296, 313, 315, 319, 321, 331, 334, 347; *House Journal*, 1873, *passim;* Iowa, *Revised Code*, 1873, p. 239 (Title X, ch. v, section 1305); McNutt, in Cloud, *Monopolies and the People*, 168; *Chicago Tribune*, 1873, February 11, p. 2, April 11, p. 2.

[3] See above, pp. 89-91. Platform is in Martin, *Grange Movement*, 513;

Republican party, reading the signs of the times, inserted a railway regulation plank in its platform,[1] and by renominating Governor Carpenter, who had advocated laws to control railroads in his messages, it succeeded in electing the state ticket, but the Anti-Monopolists secured fifty of the one hundred members of the lower house, while seventy of the members were Patrons of Husbandry. Everything seemed to point to the enactment of a radical railroad law in the session of 1874.[2]

That the order of Patrons of Husbandry meant to take advantage of its strength in the legislature was evident when the state grange held it fourth annual session in December, 1873. By this time the order numbered nearly two thousand local granges in the state and probably about one hundred thousand members, so it was in a position to speak with authority for the agricultural part of the population. Early in the session the grange adopted a resolution declaring the right of the state to establish passenger fares and freight rates and later provision was made for the appointment of a committee of twelve to memorialize the general assembly on the subject. This committee was instructed to indicate the kind of a railroad tariff bill that would meet the approval of the grange.[3]

Eight different bills aiming at the regulation of rates were introduced into the Senate at this session and referred to the railroad committee,[4] by which on February 13, a substitute bill was reported providing for the classification of railroads and containing a schedule of rates. During the consideration of this measure, which appears to have been more radical than many of the Grangers desired, numerous substitutes and amend-

American Annual Cyclopedia, 1873, p. 381; *Chicago Tribune*, August 14, 1873, p. 1. See also *Nation*, xvii. 122 (August 21, 1873).

[1] *American Annual Cyclopedia*, 1873, p. 381; *Chicago Tribune*, June 26, 1873, p. 1.

[2] *Ibid.*, and *Industrial Age*, 1873, October 18, p. 4, November 8, p. 6.

[3] Iowa State Grange, *Proceedings*, iv (December, 1873); Periam, *The Groundswell*, 263–270.

[4] *Senate Journal*, 1874, pp. 39, 53, 65, 95. For resolutions and petitions relative to railroads, see *Senate Journal*, 1874, pp. 20, 64, 69, 96; *House Journal*, 1874, pp. 115, 127, 128, 131, 160, 199, 336, 395, 451. For parts of the governor's address relative to railroads, see Iowa, *Legislative Documents*, 1874, i. no. 1, pp. 38–42. See also *ibid*. ii. nos. 30, 35, 36, and *Chicago Tribune*, January 17, 1874, p. 2.

ments were offered, including a proposition to make the *prima facie* evidence of reasonableness instead of absolute maximum and another for the establishment of a commission to draw up a schedule of rates. One of the substitutes, which was offered by Senator Howland, and which proposed to establish an investigating commission to prepare the way for future legislation, was said to have been drafted by the committee appointed by the state grange; but another Senator declared it to be a snare and a delusion and drafted in a railway office.[1] All these propositions were turned down one after another and the original bill as reported by the committee passed the Senate by vote of 40 to 8.[2] In the House a substitute for this bill, although embodying the same general features, was passed by vote of 93 to 4. The Senate accepted the substitute, with a few minor amendments which were agreed to by the House, and the measure received the approval of the governor and became law on March 23, 1874.[3]

This Iowa railroad act of 1874 [4] is perhaps the best example of an attempt to establish a fixed schedule of maximum rates and remained unrepealed longer than the similar acts of any of the other states. By sections 1 and 2 of the act all the railroads in the state were divided into three classes on the basis of gross earnings and the maximum passenger fares fixed at three, three and one-half and four cents for the roads in each

---

[1] A joint resolution had previously been adopted in the Senate by vote of 38 to 7 requesting the committee of the state grange to present its railroad bill and such information as it might possess. This was apparently looked upon as reflecting on the grange, for the House, with its preponderance of Patrons, rejected this and another similar resolution by large majorities. *Senate Journal*, 1874, p. 90; *House Journal*, 1874, pp. 153, 159, 172.

[2] *Senate Journal*, 1874, pp. 198–219. See also *Chicago Tribune*, March 11, 1874, p. 5.

[3] *House Journal*, 1874, pp. 328, 344–351, 388, 395–405, 440, 448; *Senate Journal*, 1874, pp. 277, 279, 292–295, 305. Over twenty railroad bills of various sorts were introduced in the House. *House Journal*, 1874, pp. 62, 83, 84, 90, 91, 103, 127, 161, 162, 188, 196, 232, 247, 323, 325, 341, 357, 525.

[4] *Laws*, 1874, ch. lxviii; Railroad Commission, *Reports*, i. appendix, cviii–cxx. For summaries of the law, see Dixon, *State Railroad Control*, 26; Commissioner McDill, in Cullom Committee, *Report on Interstate Commerce*, ii. 944; *American Annual Cyclopedia*, 1874, p. 416.

lasses. Section 3 contained an elaborate
rates for every distance up to 376 miles on
ar classes, with special rates for various staple
three classes of carload rates. The maximum
on roads in the three different classes were
this schedule in proportions of 90, 105, and 120
per co.   ction 5 supplemented the schedule by an elaborate
classification of freights. Other sections forbade discriminations between persons; but there was no prohibition of discrimination between places, provided all rates charged were
below the maxima fixed by the bill. The enforcement provisions
of the act were unusual: a fund of ten thousand dollars was
placed at the disposal of the governor to be used in assisting
private individuals to conduct suits for damages under the act;
and in addition, all officers or employees, convicted of being
party to violations of the act, were to be subjected to fines or
imprisonment.

Such were the carefully drawn provisions [1] of an act which
attracted attention all over the United States and even in the
financial centers of the old world. With such an act and forti-
fied by the numerous reservations of rights contained in the
railway charters and grants, it seemed as if the state of Iowa
was in a fair way to establish effective control of the railroad
business within its limits. That even the railroad companies
were convinced that the state's position was practically invul-
nerable, from the standpoint of legality, is indicated by the
greater measure of obedience which they rendered to this statute
than to the Granger laws of the other states.[2]

---

[1] Peter A. Dey, later railroad commissioner of Iowa and an opponent of this
sort of legislation, declared, " that the Iowa legislation, for fixed legislation, was the
most perfect that man could get up." Cullom Committee, *Report*, ii. 958. See
also Larrabee, *Railroad Question*, 332; Dixon, *State Railroad Control*, 27.

[2] Commissioner McDill in Cullom Committee, *Report*, ii. 945; Chicago, Burlington, and Quincy, Railroad Company, *Annual Reports*, 1876, p. 11; Governor
Carpenter, in *Legislative Documents*, 1876, i. no. 1, pp. 10–13; Governor Newbold,
in *Legislative Documents*, 1878, i. no. 1, p. 27. Dixon is quite unjustified in saying
that " the attitude assumed by the railroad companies was that either of indifference or of open hostility." Dixon, *State Control of Railroads*, 28. See, however,
p. 174, note 4, below.

The question of the justness of the rates established by the schedule of this act, to the shippers on the one hand and to the railroads on the other, has been the subject of a great deal of dispute. The railroad companies at once declared that the rates were unremunerative,[1] but Senator Larrabee writes that " this law in no case compelled railroad companies to carry freight at a lower rate than they had voluntarily carried it in the past " and that " the average rates fixed by the law were higher than the rates at which the railroads had previously carried a large portion of corresponding freight." [2] The facts seem to be that the legislature, instead of reducing all rates to the level of the lowest competitive rates, as had been attempted in Illinois in 1871, had merely endeavored to equalize rates, to strike a rough average between the lowest rates that had prevailed where there was active competition, and the higher rates from non-competitive points.[3] It must be remembered, however, that competition was left in full play and would still operate in most cases to prevent roads from raising their low rates to the maxima fixed by the schedule. On the other hand, there was a great deal of complaint, especially from the western part of the state, that the schedule established by the new law operated to the disadvantage of many shippers. This was probably due in part, however, to the efforts of the railroad companies to make the law as odious as possible. On the whole, it seems that the railroad commission, established under the law of 1878, was justified in its assertion " that the Tariff Act of 1874 was oppressive and unjust in many respects." [4]

In July, 1874, the president of the Chicago and Northwestern railroad addressed a letter to the governor in which he expressed a firm belief that the law was unconstitutional, but declared

---

[1] Chicago, Burlington, and Quincy, *Annual Reports*, 1874, p. 20, 1875, p. 26, 1876, p. 11, 1877, p. 23; Chicago and Northwestern, *Annual Reports*, 1874, p. 18.

[2] Larrabee, *Railroad Question*, 332.

[3] See *ibid.* 322; Dixon, *State Railroad Control*, 27.

[4] Railroad Commission, *Reports*, i. 51; Cullom Committee, *Report*, ii. 945, 958, 1002, 1057; Governor Carpenter, in *Legislative Documents*, 1876, i. no. 1, pp. 10–13; *Senate Journal*, 1876, pp. 157–165; Iowa State Grange, *Proceedings*, v (1874); *American Annual Cyclopedia*, 1874, p. 417, 1876, p. 412, 1878, p. 446; Larrabee, *Railroad Question*, 333–335; Tuttle, *Iowa*, 369.

the intention of the company to comply with its provisions
long enough to demonstrate its absolute injustice.[1] Similar
sentiments were expressed in a letter from the general superintendent of the Chicago, Rock Island, and Pacific railroad,[2]
and the policy thus outlined appears to have been adopted by
the railroads of the state,[3] with two or three exceptions. Of
these exceptions the most important was the Chicago, Burlington, and Quincy,[4] and in accordance with the provisions of the
law steps were taken by the attorney-general to institute a
number of suits against this road. This move was checkmated
by a temporary injunction which the railroad company procured from the United States circuit court, restraining the
prosecution of suits under the law. The question of making
this injunction perpetual came up in the May term, 1875, and
served as a test case of the validity of the law. Judge Dillon,
who heard the case, in refusing to make the injunction permanent,
based his decision on the ground that railroads were public
highways, and that whatever powers the companies possessed
to make rates were subject to the implied condition that they
be not oppressively or unreasonably exercised and also subject
to future exercise of public regulation by the state. As with
the Granger cases in the other states, an appeal was taken to the
United States Supreme Court, by which the decision of the circuit court was sustained in the October term, 1876.[5]

While the appeal to the Supreme Court was pending the
Chicago, Burlington, and Quincy appears to have conformed
its charges in general to the rates in the schedule, and from

[1] Printed in full in *Prairie Farmer*, xliv. 223 (July 18, 1874). He maintained
that the rates for some lines under the law were from thirty to forty *per cent* lower
than the rates in force in 1873.

[2] *American Annual Cyclopedia*, 1874, p. 417; Tuttle, *Iowa*, 369.

[3] See references above, p. 172, note 2.

[4] In the annual report to the stockholders, February, 1875, the president of the
Chicago, Burlington, and Quincy alluded to the railroad laws of Illinois and Iowa
and asserted that " by general acquiescence, their provisions have not to any great
extent been observed." Chicago, Burlington, and Quincy, *Annual Reports*, 1874,
p. 20.

[5] 94 *United States*, 155; Governor Carpenter, in *Legislative Documents*, 1876,
i. no. 1, pp. 10–13; Tuttle, *Iowa*, 369; *Appleton's Cyclopedia*, 1875, p. 403; *Nation*,
xx. 402, xxi. 1 (January 17, July 1, 1875).

that time forth all the energies of the railroad interests were directed toward securing a repeal of the law. Here as in the other Granger states every effort was made to convince the people that the law was disadvantageous to shippers and the general public as well as to the railroads. At that time, it was generally supposed that the state's right to regulate rates, so far as it existed at all, extended to the part of an interstate shipment which was within the state, and most of the Granger laws were drawn with this idea in view, but it was soon found that in actual practice such regulation could not be made effective. It was a very simple matter for the railroad companies, although nominally charging legal rates on the part of a shipment within the state of Iowa, to make the charge for the whole through shipment as high or higher than before the law went into effect. Through rates to Chicago were actually raised in this manner on many commodities, especially on agricultural products, and the public was given to understand that this was due to the operation of the law.[1] Again, railroads which had hitherto competed strenuously for traffic at various points seemed to forget their rivalries in the face of the danger of state control, and thus points which had previously enjoyed very low competitive rates frequently found their rates raised to the maxima allowed by the law.[2] Here again the railroad officials could point to the law as the source of the evil, and with a good deal of truth, for the equalization of rates had been one of its avowed objects. As a result of this manipulation and of some inherent defects in the schedule, a considerable sentiment was soon built up in the state in favor of the repeal of the law.

On the other hand, although the order of Patrons of Husbandry had begun to decline, the Granger sentiment in the state continued strong for a couple of years longer, and stood back of the governor in his efforts to secure compliance with the law.[3] The political parties, also, continued to demand the control of

---

[1] *Senate Journal*, 1876, pp. 157–165; Cullom Committee, *Reports*, ii. 1057; *Appleton's Cyclopedia*, 1878, p. 446.

[2] Larrabee, *Railroad Question*, 333; Dixon, *State Railroad Control*, 28.

[3] Iowa State Grange, *Proceedings*, v (1874); *Prairie Farmer*, xlv. 211 (July 4, 1874).

railroads by the state; but a hint of dissatisfaction with the law is found in the Anti-Monopoly platform adopted in June, 1874, in that it discountenanced any action calculated to work injustice or retard the progress of railroad enterprises.[1]

As was to be expected, vigorous efforts were made to secure the repeal of the railroad law when the sixteenth general assembly came together in 1876.[2] Governor Carpenter treated the question in his biennial message, describing the efforts to enforce the law and expressing the belief that its general effects were beneficial. His conclusion was that " the law should therefore in its main features be retained, and perfected as experience may unfold its weaknesses, or as may be necessary to adjust it to the future demands of commerce." [3] There seems to have been considerable sentiment in favor of revising the schedule in the law so as to make it more satisfactory to both railroads and shippers, but the railroad forces, in the hope of securing the repeal of the law opposed all amendments which retained the principle of a statutory maximum.[4] In the end this law was left unchanged; but late in the session a law was enacted, by large majorities in both houses, which provided for the release of any railroad company and its agents from criminal prosecution under the act of 1874, on condition that the company adopt the schedule and file a bond to operate under it for two years (provided it should remain in force) and not to seek to evade it by an increase on through rates, the test of such increase to be the rates in force in 1873.[5] This law was accepted by the Chicago, Burlington, and Quincy, the Illinois Central, and the

---

[1] *American Annual Cyclopedia*, 1874, p. 418, 1875, p. 402.

[2] Cf. *Appleton's Cyclopedia*, 1875, p. 412.

[3] *Legislative Documents*, 1876, i. no. 1, pp. 10–13.

[4] *Senate Journal*, 1876, pp. 51, 116, 157–165, 189, 190, 206, 227, 253, 416–419, 452; *House Journal*, 1876, pp. 103, 192, 221, 386, 452–458, 475, 482, 506, 530–532. See also Cullom Committee, *Report*, ii. 1057. That the people of the state were still deeply stirred over the subject of railroad legislation is indicated by the large numbers of petitions received by the two houses, some requesting the retention and enforcement of the act, others, its repeal or modification. See *House* and *Senate Journals*, indexes.

[5] *House Journal*, 1876, p. 593; *Senate Journal*, 1876, pp. 397, 451; *Laws*, 1876, ch. cxxxiii.

Chicago, Milwaukee, and St. Paul companies, and the statutory rates appear to have been quite generally in force during the succeeding two years.[1]

In the interval which elapsed before the meeting of the next general assembly in 1878, the order of Patrons of Husbandry declined in the state almost to extinction, and its decline was accompanied by a material decrease in popular interest in railroad regulation. On the other hand, the activity of the railroad forces in working up sentiment in favor of the repeal of the law increased as the chances of success in this way became greater and as the hope that the law might be declared unconstitutional was blasted by the Supreme Court decisions of the fall of 1876. In the summer of 1877, the president of the Illinois Central sent an agent east to enlist the assistance of eastern magazines and newspapers in a campaign for the repeal of the law and the substitution of a commissioner system of regulation similar to that which prevailed in Massachusetts and Minnesota.[2] This agent secured the publication of a long editorial in the *New York Tribune* setting forth the disastrous effects of the law on the state, and many Iowa newspapers were induced to copy this and thus circulate it among the people it was desired to reach. Other special articles and letters were also furnished to such newspapers as would make use of them, the burden of all being the advantage of the commission system of regulation over a fixed schedule of maximum rates, for the railroad forces now realized that there must be at least a pretense of the retention of state control. Agents were also sent among the people of the state to get in touch with local politicians and work for the nomination and election of candidates favorable to the railroad interests.[3] The result of this activity and of the decline of Grange influence was seen in the election of a general assembly inclined to favor a repeal or extensive modification of the legislation of 1874.

[1] Governor's message, in *Legislative Documents*, 1878, i. no. 1, p. 27; Chicago, Burlington, and Quincy, *Annual Reports*, 1876, p. 11.

[2] See account of this mission by the agent, Charles Aldrich, "Repeal of the Granger Law in Iowa," in *Iowa Journal of History and Politics*, iii. 256–270 (April, 1905).

[3] *Ibid.*

The act of 1878, by which the Granger law of Iowa was practically repealed, was passed by votes of 55 to 43 in the House and 29 to 21 in the Senate.[1] The affirmative votes on this measure appear to have come from three classes; those who were controlled by the very active railroad lobby; those who were actually convinced that the law was a detriment to the state, especially representatives from districts where additional railroad facilities were desired; and those who, like Senator Larrabee, felt that the law of 1874 had not been enforced, in spirit at least, and preferred a commission without a schedule of maximum rates to a schedule without a commission to enforce it.[2] With the law of 1878[3] the pendulum of railroad regulation in Iowa swung almost to the opposite extreme. Although the sections of the old law relating to classification of roads, passenger fares, and reports of companies were retained, the freight sections were entirely repealed, and the board of commissioners which was established was given no power except to investigate, recommend, and report to the governor and legislature.

Whether this substitution of an advisory commission for the statutory schedule of maximum rates, as a means of regulating railroads, was accomplished with the approval of a majority of the people or was the result of manipulation of the legislature by the railroad interests is a question upon which the evidence is conflicting,[4] and which cannot be answered with any degree

---

[1] For governor's messages, see *Legislative Documents*, 1878, i. no. 1, p. 27 (Newbold); *Appleton's Cyclopedia*, 1878, p. 445 (Gear). For references to petitions, which were again numerous, see *House* and *Senate Journals*, 1878, indexes. For bills introduced or legislative action, see *House Journal*, 1878, pp. 113, 117, 159, 285, 334–337, 342–345, 495; *Senate Journal*, 1878, pp. 315, 350–368, 381.

[2] Larrabee, *Railroad Question*, 334; Dixon, *State Railroad Control*, 28; Peter Dey, " Railroad Legislation in Iowa," in *Iowa Historical Record*, ix. 558; Cullom Committee, *Report*, ii. 945, 1002, 1057.

[3] Laws, 1878, ch. lxxvii; Railroad Commission, *Reports*, i. appendix, pp. clxxxvii–cxciv. For discussions of the law, see Dixon, *State Railroad Control*, part ii. ch. 1; Larrabee, *Railroad Question*, 335; Cullom Committee, *Report*, ii. 945–947; Railroad Commission, *Report*, i. 50–79.

[4] Cullom Committee, *Report*, ii. 944, 958, 1002, 1057; Larrabee, *Railroad Question*, 335; Dixon, *State Railroad Control*, 28; Railroad Commission, *Reports*, i. 3.

of certainty. Whichever may have been the case, the law was accepted by the people and for a number of years it seems to have given quite general satisfaction.[1] Undoubtedly the attitude of railroad officials toward shippers and the public in general was very different from what it had been before the passage of the Granger law and the Supreme Court decisions of 1876, and, as a general rule, the new railroad commission had little difficulty in inducing the companies to remedy such grievances as it found worthy of presentation. Thus if it had no other results, the Granger agitation at least brought about a better understanding of the rights of shippers and the public and the duties of transportation companies, which showed itself in the more conciliatory attitude of the railroads. Abuses in railway management continued to exist, nevertheless, and early in the next decade another agitation was started which culminated in the law of 1888 establishing a commission with power, the law which is still in operation in the state.[2] This movement in the eighties is outside the scope of this work, but it undoubtedly builded largely upon and was profoundly affected by the Granger movement of the previous decade.

WISCONSIN

The convention which framed a constitution for the new state of Wisconsin in 1848, mindful of the Dartmouth College decision, inserted a reservation in the article of that instrument concerning the creation of corporations which provided that " all general laws or special acts, enacted under the provisions of this section, may be altered or repealed by the legislature at any time after their passage." [3]

Even during the fifties, when the prevalent desire for railroads was leading counties, towns, cities, and even individuals to adopt generous but ill-advised measures to encourage their construction,

[1] Cullom Committee, *Report*, ii. 945–948; Dixon, *State Railroad Control*, part ii; *Appleton's Cyclopedia*, 1879, p. 314; Governor's message in *Legislative Documents*, 1880, i. no. 1, p. 28.

[2] Larrabee, *Railroad Question*, 336–342; Dixon, *State Railroad Control*, part iii. ch. i.

[3] Article XI, section 1.

the note of complaint against extortionate and discriminating rates was heard,[1] but it was not until about the close of the Civil War that the legislature began to consider seriously the advisability of making use of these reserved powers. In 1864 acts were passed to compel railroad companies to carry cord wood, to carry grain and deliver it to the consignee as directed, and to allow any warehouseman to build a side-track connecting with the company's line. Several bills for the establishment of a schedule of maximum rates were also introduced at this session but failed to receive favorable action in either house.[2] From this beginning in 1864 to nearly the end of the next decade, the railroad question occupied a prominent part in every session of the legislature, and innumerable bills were introduced touching upon the various aspects of the problem.

In the legislative session of 1866, the Assembly passed a rate bill and the Senate a bill to provide for the establishment of a commission of the advisory type. This latter measure was amended by the Assembly in such a way as to give the proposed commission some power over rates; but the Senate refused to accept the amendment, and neither measure became a law.[3] In 1867 the Assembly again passed a rate bill, the vote at this time being 71 to 11; but the Senate rejected it by vote of 17 to 9.[4] In 1870 a joint committee was appointed to investigate railroad problems, but no legislation ensued.[5] During 1872

---

[1] H. C. Campbell, in *Wisconsin in Three Centuries*, iv. 256.

[2] Wisconsin, *Assembly Journal*, 1864, pp. 214, 312, 394, 600, 604, 606, 659, 662–664, 681, 717–735, 760, 801–804; *Senate Journal*, 1864, pp. 22, 88, 178, 214, 272, 319, 448, 465, 632, 637, 638, 653, 668, 690, 694; Wisconsin, *Laws*, 1864, chs. xlix, cccxv, cccclxxii.

[3] On railways in the session of 1865, see *Assembly Journal*, 1865, pp. 160, 169, 192–194, 213, 214, 234, 315, 368, 489, 495, 562, 570, 811–813, 986, 987; *Senate Journal*, 1865, pp. 123, 255, 316, 465, 514, 570, 803, 812. For the session of 1866, see *Assembly Journal*, 1866, pp. 39, 172, 279, 289, 296, 324–337, 345, 356, 412, 478, 589, 594, 700, 732, 1125, 1135; *Senate Journal*, 1866, pp. 178, 521, 525, 653, 754, 782, 867, 883–897, 962–972, 984, 1011, 1029, 1034; *Wisconsin Democrat*, March 30, 1866; C. R. Tuttle, *Illustrated History of Wisconsin*, 600–602.

[4] *Assembly Journal*, 1867, pp. 488, 490, 1179; *Senate Journal*, 1867, pp. 21, 483, 641–649, 778, 784, 903.

[5] *Assembly Journal*, 1868, pp. 83, 736; *ibid.*, 1869, pp. 558–560; *ibid.*, 1870, pp. 30, 50, 442, 536. See also J. H. Howe, *Statement in Behalf of the Chicago and*

and 1873 there was considerable agitation outside the legislature for the regulation of rates, and Governor Washburn tried to stir that body into activity by vigorous discussions of the question in his annual messages.[1] Nevertheless none of the numerous bills introduced were passed by either house. Clearly the legislature was not yet convinced that the people were in earnest in their demand for railroad regulation, and after ten years of agitation, the advocates of restrictive laws seemed farther from their goal than they had been in 1864.

Before considering the railroad legislation of 1874, it will be necessary to notice a number of things which explain the very different attitude toward the railroad question of the legislature of that year from that of preceding legislatures. Most important of these factors was undoubtedly the rapid organization of the farmers of the state into the order of the Patrons of Husbandry.[2] This order, which numbered less than thirty active granges in the state at the opening of the year 1873, grew to over four hundred local granges by March 1, 1874; and by taking a stand in favor of railroad regulation it undoubtedly gave a great impetus to that movement. Closely connected with the spread of this organization was the formation of the Reform party, which made restrictive railroad regulation the main plank in its platform.[3] The Republican leaders had been reading the signs of the times, and their party platform, adopted in August, 1873, also declared for the regulation of railroads, the establishment of a board of commissioners, and anti-pass legislation.[4] This, however, was too late to stem the tide. The Reformers, by fusing with the Democrats, won the election and secured control of the Assembly, though the Republicans

Northwestern Railroad Company Relative to Assembly Bill No. 260, Relating to Railroad Tariffs (pamphlet, 1870).

[1] *Assembly Journal*, 1871, pp. 55, 66; *ibid.*, 1872, pp. 306, appendix, 22–24; *ibid.*, 1873, pp. 144, 616, 808, 812–814, 831, 852; *Senate Journal*, 1873, pp. 28, 39, 113, 116, 144, 279, 322, 487, 514, 533; *Prairie Farmer*, xliv. 17 (January 18, 1873); Tuttle, *Wisconsin*, 636.

[2] See table above, following p. 58.

[3] *American Annual Cyclopedia*, 1873, p. 775.   See also above, pp. 89–92.

[4] *American Annual Cyclopedia*, 1873, p. 774.

retained a majority of one in the Senate.[1] One other factor must be noted among the influences leading to the railroad legislation of 1874; in the autumn of 1873, a number of leading railroad companies were impolitic enough to raise the rates for the transportation of agricultural products, in the face of an abundant harvest and in spite of complaints that the rates were already too high.[2]

The victory of the Reform party in 1873 involved the defeat of Governor Washburn, who, as has been seen, had been recommending railroad legislation for several years; but the governor-elect, W. R. Taylor, was a prominent Granger and in his first annual message took an even stronger position in favor of laws to curb the railroad companies.[3] Advice was also received by the legislature from the state grange which held its annual session in January.[4] This was in the form of a resolution recommending an increase in the tax on gross receipts of railroads from three to five per cent and the appointment of " Commissioners with full power to regulate and prevent unjust discrimination or excessive tariff rates and to enquire into the condition of Railways chartered by the State Government, and to report facts on which to base future and judicious legislation." By order of the grange, copies of this resolution were sent to the lieutenant-governor, and to the speaker of the Assembly; and it may be taken as an authoritative exposition of the kind of railroad legislation desired by the leaders of the Patrons of Husbandry.[5]

The numerous railroad bills which were introduced at this session were referred to a joint committee, which finally presented the results of its labors to both houses in the form of a bill to prohibit any rates higher than those in force during the first

---

[1] *Chicago Tribune*, November 17, 1873, p. 3.

[2] Wisconsin Railroad Commission, *Reports*, i. 84; *Cincinnati Semi-Weekly Gazette*, September 16, 1873, p. 7; *Prairie Farmer*, xliv. 300 (September 20, 1873); Maynard, *Patrons of Husbandry in Wisconsin* (Ms.); *Grant City* (Wisconsin) *Herald*, September 25, 1873; *Wester Farmer*, September 27, 1873.

[3] *Senate Journal*, 1874, appendix, pp. 3–23.

[4] Wisconsin State Grange, *Proceedings*, ii (January, 1874).

[5] Maynard, *Patrons of Husbandry in Wisconsin* (Ms.), 52–56; *Senate Journal*, 1874, pp. 164–166.

week in January, 1872, without special permission from a railroad commission to be established. The Assembly passed this measure by vote of 69 to 14. In the Senate, however, the railroad forces rallied, and fearing their inability to prevent the passage of the bill in an open fight, they brought forward the most extreme of the other railroad bills and had it substituted for the committee bill by vote of 20 to 13. This bill, which had been first introduced by Senator Potter, contained a schedule of maximum rates very much lower than the rates then in force on the roads of Wisconsin, and was brought forward with the idea that so radical measure could not possibly become a law and that thus all railroad legislation might be prevented. Two days later this bill passed the Senate by vote of 20 to 7 but was laid aside in the Assembly as had been expected. Shortly after this the joint committee measure again came before the Senate in the shape of an Assembly bill and the same tactics were again pursued; the Potter bill being substituted for the Assembly measure. The responsibility was thus thrown upon the Granger members of the Assembly, and they faced the dilemma of returning to their constituents with no railroad legislation enacted or accepting this radical and unsatisfactory Senate measure. Apparently much to the surprise of the managers of the railroad interests, the Grangers chose the latter alternative and accepted the Potter bill.[1]

---

[1] *Assembly Journal*, 1874, pp. 23, 36, 103, 194, 367, 559, 611, 631–636, 670, 673; *Senate Journal*, 1874, pp. 9, 36, 75, 92, 145, 197, 285–297, 384–386, 423, 517, 562.

An interesting parallel can be drawn between the legislative history of the Potter law of Wisconsin and that of the " tariff of abominations" passed by Congress in 1828. The latter was the result of the attempts of southern leaders to prevent any tariff legislation and in both cases the measures adopted were distasteful to a large majority, even to most of those who voted for them. See Turner, *Rise of the New West*, ch. xix.

As early as January 17, 1874, the *Industrial Age* announced the existence of a political deal between the Republican leaders and the St. Paul railroad officials by the terms of which all railroad bills were to be killed either by direct vote or by loading them with amendments to make them obnoxious or useless. After the law was passed, O. W. Wright, a prominent leader of the Reform party, declared, " The Potter law was unquestionably designed to defeat the ends of railway legislation. If its inventors should finally be hoist with their own petard the mourners would be few." *Chicago Tribune*, May 23, 1874, p. 2. See also *ibid.*, March 11, p. 2.

The Potter law of Wisconsin [1] was one of the most famous and most condemned of all the Granger acts. It will be worth while to note its provisions with some care. The first section of the law divided the railroads of the state into three classes; A, B, and C; those placed in classes A and B being listed, and class C including all the rest, and especially the newer and less important lines. By section 2 the maximum passenger fare was fixed at three, three and a half, and four cents per mile for roads in classes A, B, and C, respectively. Section 3 provided for the classification of freight into four general classes numbered 1, 2, 3, and 4, and seven special classes: D, grain in carloads; E, flour or lime; F, salt, cement, etc.; G, lumber in carloads; H, livestock in carloads; I, agricultural implements, furniture, and wagons; J, coal, brick, sand, stone, etc., in carloads. By section 4 graduated maximum rates were fixed for the transportation of freight in the seven special classes on roads in classes A and B, no distinction being made between the two classes in this case. Section 5 provided that for all freight in the four regular classes transported on roads in classes A and B and for *all* freight transported on roads in class C, the maximum charge should be the rates in force June 1, 1873. Sections 8 to 13 inclusive provided for the appointment of three railroad commissioners, who were empowered to reclassify all freights except such as were placed in classes D, E, G, and H, and to reduce rates on any road in any class whenever a majority of the commission should believe that it could be done without injury to the road.

It will be seen then that the maximum rates on grain, lumber, and live-stock, in carloads, and on flour and lime, were fixed by the act for the more important roads and could not be raised though they might be lowered by the commission. Maximum rates were also provided for these roads for commodities in the other special classes, but these were subject to change by the commission by means of reclassification. The newer and weaker roads placed in class C were affected only by the provisions of the act which limited their passenger fares to four cents per mile

[1] *Laws*, 1874, ch. cclxxiii; Railroad Commission, *Reports*, ii. appendix A, 1–6.

and their freight charges to the rates in force June 1, 1873, and this latter limitation was also applied to freight in the four regular classes transported on roads in classes A and B. By taking the rates of June 1, 1873, maxima were secured which had been fixed by the roads themselves and yet were in many cases somewhat lower than the rates in force at the time of the passage of the act because of the raise of rates in the fall of 1873. It should also be noted that the control which might be exercised by the commission over charges, by virtue of the power given it to reclassify freights and to reduce rates, was very thorough-going.

There has been a great deal of controversy as to the actual amount of the reduction in rates made by the Potter law. At the time, the assertion was made that the framers of the law had merely taken the lowest rates in force and reduced them twenty-five per cent.[1] The president of the St. Paul Railroad Company also declared that the reduction amounted to twenty-five per cent, and drew the unwarranted conclusion that a reduction of equal proportion in the gross earnings of the company would be the result of the application of the Potter rates.[2] On the other hand the commissioners appointed under the law reached the conclusion by mathematical calculation that the enforcement of the Potter law would entail a reduction of less than five per cent of the gross earnings on freight traffic and less than thirteen per cent on passenger traffic, assuming that the amount of business remain the same.[3] The commissioners were probably the more nearly correct, for it must be remembered that all freight in the four general classes was subject only to such reduction as was involved in a return to the rates of June 1, 1873. That the rates on most of the commodities in the special classes were fixed unreasonably low as compared with rates previously in force in Wisconsin and on roads elsewhere in the country is also undoubtedly true.[4]

[1] F. R. Leland, "The Second Stage of Wisconsin Railroad Legislation," in *Nation*, xx. 189 (March 18, 1875).

[2] Railway Commission, *Reports*, i. division iii. 3 (1874). See criticism in A.B. Stickney, *The Railway Problem*, ch. xi, and Larrabee, *Railroad Question*, 232–237.

[3] Railway Commission, *Reports*, i. division ii. 21, 263.

[4] *Ibid.*, division i. 33–35; division ii. 33, 252–271.

Another bill for " An act in relation to Railroads " was passed at the session of the legislature in 1874 by votes of 19 to 6 and 46 to 16. This measure prohibited unreasonable discrimination; the consolidation of parallel or competing roads; and the issuance of free passes to state officers, judges, and members of the legislature.[1] An attempt was made by the Assembly to make a violation of the *pro rata* principle *prima facie* evidence of unjust discrimination, but this was rejected by the Senate.[2] These two acts, the Potter law and the act, " in relation to Railroads " generally known as the " anti-pass law," constitute the Granger legislation of the state of Wisconsin.[3]

As in the other states, the Granger element of Wisconsin was to find that the enactment of radical legislation was easier than its enforcement. The first step to be taken was the appointment of a board of railway commissioners. For advice upon this subject the governor turned to those who appeared to be primarily responsible for the agitation which had produced the law, the Patrons of Husbandry. On March 17, the executive committee of the state grange met at Madison at the request of the governor, and joined with a committee chosen by Patrons who had been members of the legislature in recommending the appointment of J. H. Osborn of Oshkosh, chairman of the executive committee of the state grange, for railroad commissioner for three years, and of Philo Belden for one year.[4] After considerable delay the governor finally appointed Mr. Osborn as chairman of the board with John W. Hoyt and George H. Paul as the other members.[5] Mr. Hoyt was connected with the State Agricultural Society. Mr. Paul was supposed to represent the commercial interests of the state, but was repudiated by the *Milwaukee Journal of Commerce*.[6]

[1] *Laws*, 1874, ch. cccxli; Railroad Commission, *Reports*, ii. appendix A, 7.

[2] For the legislative history of this measure, see *Assembly Journal*, 1874, pp. 53, 57, 344, 716–721, 783; *Senate Journal*, 1874, pp. 23, 26, 93, 153, 271, 495–497, 536, 573, 640.

[3] The law increasing the tax on gross earnings of railroads from three to four per cent, enacted by this legislature, is sometimes included among the Granger laws.

[4] Wisconsin State Grange, *Proceedings*, iii (January, 1875).

[5] *Senate Journal*, 1875, p. 27.

[6] *Nation*, xviii. 308 (May 14, 1874); *Industrial Age*, May 2, 1874; Maynard, *Patrons of Husbandry in Wisconsin* (Ms.), 57.

Early in May the board effected its organization and proceeded to notify the railroad companies of the classification of roads and the maximum rates fixed by the Potter law.[1] Meanwhile the leading railroad companies had submitted the Potter law to such eminent jurists as William M. Evarts and Charles O'Connor of New York and E. Rockwood Hoar and Benjamin R. Curtis of Massachusetts,[2] and relying upon the opinions of these lawyers, the officials of the St. Paul and the Northwestern appear to have reached the conclusion that the law was invalid and could not be enforced. Accordingly President Mitchell of the St. Paul and President Keep of the Northwestern addressed letters to the governor in which they took the position that the enforcement of the law would amount to confiscation, and declared the intention of their companies to disregard its provisions until these were passed upon by the courts.[3]

These statements were looked upon as a challenge by the Granger governor, who answered them promptly in a vigorous proclamation dated May 1, 1874, in which he enjoined

all railroad corporations, their officers and agents, peaceably to submit to the law, for since the Executive is charged with the responsibility of seeing that the laws are faithfully executed, all the functions of his office will be exercised to that end; and for this purpose he invokes the aid and coöperation of all good citizens.[4]

Most of the smaller roads of the state took steps to comply with such portions of the laws as related to them;[5] but the St. Paul and the Northwestern, following out their announced intention, made no effort so to revise their tariffs as to conform

[1] Railroad Commission, *Reports*, 1874, division i. 18; division ii. 1–4.

[2] *The Wisconsin Railroad Law* (pamphlet in Wisconsin Historical Society library); F. A. Flower, *Life of Matthew Hale Carpenter*, 155–158. See also, with reference to a favorable opinion of the validity of the law by Senator Carpenter, *Industrial Age*, May 23, 1874, p. 1; *Wisconsin State Journal*, May 14, 1874.

[3] Railroad Commission, *Reports*, 1874, division iii. 1–5.

[4] *Ibid.* 7. The governor followed this up with an address to the people, dated May 21, 1874, in which citizens were enjoined to pay no higher charges than the law allowed and to report all extortions to the district-attorneys. All local officers were also enjoined to enforce the law within their jurisdictions. Aid from the executive was pledged if circumstances should require it. *Ibid.* 8–10.

[5] *Ibid.* 1–14.

to the provisions of the law.   Attorney-General Sloan then made
application to the supreme court of the state for leave to bring
quo warranto proceedings against these companies.[1]   The answer
of the railroad forces to this move on the part of the state was
the application of certain Northwestern bondholders to the
circuit court of the United States for an injunction to restrain
the company, the railroad commissioners, and the attorney-
general from applying or enforcing the rates of the Potter law
on the Northwestern lines.   The case was finally argued in
July with Supreme Justice Davis and Circuit Justices Drum-
mond and Hopkins on the bench.   Among the attorneys for
the plaintiffs was Hon. C. B. Lawrence, ex-chief justice of
Illinois, who had lost his seat on the bench as a result of the
Granger movement in that state, while Attorney-General Sloan
was assisted by Hon. L. S. Dixon, ex-chief justice of Wisconsin.
Three days were devoted to the argument of the case.   The
principal contention of the plaintiffs was the confiscatory nature
of the act, while the defendants relied on the reserved powers
of the legislature to alter or repeal charters.   On July 4, the
court by a unanimous decision overruled the motion for an
injunction.[2]   Appeal was at once taken to the United States
Supreme Court and the decision of that body, when it was finally
delivered in October, 1876, several months after the Potter
law had been repealed, affirmed the decision of the lower
court.[3]

July 8, 1874, four days after the decision of the United States
circuit court, the attorney-general tried another method of
securing observance of the law.   He filed a bill in equity in
the state supreme court complaining of the violation of the law
by the Northwestern and St. Paul companies and asking that
they be enjoined to obey it.   Following an eight days' legal
battle in August, the decision was delivered by Chief-Justice
Ryan on September 15.   The court declared the law a valid

[1] Railroad Commission, *Reports*, 1874, division iii. 17–26.

[2] *Ibid.* 26–28; *American Annual Cyclopedia*, 1874, pp. 808–810; Tuttle, *Wisconsin*, 645–651.

[3] 94 *United States*, 164; Illinois Railroad Commission, *Reports*, 1877, pp. 22–24; Wisconsin Railroad Commission, *Reports*, 1875, appendix B.

enactment and writs were ordered to be issued as requested.[1] Before the close of the month, the presidents of both the North-western and the St. Paul companies signified their intention of acquiescing in the decision, and after October 1, the rates of the Potter law, so far as intra-state commerce was concerned, appear to have been in force on all the roads in the state.[2]

Governor Taylor is said to have celebrated the victory of the administration in the state courts with the firing of cannon at the capitol,[3] but he was mistaken if he thought this victory was to ensure the permanent regulation of railroad rates by the state. Even before their cause had been definitely lost in the state courts, the railroad forces turned their attention to another method of obtaining relief from what seemed to them oppressive laws, and entered on a campaign for their repeal. The methods followed in Wisconsin were very similar to those which were being pursued in the other Granger states at the same time; the railroad interests endeavored to persuade the people that the restrictive laws were not only injurious and unjust to the com-panies but that they worked to the disadvantage of the traveling and the shipping public and affected adversely the interests of the whole state.[4] The decision of the state supreme court on the validity of the Potter law brought forth a threat that the public would be given " Potter cars, Potter rails, and Potter time " ;[5] and President Mitchell of the St. Paul company, in

[1] 35 *Wisconsin*, 425; Railroad Commission, *Reports*, 1874, division iii. 28–78; *American Annual Cyclopedia*, 1874, pp. 808–810; J. B. Winslow, *Story of a Great Court*, 339–347; Tuttle, *Wisconsin*, 645–651. A list of printed briefs, etc., relative to the Wisconsin Granger cases, is in Wisconsin Historical Society, *Proceedings*, 1897, p. 143. See also Hinckley *v.* Chicago, Milwaukee and St. Paul Railway Com-pany, 38 *Wisconsin*, 194, in which a verdict of one thousand dollars damages for ejection from a train after paying fare at the legal rate was sustained.

[2] Railroad Commission, *Reports*, 1874, division iii. 79; *American Annual Cyclopedia*, 1874, p. 810. See, however, Charles W. Lea, *Grange Movement in Wisconsin* (Ms.), 31, for a different conclusion.

[3] *Nation*, xxiv. 143 (March 8, 1877).

[4] *Ibid.* xviii. 293 (May 17, 1874), xix. 17, 199–201 (July 9, September 24, 1874), xx. 53 (January 28, 1875); *American Exchange and Review*, xxv. 393 (Au-gust, 1874); Lea, *Grange Movement in Wisconsin* (Ms.), 27; *Chicago Tribune*, July 20, 1874, p. 4.

[5] *Nation*, xix. 199–210 (September 24, 1874).

his letter to the governor announcing the intention of his company to conform to the provisions of the law, reiterated the charge that it would prevent any further development of the railroads of the state. He added that the company faced the alternative of either cutting down its service or transacting business at a loss, but announced that the latter course would be followed for the time being in the hope that the laws would be repealed at the coming session of the legislature.[1] The threatened policy of retaliation seems to have been attempted in some cases, especially by cutting down the number of local trains,[2] but it was perfectly clear, as the *Nation* pointed out, that there was nothing to prevent legislation to regulate the service of railroads as well as the rates.[3] Consequently the railroads directed most of their energies toward securing control of the next legislature, which was to meet in January, 1875.

Meanwhile the officers of the state grange were taking the lead on the other side, in the endeavor to preserve the Potter law or at least the principle of state control of rates. In July the executive committee issued an address [4] on the subject which was prepared by its chairman, J. H. Osborn, who was also chairman of the state railroad commission. This paper warned the Patrons of the efforts which were being made to repeal the law and exhorted them to see that only honest men who could be relied upon to support the farmers' interests be nominated and elected to the legislature. This was followed in October by an address from the master of the state grange, John Cochrane,[5] which pointed out the essential features of the Potter law and called upon the Patrons to demand of their representatives not merely the retention of these features but additional legislation to prevent the manipulation of railroad accounts. This

[1] Railroad Commission, *Reports*, 1874, division iii. 79.

[2] Lea, *Granger Movement in Wisconsin* (Ms.), 32, referring to " country papers "; F. L. Holmes, in *Wisconsin in Three Centuries*, iv. 119.

[3] *Nation*, xix. 199–201 (September 24, 1873).

[4] Wisconsin State Grange, *Proceedings*, iii. appendix 6–12 (1875); Maynard, *Patrons of Husbandry in Wisconsin* (Ms.), 57.

[5] Wisconsin State Grange, *Proceedings*, iii. appendix, 1–6 (1875).

address was accompanied by a list of thirteen questions relating to the position of candidates for the legislature on various aspects of the railroad problem, and masters of local granges were advised to submit this list to all candidates. Considerable use appears to have been made of this *questionnaire*, the answers received being made public, and it was doubtless disconcerting to such candidates as wished to avoid the issue, for the fact of a failure to reply to the questions was also to be announced and would undoubtedly make an unfavorable impression.

The election which ensued was not a decided victory for either the advocates or opponents of state control. The struggle was at once transferred to the legislature. Neither the railroad men, who wanted a complete repeal of the Potter law, nor the radical Granger element, which desired to retain the Potter rates and to strengthen the provision for enforcement, were strong enough to put through their bills. The outcome was the adoption of two compromise measures.[1] The first of these contained a reclassification of the roads and was designed to relieve some of the weaker roads which had been placed in class B by the Potter law.[2] The other, which was known as the Quimby amendment, was a revision, generally upward, of the rates in the seven special classes established by the Potter law, especially as applied to short distances.[3]

There seems to have been little difficulty over the enforcement of the railroad laws during 1875,[4] but the companies continued the campaign for their repeal along the same lines as those followed in 1874. In this they had the assistance of

---

[1] *Senate Journal*, 1875, pp. 376, 387, 416, 431, 443, 476, 479; *Assembly Journal*, 1875, pp. 170, 457, 513, 514–518, 573, 585, 614; *Industrial Age*, 1875, March 27, p. 4, April 17, p. 4, May 1, p. 4, June 5, p. 2; *Appleton's Cyclopedia*, 1875, p. 60; Leland, in *Nation*, xx. 189 (March 18, 1875) and reply, " Good and Bad Grangers " by " A Granger " in *ibid*. 241 (April 8, 1875); A. Keep and A. Mitchell, *Memorial of the Chicago and Northwestern and Chicago, Milwaukee and St. Paul Railway Companies to the Senate and Assembly of the State of Wisconsin* (1875); Flower, *Carpenter*, 291; Tuttle, *Wisconsin*, 653.

[2] *Laws*, 1875, ch. ccxxxiv; Railroad Commission, *Reports*, 1875, appendix A, 25–30.

[3] *Laws*, 1875, ch. cxiii; Railroad Commission, *Reports*, 1875, appendix A, 14.

[4] *Ibid*. 28.

a number of influential eastern papers and a large part of the press of the state. The *Nation* continued to advise capitalists to refrain from investment in the state,[1] while the *Evansville Review*, as an example of the local papers, asserted that " since the establishment of the Potter law not a spadeful of earth has been raised towards the construction of a single line of road." [2] It mattered not that the railroad situation was nowhere nearly so bad as it was depicted, and that its unfavorable features were not shown to be results of the Potter law. The argument had its effect, and a majority of the people were probably convinced that the railroad laws were a serious detriment to the welfare of the state. On the other side, the officials of the state grange continued to support the legislation. In August Master Cochrane issued a circular defending the Potter law, together with another set of questions to be submitted to candidates for the legislature. Just before the election a pamphlet entitled *The Wisconsin Railroad Laws and some Reasons for their Repeal* was issued by the railroad forces. Master Cochrane replied to this in another circular. The *Bulletin* of the Wisconsin State Grange, which had been established as the organ of the order in the state, also defended the Potter law in editorials, denied that it had checked construction, and declared that it needed " to be perfected, not repealed." [3]

The united Democratic and Reform parties renominated Governor Taylor on a platform demanding the continued exercise of the sovereignty of the state over corporations,[4] while the Republicans nominated Harrison Ludington, who was expected to favor the repeal of the Potter law and who therefore received the united support of the railroad forces. By this time many of the people were doubtless weary of the controversy and others had been convinced that the laws were injurious, but above all the order of Patrons of Husbandry had declined very consider-

---

[1] *Nation*, xx. 190, 241, 338 (March 18, 27, May 20, 1875).

[2] *Evansville Review*, September 20, 1875, cited in Lea, *Grange Movement in Wisconsin* (Ms.), 31–34.

[3] Wisconsin State Grange, *Bulletin*, September, October, November, 1875.

[4] *Appleton's Cyclopedia*, 1875, p. 764; *Wisconsin Statesman*, September 18, 1875, p. 3.

ably in numbers and influence.[1]   The result was the election of Ludington and a Republican majority in both houses of the legislature.[2]

When the new legislature met, in January, 1876, Governor Ludington depicted the sad condition of the railroads and recommended the repeal of the Potter law and the Quimby amendment, and the enactment of a law to prohibit and punish unjust discrimination and extortion and to provide for a supervisory commission.[3]   During the same month the state grange held its annual session and presented a resolution to the legislature to the effect that only such railroad legislation should be enacted as was necessary for the enforcement of the Potter law.[4]   In February another body of farmers met in what was called the Wisconsin Agricultural Convention and adopted a resolution protesting against the proposed repeal of the Potter law, but recommending its modification if it were deemed unjust to the railroads.[5]   It is clear that many in the state still approved of the law; for in addition to these resolutions, thirty-nine memorials were received by the Senate and twenty by the Assembly opposing its repeal or modification.   On the other hand, the Assembly received three and the Senate twelve memorials favoring its repeal or the substitution of a less drastic measure.[6]

Early in the session what was known as the Vance bill was introduced by the railroad supporters.   The remnants of the Granger forces filibustered against this measure, but they were unable to prevent its passage, the vote being 56 to 30 in the Assembly and 20 to 7 in the Senate, and it became law upon publication, March 1, 1876.[7]   This measure was practically a total surrender of the principle of effective control of railroad

---

[1] *Nation*, xxii. 57 (January 27, 1876).   See table above, following p. 58.

[2] Lea, *Grange Movement in Wisconsin* (Ms.), 33; *Wisconsin Statesman*, November 13, 1875, p. 2; Campbell, in *Wisconsin in Three Centuries*, iv. 277.

[3] Wisconsin, *Documents*, 1876, i. 9–12.

[4] Wisconsin State Grange, *Proceedings*, iv (1876).

[5] Wisconsin State Agricultural Society, *Transactions*, xiv. 362–370 (1876); *Assembly Journal*, 1876, p. 289.

[6] See *Assembly Journal*, 1876, index, p. 91; *Senate Journal*, 1876, p. 578.

[7] *Ibid.* 357, 365; *Assembly Journal*, 1876, pp. 78, 200, 215, 264–269, 304.

rates by the state and marks the end of the Granger railroad legislation of Wisconsin.[1] The new law provided for a single commission with merely supervisory powers in the place of the board established by the Potter law; there were sections prohibiting unreasonable charges and discrimination for like services from the same place; and the three principal roads of the state were limited in freight rates to the tariff in force on the St. Paul on June 15, 1872, a maximum which the roads had no desire to exceed. Finally all the sections of the Potter law except such as were merely formal or pertained to the powers of the commission to investigate and report, together with all the other restrictive legislation of 1874 and 1875, including the anti-pass law, were repealed. March 3, Governor Ludington appointed Dana C. Lamb as railroad commissioner.[2] The railroad question did not trouble the political waters of Wisconsin again for several years.

SUMMARY OF STATE LEGISLATION

The four states in which the movement for restrictive railroad legislation during the seventies has been traced are those in which it achieved the most important results and in which it was most closely connected with the movement for agricultural organization. But the demand for the regulation of railroads made its appearance in nearly every state of the Union during the decade, and in a number of other states besides the four already considered there was a more or less direct connection between this movement and the parallel one for agricultural organization, which, as has been seen, was equally widespread. This was particularly true in some of the other states of the upper Mississippi Valley, such as Missouri and Nebraska, and also in California and Oregon on the Pacific slope.

In Missouri the agitation for state control of railroads presents many similarities to the contemporary movement in the neighboring state of Illinois. At the very beginning of the decade

[1] *Laws*, 1876, ch. xxxvii.   See also *Appleton's Cyclopedia*, 1876, p. 806; *Nation*, xxiii. 3 (July 6, 1876); *Wisconsin Statesman*, March 11, 1876, p. 1.

[2] *Senate Journal*, 1876, p. 489.

a demand for restrictive legislation made its appearance in the state and the Legislative Farmers' Club, organized at the session of 1871–72, had united action upon this subject as one of its purposes.[1] Nothing was accomplished, however, until the summer of 1874, when the farmers of the state began to desert the old political parties and joined together to form the Independent party with railroad regulation as its principal issue.[2] In October the state grange, representing about two thousand local granges and nearly one hundred thousand farmers as members of the order, declared for the effective regulation of railways;[3] and the legislature responded at its next annual session in 1875 by passing a railroad act for which the Illinois law of 1873 and the Potter law of Wisconsin were used as models.[4] This act fixed maximum rates for freight and passenger transportation and established a railroad commission with extensive powers, but here, as in the other states, considerable difficulty was experienced in enforcing the law. More important than this legislation were the provisions relating to railroads which the radical element succeeded in inserting in the new state constitution adopted in the fall of 1875.[5] These provisions, which reflect the influence of similar provisions in the Illinois constitution of 1870, declare railroads to be public highways and the companies common carriers and subject to all the liabilities as such, prohibit any railroad from charging more for a less than for a greater distance, and make it obligatory upon the legislature to establish reasonable maximum rates and to pass laws to prevent unjust discrimination and extortion. The granting of free passes to state officers is also prohibited. The railroad sections of this constitution and the ensuing

---

[1] *Rural World*, xxvi. 396 (December 16, 1871).

[2] See above, p. 97.

[3] Missouri State Grange, *Proceedings*, iii. 17, 46, 61–65 (October, 1874). See also *ibid*. iv. 21, 48, 60, 71, 99 (December, 1875); *Chicago Tribune*, 1874, January 10, p. 2, January 12, p. 8; *American Annual Cyclopedia*, 1873, p. 519, 1874, p. 578.

[4] Wisconsin Railroad Commission, *Reports*, 1875, p. 38; Iowa Railroad Commission, *Reports*, 1878, p. 53; *Appleton's Cyclopedia*, 1875, p. 519.

[5] *Ibid*. 523. See Missouri constitution of 1875 in Thorpe, *Constitutions*, iv. 2264–2267 (Article XII, sections 2, 4, 12, 13, 17, 21, 24).

legislation met with the usual denunciation by railway officials
and were by no means always enforced,[1] but they indicated
the determination of the people of Missouri and especially the
farmers to subject railway corporations to state control, and
they laid the basis for later and more efficient legislation.

In Kansas and Nebraska the situation was somewhat different.
These states were still largely undeveloped and the desire for
more railroad facilities was so overpowering that little attention
was paid to the question of regulation during the decade of the
seventies. The order of Patrons of Husbandry, it is true,
flourished vigorously in both states, and in Kansas there was
also an Independent or farmers' party,[2] but these organizations
were here interested in business coöperation, financial legislation,
and general political " reform " rather than in the railroad problem, although the state granges did occasionally reflect the
struggle which was going on in the other states of the Northwest
by adopting resolutions expressing approval in general terms of
state and national regulation of railroads.[3] In 1871 the people
of Nebraska rejected a proposed constitution which contained
articles prohibiting local aid to railway companies and the consolidation of parallel or competing lines.[4] In 1875, however,
another attempt to provide the state with a new constitution
was successful, and this instrument reflects both the changing
sentiment in the state and the influence of the constitutional
and legislative enactments relative to railroads in the other
northwestern states.[5] As in many other state constitutions
adopted during this decade, railroads were declared to be public
highways and railroad companies common carriers, and the
consolidation of parallel or competing lines was prohibited.
The legislature was empowered to pass laws establishing rea-

---

[1] Thomas Allen, *The Railroad Problem* (pamphlet, 1875); *Appleton's Cyclopedia*,
1878, p. 579; Cullom Committee, *Report*, i. 112, ii. 797–800. See also Missouri
Railroad Commission, *Reports*, 1875, *et seq.*

[2] See above, pp. 58, 92, 97.

[3] Kansas State Grange, *Proceedings*, i (July, 1873); F. H. Dixon, " Railroad
Control in Nebraska," in *Political Science Quarterly*, xiii. 617–647 (December,
1898).

[4] *American Annual Cyclopedia*, 1871, p. 538.

[5] Thorpe, *Constitutions*, iv. 2381.

sonable maximum rates and was required to pass laws to prevent unjust discrimination, extortion, and other abuses of railway management. In spite of the mandatory character of this last provision. the agitation for restrictive legislation did not become intense until near the close of the decade and no legislation was secured until 1881.[1] In Kansas, likewise, the first law providing for state regulation of railroads was not enacted until 1883.[2]

On the Pacific coast, the farmers' organizations played a considerable part in movements for railway regulation during the decade of the seventies. The desire to curb the Central Pacific railroad, which practically controlled the transportation situation in California, was one of the causes for the organization of the farmers of the state into clubs and granges, and for the formation of the People's Independent party in 1873. At its very beginning the state grange resolved " to labor for the reduction of railroad fares and freights, by using all legitimate means to obtain the necessary legislation " and its proceedings are filled with resolutions, addresses, and reports of transportation committees discussing the railroad problem and demanding the establishment of maximum rates and other restrictive legislation.[3] In 1874 restrictive bills passed both houses of the legislature but neither became law.[4] At the next session in 1876, however, what was known as the O'Connor bill was enacted into law.[5] This measure established an appointive railroad commission. defined and prohibited extortion and discrimination, and limited the granting of free passes. The commission, however, was given no specific control over rates, the provisions of the bill proved to be too general to be of any value, and the contest was carried into the constitutional convention of 1878.

[1] Dixon, in *Political Science Quarterly*, xiii. 617–647 (December, 1898); Cullom Committee, *Report*, i. 113, ii. 1133.

[2] *Ibid.* i. 102.

[3] Carr, *Patrons of Husbandry*, 81, 87, 95, 134, 139, 143, 152, 176; *Nation*, xxi. 2 (July 1, 1875); *California Patron*, July 18, 1877, p. 5; *Prairie Farmer*, xliv. 355 (November 8, 1873).

[4] *American Annual Cyclopedia*, 1874, p. 100.

[5] *Appleton's Cyclopedia*, 1876, p. 83; H. H. Bancroft, *History of California*, vii. 826–828; Cullom Committee, *Report*, i. 87.

The control of this body was in the hands of the Kearneyite or Workingmen's party aided by the organized farmers of the state, and the outcome, so far as railroad regulation was concerned, was the enactment of the most radical provisions ever embodied in a state constitution.[1] All railroad and other transportation companies were declared to be common carriers and subject to legislative control; and the granting of passes to state officers, pooling with other carriers, and discrimination between places or persons, were prohibited. The constitution also made provision for an elective railway commission with the power of fixing maximum rates, which should be deemed by the courts to be conclusively just and reasonable. A law along the line of these provisions was enacted in 1880; but the agitation which had produced them soon died down, and the commission does not appear to have subjected the management of railroads to any considerable restrictions.[2]

In Oregon also, the Patrons of Husbandry were active in demanding railroad regulation during the seventies, and the farmers' Independent party, which played a considerable part in the election of 1874, declared for legislation fixing railroad charges.[3] In 1875, the platforms of all three parties, Democratic, Republican, and Independent, declared for legislation to control railroads;[4] but no law was forthcoming. Again in 1876 the state grange denounced the "exorbitant rates" and "oppressive monopoly" of the railroad companies and called upon the local granges to petition the legislature for relief.[5] Nothing was accomplished by this agitation, and it was not until 1885 that a restrictive railway measure was enacted in Oregon.[6] On the other hand, a reflection of the Granger railway legislation of the North Central states is seen in the railroad provisions of the constitution adopted by the new state of Colorado in

---

[1] Bancroft, *California*, vii. ch. xv; Thorpe, *Constitutions*, i. 437–442; Cullom Committee, *Report*, i. 86.

[2] Cullom Committee, *Report*, i. 87; Bancroft, *California*, vii. 399, 403–406.

[3] *Chicago Tribune*, April 17, 1874, p. 5.

[4] *Appleton's Cyclopedia*, 1875, p. 609.

[5] Oregon State Grange, *Proceedings*, iii. 16, 22, 42 (September, 1876).

[6] Cullom Committee, *Report*, i. 119.

1876.[1] These provisions, which empowered the general assembly to alter or repeal charters and forbade unreasonable discrimination, do not appear to have been the result of any particular agitation at the time and were not followed up by restrictive legislation until the middle of the next decade.

The Granger movement for railroad regulation had its origin, as has been seen, in Illinois and the neighboring states of the upper Mississippi Valley during the later sixties. At about the same time another movement for the regulation or rather supervision of railroads was getting under way in another part of the country. It will be desirable to glance at this movement briefly because its influence was mingled with the Granger influence in the railway legislation of many of the eastern and southern states, and indeed of several of the Granger states themselves after the movement which began there had spent itself. Even before the Civil War, railroad commissions for various purposes had been established in several of the New England states; but it was not until the latter part of the decade 1860–70, when the abuses of railway management were arousing the people throughout the country, that any serious attempt was made to secure state supervision. In 1869 Massachusetts established a railroad commission to which practically no mandatory authority was given, but which, by the application of the force of publicity, was able to exercise considerable influence over the management of railroads; and this commission, like the mandatory commission of Illinois established by the laws of 1871 and 1873, has served as a model for similar boards in a number of other states.[2]

The movement which led to the establishment of this Massachusetts commission seems to have started with the commercial rather than the agricultural class, and no evidence has been found that the order of Patrons of Husbandry in Massachusetts interested itself at all in the subject of railroad regulation during the period. In New Hampshire and Vermont also, the Grangers

---

[1] Thorpe, *Constitutions*, i. 504–506.

[2] On the Massachusetts commission, see Adams, *Railroads*, 137–143; Johnson, *American Railway Transportation*, 352–355; Massachusetts Railroad Commission, *Reports*, 1870, *et seq.*; Cullom Committee, *Report*, i. 66–71.

were not at first especially interested in the railroad problem and in each of these states the state granges accepted and thanked the railroad companies for reduced rates to the annual sessions.[1] Later in the decade, however, these state granges are found complaining of high rates and discriminations in railway service and asking for legislation to remedy the evils. The New Hampshire State Grange addressed a petition to the legislature along these lines in 1879 and it was claimed that the passage by the House of Representatives of a bill to equalize railroad rates and abolish free passes was a result of this petition.[2] This measure was rejected by the Senate but a " short haul " law was enacted prohibiting higher transportation rates for a less than a greater distance on the same line.[3] The influence of the Grange may also have been a factor in securing the Vermont " short haul " law of 1882, and the New Hampshire law of 1883 establishing a commission with power to fix maximum rates.[4]

The farmers do not appear to have played any special part in the movement in New York which led to the Hepburn report of 1879 and the law of 1882, and the law itself was of the Massachusetts or supervisory rather than the Granger type.[5] In Pennsylvania, however, the constitution adopted in 1873 shows clearly the influence of the Illinois constitution of 1870 in provisions forbidding free passes, unjust discrimination, and the consolidation of competing lines.[6] The legislation which ensued in 1874 was of a very conservative character,[7] and there seems to be no indication that the Grange or any other farmers' organ-

---

[1] New Hampshire State Grange, *Proceedings*, iii. 37 (December, 1876); Vermont State Grange, *Proceedings*, iv. 29 (December, 1875).

[2] New Hampshire State Grange, *Proceedings*, vii (1880).

[3] Cullom Committee, *Report*, i. 116.

[4] *Ibid.* 117, 132.

[5] Hugo Meyer, *Government Regulation of Railway Rates*, 216–230. See also *Industrial Age*, November 22, 1873, p. 4, and New York State Grange, *Proceedings*, ii (January, 1875).

[6] See Article XVI, section 10, and Article XVII, sections 1, 3, 4, 8, 10, in Thorpe, *Constitutions*, v. 3144–3147. Cf. Illinois State Farmers' Association, *Proceedings*, ii. 34–36 (December, 1873); Wisconsin Railroad Commission, *Reports*, 1874, p. 80.

[7] Cullom Committee, *Report*, i. 122–124. See also *Appleton's Cyclopedia*, 1879, p. 719.

ization was actively engaged in agitating for railroad regulation in Pennsylvania.

In Ohio, Indiana, and Michigan, however, the sentiments of the farmers on the railroad question were somewhat the same as in Illinois and Wisconsin and they made use of their organizations to agitate for restrictive legislation, but without any considerable success. A law was enacted in Ohio in 1873 fixing a maximum freight rate of five cents per ton mile and containing a "short haul" clause:[1] but no provision was made for its enforcement and the agitation on the part of the farmers' organizations continued.[2] When the state grange met for its first annual session in 1874, a proposition to ask for reduced rates on the return fare was voted down on the ground that the members should not put themselves under obligations to the railroad companies. This was followed up at the next session in March, 1875, by a resolution demanding legislation to subject railroad corporations to the control of state authority,[3] but the legislature failed to respond.

In Indiana a somewhat similar situation prevailed. The state grange complained of the mismanagement of railroads in 1873, and in 1874 adopted a resolution asking for laws to make the railroads " serve the people instead of ruling them, and compel them to carry passengers and freights at rates in proportion to the actual cost of the road, and local in proportion to through freights ";[4] but no legislation of the sort was secured during the decade. Michigan enacted a law in 1873 establishing a single commissioner with supervisory powers and limiting

[1] Cullom Committee, *Report*, i. 119; Wisconsin Railroad Commission, *Reports*, 1874, p. 80. Ohio had a single railroad commissioner with advisory powers as early as 1867. *Ibid*. In January, 1873, a state agricultural convention requested legislation to limit freight and passenger charges and prevent discrimination. *Cincinnati Semi-Weekly Gazette*, January 10, 1873. This may have had some influence on the ensuing legislation.

[2] *Chicago Tribune*, June 18, 1873, p. 5. See also *Cincinnati Semi-Weekly Gazette*, September 26, 1873, p. 5 (" The Ohio Campaign ") and October 28, 1873, p. 4 (" Capturing the Grangers ").

[3] Ohio State Grange, *Proceedings*, i. 9, 22, 26 (1874), ii. 19, 27 (1875); Ellis, in *Ohio Farmer*, c. 472 (December 19, 1901).

[4] *Prairie Farmer*, xliv. 403 (December 30, 1873); Indiana State Grange, *Proceedings*, iv. 30 (November, 1874).

passenger fares to three cents per mile.[1] The farmers were not satisfied with this and in January, 1874, the state grange demanded " such legislation as will . . . compel all railroad companies to carry passengers and freight at reasonable uniform rates." [2] No response was made by the legislature to this demand, and the Grange does not appear to have been a factor of considerable importance in securing any of the Michigan railway legislation.

In the states of the South the railroad enactments of the period seem to have been, for the most part, reflections of the Granger enactments of the northwestern states rather than the results of internal agitation. Besides Missouri, which has already been considered, seven southern states adopted new constitutions during the years 1871–80 [3] These states were Alabama, 1875; Arkansas, 1874; Georgia, 1877; Louisiana, 1879; North Carolina, 1876; Texas, 1876; and West Virginia, 1872; and in all but two of the new constitutions — those of North Carolina and Louisiana — the influence of the Illinois constitution and the other railroad enactments of the northwestern states is clearly discernible. Most of these constitutions, and this includes that of Louisiana also, declare railroads to be public highways, and the companies common carriers, but the most distinctively Granger sections are those which make it the duty of the legislatures to pass laws to regulate freight and passenger charges and to prevent discriminations. Mandatory provisions of this sort are found in every one of the five constitutions. In addition, the constitutions of Alabama, Texas, and West Virginia forbade the consolidation of parallel or competing lines,[4] and those of Alabama and Arkansas contained provisions against the issuance of free passes to public officials. The constitution of Arkansas also contained a " short haul "

---

[1] Cullom Committee, *Report*, i. appendix, 34–36; Iowa Railroad Commission, *Reports*, 1878, p. 53; Michigan Railroad Commission, *Reports*, 1873, *et seq.*

[2] Michigan State Grange, *Proceedings*, i. 31 (1874). See also *ibid.* ii. 31, vi (1875, 1878).

[3] For these constitutions, see Thorpe, *Constitutions*.

[4] In the case of West Virginia this was permitted with the consent of the legislature.

clause applying to all traffic on the same line in the same direction, and rebating was prohibited by the constitution of Georgia.

Legislation in accordance with these constitutional requirements followed in most of the states. Here again the influence of the more distinctively Granger legislation of the northwestern states is seen. The West Virginia act of 1873 divided the railroads into classes and established complete schedules of freight rates;[1] the Arkansas act of 1873, adopted a year before the new constitution went into effect, and the Texas acts of 1876, 1879, and 1882 established maximum rates in general terms; and the acts of Georgia in 1879 and Alabama in 1881 established railroad commissions with power to regulate rates.[2] Although this legislation was influenced indirectly by the Granger movement, the farmers of the South, and more particularly the Patrons of Husbandry, do not, as a rule, seem to have played any considerable part in the movement.[3] Thus the state grange of Texas, at its organization in 1873, declared that it was not antagonistic to railroads but recognized the benefits conferred by them, and later it endeavored to secure congressional aid for a Texas and Pacific railway;[4] while the *Southern Farmers' Monthly* in 1880 advised the farmers of Georgia to keep out of the controversy over railroad legislation in that state.[5]

There are some instances, however, of Grange agitation for railroad regulation in the southern states; in Arkansas, for example, the state grange memorialized the legislature in 1877

[1] This act remained on the statute books for some time, but it is said to have been ineffective. Cullom Committee, *Report*, i. 134.

[2] Cullom Committee, *Report*, i. 78-86, 131; *Appleton's Cyclopedia*, 1879, p. 420. For railroad opposition to this legislation, see E. P. Alexander, *Reply to Circular No. 19 of the Railroad Commission of Alabama* (pamphlet, 1881) and H. S. Haines, *The Railroads and the State* (pamphlet, 1879).

[3] This conclusion is based upon the examination of a large number of proceedings of southern state granges and southern agricultural papers of the period.

[4] Texas State Grange, *Minutes*, 7, 10 (October, 1873 and April, 1874), *Proceedings*, i. 11, 28 (1874); National Grange, *Proceedings*, viii. 85-88 (February, 1875); *Resolutions of Legislatures, Boards of Trade, State Granges, etc., Favoring Government Aid to the Texas and Pacific Railway* (pamphlet, 1874).

[5] *Southern Farmers' Monthly* (Savannah), iii. 214 (July, 1880).

for a law establishing maximum rates, but at the same time committees were appointed to secure reduced rates by negotiating with the railroads and by contracting to give all business of Grangers to certain lines,[1] a treating with the enemy which would not have been countenanced by the northwestern granges for a moment. In Virginia and Tennessee, likewise, the state granges were interested in efforts to secure reduced rates by negotiations with the companies; but the Virginia Grange appointed a committee in 1874 to memorialize the legislature for a law prohibiting free passes.[2] The next year the Virginia legislature did pass an act designed to prevent discrimination in charges, but this was superseded in 1877 by the establishment of a commission of the Massachusetts type with supervisory and advisory powers.[3] The state grange of South Carolina appealed to the legislature in 1877 and 1878 for laws to prevent discrimination and other evils in railroad management. A conservative law, but one which was approved by the officials of the grange, was enacted in 1878.[4] The influence of the Patrons may also have been a factor in securing the more radical restrictive legislation of 1881.[5] In Kentucky and Tennessee, also, the agitation of the neighboring states was reflected in attempts to enact radical railroad laws about 1875, and the Grangers seem to have taken part in these to some extent, but no legislation was secured in either state during the decade.[6]

As a result of this survey of state legislation for the control of railroads during the decade of the seventies it is evident that the Granger movement was a considerable factor in procuring and shaping the course of this legislation in a large number of states, while its indirect influence can be traced in the railroad

[1] Arkansas State Grange, *Proceedings*, v. 15, 24 (1875).

[2] Virginia State Grange, *Proceedings*, Special session, 24, 34 (1874); Tennessee State Grange, *Proceedings*, ii. 39 (1875).

[3] Wisconsin Railroad Commission, *Reports*, 1875, p. 39; Cullom Committee, *Report*, i. 132–134.

[4] South Carolina State Grange, *Minute Book* (Ms.), 75, 88, 100.

[5] Cullom Committee, *Report*, i. 125.

[6] Tennessee State Grange, *Proceedings*, ii. 31, 39, 48, 57, 61, 62, 66 (February, 1875); Wisconsin Railroad Commission, *Reports*, 1875, p. 40; Cullom Committee, *Report*, i. 107, 127.

enactments of nearly every state which has attempted to solve the problem, either during the period or since. Several of the principal features of American railway legislation can be looked upon as primarily Granger in their origin. Among these are (1) the establishment of schedules of maximum rates by direct legislative enactment, a method which has been generally superseded so far as freight charges are concerned by (2) the establishment of a commission with authority to draw up schedules of maximum rates; (3) the establishment of the maximum rates. whether fixed by the legislature or by a commission, as *prima facie* evidence of reasonableness before the courts; (4) the attempt to prevent discrimination between places by *pro rata* or " short haul " clauses; (5) the attempt to preserve competition by forbidding the consolidation of parallel lines; (6) the prohibition of the granting of free passes to public officials. Some of these features have been found by experience to be unsatisfactory or inconsistent with each other — for example the attempt to preserve competition as a vital force in keeping down rates and at the same time to prevent discrimination between places has been practically a failure — but, on the whole. it is not too much to say that the fundamental principles upon which American regulation of railroads by legislation has developed were first worked out in the Granger states of the Northwest during the decade of the seventies.

CHAPTER VI

GRANGER RAILWAY LEGISLATION (CONTINUED)

THE GRANGER CASES AND THE SUPREME COURT

PERHAPS the most important results of the Granger railroad legislation are to be found in the series of decisions of the United States Supreme Court in what have always been known as the Granger cases. These cases were the first to bring before this high judicial tribunal the question of the right of a state government to fix maximum rates for railroad freights and fares and warehouse charges, and though parts of these decisions have been reversed by later decisions, the fundamental principle of the right of a state to regulate a business which is public in its nature, a principle which was established by these cases, has been maintained and constantly applied ever since. No true conception of the present status of the law as to railway regulation can be obtained without an understanding of the principles involved in the Granger cases.

In the October term of the Supreme Court of the United States, 1876, decisions were handed down together in the cases of Munn v. Illinois; Chicago, Burlington, and Quincy Railroad Company v. Iowa; Peik v. Chicago and Northwestern Railroad Company and Lawrence v. Same; Chicago, Milwaukee, and St. Paul Railroad Company v. Ackley; Winona and St. Peter Railroad Company v. Blake; Southern Minnesota Railroad Company v. Coleman; and Stone v. Wisconsin.[1] In a dissenting opinion on the last of these cases Justice Field spoke of them as the "Granger cases," presumably because the legislation of Illinois, Wisconsin, Iowa, and Minnesota which gave rise to them had been generally spoken of as the Granger laws. With

[1] 94 *United States Reports*, 113 *et seq.*; Illinois Railroad Commission, *Reports*, 1877, pp. 5-27.

these cases might be included Ruggles *v*. Illinois,[1] decided in 1883, in which also one of these laws was in question, and which was decided on the same principles.[2]

In the first of these Granger cases, Munn *v*. Illinois, the question involved was not the right of a state to regulate railroads but the validity of the Illinois law of 1871 fixing maximum rates for the storage of grain in the elevators of Chicago. In this decision, however, were laid down the fundamental principles which were followed in the other cases arising out of the railroad laws, and, moreover, the warehouse act in question was as much a Granger law as any of the restrictive railroad acts. The way in which this case arose has been described in a previous section.[3] The supreme court of Illinois had decided the case against the warehousemen in 1874 and it had then been carried to the United States Supreme Court. There the attorneys for the appellants claimed that the act in question was repugnant to three separate sections of the federal constitution: Article I, section 8, which conferred upon Congress the power to regulate interstate commerce; Article I, section 9, which forbade preference to the ports of one state over those of another; and Amendment XIV, which prohibited a state from depriving any person of property without due process of law.

The opinion of the court, delivered by Chief-Justice Waite, considered the last of these objections first. It was pointed out that it had long been customary, both in England and America,

---

[1] 108 *United States*, 526. This case presented no new features but came up too late to be decided with the other Granger cases. See above, p. 152.

[2] For discussion of the principles involved in these cases, see James K. Edsall, " The Granger Cases and the Police Power," in American Bar Association, *Reports*, x. 288–316 (1887); W. E. Dunbar, " State Regulation of Prices and Rates," in *Quarterly Journal of Economics*, ix. 305–332 (April, 1895); Alton D. Adams, " Reasonable Rates," in *Journal of Political Economy*, xii. 79–97 (December, 1903), reprinted in W. Z. Ripley, *Railway Problems*, ch. xxiii; H. S. Smalley, *Railroad Rate Control in its Legal Aspects* (American Economic Association, *Publications*, 3d series, vii. no. 2), reprinted in part in Ripley, *Railway Problems*, ch. xxiv; Albert Stickney, *State Control of Trade and Commerce by National or State Authority*, ch. iv; J. F. Hudson, *The Railways and the Republic*, ch. iv; *Nation*, xxiv. 143 (March 8, 1877). See also David A. Wells, " How will the Supreme Court Decide the Granger Railroad Cases ? " in *Nation*, xix. 282–284 (October 29, 1874).

[3] See above, p. 143.

to fix by law maximum rates of charges for ferries, common carriers, hackmen, bakers, millers, wharfingers, innkeepers, etc., and that such regulation had never been considered as necessarily depriving the owner of property without due process of law. The basis of this right of regulation is to be found in the fact that the property in question has been devoted to a use in which the public has an interest and is therefore subject to be controlled by the public for the common good. It then remained to consider whether the business of warehousemen in Chicago was one in which the public had such an interest as would justify its regulation by the state. After pointing out its great extent and importance, the large number of people affected by it, and the fact that it might be a virtual monopoly, the court reached the conclusion that " if any business can be clothed ' with a public interest and cease to be *juris privati* only,' this has been."

The attorneys for the warehousemen had insisted that, even admitting the public interest in the business, the owners were entitled to a reasonable compensation for the use of their property and that what is reasonable is a judicial and not a legislative question. To this the court replied that the practice had been otherwise, and that if the right to regulate existed at all, it implied the right to fix maximum charges. " We know that this is a power which may be abused, but that is no argument against its existence. For protection against abuses by legislation, the people must resort to the polls, not to the courts."

In answer to the objection based upon the power of Congress to regulate interstate commmerce, it was admitted that the warehouses might incidentally become connected with interstate commerce; but it was declared that " certainly until Congress acts in reference to their interstate relations the state may exercise all the powers of government over them, even though in so doing it may indirectly operate upon commerce outside its immediate jurisdiction." Finally the remaining objection, based upon section 9 of Article I, of the federal constitution, was brushed aside with the remark that the section in question was a limitation upon the powers of Congress and in no respect affected the states. The judgment of the supreme court of Illinois was therefore affirmed.

To this decision of the court, Justices Field and Strong dissented and Justice Field prepared a long dissenting opinion which was concurred in by Justice Strong. In this opinion, the ground was taken that the act in question was invalid because it amounted to a deprivation of property without due process of law. The basis of the precedents cited of the regulation of ferries, common carriers, etc., was declared to be, not the public interest in the business, but the fact that there was some special privilege granted by the state which of course gave to the state the right to regulate the conditions under which the privilege should be enjoyed. The warehousemen of Chicago enjoyed no such special right or privilege, and therefore their charges could not justly be interfered with.[1]

The court next took up the railroad cases. The public nature of the railway business had been specifically declared by the Supreme Court in 1872 in the case of Olcott *v.* The Supervisors [2] and so it was possible to apply the general principle enunciated in Munn *v.* Illinois. There was, however, another point to be considered. The famous Dartmouth College case [3] had determined that a charter was a contract in the meaning of Article I, section 10, of the United States constitution, which prohibits a state from impairing the obligation of contracts. and the railroads, through their attorneys, maintained that the charters granted to them, either directly or by implication, the right to fix the charges, and that in consequence the state was

---

[1] The dissenting judges hardly established their contention, for it is difficult to see why the state could not consider the right to operate a warehouse as a special privilege as well as the right to conduct a ferry, an inn, or a bakeshop. It seems that the doctrine of public interest is really the basis for requiring special grants, franchises, or licenses in all these cases. The dissenting opinion does make it plain, however, that the majority of the court had laid down no satisfactory rule for distinguishing between a business that is *juris privati* and one that has been " clothed with a public interest." Cf. Dunbar, " State Regulation," in *Quarterly Journal of Economics*, ix. 305–332.

[2] 16 *Wallace*, 678. See above, p. 11.

[3] 4 *Wheaton*, 518.

estopped from interfering. In the first of these cases — Chicago, Burlington, and Quincy Railroad Company *v.* Iowa, an appeal from the Circuit Court of the United States for the district of Iowa — the opinion of the court applied the principle of Munn *v.* Illinois. It was admitted that the charter was a contract which could not be impaired by a state law; but it was pointed out that the charter in question was obtained under the general incorporation law of Iowa, which reserved to the legislature the right to make rules and regulations.

In Peik *v.* Chicago and Northwestern Railway Company and Lawrence *v.* same, both Wisconsin cases, the special point involved was a provision in the charter of the company by which it was specifically authorized " to demand or receive such sum or sums of money for the transportation of persons and property, and for the storage of property, as it shall deem reasonable." The railroad attorneys maintained that by this express grant the state was estopped from regulating the charges of the company. It was shown, however, that the state constitution, in force when the charter was granted, contained a provision declaring that all acts creating corporations " may be altered or repealed by the legislature at any time after their passage," [1] and the court held that this restriction permitted the legislature to place the corporation on the same footing as a natural person.

The question of interstate commerce was brought up in these cases again, as the Wisconsin law applied to all shipments taken up or set down within the state. The court here went even further than in Munn *v.* Illinois by declaring that " until Congress acts in reference to the relations of this company to interstate commerce, it is certainly within the power of Wisconsin to regulate its fares, etc., so far as they are of domestic concern." With regard to the reasonableness of the rates fixed, the court declared as in Munn *v.* Illinois that it was bound by the limit fixed by the legislature and " if it has been improperly fixed, the legislature, not the courts, must be appealed to for the change." The principles of Munn *v.* Illinois and Chicago,

[1] See above, p. 179.

Burlington, and Quincy Railway Company *v.* Iowa were therefore applied and the decrees of the lower court affirmed.

In another Wisconsin case — Chicago, Milwaukee, and St. Paul Railway Company *v.* Ackley — the question involved was the right of the company to recover more than the maximum fixed by the law, for transportation performed, by showing that the charge was no more than reasonable compensation. In accordance with the previous decisions the court determined that " the limit of recovery is that prescribed by the statute." The Minnesota cases — Winona and St. Peter Railway Company *v.* Blake and Southern Minnesota Railway Company *v.* Coleman — presented no new points, there being nothing in the charters " limiting the power of the State to regulate the rates of charge " ; and the case of Stone *v.* Wisconsin merely decided that a railroad charter granted by the territory, but not accepted nor the company organized until after the admission of the state, was subject to the reserved right of alteration contained in the state constitution.

To all of these cases Justices Field and Strong dissented and in connection with the last a dissenting opinion was presented covering the whole series. In Munn *v.* Illinois, as has been seen, these justices dissented on the ground that the business in question did not depend upon any special grant or privilege. This, of course, would not apply to the railroad cases, so the justices here based their dissent on the contractual character of the charters, holding that implied rights and privileges were as inviolable as those expressed. It was further asserted that the reserved power to alter all laws creating corporations " should not, in common honesty, be so used as to destroy or essentially impair the value of mortgages and other obligations executed under express authority of the state."

Taking the decisions of these Granger cases as a whole, the following propositions are established:

(1) A state may, under the police power, regulate, to the extent of fixing maximum charges, any business which is public in its nature or which has been " clothed with a public interest."

(2) The warehouse business (in Chicago) and the business of operating a railroad are sufficiently of a public nature to be subject to such regulation by the state.

(3) At least until Congress acts in the premises, a state may regulate interstate commerce so far as its citizens are affected.

(4) Although a railroad charter is a contract, it does not interfere with the right of a state to regulate charges unless it contains a direct stipulation to that effect, and the charters are subject to reservations contained in the general laws under which they are obtained or in the state constitutions.[1]

(5) The courts are not competent to review the question of the reasonableness of charges fixed by the legislature, or in other words the power of the state to regulate rates is subject to no restraint by the courts.

Of these five propositions, the first, second, and fourth have been reaffirmed in many later cases, have been consistently followed by the state courts, and can be considered as permanently established. The third and fifth, on the other hand, have been completely reversed by later decisions of the United States Supreme Court.

It was not until eleven years after the decision of the Granger cases that Congress finally enacted a law to regulate interstate commerce. During most of this period the courts and the legislatures, as a rule, acted upon the assumption that it was within the province of a state to regulate inter- as well as intrastate commerce in so far as its citizens were affected thereby. Indeed it seems to have been believed by some that the whole field of railroad regulation might be covered by state action and that there would be no need of federal regulation. In 1886, however, the case of the Wabash, St. Louis and Pacific Railway

[1] The question as to whether a legislature could grant a valid charter containing a contract which would restrain future legislatures from regulating charges, and thus in effect limit the police power of the state, was not involved in any of these cases but the implication from the opinion in Peik *v.* Chicago and Northwestern Railway Company would seem to be that it could. See, however, Edsall, "The Granger Cases and the Police Power," in American Bar Association, *Reports*, x. 301–316.

Company *v.* Illinois,[1] decided by the supreme court of Illinois along the lines of the decisions in the Granger cases, was carried to the United States Supreme Court, and gave rise to a decision that no state can exercise any control over commerce which passes beyond its limits. This decision, which has ever since been accepted as the correct interpretation of the federal constitution on the subject, put an end to the attempts of state governments to regulate interstate commerce and gave an added impetus to the movement which resulted in the enactment by Congress of the interstate commerce act of 1887.[2]

The principle that the right of a state to fix maximum rates is unlimited and therefore not subject to judicial review was practically unquestioned for nine years after the decision of the Granger cases. In 1885, however, Chief-Justice Waite, in delivering an opinion in the Mississippi case of Stone *v.* Farmers' Loan and Trust Company,[3] intimated that the courts would interfere to prevent such regulation as would amount to " a taking of private property for public use without just compensation, or without due process of law." This was a mere *obiter dictum* in this case; but it left the status of the law on the point in doubt until finally, in 1890. in Chicago, Milwaukee and St. Paul Railway Company *v.* Minnesota,[4] the Supreme Court declared a Minnesota law invalid because it denied a judicial hearing as to reasonableness of rates There has been considerable doubt as to the exact scope of this decision. Justice Bradley prepared a long and vigorous dissenting opinion, concurred in by Justices Gray and Lamar, in which he declared that it practically overruled the Granger cases. On the other hand, in Budd *v.* New York, decided in 1892, the court seemed to return in a measure to the older position and denied that the Granger cases had been reversed. Step by step, however, the courts have since been building up the doctrine of judicial

[1] 118 *United States,* 557.
[2] Cf. Hudson, *The Railways and the Republic* (3d ed., 1889), 329 and note; Cullom Committee, *Report,* i. 34–38; Johnson, *American Railway Transportation,* 359–361.
[3] 116 *United States,* 307.
[4] 134 *United States,* 418.

review of the reasonableness of rates fixed by legislation, a doctrine which has materially limited the rights of the state to regulate railway charges.[1]

In spite of these later developments, the fundamental principle of the Granger cases still stands, and no one today questions the existence of a right on the part of a state to regulate, to the extent of fixing reasonable maximum charges, railroads and other businesses of a public nature. Upon the establishment of this right has depended the voluminous restrictive railroad legislation of the last forty years.

THE AGITATION FOR FEDERAL REGULATION [2]

The Granger agitation for government control of railroads had not been under way very long before it became evident to many that the problem was national in its scope and that the evils complained of could not be entirely removed by even the most radical state legislation. It was believed by some that a state might exercise jurisdiction over any railroad traffic taken up or set down within its borders; the early Granger laws were framed with this intention; and the United States Supreme Court upheld this opinion in 1876.[3] It soon became evident, however, that economic conditions made any effective regulation of interstate traffic by state laws practically impossible, and that any serious attempt to enforce such legislation by several states would lead to great confusion.[4] It was natural, then, that there should be a demand for federal legislation to supplement the Granger laws which were being passed in the western states.

---

[1] Smalley, *Railroad Rate Control* (American Economic Association, *Publications*, 3d series, vii. no. 2); Adams, "Reasonable Rates," in *Journal of Political Economy*, xii. 79–97; Dunbar, "State Regulation," in *Quarterly Journal of Economics*, ix. 305–332.

[2] On this general topic see L. H. Haney, *A Congressional History of Railways, 1850–1887*, chs. xix, xxi, xxii. This section was written before a copy of the above came to hand.

[3] See above, pp. 208–213.

[4] See E. J. James, *The Agitation for Federal Regulation of Railways* (American Economic Association, *Publications*, 1st series, ii. no. 3).

The first serious consideration of the regulation of railroad rates by Congress was in the second session of the Fortieth Congress (1867–68). At this session the Senate committee on commerce was instructed to consider the expediency of establishing maximum rates on interstate roads,[1] and the House committees on judiciary and on roads and canals were instructed to inquire into the constitutional power of Congress to regulate rates on railroads engaged in interstate commerce.[2] The first two of these committees failed to report, but on June 9, 1868, the House committee on roads and canals submitted the first report which was ever made to Congress on the subject of railroad regulation.[3] In this report, the committee declared not only that Congress had the power to regulate interstate traffic on railroads, but that such regulation would be expedient. The appointment of a select committee to consider the subject and prepare a bill was suggested in the report, but the House took no further action.[4] Resolutions instructing committees to investigate the subject were also adopted by both houses of the Forty-first Congress,[5] and the first bills looking toward a general system of federal control of railroad rates were introduced into the House of Representatives in the second session of the Forty-second Congress.[6] One of these, introduced by Mr. McCrary of Iowa, was entitled, a bill " to require uniform charges for transporting freight and passengers by railroad companies and other common carriers, and to prevent unjust

[1] *Senate Journal*, 40 Congress, 2 session, 76; *Congressional Globe*, 343.

[2] *House Journal*, 456, 640, *Congressional Globe*, 1632, 2331. It is interesting to note that the Senate resolution indicates no doubt as to the constitutional power of Congress to regulate interstate rates on railroads, but proposes to inquire into the expediency of such legislation, while the House resolutions seem to take it for granted that such regulation would be desirable, if constitutional, and call for an investigation of the power of Congress in the premises.

[3] *House Journal*, 828; *Congressional Globe*, 2977; *House Reports*, ii. no. 57; James, *The Agitation for Federal Regulation*, 33.

[4] The report was accompanied by a twelve page minority report signed by Kerr of Indiana and Barnum of Connecticut, which took issue with the majority report on both the constitutionality and expediency of the proposed legislation.

[5] *House Journal*, 41 Congress, 2 session, 84; *Senate Journal*, 3 session, 569, 1943.

[6] *House Journal*, 197, 561, 654.

discrimination in favor of or against particular persons or places." None of these bills was reported by the committee to which it was referred.

Meanwhile the agitation for state control of railways, which came later to be known as the Granger movement, had been getting under way in the West and had already produced the radical provisions of the Illinois constitution of 1870, and the Illinois and Minnesota laws of 1871.[1] The newspapers and magazines began to be filled with articles discussing the abuses which had appeared in railroad construction and management; and the opinion grew that there was a railroad problem to be solved and that the federal government should aid in its solution. The aspect of the problem which attracted the most attention at this time was that of securing cheap transportation to the eastern markets for the products of the western farmers;[2] and, as it was quite generally believed that insufficient facilities and lack of competition were the causes of the prevalent high rates, the duty of Congress seemed to many to be to construct or aid in the construction of additional canals and trunk railroads from the Mississippi River to the seaboard.

President Grant in his annual message of December, 1872,[3] called attention to the fact that " various enterprises for the more certain and cheaper transportation of the constantly increasing Western and Southwestern products to the Atlantic seaboard " would come before Congress at that session, and recommended the appointment of a committee to gather information on the subject. In the House an attempt was made to authorize the appointment by the president of a commission of three members to collect information concerning interstate railroads.[4] It was proposed that this commission should investigate the earnings, expenditures, rates of charge, and operations

[1] See above, pp. 123–205.

[2] Cf. Johnson, *American Railway Transportation*, 367; James, *The Agitation for Federal Regulation*, 34. See also, Martin, *Grange Movement* (published in 1874).

[3] Richardson, *Messages and Papers of the Presidents*, vii. 195.

[4] *House Journal*, 42 Congress, 3 session, 263, 266, 275, 302; *Congressional Globe*, 893, 1057.

of railroads and report to the president its findings, including statements of what rates ought to be charged, whether they should be uniform per mile or not, and what legislation might be necessary on the subject. This measure failed to pass the House, but the Senate adopted a resolution for the appointment of a select committee of seven on transportation routes to the seaboard, to consider the part of the president's message relating to cheap transportation. The committee was appointed by the vice-president, with Senator Windom of Minnesota as its chairman, but was able to accomplish little during the session.[1]

The Senate also adopted several resolutions instructing its committees on judiciary and on commerce to inquire into and report by bills or otherwise upon the constitutionality and expediency of legislation to regulate rates on interstate commerce, and the right of Congress to construct and operate or authorize the construction of interstate railroads.[2] The committee on judiciary appears to have paid no attention to these resolutions; but the committee on commerce presented a report, February 20, 1873, in which it declared that it lacked the necessary information to report a bill even if prepared to report favorably " which they were not." [3] This was accompanied by a minority report from the chairman of the committee, Senator Vickers of Maryland, which argued at length against the constitutionality and expediency of federal regulation of railroads. This ended the attempts to take action at this session; but shortly before adjournment an important step was taken, when the Senate committee on transportation routes to the seaboard was increased to nine members; was authorized to sit during the recess at such places as it might designate, to employ a clerk and a stenographer, and to send for persons and papers; and was instructed to investigate and report to the Senate at the next session of Congress on the subject of transportation from the interior to the seaboard.[4]

[1] *Senate Journal*, 42 Congress, 3 session, 41, 73, 74, 75.

[2] *Ibid.* 29, 35, 72, 73.

[3] *Ibid.* 413; *Congressional Globe*, 1522; *Senate Reports*, no. 462.

[4] *Senate Journal*, 609, 615, 616, 625, 627.

That the time was ripe for this investigation was evident from the attention which the railroad question was attracting in 1873. The Granger movement was then at its height in the western states and the organizations which had been agitating for state legislation were beginning to call for action by the federal government as well. Thus the National Grange, at its first delegate session in 1873, established a committee on transportation and coöperation and in the next month the Iowa State Grange resolved to petition Congress " to regulate without delay, by a just and equitable law, the freights and fares of all railroads within the United States." [1] The governors of both Minnesota and Missouri in messages to the legislatures early in 1873 recognized the inadequacy of state legislation to control railroads and recommended that Congress be memorialized to assist by regulating commerce among the several states.[2] In the legislature of Illinois a joint resolution was adopted instructing the Senators and requesting the Representatives to work for a law regulating interstate commerce on railroads.[3] In Iowa, also, a similar resolution was adopted by the legislature, after being amended to reserve the right of the state to regulate rates within its borders.[4]

Besides these calls from the West for federal action on the railroad question, there were a number of movements of more national scope under way in 1873, which had " cheap transportation " among their objects. Of these, the most important was the National Cheap Transportation Association organized in New York City, May 6 and 7, 1873.[5] Delegates are said to have been present at this meeting from Illinois, Iowa, Michigan, and Indiana, and other states of the Mississippi Valley, as well as from most of the eastern states. The purpose of the

---

[1] National Grange, *Proceedings*, vi. 10, 20; *Prairie Farmer*, xliv. 51 (February 15, 1873).

[2] Minnesota, *Executive Documents*, 1872, i. 5–10; *American Annual Cyclopedia*, 1873, p. 519.

[3] Illinois, *Public Laws*, 1873–74, p. 152.

[4] Iowa, *Senate Journal*, 1873, pp. 29, 48–51, 74.

[5] Periam, *The Groundswell*, 317–326; *American Annual Cyclopedia*, 1873, pp. 547, 754; *Nation*, xvi. 329, 383 (May 18, June 5, 1873); *Prairie Farmer*, xliv. 153 (May 17, 1873); *Industrial Age*, August 20, 1873, p. 7.

association is made clear in the resolutions adopted. These, after pointing out the unsatisfactory character of existing rates of transportation, due in part to insufficiency of avenues, declare:

that the duty of the hour, and the mission of this association is to obtain from Congress and the several State Legislatures such legislation as may be necessary to control and limit by law, within proper constitutional and legitimate limits, the rates and charges of existing lines of transportation.

Other resolutions advocated an increase in the means of transportation and recommended the establishment of subsidiary state, county, and local associations to assist in the solution of the problem. Josiah Quincy of Massachusetts, who seems to have been the leading spirit of this meeting, was made president of the association; and in November, 1873, he issued a call for a second meeting to be held in Washington, in January, 1874.[1] In September, 1873, another meeting was held in New York City at which a New York Cheap Transportation Association was formed and resolutions adopted. Senator Windom and other members of the Senate committee on transportation routes to the seaboard are said to have been present at this meeting.[2]

On May 20, 1873, a convention, called by Governor Smith of Georgia, met in Atlanta to discuss projects of cheap transportation between the South and the grain-growing states of the Northwest.[3] This convention was attended by governors of several southern and western states and by delegates from cities, granges, and other organizations, but its solution of the transportation problem was the construction of more roads and canals rather than the regulation of existing railroads. About a week later, May 28, 1873, the National Agricultural Congress met in Indianapolis and devoted most of its time

[1] In this call the railroad question was discussed at length and the conclusion reached that Congress should make a thorough investigation of the subject and consider the expediency of enacting laws to regulate railroads. *Prairie Farmer,* xliv. 353, 412 (November 8, December 27, 1873).

[2] *Ibid.* 299, 300 (September 20, 1873).

[3] *American Annual Cyclopedia*, 1873, pp. 319, 754-757.

and attention to the transportation problem.[1]   It also favored the construction of more railroads and canals; but adopted a resolution recommending :

that efforts be made and persevered in, until all railway corporations shall be subjected to the regulation of the General and State Governments, so as to insure the absolute and perpetual prohibition and prevention of extortionate charges and unjust discrimination.

Late in October of the same year, a Northwestern Farmers' Convention was held in Chicago with two hundred delegates present, mainly from Illinois but a few from the other states of the Northwest.[2]   The first object of this convention was stated by Mr. Flagg, the president of the Illinois State Farmers' Association, to be: " Cheap Transportation, embracing water transportation; regulations by legislation, State and National, of existing railways; Governmental railways."   Among the resolutions adopted by this convention was one requesting Congress " without needless delay to pass a maximum freight and passenger law regulating traffic between the States," and protesting " against the further granting of any subsidies whatever to private corporations of any kind."   Another resolution favored the construction and operation of canals by the national government.   In addition, the convention, by invitation of Senator Windom, appointed a committee to meet with the Senate committee on transportation routes to the seaboard and supply it with information and suggestions.

These various conventions, which are manifestations of the widespread interest in the transportation question during 1873, served to extend and keep alive that interest.   As a result, much attention was attracted by the investigations and report of the Windom committee, which began its sessions in New York in September.   Some complaint was heard of the railroad con-

[1] *American Annual Cyclopedia*, 1873, pp. 376–378, 754–757; *Nation*, xvi. 377 (June 5, 1873).

[2] For the proceedings of this convention in full, see Windom Committee, *Report*, ii. 653–673.   See also Martin, *Grange Movement*, 509; *American Annual Cyclopedia*, 1873, p. 368; *Prairie Farmer*, xliv. 315, 345–347 (October 4, November 1, 1873); *Chicago Tribune*, 1873, October 23, p. 3, October 24, p. 1; *Industrial Age*, September 27, 1873, p. 4.

nections of several members of the committee,[1] but it seems to have made as thorough an investigation of the subject as the time and the means at its disposal would permit. It met at various places in the East and in the Mississippi Valley, and also in the city of Washington; and took testimony from railroad officials, merchants and manufacturers, state railroad commissioners, and representatives of farmers' organizations. At the session in St. Louis in October, Hon. Willard C. Flagg and Samuel P. Tufts appeared as delegates from the Northwestern Farmers' Convention. Mr. Flagg presented the committee with a copy of the proceedings of the convention and also discussed the organization and objects of the Illinois State Farmers' Association of which he was president. The testimony of Mr. Tufts is especially interesting as representing the attitude of the more radical element among the western farmers.[2] Three propositions were advocated by Mr. Tufts: (1) Congress should enact maximum freight and passenger tariff laws with three cents per mile as the limit for passenger fares; (2) no subsidies should be given to manufacturing or transportation companies, and there should be no class legislation; (3) anyone interested pecuniarily in any commercial throughfare should be made ineligible to Congress. When questioned as to the constitutionality of the first of these propositions, in view of the binding force of contracts, he declared that the western people believed that all power rested with the people, and if the courts should declare this unconstitutional, " then do as they did in the Dred Scott decision, wipe the Supreme Court out and get one that would decide it."

The primary object of the Windom committee was the investigation of the problem of " cheap transportation " ; but it also took cognizance of all other phases of the railroad question which presented themselves, and its report contains the first comprehensive plan for the regulation by the federal government of interstate traffic on railroads.[3] The key to this report,

---

[1] *Nation*, xvii. 153, 250 (September 4, October 16, 1873).

[2] Windom Committee, *Report*, ii. 673–676. He stated that his views were derived from intercourse with other farmers in their clubs and conventions.

[3] See James, *The Agitation for Federal Regulation*, 35–37.

which was presented to the Senate, April 24, 1874, is to be found in the conclusion " that the problem of *cheap* transportation is to be solved through *competition*." As a consequence, a large part of the report was devoted to a discussion of various proposed waterways and freight railroads to be owned or controlled by the government.[1] With regard to legislation establishing rates and fares on existing lines, the committee declared that more definite and detailed information was needed than was in the possession of Congress or itself. It did, however, recommend a number of restrictive measures, which it declared " may be enacted with entire safety, reserving other matters of legislation for further inquiry and consideration." [2] Among these measures, the most important are: complete publicity of rates with prohibition of increases without reasonable notice to the public; prevention of the consolidation of parallel or competing lines; prohibition of discrimination against lake or river ports; and the establishment of a bureau of commerce to collect information and report to Congress on such subjects as rates and fares; classifications, rebates, and discriminations; receipts and expenditures; amount and value of railroad stocks and bonds; and amount and value of commodities transported.

Before this report was presented, a resolution had been introduced and discussed in the Senate for instructing the Windom committee to report a bill creating a commission to investigate and report as to what legislation was constitutional, necessary, and practicable for the regulation of interstate commerce.[3] No action was taken on this resolution; and the same was true of the McCrary bill received from the House, and of a bill introduced by Senator Dorsey of Arkansas which proposed to establish a national bureau of railroads, both of these measures being referred to the Windom committee.[4] Shortly after the committee's report was received, three other bills providing in various ways for the regulation of interstate commerce were introduced, but the Senate failed to take any action on the subject.

---

[1] Windom Committee, *Report*, i. 242.   [2] *Ibid*. 240–242.

[3] *Senate Journal*, 43 Congress, 1 session, 165, 173, 188; *Congressional Record*, 941–944.

[4] *Senate Journal*, 383, 461.

In the country at large, however, the demand for national legislation for the control of railroads was steadily increasing. On December 17, 1873, the Illinois State Farmers' Association declared that " we oppose any legislation by Congress, under the plea of regulating commerce between the States, which shall deprive the people of their present controlling influence through state legislation." [1] That this sentiment was not the prevalent one among the farmers of the Northwest is indicated by the fact that the state grange of Illinois, which met about a week earlier, adopted a resolution declaring that Congress should exercise its power to regulate interstate commerce by controlling railroads,[2] and the Iowa State Grange about the same time refused to adopt a resolution asserting the exclusive right of the state legislature to regulate railroads, on the ground that the constitution of the United States gives to Congress the power to regulate commerce between the states.[3] The Michigan State Grange also, at its first annual session in January, 1874, demanded " such legislation as will control and regulate the carrying trade of our country and compel all railroad companies to carry passengers and freight at reasonable and uniform rates," [4] which would seem to call for federal as well as state action.

The prevailing sentiment among the farmers of the West is also indicated by resolutions adopted by the state legislatures, for at this time most of these legislatures were controlled by the Granger element. Thus the general assembly of Illinois, early in 1874, adopted a joint resolution calling upon Congress to prevent unjust charges and discriminations on railroads engaged in interstate business,[5] and the legislature of Iowa about the same time declared in favor of congressional legislation to regulate freights and fares which could not be reached by state laws.[6] The demand for congressional action was not confined to the

[1] Illinois State Farmers' Association, *Proceedings*, ii. 100–109 (1873); *American Annual Cyclopedia*, 1873, p. 369.
[2] *Prairie Farmer*, xliv. 403 (December 9, 1873).
[3] Iowa State Grange, *Proceedings*, iv (1873).
[4] Michigan State Grange, *Proceedings*, i (1874).
[5] Illinois, *House Journal*, 1874, p. 199; *Senate Journal*, 1874, p. 313.
[6] Iowa, *House Journal*, 1874, pp. 420–422; *Senate Journal*, 1874, p. 313.

West, however, for the state Republican convention of Massachusetts adopted a resolution asserting the power of Congress over interstate commerce and calling upon it to exercise its powers so as to reduce freights and fares to proper rates.[1]

In pursuance of the call of President Josiah Quincy, the National Cheap Transportation Association met in Washington in January, 1874,[2] while Congress was in session. All granges, farmers' clubs, workingmen's unions, and merchants' and manufacturers' associations, in sympathy with the movement, were invited to send delegates, and a number of men prominent in the agricultural organizations of the western states were present at the meeting. The resolutions adopted by the association declared that relief from excessive rates and other abuses must be brought about by regulation and competition, and advocated the creation of a national bureau of commerce and transportation to take charge of the first of these propositions. Various projects for the construction of government canals and railroads were recommended to Congress and a committee was appointed to urge the desired legislation. The subject of transportation also received consideration at the meeting of the National Grange in St. Louis in February, 1874.[3] Master Adams discussed it at some length in his address and made it clear that he preferred restrictive legislation to the construction of new railroads and canals, as a solution of the problem. Colonel Smedley of Iowa presented, as the report of the committee on transportation and coöperation, a series of resolutions, one of which requested Congress to " so regulate the internal commerce between the States as to make the tax upon internal transportation approximate more justly the actual cost." This was adopted along with the rest of the report.

The greater responsiveness of the House of Representatives to public sentiment, as compared with the Senate, is well illus-

---

[1] *Congressional Record*, 43 Congress, 1 session, 2458.

[2] *Nation*, xviii. 52 (January 22, 1874); *Prairie Farmer*, xliv. 353, 412 (November 8, December 27, 1873). See also report of Colonel A. B. Smedley, delegate from Iowa, in Iowa, *Legislative Documents*, 1874, ii. no. 30. Smedley was prominent in Grange circles and was later master of the state grange.

[3] National Grange, *Proceedings*, vii. 14–16, 30, 58, 78 (1874).

trated by its action upon the railroad question in the first session of the Forty-third Congress (1873-74). Some nine different bills and one joint resolution embodying various propositions for the regulation of railroads were introduced at this session,[1] and the subject finally came before the House in the form of a bill " to regulate commerce among the several states," [2] reported by Mr. McCrary of Iowa, chairman of the committee on railroads and canals.[3] This measure proposed to prohibit extortion and unfair discrimination by railroads engaged in interstate commerce, and in order to determine what were reasonable rates, a commission of nine was to be established to make schedules of maximum rates for each railroad. Anyone aggrieved by higher charges, might bring suit against the railroad company in the courts and in such suits the commissioners' schedules were to be taken as *prima facie* evidence of reasonableness, but the corporations were to be permitted to prove the reasonableness of the charges if they could do so. No method was provided, as in the Illinois law of 1873, for *prima facie* evidence as to unjust discrimination,[4] but in other respects the two measures were similar in principle.

This McCrary bill was introduced in the House on January 20, 1874; but before it came up for consideration a resolution was adopted by a vote of 172 to 64 declaring that Congress possessed the constitutional power to regulate interstate commerce and that existing conditions demanded the prompt exercise of that power.[5] The debate on the McCrary bill was very extensive and involved various questions of constitutionality, state rights, and expediency.[6] Some of the representatives were in

---

[1] *House Journal*, index, p. 1543.

[2] The bill is printed in full in *Congressional Record*, 1946.

[3] McCrary had introduced one of the railroad bills in the previous Congress. He was a lawyer and later became consulting attorney for the Atchison, Topeka and Santa Fe Railroad Company. *Biographical Congressional Directory*, 667.

[4] The section prohibiting unjust discrimination seems to have been tacked on to the bill. It is clear that the interest at this time was in " cheap transportation " rather than in the prevention of discrimination.

[5] *House Journal*, 408-410.

[6] For the course of the McCrary bill in Congress, see *House Journal*, 272, 362, 520, 552, 556, 575, 595, 598, 610, 611, 614, 616, 618, 628, 656, 657, 659, 665; *Senate*

favor of more radical measures, providing for conclusive rates or for equal rates for equal distances, but all amendments were shut off by the previous question and the bill passed the House March 26, 1874, by vote of 121 to 115.[1]   In the Senate, as has been seen, the measure was referred to the Windom committee. This committee reported it back late in the session with amendments, but no action was taken.

The failure of Congress to enact the McCrary bill into law was followed by a lull in the agitation for federal control of railroads. The Granger element in the western states seems to have been more interested for the time being in efforts to enforce the state laws, and the failure or repeal of most of these laws naturally dampened the ardor of the advocates of restrictive legislation. The agitation never disappeared entirely, however, and occasional demands for federal action continued to come from the West. Thus the Anti-Monopoly state convention of Iowa, in June, 1874, demanded legislation both state and national, to " secure the industrial and producing interests of the country against all forms of corporate monopoly and extortion." [2] The Iowa Republicans also, in July, 1874, asserted that Congress possessed the power to regulate interstate commerce and should exercise it to prevent extortion and unjust discrimination.[3] The state granges of the West and the National Grange continued to discuss and pass resolutions on the railroad question and to call for national legislation,[4] but the order of Patrons of Husbandry was now rapidly declining in numbers and in influence. The National Cheap Transportation Association, likewise, held sessions in Richmond, Virginia, in December, 1874, and in Chicago in December, 1875; adopted

Journal, 383, 661; *Congressional Record*, 783, 1963–1968, 2044–2050, 2144–2164, 2171–2180, 2206–2209, 2230–2251, 2414–2437, 2459–2471, 2491–2493, and appendix, 6, 38, 75, 99, 137, 144, 149, 152, 161, 163, 169, 288, 495.

[1] The *Nation*, xviii. 211 (April 2, 1874) stated that the railroads paid no attention to the McCrary bill, because, if passed, it could not be enforced.   See also *ibid*. 17, 34, 87–89 (January, 8, 15, February 5, 1874).

[2] *American Annual Cyclopedia*, 1874, p. 418.

[3] *Ibid*. 419.

[4] National Grange, *Proceedings*, viii. 11, 85–90, 102, 107, 124, ix. 24, 40, 47, 58, 68, 152, 161, x. 12, 159 (February, November, 1875, November, 1876).

resolutions; and appointed committees to urge railroad legislation upon Congress; but the Chicago meeting seems to have been the last appearance of this organization.[1]

In Congress itself, but little interest was manifested in the subject from 1874 to 1878, and the various bills and resolutions failed to receive any attention. Finally, however, in the second session of the Forty-fifth Congress (1877–78), a bill for the regulation of interstate commerce was reported in the House by Mr. Reagan of Texas [2] as chairman of the committee on commerce and received consideration. This measure is extremely verbose and difficult to interpret, but it seems to embody the following provisions: (1) no railroad to discriminate between persons engaged in interstate commerce, or to grant rebates; (2) no railroad to charge higher rates for a short than for a longer haul on the same line; (3) no railroad to charge higher rates for interstate traffic than it charged for traffic wholly within a state; (4) schedules of rates to be publicly posted and variations therefrom prohibited.[3] A comparison of the provisions of this bill with those of the McCrary bill of 1874 indicates a change which had taken place in the transportation problem. In the early part of the decade the principal object of agitation and of the proposed laws such as the McCrary bill was " cheap transportation," especially for through traffic from the interior to the seaboard. By the time the Reagan bill made its appearance, the emphasis was laid upon the elimination of unjust discriminations between persons and places. This was a result of great reductions in through freights during the interval; and the force of competition, which had helped to bring about this reduction, was also responsible in large part for the increased discriminations.[4]

---

[1] *Prairie Farmer*, xlv. 363 (November 14, 1874); *American Annual Cyclopedia*, 1874, p. 799, 1875, p. 672.

[2] Reagan was a member of the order of Patrons of Husbandry. He later served on the railroad commission of Texas. See *Biographical Congressional Directory*, 761.

[3] The bill is printed in full in *Congressional Record*, 3412.

[4] See James, *The Agitation for Federal Regulation*, 37–39; Johnson, *American Railway Transportation*, 368.

Considerable opposition to the Reagan bill developed during the discussion. It was denounced by some as a measure in the interests of the corporations.[1] The principal objections, however, were the complicated language in which it was phrased and the fear that it might be construed to interfere with commerce wholly within a state. Later in the session, Reagan introduced a substitute measure, couched in simpler language and definitely excluding commerce within a state from its provisions, but with an added section prohibiting pooling. Time was lacking for the consideration of this substitute and it went over to the next session. By this time, the stream of petitions and memorials for restrictive railroad legislation, which had been trickling into Congress since early in the decade. had become a flood,[2] and the Reagan bill was quickly revived in the third session of the Forty-fifth Congress (1878–79).[3] Mr. Reagan's substitute measure was accepted by the House and the bill passed by vote of 130 to 104. In the Senate the measure was referred to the committee on commerce where it was allowed to sleep undisturbed, although one senator attempted to secure a report by introducing a resolution requesting early action.

The National Grange memorialized Congress in November, 1878, " to enact general laws, prohibiting unjust discrimination and to regulate the rates of freight and passage," and steps were taken in November, 1879, to inaugurate a general campaign of petitions to Congress among the farmers.[4] Partly as a result of this action, the Forty-sixth Congress was again flooded with petitions, memorials, and resolutions from citizens, granges, state legislatures, and boards of trade for the passage of the Reagan bill or some other measure for the regulation of interstate

[1] For the career of the Reagan bill at this session see *House Journal*, 241, 525, 991, 1039, 1043, 1068, 1089, 1102, 1149, 1170, 1184; *Congressional Record*, 442, 1340, 3096, 3275–3280, 3324–3327, 3392–3413, 3435–3521.

[2] *Senate Journal*, 44 Congress, 1 session, 411, 422, 428, 445; *House Journal*, 45 Congress, 2 session, 680, 763; *Senate Journal*, 45 Congress, 3 session, 538 (index); *House Journal*, 45 Congress, 3 session, 775 (index).

[3] *House Journal*, 70; *Senate Journal*, 48, 49, 131, 228, 254; *Congressional Record*, 93–102, 113, 117, 531, 1045, 1182.

[4] National Grange, *Proceedings*, xii. 67, 72, 96–98, xiii. 24, 39, 86, 121, 124, 135, 145 (1878, 1879).

commerce.[1] Mr. Reagan again introduced his bill early in the first session (1879), and several other railroad bills were introduced in both houses, but none of them was reported from the committees.[2] The next session (1879–80) saw the introduction of another batch of bills and resolutions on the subject. Finally, toward the close of the session, the House committee on commerce reported three bills, one of which was similar in its provisions to the Reagan bill.[3] These did not come up for consideration until the third session of this Congress (1880–81), when, after a brief debate in the House, the subject was dropped again.[4]

It seems probable that one reason for the failure to get the Reagan bill enacted into law was the feeling that it was but a half-way measure at best. This is indicated by the action of the National Grange at its session in November, 1880.[5] A resolution was reported by a committee, favoring the passage of the bill " now pending before Congress and commonly known as the Reagan bill." By vote of 33 to 11, the Grange amended this by adding the words " so amended as to prevent extortionate freights on all lines of railroad engaged in interstate commerce," and finally a substitute was adopted which made no mention of the Reagan bill. Later on, however, another resolution was adopted declaring:

That while the bill now pending before Congress to regulate inter-State commerce, commonly known as the Reagan Bill, does not, in the judgment of the National Grange, correct all the evils of railroad transportation, yet we accept it as a beginning of railroad legislation, and urge upon Subordinate Granges and farmers to petition their representatives in Congress to support and vote for it.[6]

[1] *House Journal*, 1 session, 712 (index under " Interstate commerce "); 2 session, 1645; 3 session, 687; *Senate Journal*, 1 session, 340; 2 session, 116, 152; 3 session, 531.   See also remarks of Mr. Conkling in *Congressional Record*, 2508.

[2] *House Journal*, 115, 140, 150, 160; *Senate Journal*, 30.

[3] *House Journal*, 35, 69, 71, 155, 180, 229, 246, 346, 433, 594, 630, 903, 1215; *Senate Journal*, 371, 437, 450; *Congressional Record*, 1154, 1862, 1864, 2506–2510.

[4] *House Journal*, 37, 59, 126, 150, 187, 312, 458, 554; *Congressional Record*, 17, 48, 362–366, 1154.

[5] National Grange, *Proceedings*, xiv. 28–31, 46–48, 62, 69, 74–79, 89–94, 144, 151, 156 (1880).   See also *ibid*. xv. 19–22, 97–101, 143, xvi. 13 (1881, 1882).

[6] A resolution was also adopted thanking those members of Congress who had supported the Reagan bill.

The failure of the Reagan bill by no means put an end to the agitation for federal regulation of railroads, but it does mark the end of that part of the agitation to which the term " Granger " can be distinctively applied. In some ways, indeed, it might be more appropriate to confine that term to the agitation which centered around the Windom committee report and the McCrary bill, and which was contemporaneous with the Granger legislation of the northwestern states. At any rate, after 1880, the influence of the agricultural element in the agitation for railroad regulation seems to have been relatively slight. This was due in part to the fact that the order of Patrons of Husbandry was giving way to other farmers' organizations interested more in financial questions than in railroad regulation; but still more to the growing interest which the manufacturing and commercial classes were displaying in the transportation problem. At session after session of Congress railroad bills were introduced and discussed, and in 1885 the Senate and House each passed different bills. In the same year the Senate established another select committee, with Senator Cullom of Illinois as chairman, to investigate the subject of railroad transportation during the recess of Congress; and the report of this Cullom committee, made in 1886, together with the Wabash decision by which the Supreme Court denied to the states any authority over interstate traffic, led to the enactment of the interstate commerce act of 1887.[1]

The claims of certain Grange enthusiasts that the credit for this act belongs to the order of Patrons of Husbandry [2] can hardly be substantiated. for an examination of the report of the Cullom committee shows that the demand for regulation of railroads was fully as insistent among merchants and manufacturers at this time as among farmers. It is true, however, that the Patrons of Husbandry and other agricultural organizations of the seventies, to whose agitation for railroad regulation, both state and national, the general term " Granger movement "

[1] James, *The Agitation for Federal Regulation*, 39–50; Johnson, *American Railway Transportation*, 368–370; Larrabee, *The Railroad Question*, 353; Cullom Committee, *Report* (49 Congress, 1 session, *Senate Reports*, no. 46).

[2] Darrow, *Patrons of Husbandry*, 50; Messer, *The Grange*.

is applied, should be given credit for inaugurating the first important movement for federal regulation of railways. This movement, though unsuccessful in itself, was a forerunner of and paved the way for the more extensive agitation which finally produced the interstate commerce act.

EFFECTS

In concluding this survey of the Granger railroad legislation, there are a number of questions of a controversial nature which present themselves for consideration: (1) to what extent did the Granger laws accomplish their purpose of securing reduction and equalization of rates; (2) what was the effect of the legislation upon the business of the railroad companies; (3) to what extent did it prevent the construction of additional railroad lines ?

Some attention has already been devoted to the first of these questions in the preceding chapters and it is clear that several of the laws could have had practically no direct effect in reducing or equalizing rates, because they were not enforced. In the cases where the laws were enforced, there can be no doubt that they did, for the time being, effect some very material reductions in rates and put an end to some of the most glaring discriminations between persons and places.[1] On the other hand, the railroad companies took advantage of every loop-hole in the law or schedules to make their charges more instead of less burdensome, not so much for the purpose of increasing their revenues as with the idea of making the laws themselves unpopular.[2] The period, moreover, during which the laws were in force was generally very short indeed, because of their hasty repeal, and in case they did remain in force for any considerable length of time, as in Illinois, it seems probable that competition and other economic forces would have effected reductions in the rates without the operation of the laws. In general, then, it appears that the direct results of the laws in reducing rates were

[1] Illinois Railroad Commission, *Reports*, 1875, p. 22, 1876, p. 12; *Appleton's Cyclopedia*, 1878, p. 579.

[2] See above, pp. 154, 163, 175.

inconsiderable, but that they did put a check upon unjust discriminations while they remained in force.

Indirectly, however, the Granger laws and the agitation which produced them, seem to have had a considerable effect upon rates, particularly during the years immediately following the repeal of the laws. The desire to prevent a recurrence of the agitation was undoubtedly one factor in bringing about the rapid reductions of railroad rates during the later seventies, and certainly the general attitude of railroad officials toward the public was then very different from what it had been at the beginning of the Granger movement.[1]

At the time of the Granger agitation, it was universally asserted by the railroad officials and their supporters that the enforcement of the laws would so curtail the revenues of the companies as practically to ruin them and would prevent all further railway construction in the states affected. In the cases where the laws were enforced it was declared that the predictions had been realized. These assertions are to be found over and over again in the annual reports of the railroad companies,[2] in memorials to the legislatures,[3] in messages of anti-Granger governors,[4] and in newspapers and periodicals;[5] but

---

[1] Illinois Railroad Commission, *Reports*, 1876, pp. 15, 22; Governor's message (Illinois), *Senate Journal*, 1877, p. 19 or *House Journal*, 1877, p. 30.

[2] For example see Chicago and Northwestern Railway Company, *15th Annual Report* (1874), or extracts from same in *Yesterday and Today, a History of the Chicago and Northwestern Railway Company*, 59–61.

[3] Illinois, *Reports to the General Assembly*, 1873, iv. 971. See above, p. 154.

[4] Governor Gear of Iowa, in his biennial message to the legislature, January, 1880, declared: " That the law of the Fifteenth General Assembly had a tendency to restrict capital from seeking investment in railway construction in the state is evidenced by the fact that during the four years it was in operation only 310 miles of railway were constructed, and since the enactment of the present law nearly 700 miles have been constructed; over ninety *per cent.* of the cost of which has been defrayed by the investment of foreign capital." Iowa, *Legislative Documents*, 1880, i. no. 1, p. 28.

This is an excellent example of the way in which the Granger legislation was made responsible for the results of the panic of 1873. See also message of Governor Ludington of Wisconsin in *Governor's Message and Accompanying Documents*, 1876, i. 9–12.

[5] The *Nation* was especially diligent in this connection. See especially xvi. 309, 384, 397, xvii. 49, 156, 218, xviii. 55, 293, xix. 17, 199–201, xx. 53, 201, xxi.

always they seem to be mere assertions without any attempt to present positive proof either by the use of statistics or in any other way. On the other hand, the proceedings of granges and other agricultural organizations, the Grange press,[1] the messages of Granger governors,[2] and the reports of the Granger railroad commissions,[3] are equally filled with contrary assertions and with equal absence of conclusive proof.

This controversy did not end with the cessation of the Granger movement. The railroad forces seized upon the Potter law and kindred acts as " horrible examples " to hold before the people whenever there appeared to be any danger of legislative interference; or, as A. B. Stickney, himself a railroad president, expressed it, " the Granger laws have served the purpose of a ' bloody shirt ' to conceal incompetence in railway management for twenty years at least." [4] The railroad side of the argument, moreover, occupied a conspicuous place,[5] while the Granger side

---

157 (1873–75). Some of these statements are inconsistent with the statistics presented in *ibid.* xx. 1 (July 1, 1875). See also *American Exchange and Review*, xxv. 393 (August, 1874). For the attitude of local papers, see *Evansville* (Wisconsin) *Review*, September 22, 29, 1875, quoted in Lea, *Grange Movement in Wisconsin* (Ms.), 31–34.

[1] *Grange Bulletin* (Wisconsin), October, 1875.

[2] See especially the annual message of Governor Taylor of Wisconsin, January 15, 1875 in *Governor's Message and Accompanying Documents*, 1875, i. 24–33. Governor Newbold of Iowa in 1878 declared that " during the years 1874, 1875, and 1876, the increase of railroad mileage in Iowa was greater, both absolutely and relatively, than in either of our sister states on the north and west, while those of our neighbors that showed most decided increase were Illinois and Wisconsin, both having laws regulating railroads." Iowa, *Legislative Documents*, 1878, i. no. 11, p. 27.

[3] " No contemplated roads have been to our knowledge, abandoned because the State has assumed to protect its citizens from ' extortion and unjust discrimination.' On the contrary, new roads were opened with remarkable rapidity wherever there seemed a remote chance of reimbursement up to the time of the panic in September, 1873." Illinois Railroad Commission, *Reports*, 1876, p. 12. See also *ibid.* 18–21, 1872, p. 18, 1875, pp. 11, 22.

[4] Stickney, *Railway Problem*, 121.

[5] For example, C. F. Adams, " The Granger Movement " in *North American Review*, cxx. 394–424 (April, 1875), though apparently judicial in spirit really presents a very distorted view of the movement and its effects. This and the articles and editorials in the *Nation* have undoubtedly been the principal sources of the views of later writers.

was buried in forgotten pamphlets and local newspapers, with
the result that most later investigators, even including many
who desired to be impartial, have accepted the railroad point
of view and denounced the Granger acts as violations of economic
law and injurious to both the railroads and the public.[1]

There have been a few exceptions to this prevailing opinion.
As early as 1876, an anonymous writer who signed himself
" Wisconsin Granger," in an article in the *International Review*
declared that the Potter law did not

reduce rates below a non-remunerative standard. It did not destroy railroad values nor did it reduce them to any material extent nor check railway
construction. The actual gross reduction under the law was not over five
per cent. . . . The actual test of the law increased the net earnings by
reducing expenditures and increasing business, and proved wholly beneficial.

Had it stopped here, there would have been nothing to distinguish this statement from the numerous Granger assertions
of the period, beyond the fact that it appeared in a prominent
magazine, but the writer went further and added a footnote in
which he presented statistics to show that the railways of Wisconsin during the Granger period compared favorably with the

---

[1] Probably the most widely known and quoted statement of the effects of the
Granger legislation is the following from Hadley, *Railroad Transportation*, 135.
" But a more powerful force than the authority of the courts was working against
the Granger system of regulation. The laws of trade could not be violated with
impunity. The effects were most sharply felt in Wisconsin. The law reducing
railroad rates to the basis which competitive points enjoyed left nothing to pay
fixed charges. In the second year of its operation, no Wisconsin road paid a divi-
dend; only four paid interest on their bonds. Railroad construction had come to
a standstill. Even the facilities on existing roads could not be kept up. Foreign
capital refused to invest in Wisconsin; the development of the State was sharply
checked; the very men who had most favored the law found themselves heavy
losers. These points were plain to every one. They formed the theme of the
Governor's message at the beginning of 1876. The very men who passed the law
in 1874, hurriedly repealed it after two years' trial. In other states, the laws were
either repealed, as in Iowa, or were sparingly and cautiously enforced. By the
time the Supreme Court published the Granger decision, the fight had been settled,
not by constitutional limitations, but by industrial ones."

For a large number of other quotations to the same effect, see C. R. Detrick,
" The Effects of the Granger Acts," in *Journal of Political Economy*, xi. 237–247
(March, 1903). See also F. L. Holmes, " Development of Transportation Facili-
ties," in *Wisconsin in Three Centuries*, iv. 119, on the effects of the Potter law.

railroads of other states in extensions and in payment of interest on indebtedness.[1]

In 1891, appeared a book by A. B. Stickney, president of the Chicago and Great Western railroad, in which the fairness of the Granger laws was upheld and the position taken that the evils which had been laid at their door were really results of competition and of bad management on the part of railway officials.[2] Two years later, ex-Governor Larrabee of Iowa, who had played a part in the Granger and later railroad legislation in that state, published *The Railroad Question*, in which he also asserted that the Granger acts were fair and reasonable, and declared that if the earnings or construction of railroads had been affected at all, " it was due solely to a conspiracy on the part of the railroad managers to misrepresent and pervert the legislation in these states." [3]

Finally, in March, 1903, an article by Charles R. Detrick appeared in the *Journal of Political Economy* in which the whole subject of the effects of the Granger acts upon the railroads is examined in the light of statistics.[4] The investigation of the subject is rendered difficult by the fact that the Granger laws were in force during the period of financial depression following the panic of 1873 and it is necessary to determine to what extent each of these factors was the cause of the prevailing conditions among railroads. The problem is handled by Mr. Detrick by comparing statistics of railway construction and earnings in the Granger states and in various other groups of states. As a result of this study, the following proposition can be considered as definitely established: the percentages of increase in railroad mileage and in average net earnings of railway companies during

[1] " The Grange and the Potter Law," in *International Review*, iii. 665–673 (October, 1876). See especially pp. 665–667.

[2] Stickney, *Railway Problem*.

[3] Larrabee, *Railroad Question* 246.

[4] C. R. Detrick, " The Effects of the Granger Acts," in *Journal of Political Economy*, xi. 237–256 (March, 1903). The statistics in this article have been used by Senator R. M. La Follette in discussions of the Granger movement in several of his pamphlets, magazine articles, and speeches. For a reply to one of these by the general solicitor of the Chicago, Milwaukee, and St. Paul Railway Company, see Burton Hanson, *Unfair Railway Agitation*.

the period were at least as great in the four Granger states —
Illinois, Wisconsin, Minnesota, and Iowa — as in four other
western states — Indiana, Michigan, Nebraska, and Missouri, —
or in six representative middle states, or ten representative
southern states.

It might seem from this that the railroad claims are completely
refuted. There are, however, a number of other points to be
considered. In the first place, in several of the states which are
used by Mr. Detrick for comparison with the " Granger states,"
there were vigorous agitations for railway legislation of the
same sort and Missouri actually enacted a Granger act in 1875.[1]
If the Granger laws did affect the prosperity of railroads and the
confidence of the people in them at all, it is probable that that
effect was nearly, if not quite, as great in neighboring states
where similar agitations were under way, as in the states which
had actually passed the laws. There seems to be sufficient
evidence to justify the claim that the Granger agitation did tend
to make capitalists, and especially European capitalists, hesitate
about investing money in western or perhaps in any American
railroads.[2] If so, however, it is probably true, as ex-Governor
Larrabee of Iowa asserted, that this was caused rather by the
alarm sent forth by the railroad companies and their sympathiz-
ers than directly by the laws themselves.[3] There is no doubt
but that the nature and effect of the laws were greatly, and
probably intentionally, exaggerated, and the *Nation* did not
hesitate to advise capitalists to refrain from investing in western
railroad securities.[4] The contemporary business depression,
however, which followed in the wake of the panic of 1873, together
with the exposures of fraud in railway financing, were of so much
greater influence in causing lack of confidence in railway securities, that it is impossible to reach any very definite conclusions

[1] See above, pp. 194–196.

[2] *Chicago Tribune*, 1873, June 7, p. 5, June 28, p. 3; 1874, July 20, p. 4; *Nation*,
xvi. 384, 397, xvii. 218, xviii. 293, xx. 53, 338, xxi. 157 (1873–75).

[3] The same idea was expressed by Governor Taylor of Wisconsin in his annual
message, January 15, 1875, in *Governor's Message and Accompanying Documents*,
i. 28–30.

[4] *Nation*, xx. 190, 242 (March 18, April 8, 1875).

as to the effects of the Granger agitation in that direction.[1] It may be true that the efforts in the West to subject railroads to state control were factors in prolonging the depression and preventing the earlier resumption of railway construction. That, however, has never been proved, and probably is not susceptible of proof. Certainly the claims which would make the Granger movement primarily responsible for the stoppage of construction and the general railroad depression during the years from 1873 to 1876, are greatly exaggerated.

On the whole, it seems that the immediate economic effects of the Granger agitation for railroad regulation were small: it did secure some temporary reductions in rates and check some of the worst discriminations; it probably reduced railway earnings to some extent, although the decreased rates were in part offset by increased business of which they were a cause;[2] and it may have been a slight contributing factor in checking railway construction in the western states. The indirect and political results of the movement, however, were more important: it led to decisions of the United States Supreme Court which established the right of states to control railroads; and it laid the foundation for later legislation. In judging the results of this movement and comparing it with the more recent and more successful attempts at state regulation, allowance must be made for the fact that the problem had just begun to be studied in the seventies. The railroad laws of the present time are, as a rule, drawn up with care by men who have made a study of railroad economics and are administered by trained experts. The measure of success which these laws have attained attests the soundness of the fundamental principles first developed in the Granger acts of the seventies.

[1] " Nothing is more certain than that any cloud which now hangs over American credit in England and Holland is due to the extensive defaults in American railroad bonds, to the dishonest management of American railroad corporations, and to the hostile legislation of Western states, and the wild and furious denunciations of capitalists and money-lenders indulged in by Western politicians during the last two or three years." *Nation*, xxi. 157 (September 9, 1875).

[2] Wisconsin Railroad Commission, *Reports*, 1874, p. 34.

CHAPTER VII

BUSINESS COÖPERATION

Up to the close of the Civil War, the farmers of the West were generally content to confine their business operations to the raising of crops and stock. They disposed of their surplus products in the most convenient market and purchased the few supplies needed from the nearest store-keeper, without bothering their heads about the extortions of manufacturers or the profits of middlemen. During the decade of the seventies however, there was a determined effort on the part of the farmers to establish direct relations between producers and consumers, with reference to both the products which they wished to dispose of and the supplies they had to purchase. The explanation of this is to be sought in changing economic conditions. The western farmers in the pioneer period were independent in their economic relations with the outside world, and indeed each farm was almost a self-sufficing unit. But the rapid development of the country and the increase in transportation facilities changed all this, and by 1870 the farmers had become largely producers of staple crops for market and nearly as dependent upon outsiders for supplies as were those engaged in other occupations. With no adequate conception of the actual services performed by the middlemen or the complexities of the business of distribution,[1] and with the example of successful coöperation in England to urge them on, the western farmers believed it possible to regain their economic independence by themselves assuming the management of those industries which touched them most closely. Two things were prerequisite for this — organization, and a certain amount of mutual confidence — and these were furnished by the rapid growth of farmers' clubs and especially of the order of Patrons of Hus-

[1] Cf. Fetter, " The Theory of the Middleman " and Kieley, " The Middleman in Practice," both in Bailey, *Cyclopedia of American Agriculture*, iv. 239–243.

bandry during the early seventies. The result was the establishment of an almost incredible number of coöperative or pseudo-coöperative enterprises under the control of the farmers' organizations. These enterprises included local, county, and state agencies for the purchase of implements and supplies and the sale of farm products, local grain elevators and coöperative stores, the manufacture of farm machinery, banking, insurance, and even organizations for bringing about direct trade between the American producer and the European consumer.

Most of the enterprises were short-lived and many brought disaster to those involved; but they are, nevertheless, distinctly worthy of study, not only as an illuminating, though pathological, chapter in the history of coöperation, but also as an integral part of the movement for agricultural organization which swept the country in the seventies. To trace in detail the history of these coöperative enterprises in the various states would require a volume in itself, and it will be necessary to confine this account to a brief sketch of the development of this feature of the Granger movement with some consideration of its scope, characteristics, and results.

Grange Agencies

Even as early as October, 1867, two months before the establishment of the preliminary National Grange, one of Kelley's correspondents had suggested that the proposed order should be so framed as to confer a pecuniary benefit upon its members. Kelley himself appears to have looked with favor upon this idea; but it was opposed by others of the " founders " and the constitution and early circulars of the order dwelt almost entirely upon the social, fraternal, and intellectual benefits to be conferred. When the work of organizing local granges was begun, however, the farmers were inclined to ask, " What pecuniary benefit are we to gain by supporting the organization ? " and it was not long before the circulars were revised to lay emphasis on the possibilities of protection and coöperation which the order presented.[1]

[1] Kelley, *Patrons of Husbandry*, 35, 79, 112–114, 129.

Thenceforth, business coöperation was a leading feature of the movement and one of the principal incentives for the growth of the order. Whenever a local grange was formed, almost the first step taken was to adopt some plan of coöperative buying and selling. Often, especially during the early years, all that was done was to make arrangements with certain local dealers for special rates in return for the cash trade of all the members.[1] This plan never worked very long and generally made way for the establishment of a local agency. In some cases, the agent simply attended to forwarding the cash orders of the members to a manufacturer or jobber or to the state agency, if established, and distributed the shipments when they arrived. For these services the agent might receive a small commission or he might be paid a small salary by the grange. More often, perhaps, he got no compensation but the opportunity to purchase his own supplies at a reduced price and the satisfaction of helping his neighbors. In other cases, the agency was supplied with a small amount of capital by the grange or by a stock company of members, and then it approached more nearly to the dignity of a coöperative store.

Often the granges of a county or other district found it advantageous to join together in a county council or Pomona grange and established a county or district agency to assist the members in their buying and selling.[2] These larger agencies varied in methods much as did the smaller ones connected with a single grange. At first most of their energies were devoted to inducing manufacturers and wholesale dealers to make special terms. In this, of course, they were more successful than the local agencies because of their ability to control a larger trade. Later many of the county and district associations developed into coöperative stores of one form or another. Whatever the method, the object in view was the same throughout: to secure supplies at lower prices by bulking orders and dealing as directly as possible with manufacturers and jobbers; and to eliminate

---

[1] A " Trading Card " of the Winnebago County (Wisconsin) Council, Patrons of Husbandry, is in the library of the Wisconsin Historical Society.

[2] See Kelley, *Patrons of Husbandry*, 298.

some of the profits of the middlemen by shipping produce directly to the large markets instead of disposing of it to the local dealers and commission men. The aggregate business done by or through these local agencies throughout the country was certainly enormous during the years 1873, 1874, and 1875, and they no doubt effected very considerable savings for the members. Their operations, moreover, naturally tended to force local dealers to lower their prices in order to meet the competition, and so were beneficial to many who were not members of the order.[1]

But the Grangers were never satisfied with local coöperation. If so much could be accomplished by the united efforts of the members of a single grange or in a single county, what was to prevent the coöperation of all the Patrons in a state or the United States from accomplishing many times as much? As a result state agencies were established in state after state, until by December, 1874, twenty-six state granges had adopted some sort of an agency system.[2] The methods of operation of these agencies were even more diverse than those of the local agencies, and can perhaps best be made clear by sketching the careers of a few of them as types.

When the first state grange was organized in Minnesota in 1869, business coöperation was one of the principal subjects discussed, and the general sentiment was strongly in favor of the appointment of a state agent to purchase supplies and dispose of produce for the Patrons. Kelley and others of the " founders " feared that such a move might be premature, and when the subject of appointing state agents and a general business agent for the order was brought up at the so-called first annual session of the National Grange in April, 1869, it was laid on the table.[3] If the National Grange had taken hold of the subject at this time and worked out a comprehensive system of coöperation for the order, it might possibly have guided the

---

[1] The *Prairie Farmer* for 1873, 1874, and 1875 contains many reports of the work of different local agencies. See especially xliv. 369, 387, 395, xlv. 11 (November, 1873–January, 1874).

[2] See list of state agents in *Prairie Farmer*, xlv. 411 (December 26, 1874).

[3] Kelley, *Patrons of Husbandry*, 168, 170, 171, 176, 183, 186.

movement along more conservative lines and prevented much of the confusion and disaster that followed. As it was, however, each state grange was left to work out its own salvation in the matter of business coöperation, and Minnesota led the way.

In the same month in which the " founders " laid the subject of coöperation on the table, Master Smith of the Minnesota State Grange appointed C. A. Prescott of St. Paul as state business agent and issued a circular which announced that the agent would sell produce and make purchases for members.[1] The agent proceeded to issue weekly bulletins giving prices of produce and sent a circular to manufacturers of agricultural implements inviting them to send samples to be tested and reported upon by the state grange.[2]   The appointment of Prescott as agent was confirmed by the state grange when it met in July, 1869,[3] but no further record of the operations of this earliest agency, prior to 1873, has been found.   In February, 1873, the state grange appointed a committee to develop a feasible plan for coöperation in the purchase of farm implements,[4] and later in the year another state agent, J. H. Denman, was engaged in visiting manufacturers and wholesale dealers in order to secure special terms for members of the order.[5] At the meeting of the state grange in December, 1873, Denman was elected state purchasing agent for the ensuing year with a salary of not to exceed sixteen hundred dollars to be derived from commissions on sales.[6] The Minnesota agency never succeeded in doing business on as large a scale or securing as favorable terms as did some of the other grange agencies, partly because the number of granges in the state was comparatively small; nevertheless, the Patrons of the state claimed to have

---

[1] The agent received a commission on business transacted.   The first purchase is said to have been a jackass for one of the officers of the state grange.   Kelley commented: " This purchasing business commenced with buying jackasses; the prospects are that many will be *sold*."   Kelley, *Patrons of Husbandry*, 180.

[2] *Minnesota Monthly*, i. 134, 213 (April, June, 1869).

[3] *Ibid*. 249 (July, 1869).

[4] Minnesota State Grange, *Constitution*, 1873, pp. 13–16.

[5] *Prairie Farmer*, xliv. 355 (November 8, 1873).

[6] *Ibid*. 412 (December 27, 1873).

saved large amounts of money through the operations of the state and local agencies.[1]

Iowa was the first state in which Grange coöperation achieved a marked success. Local agencies existed in the state from the very beginning of the organization of granges and in 1872 a state business agency was established at Des Moines, with J. D. Whitman as state agent, and a Chicago firm was chosen to receive shipments of produce from Iowa Grangers. Whitman appears to have been energetic and capable. He soon succeeded in building up a large business in the sale of farm implements and supplies to Patrons. Negotiations were entered into with manufacturers and wholesale dealers, and the special rates secured communicated to the granges by means of confidential circulars. Whenever possible the state agent seems to have turned the orders over to these firms to be filled, but some of the shipments were made through the agency. Many orders were also sent by local grange agents or individual Patrons directly to the manufacturers or wholesalers. At first the state agent seems to have worked without any capital, but as the business developed he was allowed to use part of the funds of the state grange. This enabled him to take advantage of opportunities to secure very low rates by making large purchases outright and then filling orders as they came in.[2]

Even as early as December, 1872, before the state agency had gotten into operation, glowing reports were made of the savings effected by the Patrons of Iowa.[3] It was declared that one-third of the grain elevators and warehouses in the state were owned or controlled by the Granges and that five million bushels of grain and large numbers of cattle and hogs had been shipped direct to Chicago through grange agents, upon which a saving of from ten to forty per cent had been effected. On the purchases of agricultural implements alone

---

[1] Martin, *Grange Movement*, 487.

[2] Iowa State Grange, *Proceedings*, iv, v. 11 (1873, 1874); *Prairie Farmer*, xliv. 377, 411 (November 29, December 27, 1873); Martin, *Grange Movement*, 473–485.

[3] S. Leavitt, *Township Coöperation* (pamphlet), 3, quoting a letter from Des Moines to the *New York World*. Same in *Rural Carolinian*, iv. 493 (June, 1873).

the farmers of the state were said to have saved a total of $365,000 and an example was given of a reaper which had been retailing at $240 but was sold to granges at $140. During 1873 the business of the local agencies increased by leaps and bounds under the stimulus of the state agent. At the state grange meeting in December of that year, the executive committee reported that the agents of the order in the state had done a business during the year of five million dollars, and effected a saving of at least fifteen per cent on family supplies and twenty per cent on agricultural implements.[1]

During 1874 the operations of the business agencies continued to increase, but the state grange also embarked in the business of manufacturing farm machinery and that was the beginning of the end.[2] In 1875 the crash came — the failure of the implement works bankrupted the grange, and though the state agency continued for a while to do a large business, it had gotten beyond its depth and was hampered by the lack of capital. An attempt to provide it with twenty-five thousand dollars by the sale of stock to Patrons at ten dollars a share was a failure, and the rapid decline of the order after 1875 soon snuffed it out along with most of the local agencies.[3]

In Illinois, also, the beginning of coöperation was practically contemporaneous with the organization of the first active granges in Lee and Whiteside counties and successful operations were reported even before the organization of the state grange in 1872.[4] In this state the situation was somewhat complicated by the existence of large numbers of open farmers' clubs, side by side with the Grange. The members of these organizations were as eager to attempt coöperation as were the Patrons and in many instances county or district farmers' associations, made up of both clubs and granges, were organized to manage the business feature.[5] Some of these were very successful for

---

[1] Iowa State Grange, *Proceedings*, iv (1873).

[2] *Ibid.* v. 11, 16–26 (1874); National Grange, *Proceedings*, x. 38 (November, 1875).

[3] Iowa State Grange, *Proceedings*, vi. 11–15, 29, 35, 41, 45, 46 (1875).

[4] Paine, *Granger Movement in Illinois*, 39, note.

[5] The purpose of these associations is clearly indicated by the following resolu-

a few years, as, for example, the Central Farmers' Association of Centralia. This organization was formed in January, 1873, and a purchasing agent was appointed in March. The agent experienced considerable difficulty in getting terms from implement manufacturers, because most of them had already made arrangements with dealers for the year. Opposition was also experienced from the local merchants; but the farmers persisted and in November, 1873, the secretary of the association was able to report the sale of about one hundred thousand dollars' worth of implements alone, through the agency, with a saving to the farmers living within a radius of fifteen miles of Centralia of twenty-five thousand dollars over prices which had formerly prevailed.[1]

The Illinois State Farmers' Association, though primarily interested in politics, also gave some attention to coöperation and at one time attempted to establish a state agency to serve the clubs and granges. This experiment was a failure,[2] and no very considerable degree of success attended the attempts of the state grange to establish a purchasing agency for the Patrons. The first state grange agent, who was appointed as early as December, 1872, merely negotiated for special terms for Patrons and issued circulars of information to the local granges and agencies.[3] During 1874 and 1875 more extensive operations were attempted; but the agent and the executive committee disagreed as to methods to be pursued, and the local agents were inclined to take advantage of temporary concessions made elsewhere, instead of dealing through the state agency. At the fourth annual meeting of the grange, in December, 1875, it was generally conceded that the state agency had been a failure. The reports indicated clearly, moreover, that the local

tion which was adopted by one of them at its organization in 1873: " *Resolved,* That we buy everything we need direct from manufacturers and wholesale houses, and buy by large quantities and pay cash, and that we sell our produce in large quantities together, when sold, endeavoring thereby to get better prices, lower freights, etc." *Prairie Farmer,* xliv. 83 (March 15, 1873).

[1] *Ibid.* xliv. 4, 369 (1873). For the operation of other local agencies, see *ibid.* xliii. 385, xliv. 43, 52.

[2] *Ibid.* xliv. 124, xlvi. 35 (1873, 1875); *Industrial Age,* January 31, 1874, pp. 5, 7.

[3] *Prairie Farmer,* xliv. 83, 91, 131 (March, April, 1873).

agencies, with the exception of a few which had organized as stock companies, had proven unsatisfactory and were declining.[1] At this session the donation from the National Grange [2] was turned over to the executive committee to be used for business purposes and the committee was authorized to establish a new agency to be located in the city of Chicago and placed in charge of a salaried agent who should be under bonds. This plan was tried during 1876 with considerable success, according to the reports made to the state grange in December of that year,[3] and the new agency continued operations on a small scale well down into the eighties.[4]

Meanwhile the work done by state agencies in other states had been taken over in part in Illinois by a number of commercial firms of Chicago which early began to advertise that they were prepared to fill orders for clubs and granges at wholesale prices. Prominent among these were the firms of Z. N. Hall, which for several years furnished the granges with groceries at wholesale prices and other supplies for a small commission, and Montgomery Ward and Company, which has since developed into one of the largest mail order houses in the country.[5] For facilitating the direct shipment of produce by the local granges or agencies to Chicago a contract was made by the state grange with the commission firm of Reynolds, Corbett, and Thomas, by which it was officially recognized as Grange agent. When this firm failed, late in 1874, though without loss to shippers, its members declared that the Grange support had not been such as to warrant further experiments of the kind.[6] The executive committee of the state grange succeeded, neverthe-

---

[1] *Prairie Farmer*, xlv. 52, 202 (February 14, June 27, 1874); Illinois State Grange, *Proceedings*, iv. 12, 15, 17, 23–31 (1875).

[2] See above, p. 68.

[3] Illinois State Grange, *Proceedings*, iv. 42, 44, v. 9, 48–50, 55–57, 90–101 (1875, 1876).

[4] A. G. Warner, "Three Phases of Coöperation in the West," in American Economic Association, *Publications*, ii. no. 1, p. 34 (March, 1887) and in Johns Hopkins University, *Studies*, vi. 384.

[5] *Prairie Farmer*, xliv. 91 (adv.), 92, 348, 411 (adv.), xlvi. 172 (1873, 1874).

[6] *Prairie Farmer*, xlv. 52, 396 (February 14, December 12, 1874); *Industrial Age*, December 12, 1874, p. 5.

less, in making a similar arrangement with another Chicago firm, which was placed under bond for one hundred and fifty thousand dollars, and in the course of time commercial firms at Peoria and St. Louis were also given official recognition as state agents.[1]

Another feature of the coöperative movement in Illinois is of interest. There was considerable talk among the farmers to the effect that prices were fixed by rings and monopolies, and it was quite common for the agitators to advise the farmers to retaliate by forming organizations to control the prices of farm products. One of the first attempts in this direction was made by the Northwestern Farmers' Convention which met in Chicago in October, 1873. Among the resolutions adopted was one recommending to the farmers of the Northwest that they withhold their hog products from the market until the price should reach five dollars per hundred pounds.[2] What was the result of this attempt to raise prices by regulating the supply does not appear, but it may be assumed that it was a failure. Many farmers were so situated that it was not feasible for them to withhold their hogs from market. The organization, moreover, was too incomplete to give such a movement a chance of success.[3] Later on various county and subordinate granges in Illinois and other western states attempted to control prices by agreeing to " hold their hogs," and in January, 1878, the state grange recommended that hogs be withheld from market for thirty days, unless certain specific prices should be previously offered.[4] No evidence has been found which would indicate that any of these attempts were successful.[5]

---

[1] Illinois State Grange, *Proceedings*, iv. 12, v. 5? (1875, 1876).

[2] *Prairie Farmer*, xliv. 347 (November 1, 1873). The proceedings are also to be found in Windom Committee, *Report*, ii. 646–688. There were a few delegates present from other states, but the convention was mainly a gathering of Illinois farmers.

[3] See *Prairie Farmer*, xliv. 353 (November 8, 1873).

[4] Paine, *Granger Movement in Illinois*, 44. See also *Prairie Farmer*, xlvi. 372 (1875); *Wisconsin Statesman*, July 31, 1875, p. 3.

[5] These experiments are of interest in view of the recent attempts of the American Society of Equity to control the price of grain in the same way. For Granger propositions for controlling the price of grain, see *Prairie Farmer*, xliv. 249, 265 (August 9, 23, 1873); *Chicago Tribune*, August 18, 1873, p. 3.

The operations of Grange agencies in the other states of the Middle West may be briefly summarized. Both state and a profusion of local agencies existed in every state from Kansas to Ohio, but they were similar in their general features to those already described in Iowa and Illinois. The Ohio agency did a large business for several years under the direction of W. H. Hill as state agent, located at Cincinnati, but dissensions arose, and it was closed out by the state grange about 1878.[1] The Indiana agency was first established on a commission basis. Later the state grange paid the agent a regular salary and allowed him to use fifteen thousand dollars of its funds as capital. During 1875 the business of this agency amounted to three hundred thousand dollars, and in 1876 it was still larger; but bad management soon brought it to bankruptcy, entailing a loss of several thousand dollars upon the state grange.[2] In Michigan the state grange was generally conservative in business matters and most of the Grange coöperation was carried on through county councils and local agencies, the state agent confining himself to making contracts with manufacturers and dealers. One of these contracts is said to have broken up the " plaster ring " and saved the farmers a large amount of money on their purchases of land plaster. In the later part of the decade arrangements were made with commercial firms in Detroit and Chicago to act as Grange agents for filling orders and selling produce. A special agency was also established in Ypsilanti in 1878; but the business was so small that the executive committee was obliged to permit the agent to run it as a general commission house in order to clear expenses.[3] In Wisconsin the first state grange agent was appointed as early as 1871. The work of the agency was confined to making contracts and

---

[1] On the Grange agencies of Ohio, see Ohio State Grange, *Proceedings*, i–iii (1874–76); W. H. Hill, *Revised and Consolidated Price List and Grange Book of Reference;* Ellis, " History of the Grange in Ohio," in *Ohio Farmer*, c. 348, ci. 32, 274, 298, 370 (1901, 1902); Warner, " Three Phases of Coöperation in the West," in Johns Hopkins University, *Studies*, vi. 371.

[2] Indiana State Grange, *Proceedings*, iv. 12, 15, 16, 26, 29, 31, 35–37 (1874), xxxiv. 98 (appendix); Illinois State Grange, *Proceedings*, iv. 17 (1875); *Rural Carolinian*, v. 592; Warner, in Johns Hopkins University, *Studies*, vi. 382.

[3] Michigan State Grange, *Proceedings*, i–vii (1874–80).

to general supervision of the business features of the order, until 1876, when a regular business agency for filling orders and receiving consignments of produce was established in Milwaukee. This agency did a considerable business for a few years and persisted during the decade of the eighties. In 1886, however, the agent reported that the business was not confined to members of the order and that the service of the agency was most considerable as a bureau of information as to prices and a regulator of local trade.[1] The operations of the Grange agencies in Kansas,[2] Nebraska,[3] and Missouri [4] were similar to those in Iowa though on a smaller scale, and were all brought to a close by the collapse of the order in these states in the later seventies. In Missouri the Patrons had at one time besides the ordinary purchasing agent, a commission agent and a live stock agent in St. Louis.

The business operations of the order in California were extensive and different in many ways from those attempted in other parts of the country, and consequently it will be worth while to sketch them in some detail.[5] The primary purpose of the California farmers in organizing the State Farmers' Union, out of which grew the state grange of the Patrons of Husbandry, was to bring about coöperation in the marketing of products, especially grain, and in the purchase of grain sacks and other supplies. Various plans were laid by the Farmers' Union during 1872 and 1873 for different forms of coöperation, but the actual

---

[1] On Grange coöperation in Wisconsin, see Wisconsin State Grange, *Proceedings*, ii–viii (1874–80); *Prairie Farmer*, xliv. 211, 369, xlv. 139, xlvi. 283 (1873–75); Maynard, *Patrons of Husbandry in Wisconsin* (Ms.), 16–29, 52, 66; Lea, *Grange Movement in Wisconsin* (Ms.), 14; Wisconsin Bureau of Labor and Industrial Statistics, *Reports*, ii. 208–211 (1885–86); Albert Shaw, " Coöperation in the Northwest," in Johns Hopkins University, *Studies*, vi. 316–318.

[2] See Kansas State Grange, *Proceedings*, iii. 3, 4, 7–11, 32, 34–37 (1875) and J. K. Hudson, *Patrons' Handbook*, 26.

[3] Nebraska State Grange, *Proceedings*, iv. 7–12, 22–25, 31–36 (1874); *Prairie Farmer*, xlv. 235 (July 25, 1874).

[4] Missouri State Grange, *Proceedings*, iii. 16, 34–43, iv. 11, 21–23, 78–80, 103, 108–113, 119–131 (1874, 1875).

[5] Most of the documents and other material upon which the following account of business operations in California is based, can be found in Carr, *Patrons of Husbandry*, chs. ix, xii, xiv–xvi. See also *Prairie Farmer*, xlv. 291, 331, 347, 355, 361, 387, xlvi. 21, 75 (1874–75).

operations devolved upon the state grange, which was organized in July, 1873. The way in which the business feature dominated the movement in California is seen in the declaration adopted at this time, by which the specific objects of the state grange were said to be to establish farmers' banks and Grange stores; to arrange for the purchase of farm machinery directly from manufacturers and the shipment of products directly to consumers; gradually to substitute the cash for the credit system; and eventually to introduce the shipment of grain in bulk instead of in sacks.[1]

In carrying out this program, the executive committee of the state grange made arrangements with the firm of Morgan's Sons to act as shipping agents for the Patrons, and appointed a state agent under bonds, who devoted himself, in addition to supervising the operations of the shipping agent, to making favorable terms with dealers in implements and importers of grain sacks and other supplies. Morgan's Sons also entered the field as direct purchasers of grain, and a lively competition sprang up between them and the old " wheat ring," which pushed the price of wheat up steadily. As a result of the operations of this firm and the purchasing agency during the year 1873–74 it was claimed that over five million dollars were saved for the farmers of the state.[2]

The wheat crop of 1874 in California was very large, being nearly double that of the preceding year, and Morgan's Sons apparently got beyond their depth in attempting to handle the Granger consignments. Seventeen cargoes in all were shipped for the Patrons in 1874 and fifteen more were in port under charter to load when, through a combination of circumstances, the firm of Morgan's Sons was forced into bankruptcy. It might be thought that this experience would be enough for the Grangers, for their losses were considerable, and it was, probably, the most potent cause for the rapid decline of the order in the state during the next few years. The leaders, however, were only spurred on to greater effort. A special

---

[1] Carr, *Patrons of Husbandry*, 134; *Chicago Tribune*, July 26, 1873, p. 5.

[2] Carr, *Patrons of Husbandry*, 160, 177.

meeting of the state grange was held in November, 1874, at which it was determined to incorporate a " Grangers' Business Association " to take the place of the bankrupt firm as shipping agent for the Patrons. The business agency and the recently established dairy agency were to be departments of the association.

This association was incorporated in February, 1875, with a nominal capital stock of one million dollars, divided into shares of twenty-five dollars each.[1] The articles of incorporation declared its purposes to be to deal in all kinds of agricultural produce, farm implements, and general merchandise, and to ship grain and other merchandise to foreign ports, " as factors and broker and not otherwise." The by-laws of the association provided that none but Patrons could be stockholders or directors, and this seems to have been all that distinguished it from an ordinary stock company, for the profits, if any, were to be divided among the stock-holders in the usual way. Great things were expected of the Grangers' Business Association of California,[2] for the order was at the highest point of membership in the early months of 1875. By July, 1876, however, the number of granges in the state had declined from 263 to 173,[3] and the decline continued during the following years. This must have seriously crippled the operations of the new stock company, but it was reported as still in existence and doing a considerable business in 1881.[4]

In Oregon alone, of the other states of the Far West, were there enough granges to make possible any considerable attempts at distributive coöperation. The methods followed in this state were similar to those in California; a state agency, with a fund of over five thousand dollars raised by subscriptions from granges, did an extensive business in 1875 and 1876; and Grange shipments were made through a commercial firm. Some of the Patrons of Oregon appear to have suffered losses

[1] For articles of incorporation and by-laws, see Carr, *Patrons of Husbandry*, 207–210.

[2] *Ibid.* 205–207; Illinois State Grange, *Proceedings*, 17 (1875).

[3] See table above, following p. 58.

[4] National Grange, *Proceedings*, xv. 36 (1881).

through the failure of Morgan's Sons, and in 1882 the master of the state grange reported that the business ventures had not been successful and had entailed a considerable debt upon the state grange.[1]

Numerous Grange agencies were also established in the southern states; but they operated, as a rule, on a smaller scale than did those of the Middle West. In Maryland the executive committee of the state grange made arrangements in 1874 to enable the members of the order to purchase fertilizers at wholesale rates, and soon after a Baltimore firm was placed under bonds to act as business agent for the Patrons of the state. This firm was reported to have done a Grange business of $185,-000 in 1875; but the arrangement apparently was not satisfactory for in 1876 a warehouse was rented in Baltimore and a member of the order put in charge on a salary basis. A fund of about sixteen hundred dollars was raised by subscription among the local granges and the agency did a business of $358,000 during 1877. Complaints were made that the support of the agency by the Patrons was not universal; but it seems to have had a successful career, and in 1881 was reported as having a " surplus capital " of over ten thousand dollars. In 1882 plans were being laid for reorganizing the business on the Rochdale plan.[2]

In West Virginia the Grange was not strong enough to establish an independent agency, but in 1877 five hundred dollars were contributed to the fund of the Maryland agency. Trouble soon arose, however, because the West Virginia Grange was not allowed any share in the control of the agency, and it withdrew after a few months.[3] In Virginia, the Carolinas, and Florida, little seems to have been accomplished in the way of distributive

---

[1] Oregon State Grange, *Proceedings*, iii (1876); Illinois State Grange, *Proceedings*, iv. 17 (1875); National Grange, *Proceedings*, xvi. 39 (1882).

[2] Maryland State Grange, *Proceedings*, i (March, 1874), special session (December, 1875); Maryland State Grange Agency, *Circular* (March 20, 1876); *American Farmer*, v. 138, vi. 33, vii. 12–14, 147, viii. 7–12, 148 (1876–79); National Grange, *Proceedings*, xv. 38, xvi. 31 (1881, 1882); R. D. Randall, " Coöperation in Maryland and the South," in Johns Hopkins University, *Studies*, vi. 506.

[3] *American Farmer*, vii. 13, viii. 148; National Grange, *Proceedings*, xv. 44 (1881).

coöperation beyond making arrangements for securing fertilizers at reduced prices.[1]   In Kentucky and Tennessee, however,
more extensive operations were undertaken by the order.   The
Kentucky State Grange rented a warehouse in Louisville and
put it in charge of an agent on a commission basis, part of the
rent of the building being defrayed by leasing space in it to
manufacturers for the exhibition of machinery.   In 1875 the
agency was reported as doing a business of between two and
three hundred thousand dollars.   Plans were then laid for changing the agency to a salary basis and for raising a fund of twenty-
five thousand dollars by the sale of bonds.   The Tennessee
Patrons shared in the work of the Kentucky agency for a while
and commercial firms in New Orleans, Memphis, and Atlanta
also received recognition from the state grange.   In 1875,
however, the executive committee was ordered to arrange for
the establishment of an independent state agency, with subordinate agents for each of the three grand divisions of the state.
In neither of these states did the business ventures have any
lasting success, and their failure discredited the order there
for many years.[2]

The state granges of Alabama and Mississippi adopted the
plan of choosing established firms in the various commercial
centers of the state or neighboring states and placing them
under bonds to act as Grange agents.   The Alabama State
Grange had, in addition, a similar agent in New York, and the
Mississippi Grange, one in Liverpool, England, to look after
consignments of cotton.[3]   The executive committee of the
Georgia State Grange made arrangements with the various

[1] Virginia State Grange, *Proceedings*, i (1873–74); Illinois State Grange, *Proceedings*, iv. 17 (1875); North Carolina State Grange, *Proceedings*, ii–iv (1875–77);
South Carolina State Grange, *Minute Book* (Ms.); *Prairie Farmer*, xlv. 411 (December 26, 1874).

[2] Tennessee State Grange, *Proceedings*, ii (1875); Illinois State Grange, *Pro-
ceedings*, iv. 17 (1875); National Grange, *Proceedings*, xv. 37, 43 (1881); *Prairie
Farmer*, xlv. 411 (December 26, 1874); Randall, in Johns Hopkins University,
Studies, vi. 505.

[3] Alabama State Grange, *Proceedings*, ii, iii (1874, 1875); Mississippi State
Grange, *Proceedings*, v (1875); *Prairie Farmer*, xlv. 411 (December 26, 1874);
Hawkins, " The Grange in the South," in Allen, *Labor and Capital*, 487.

cotton buyers as early as 1873 to enable Patrons to sell their cotton by contract and in bulk.[1] In Louisiana a member of the order was established as Grange agent at New Orleans and did a business on a commission basis during the year 1875 amounting to $744,000.[2] In Arkansas and Texas the business ventures were mainly in the hands of local agencies during the early years and the failure of many of these cooled the ardor of the members. The executive committee of the Texas State Grange issued circulars informing Patrons of special offers made by merchants or manufacturers and the Arkansas State Grange established an agency at Little Rock in 1876, but its business was too small to warrant its continuance.[3]

In the eastern states the Grange did not make much headway until after the middle of the decade, when the Rochdale plan of coöperative stores had quite generally superseded the agency plan. Still there were many local agencies in more or less successful operation in these states, and Maine, New Hampshire, and Vermont each had state purchasing agents for a time. The Maine and New Hampshire agents confined themselves to making arrangements with different firms for doing business for Patrons at reduced rates, but the operations of the Vermont agency were somewhat more extensive. The by-laws of the Vermont State Grange made definite provision for a business committee in each subordinate grange and these seem to have operated through the state agent. The purchasing business of the state agency amounted to between seventy and eighty thousand dollars in 1874 and was more than doubled the next year.[4] The executive committees of the state granges of Massachusetts and New York made trade arrangements for Patrons with various firms, and in New York several commission

---

[1] *Rural Carolinian*, v. 152 (November, 1873).

[2] Louisiana State Grange, *Proceedings*, iii (1875); *Prairie Farmer*, xlv. 411 (December 26, 1874), xlvi. 259 (August 14, 1875); *Rural Carolinian*, v. 512 (August, 1874).

[3] Arkansas State Grange, *Proceedings*, v (1877); Texas State Grange, *Minutes* (October, 1873), *Proceedings*, i (August, 1874); National Grange, *Proceedings*, xv. 35, 43 (1881).

[4] State grange proceedings: Maine, i, ii (1874, 1875); New Hampshire, i–iii (1873–76); Vermont, i–iii (1872–75).

houses were recognized as Grange agents in return for offers of special rates to Patrons.[1]

It appears, therefore, that state grange agents for distributive coöperation, of one sort or another, were established in the decade of the seventies throughout the United States from Maine to California: in the Middle West every state had a regular Grange purchasing agent who was himself a member of the order, and some had also arrangements with bonded firms in different commercial centers; on the Pacific coast the interest centered in schemes for direct shipment of grain to Liverpool, but the state agents of California and Oregon also did a considerable business in purchasing implements and supplies; in the South the efforts were directed mainly toward securing reliable firms for handling the staple crops at reasonable rates, and making arrangements for the purchase of fertilizer, but the state agencies of Maryland, Kentucky, and Louisiana did an extensive business in purchasing implements and general supplies; in New England and the Middle States, the work of the state agencies, except in Vermont, was inconsiderable. As a general rule these agencies made their appearance in a state within a year after the organization of the state grange, did a flourishing business for a few years while the order was growing rapidly, and then either came to a disastrous ending or gradually lost ground with the decline of the order itself in the later part of the decade. While they were in active operation they undoubtedly effected great reductions in the cost of implements and supplies and saved the Patrons a considerable amount in commissions on produce; but in this connection the work of the local agencies, county and district associations, must not be forgotten. Less ambitious and generally with less capital, if any, they often served their immediate neighborhoods more effectively than did the state agencies.

[1] Massachusetts State Grange, *Quarterly Bulletin*, January, 1876; *Proceedings*, v (1877); New York State Grange, *Proceedings*, ii, iii (1875, 1876).

The National Grange and Coöperation

The failure of the National Grange to enter actively into the early schemes for business coöperation has been noted. In January, 1871, however, Secretary Kelley distributed a lot of circulars to subordinate granges informing them of offers to sell seeds at wholesale prices, and the next year a circular was issued inviting manufacturers of agricultural implements who desired to trade directly with granges to send their wholesale price lists for publication in a confidential bulletin.[1] At the sixth annual session of the National Grange in January, 1873, the subject of coöperation was referred to the executive committee. During the following year this committee visited manufacturing establishments in various parts of the country and issued three business circulars informing subordinate granges of special terms offered. At the next session, in February, 1874, the executive committee recommended the establishment of a national business agency, which among other duties should publish " a complete business directory of the order " showing all arrangements made by the national and state granges. The subject of coöperation received considerable attention at this session; but the only positive action taken, aside from the declaration of an intention to " dispense with a surplus of middlemen," was the adoption of a resolution instructing the executive committee to give special attention to furnishing Patrons with implements and supplies at low prices and to make arrangements for a mutual exchange of products between different sections of the country.[2]

The executive committee at this time consisted of William Saunders, one of the founders and past-master of the National Grange, D. Wyatt Aiken of South Carolina and E. R. Shankland of Iowa, and these men were untiring in their efforts to advance the business interests of the order during 1874. They devoted themselves first to the compiling of national price lists

[1] Kelley, *Patrons of Husbandry*, 302–305, 385.
[2] National Grange, *Proceedings*, vi. 10, 20, vii. 13, 29–32, 57, 79 (1873, 1874); *Rural Carolinian*, v. 206 (January, 1874).

containing terms offered by manufacturers throughout the country. It was understood that these terms should be considered as confidential but it soon proved impossible to keep the circulars from falling into the hands of outside parties. As a result, many of the manufacturers withdrew their offers, and the executive committee decided to make no further attempts in this direction until some plan could be developed by which the arrangements could be kept secret. The committee then turned its attention to encouraging the state granges to invest their funds in state agencies and manufacturing establishments and to securing for the order the right to manufacture certain makes of the more expensive agricultural implements.[1]

In addition to the work of the executive committee some of the other officers of the National Grange at times allowed their names to be used in endorsing certain commercial firms as Grange agents and in one case with disastrous results. The firm of Farley and Company of New York City was appointed Grange agent by the state granges of North Carolina and Mississippi and was recommended to Patrons all over the country in a circular signed by Secretary Kelley of the National Grange. Farley was master of Manhattan Grange, but the firm seems to have been wholly fraudulent. Orders for supplies accompanied by money and consignments of produce were received from Patrons in many parts of the South and East without any returns being made. As a result the confidence of many in the order and especially in the officers of the National Grange was shaken. The North Carolina State Grange reimbursed the Patrons in that state for their losses, and claims were presented to the National Grange at its eighth session in February, 1875. The matter was thoroughly aired at this and the following sessions, but the Grange finally decided that it was not responsible for the endorsement of the firm. The charter of Manhattan Grange was revoked, however, and resolutions were adopted directing that in the future no officers other than the executive committee should endorse agents and no firms should be recommended

[1] National Grange, *Proceedings*, viii. 23–26, 29–31 (February, 1875); Virginia State Grange, *Proceedings*, i. 22 (April, 1874); Aiken, *The Grange*, 12.

unless under sufficient bonds to secure the members of the order from possible loss.[1]

At the eighth session of the National Grange, in February, 1875, business coöperation was the all-absorbing theme among the delegates, but the work of the National Grange in this direction was crippled by the loan of fifty thousand dollars to the state granges to assist them in carrying on the extensive agencies and manufacturing enterprises undertaken. A plan recommended by the executive committee for the appointment of three national purchasing agents in New York, Chicago, and New Orleans, with salaries to be paid by the National Grange, was rejected. The operations of the committee during the year were approved, however, and encouragement was given for continuing them along the same lines.[2]

During the summer of 1875, a sub-committee of the executive committee visited a number of states for the purpose of deciding upon a location for the headquarters of the National Grange, and advantage was taken of this opportunity to investigate the workings of the state business agencies. This sub-committee reported that many of the agencies were unsatisfactory, especially those doing business on a commission basis, which differed little from ordinary commission firms, and recommended the inauguration of a permanent, uniform coöperative business system in the order. As a result of this investigation the executive committee adopted a series of resolutions condemning the commission system as at variance with coöperative principles and recommending the abolition of all commission agencies and the establishment in each state of a single salaried state agent. When the National Grange met in November, 1875, it expressed its approval of this action by adopting a similar resolution, with the added recommendations that the agents be members of the order, that they be placed under bonds, that they coöperate

---

[1] On this episode, see National Grange, *Proceedings*, viii. 51, 90, 98, 104, ix. 100, 135, 141, 155, x. 23, 101 (1875–76); State grange proceedings: North Carolina, iii. 12, 27, 36 (1876); New York, ii. 13, 22–24, 42–44, 56 (1875); Ohio, iii. 7 (1876).

[2] National Grange, *Proceedings*, viii. 23–31, 55, 65, 70, 77, 99 (February, 1875); Woodman, "Early History of the Grange," in *American Grange Bulletin*, xxx. nos. 38, 41 (March 7, 28, 1901).

with each other by exchanging price lists, and that they buy and sell for Patrons of other states on the same terms as for those of their own.[1]

In response to another resolution of the National Grange the executive committee at this session reported a system of rules for the government of coöperative associations within the order. These rules embodied what is generally known as the Rochdale plan. The principal features were the organization of a stock company with shares of five dollars each to be held only by members of the order and in limited amounts; each holder of a share or more of stock to be a member of the association and have an equal voice in its management regardless of the amount of stock held; sales to be for cash and at the usual retail rates; and profits, after payment of a limited interest on stock, to be divided among purchasers in proportion to amounts purchased, the proportion to non-members to be only one-half that to members of the association. These rules were intended to be used in the organization of local coöperative stores by a single grange or by the granges of a neighborhood, but it was also expected that more extensive wholesale associations might be formed along the same lines, the stock to be held in part by the local associations. The rules were explained at length to the National Grange by one of the members of the executive committee and after thorough discussion the Grange decided to recommend them to Patrons throughout the country. In addition the executive committee was authorized to have them printed, together with such forms and blanks as it might deem necessary, for distribution to interested Patrons.[2]

Another scheme for a comprehensive form of distributive coöperation made its appearance at this session of the National Grange. During the summer the members of the executive committee had been in correspondence with representatives of the English Coöperative Union by whom a suggestion was made " that the time had come for a system of international exchanges between the coöperations [coöperators ?] of England

---

[1] National Grange, *Proceedings*, ix. 20–33, 141 (November, 1875).

[2] *Ibid.* 23, 93–100, 130, 171.

and the Mississippi Valley." Negotiations were carried on by the executive committee with the approval of the National Grange, and finally a delegate was sent to England to perfect the arrangements. The outcome of the whole matter was the organization of the " Anglo-American Coöperative Company " which was to have an American branch under the supervision of the National Grange. The scheme was presented to the National Grange at its tenth session in November, 1876, and was recommended by it to the Patrons in connection with a comprehensive plan for coöperation, embracing local coöperative stores, state and interstate coöperative associations, and finally, at the top, the American branch of the Anglo-American Coöperative Company. The inauguration of this scheme for international coöperation depended upon the raising of a certain amount of capital in America; but by this time the order of Patrons of Husbandry had declined so much in numbers and prestige that this was impossible and the plan never went into operation.[1]

COÖPERATIVE STORES

By the time of the tenth annual session of the National Grange in November, 1876, the members had pretty generally lost faith in Grange agencies of any sort and in Grange manufacturing, but most of them had become converts to the Rochdale system of coöperation. From this time on the National Grange devoted much of its energies to disseminating literature concerning this system and to encouraging the organization of coöperative stores and associations and their substitution for existing Grange agencies and corporations.[2] Long before the promulga-

---

[1] National Grange, *Proceedings*, ix. 89–93, x. 8–10, 25, 48–67, 124–130, 144–152, 162, 167–169, 172, xi. 12, xii. 95 (1875–78); Aiken, *The Grange*, 13.

In September, 1876, the Oregon State Grange planned the organization of a "Coöperative Association of the Northwest " to be ultimately connected with the Anglo-American Company. In January, 1877, the Arkansas State Grange recommended the organization of corporations which should take stock in and serve as distributing agencies for the Anglo-American Company. Oregon State Grange, *Proceedings*, iii; Arkansas State Grange, *Proceedings*, v.

[2] National Grange, *Proceedings*, ix–xvi (1875–82); *Rules for Patrons' Coöperative Associations . . . Recommended by the National Grange* (pamphlet, 1876);

tion of the rules for coöperative associations by the National Grange, stock companies made up solely of members of the order had existed in many parts of the country, for the purpose of providing capital for local stores or for agencies. Almost invariably these early stores attempted to operate by selling goods to members of the order at very low prices, but the profits, when there were any, were divided among the stockholders in proportion to the amount of stock held. Corporations of this sort operated under serious disadvantages. Their low prices aroused the antagonism of neighboring merchants and involved them in intense competition; and there was no incentive to hold the trade of Patrons when better bargains were offered elsewhere. As a consequence most of these organizations either were forced out of business or raised their prices and gave up all pretense of being coöperative.

The Rochdale system was an improvement on these corporations in many ways. By selling at ordinary rates the intense competition of the neighboring merchants was prevented; by issuing stock in small shares and giving an equal voice in the management to each shareholder, large numbers were given a personal interest in the concern; and by division of profits among purchasers, the same if not greater savings could be effected as by attempting to sell at cost. It was a distinct misfortune, both for the order of Patrons of Husbandry and for the advancement of coöperation, that the National Grange did not begin to propagate the principles of the Rochdale system until after the ineffectiveness and often disastrous consequences of the early attempts had disgusted many of the Patrons with the idea of coöperative stores and the rapid decline of the order had begun. As it was, the rules for coöperative associations issued by the National Grange were eagerly sought by Patrons everywhere and hundreds of coöperative stores, with a few more extensive associations, were organized wherever the Grange continued to flourish. In the course of time many

J. W. A. Wright, *Address on Rochdale and Grange Coöperation* (pamphlet, 1877); Wright, *Coöperation; Europe and the Grange* (pamphlet, 1876?); Aiken, *The Grange*, 13.

of these failed, either through bad management or failure to practise some of the essential features of the system, but many of them had long and successful careers and were probably efficient factors in preventing the total extinction of the order of Patrons of Husbandry in the latter seventies and early eighties. A brief survey of the operations of these coöperative associations in different parts of the country will be of value.

In the states of the Middle West large numbers of Patrons' coöperative stores were established in the years 1874 and 1875, often, however, without the essential feature of the Rochdale system, division of profits in proportion to purchases.[1] As a consequence of this and other factors most of these establishments were short lived; some, however, were reorganized on the Rochdale plan, and a few which were exceptionally well managed survived and continued to do business for a number of years on their original plan of selling at cost.

In Ohio it is said that there was at one time a Grange store in practically every county in the state; but no record has been found of any of them continuing in business for more than a few years. Just at the close of the decade, however, a " Cincinnati Grange Supply House " was established under the auspices of the state grange to take the place of the state agency which was being closed out. This corporation was organized on the Rochdale plan so far as the laws of Ohio permitted. It was intended that it should serve as a general supply house for the granges and coöperative stores of Ohio, Indiana, Kentucky, and West Virginia and should lead to the establishment of tributary stores all over the Middle West. By this time, however, the enthusiasm and class spirit which the Grange had engendered among the farmers of the West had largely passed away and the house does not appear to have done a very extensive business at any time. In 1883 a branch house was established at Cleveland, which was not a success, and in 1886, as a result of bad management, faulty organization, and lack of

---

[1] *Prairie Farmer*, xliv. 43, xlv. 97, 139, xlvi. 21, 75, 107 (1873–75); *Industrial Age*, March 7, 1874, p. 7; *Western Rural*, xiii. 196, 356 (1875); Illinois State Grange, *Proceedings*, iv. 17 (1875).

patronage, it was found necessary to appoint a receiver to liquidate the affairs of the association.[1]

In the other states of the Northwest, also, large numbers of so-called coöperative stores were established; but the only ones which appear to have had any considerable success were a few established late in the decade which followed the rules recommended by the National Grange as closely as the state laws would permit. Good examples of these are the Huntington Coöperative Store, established by Patrons at Huntington, Indiana, about 1879, and one at Brandon, Wisconsin, established in 1877. Both of these were reported as doing a large business about the middle of the next decade. In Iowa, the Farmers' Exchange of Grinnell, which was started in 1873 with a membership limited to Patrons, survived the collapse of the order in that state, but was obliged to admit others to membership after 1878. The Rochdale system was never adopted in this store; but provision was made for limiting the voting power of large stockholders, and, largely because of skilful management, the store continued to do an extensive business during the decade of the eighties.[2]

In Kansas, also, the first crop of Grange stores went to pieces about the middle of the decade; but in 1876 some of the leading Grange workers of the state brought about the organization of the Johnson County Coöperative Association at Olathe upon the Rochdale plan as embodied in the rules recommended by the National Grange. The success of this store was phenomenal.

---

[1] Warner, in Johns Hopkins University, *Studies*, vi. 372–378; S. H. Ellis, "History of the Grange in Ohio," in *Ohio Farmer*, ci. 32, cv. 399 (1902, 1904).

[2] National Grange, *Proceedings*, xv. 45, xvi. 34, 46 (1881, 1882); Illinois State Grange, *Proceedings*, v. 74, 94–96 (1876); Michigan State Grange, *Proceedings*, viii. 16 (1880); Warner, in Johns Hopkins University, *Studies*, vi. 382–384; Shaw, in *ibid.* 316; Wisconsin Bureau of Statistics, *Reports*, ii. 208–211 (1885–86).

In November, 1876, a meeting of managers of the coöperative stores of the Northwest was held in Chicago in connection with the session of the National Grange. Representatives were present from about twenty different stores and associations located in Illinois, Indiana, Iowa, Michigan, Tennessee, Arkansas, and New York. Steps were taken for the organization of a " Northwestern Coöperative Association " to be located in Chicago and to serve as a wholesale house for the local stores, but the association does not appear to have been established. Probably it was not possible to dispose of enough stock to secure a working capital. Illinois State Grange, *Proceedings*, v. 102–107.

Its capital rose in ten years from eight hundred and fifty dollars to over forty thousand dollars; nearly two hundred and seventy thousand dollars' worth of goods were sold in 1883; and a three-story modern building equipped with a hall for the local grange was erected at a cost of seventy-five thousand dollars. The success of this attempt at coöperation led to the establishment of some twenty or thirty similar coöperative stores in the state. Some were under the control of the Grange and some independent, but nearly all were successful when based upon the Rochdale plan. It is probable that this movement was an important factor in the revival of the order of Patrons of Husbandry in Kansas during the early eighties.[1]

In California a considerable number of Grange corporations were organized in 1873 and 1874 for the purpose of running local coöperative stores, and several more extensive coöperative associations were organized in the commercial centers. Among the most successful of these were the Farmers' Coöperative Union of San José, the Grangers' Union of Stockton, and a Grangers' coöperative association for Southern California at Los Angeles. The method of operation of all of these was probably about the same and the last will serve as an example. The capital of this association was fixed at one hundred thousand dollars divided in shares of fifty dollars each, which could be held only by Patrons and not more than ten by any one person. The holding of one share of stock admitted a Granger and his family to all the privileges of the company. Goods were sold to members at as near cost as possible but to outsiders at the usual rates. While this was not the Rochdale system, it contained a number of distinctively coöperative features and most of the Grange coöperative associations of California were reported as " meeting with marked success " as late as 1882.[2]

The earliest attempt at the organization of a Grange coöperative association in the southern states seems to have been the Direct Trade Union, which was incorporated in Georgia in

---

[1] Warner, in Johns Hopkins University, *Studies*, vi. 384; National Grange, *Proceedings*, xv. 37, xvi. 30 (1881, 1882).

[2] Carr, *Patrons of Husbandry*, 165–168; National Grange, *Proceedings*, xvi. 27 (1882).

1874 to handle shipments of cotton and import foreign goods for the Patrons of the South. The only feature which distinguished this Union from an ordinary stock company was the limitation of shares to Patrons of Husbandry and the declared intention of charging only the lowest possible commissions. Stock was subscribed for by Patrons of Alabama, Tennessee, Georgia, and North Carolina and operations began early in 1874. Many southern Patrons appear to have been benefited by shipping through this Union in 1874 and 1875; but there were some losses, complaints were made of mismanagement, and this attempt at coöperation seems to have been given up in 1876.[1]

Few coöperative stores were established by the Grange in the South during the early years; but after the promulgation of the rules by the National Grange in 1875, they began slowly to make their appearance. By 1882 Grange coöperative stores or associations had been formed on the Rochdale plan in Alabama, Georgia, Missouri, North Carolina, Tennessee, and Texas and probably in some of the other states, and all were reported to be successful.[2] In Texas, however, appeared what was destined to be the most successful example of distributive coöperation in the United States.[3] Here as in the other southern states, the Grange stores on the Rochdale plan began to make their appearance about the middle of the decade, and in 1878 representatives of these got together and organized the Texas Coöperative Association to handle shipments of cotton and the wholesale business in general. This association, which was also organized on the Rochdale plan, started with a paid-up stock of two hundred and fifty dollars in 1878, and grew steadily until in 1887 it had a paid-up capital of over fifty thousand dollars, did a business of over five hundred thousand dollars, and divided almost twenty thousand dollars of net profits.

[1] *Rural Carolinian*, v. 426, 483, 592 (1874); *Prairie Farmer*, xlv. 259 (August 15, 1874); State grange proceedings: Alabama, ii. 12, 17, 22, 25 (1874); Tennessee, ii. 22, 30, 38, 39 (1875); North Carolina, ii. 11, 27, 28, 33, 39, iii. 6, 12, 20, 31 (1875, 1876).

[2] National Grange, *Proceedings*, xv. 35, 43, xvi. 28, 36, 38 (1881, 1882).

[3] On the Texas Coöperative Association, see *ibid*. xv. 43, xvi. 43; Wisconsin Bureau of Statistics, *Reports*, ii. 158–160 (1885–86); Randall, in Johns Hopkins University, *Studies*, vi. 503–505.

Great as was this success, it was out-distanced by that of the local coöperative stores in the state. By 1882 there were ninety-two of these which held stock in the general association, and by 1887 the number increased to about one hundred and fifty. The total capital of these stores at that time was about seven hundred and fifty thousand dollars, and in 1885 their combined sales amounted to nearly two million dollars, from which profits of over two hundred and fifty thousand dollars were divided. Indeed the success of the coöperative movement in Texas was so great that the business interests of the state combined in 1885 and secured a change in the laws which prevented the further organization of local associations. Another result of this success was the flourishing condition of the order of Patrons of Husbandry in Texas during the eighties, when it was making little progress in other parts of the South and West.

In the eastern states, also, the advocacy of Rochdale coöperation by the National Grange bore fruit. The Grange in this section had no record of past failures in coöperation to live down, and Grange stores were organized during the later seventies and early eighties in Maine, New Hampshire, Massachusetts, Connecticut, New York, Pennsylvania, and Delaware. In 1877 a Patrons' Coöperative Corporation was established at Portland, Maine, to do a wholesale business in groceries, grain, provisions, and farm supplies. A large part of the capital was furnished by the state and subordinate granges. This corporation does not appear to have been organized on strictly Rochdale principles, but it did a large business for a number of years, supplying Grangers and Grange stores with goods at low prices. While this form of coöperation did not sweep everything before it in the East as it did in Texas, still, generally speaking, these Grange stores appear to have been successful in a small way.[1]

Of all the activities undertaken by the National Grange with the view of advancing the pecuniary interests of the members

---

[1] National Grange, *Proceedings*, xv. 36, 38, 40–42, xvi. 28, 33 (1881, 1882); E. W. Bemis, " Coöperation in New England," in Johns Hopkins University, *Studies*, vi. 33–36; Massachusetts State Grange, *Quarterly Bulletin*, January, 1876; State grange proceedings: Maine, vi. 16, 18, 26, 37 (1879); New Hampshire, i–vi (1873–79); Massachusetts, v. 20 (1877).

of the order, by far the most effective and enduring was its promulgation of the rules for Patrons' coöperative associations, together with its consistent advocacy of the Rochdale system. Plans for extensive agencies and manufacturing plants and for international coöperation may have come to naught, but the successes achieved by coöperative associations where the rules were followed bear witness to the ultimate wisdom of the members of the National Grange.

GRANGE MANUFACTURING

Unfortunately for the welfare of the order, the Grangers were not satisfied with distributive coöperation. When the purchasing agencies were getting under way they often experienced considerable difficulty in making arrangements with manufacturers for machinery at wholesale rates.[1] The manufacturers had a system of disposing of their wares through agents with exclusive territory, and such arrangements as the Grangers wished to make, though perhaps on the face of them advantageous to the manufacturers, meant serious interference with this system and perhaps loss in the end. In the course of time the Grange agents generally succeeded in finding some manufacturer or dealer who would make suitable terms, so far as the smaller and less expensive implements or machines were concerned, but the manufacturers of harvesters persistently held back. Just at this time the treasuries of the national and state granges were overflowing with money, which had been collected from dispensations and dues. How better could these funds be invested than in independent Grange factories which could be used to " smash " the " Harvester Ring," the " Plow Ring," and other combinations which were adverse to the interests of

---

[1] For example, at a meeting of plow manufacturers in November, 1873, an agreement was signed by twenty-two firms that no plows should be sold to clubs or granges except at retail prices, but local agents were advised to give reduced rates for cash sales in large quantities. The granges and farmers' clubs responded with resolutions of boycott against the firms in the " Plow Ring." *Prairie Farmer*, xliv. 379, 403, xlv. 19, 84 (1873–74). For other instances, see *Chicago Tribune*, August 21, 1873, p. 2; Lea, *Grange Movement in Wisconsin* (Ms.), 14, quoting *Evansville* (Wisconsin) *Register*, June 17, 1873.

the farmers ? So at least reasoned the leading Patrons; and when the order was once embarked in this direction, all sorts of schemes for Grange manufacturing made their appearance.

As early as 1872 the state grange of Nebraska made arrangements for the manufacture of headers under its auspices. The header was a comparatively simple machine, which was used for a while in some parts of the West for gathering merely the heads of the grain. For a year or two this enterprise appeared to be a success, and the machines, which had previously retailed for from $225 to $300, were now furnished to Patrons for $150. Later, however, the state grange undertook the manufacture of cultivators and harvesters and as a result of overstocking, defective machines, and bad management, it suffered a severe financial loss. Even the assistance from the National Grange in the form of loans and donations was not sufficient to retrieve the disaster, and the Grange disappeared from Nebraska.[1]

The most important attempt at manufacturing agricultural machinery by the Patrons of Husbandry originated in Iowa. When, in 1873, the state agent found it practically impossible to induce the manufacturers of harvesters to sell to the order at wholesale rates, the idea occurred to some one that the Grange might manufacture its own harvesters. A man was discovered in Wisconsin who owned a patent on a machine known as the Werner harvester, and State Agent Whitman with E. R. Shankland of the executive committee of the National Grange were sent to Wisconsin to make arrangements for its control. The outcome was the purchase of the patent for one thousand dollars and a royalty of two dollars on each machine manufactured. Arrangements were at once made for the establishment of foundries in various places in Iowa, Minnesota, and Nebraska to manufacture the harvesters under contract for the different state granges. During the summer of 1874 about 250 in all of these machines were manufactured and were furnished to Patrons at $140, or about half the prevailing price for harvesters.

[1] Nebraska State Grange, *Proceedings*, iv (1874); National Grange, *Proceedings*, viii. 30, 68, 82, 105 (February, 1875); Warner, in Johns Hopkins University, *Studies*, vi. 368; Woodman, " Early History of the Grange," in *American Grange Bulletin*, xxx. no. 38 (March 7, 1901).

The Werner harvester was said to be a good one and appears to have given satisfaction in most cases; some of the machines, however, proved to be defective; others were received from the foundries too late to be used in the harvest; and in nearly every case the state granges involved found at the close of the season that they had lost money by the venture. In 1875 new complications arose; the Marsh Harvester Company threatened suits for infringement of patents; and the contracts for manufacture appear to have been annulled.[1]

During the summer of 1874, when the manufacture of the Werner harvesters was to all appearances a great success, the members of the executive committee of the National Grange, and especially E. R. Shankland, the member from Iowa, conceived the design of having practically all machinery used by farmers manufactured under the auspices of the Grange. They went about the country buying up patents for the order on all sorts of implements; cultivators, seeders, hay racks, a combined reaper and mower, and so on; and care was not always taken to have the machines thoroughly tested or to be sure that the patents were valid. Some of these patents were purchased by the National Grange and others by state granges, and a lack of definite understanding between the two as to the exact obligations incurred paved the way for future difficulties. In state after state the order entered eagerly upon the manufacture of these agricultural implements; harvester factories, plow and wagon factories, sewing machine factories, threshing machine factories, and general implement factories were planned in Kansas, Iowa, Missouri, Wisconsin, Illinois, Indiana and Kentucky, and some of them actually established; but capital was difficult to procure, the state granges were short of funds, a few failures dampened the enthusiasm, and by the close of 1875 the idea of the manufacture of agricultural implements by the Grange was practically abandoned.[2]

---

[1] National Grange, *Proceedings*, viii. 30, 68, 82, 105 (February, 1875); *Prairie Farmer*, xliv. 411, xlv. 139, 347 (1873–74); *Western Rural*, xiii. 188 (June 12, 1875); State grange proceedings: Iowa, iv, v (1873, 1874); Kansas, iii (1875); Nebraska, iv (1874).

[2] National Grange, *Proceedings*, viii. 29–31, ix. 21, 37, 39, x. 38 (1875–76);

The main object of all these manufacturing schemes was to provide members of the order with the products of the factories at a low price; but there was another sort of Grange factories, the object of which was to provide a market for the raw materials produced by the farmers. Grist-mills, cheese and butter factories, linseed oil factories, starch factories, pork-packing establishments, and even hemp factories and cotton mills in the South, were projected under the auspices of the order in great profusion, and many were established. Most of these enterprises were local in character, the capital being furnished by the organization of a stock company among the Patrons of a neighborhood, and as a general rule they seem to have been more successful than the more ambitious agricultural implement factories. Farmers' coöperative creameries and cheese factories had made their appearance in some parts of the West even before the rise of the Grange, but their number was greatly increased by the order and they undoubtedly helped to bring prosperity to many a neighborhood.[1]

BANKING AND INSURANCE

Another business in which the Grangers proposed to invest their surplus capital was that of banking. Projects for Grange banks were discussed in several of the southern and western states,[2] and a New York speculator proposed the establishment of a " Grangers' Mortgage Bank " in that city,[3] but the only state

---

Prairie Farmer, xlv. 139, 355 (1874); *Western Rural*, xiii. 380 (November 27, 1875); Woodman, in *American Grange Bulletin*, xxx. nos. 38, 41, 43, 48 (1901); Maynard, *Patrons of Husbandry in Wisconsin* (Ms.), 66; State grange proceedings: Iowa, iv–vi (1873–75); Nebraska, iv (1874); Texas, i. 25 (1874).

Some of the state granges refused to be drawn into these manufacturing schemes. See Michigan State Grange, *Proceedings*, ii (1875); Missouri State Grange, *Proceedings*, iii, iv (1874, 1875); *Prairie Farmer*, xlv. 243, 371 (1874).

[1] National Grange, *Proceedings*, viii. 39 (1875); North Carolina State Grange, *Proceedings*, ii–iv (1875–77); *Prairie Farmer*, xliv. 57, 377, xlv. 139, 186, xlvi. 355 (1873–75); *Wisconsin Statesman*, July 31, 1875, p. 3; Maynard, *Patrons of Husbandry in Wisconsin* (Ms.), 66; Shaw, in Johns Hopkins University, *Studies*, vi. 340; Warner, in *ibid.* 378–382.

[2] Virginia State Grange, *Proceedings*, i (1874); North Carolina State Grange, *Proceedings*, ii, iv (1874, 1877).

[3] E. J. Nieuwland, *High Interest Monopoly and its Remedies* (leaflet, 1874).

in which anything was done in this direction during the seventies was California. The farmers of that state complained that the existing banks discriminated against them and aided the speculators in their efforts to manipulate the markets. They got together, therefore, in 1874, and organized the Grangers' Bank of California with the purpose of enabling the Patrons to secure loans of money on " the landed security of the agriculturist," " upon as favorable terms as it can be obtained in the city for commercial purposes." Only Patrons of Husbandry could be stockholders or directors of this bank, and the rights of small stockholders were guarded by provisions restricting the voting power of those holding more than fifty of the one hundred dollar shares. The bank went into operation on August 1, 1874, and within a year had two million dollars on deposit and a paid up capital of about half a million dollars. It seems to have had a successful career, and is reported to have saved the farmers of the state a large amount of money at a time of depression in the wheat market, by loaning them three million dollars and thus enabling them to hold their wheat for a rise in the market.[1] Two other Grange banks were established in 1874 in Colusa and Solano counties, California,[2] and in 1883 a Patrons' Coöperative Bank was established at Olathe, Kansas, where a very successful coöperative store was already in existence.[3]

The subject of mutual insurance early attracted the attention of the Patrons of Husbandry.[4] Farmers' mutual fire insurance companies had been in existence in many parts of the country before the appearance of the Grange, and it soon became evident

[1] For the organization and by-laws of this institution, see Carr, *Patrons of Husbandry*, 160–165. See also *ibid.* 175; National Grange, *Proceedings*, xv. 36 (1881); *Prairie Farmer*, xlvi. 355 (November 6, 1875); M. Whitehead, " Patrons of Husbandry," in New Jersey Bureau of Statistics of Labor and Industries, *Reports*, ix. 344 (1886).

[2] Carr, *Patrons of Husbandry*, 165, 167.

[3] Warner, in Johns Hopkins University, *Studies*, vi. 386; Whitehead, in New Jersey Bureau of Statistics, *Reports*, ix. 344 (1886).

[4] References on insurance are scattered through the proceedings of nearly all of the state granges. See also National Grange, *Proceedings*, xv. 36, 38, 44, 45, xvi. 38 (1881, 1882); *Country Gentleman*, xlv. 110 (February 12, 1880); Whitehead, in New Jersey Bureau of Statistics, *Reports*, ix. 345 (1886); Shaw, in Johns Hopkins University, *Studies*, vi. 318, 341–344.

that they were especially suited to the purposes of that organization. As a rule these Grange fire insurance companies were
confined to a single township or county and were very simple
in form. Small fees were paid for admission to the company
and proportional assessments made upon members whenever
a loss occurred.[1] Organizations of this sort were formed by the
Patrons of Husbandry in every state in the Union in which the
order flourished. The careers of many of them in the western
states were checked by the dissolution of local granges during
the later seventies; but in the East, where the order suffered
no set back at this time, they continued to flourish and multiply,
and many of them are still in existence.[2] In a number of the
states more ambitious schemes for fire insurance were attempted
by the state grange or by Patrons' stock companies. Thus the
California Mutual Fire Insurance Company was organized
by Patrons of that state in 1874 as a stock company, with a
capital of one hundred thousand dollars and with a somewhat
complicated method of doing business.[3] Grange fire insurance
companies which were state-wide in their scope were also organized in Kansas in 1874,[4] New Hampshire in 1878,[5] and Maine in
1879.[6] The Maine company seems to have been formed by
the consolidation of the several local companies previously
existing in that state.

The first and one of the most flourishing Grange life insurance
companies organized was the Patrons' Mutual Aid Society of
Elmira, New York.[7] The mode of operation of this society,
which was established in December, 1874, was fairly simple.

[1] See constitution of a company formed at Muscatine, Iowa, in 1873, in *Prairie
Farmer*, xliv. 387 (December 6, 1873).

[2] F. W. Card, " Coöperative Fire Insurance and Telephones," in Bailey, *Cyclopedia of American Agriculture*, iv. 303–306.

[3] Carr, *Patrons of Husbandry*, 168–172, 175.

[4] Kansas State Grange, *Proceedings*, iii (1875); J. K. Hudson, *Patrons' Handbook*, 27.

[5] New Hampshire State Grange, *Proceedings*, i–iii, v, vii (1875–80).

[6] Maine State Grange, *Proceedings*, vi. 26, 29.

[7] Patrons' Aid Society of Elmira, New York, *By-Laws*, adopted December,
1874, *By-Laws*, as amended March 16, 1876, *Sixth Annual Report* (1881); New
York State Grange, *Proceedings*, iii (1876).

It was open to Patrons only and entrance fees ranging from three to fifteen dollars, depending upon age, were collected from applicants. These fees were kept as a reserve fund, but when the fund exceeded ten thousand dollars the surplus was to be used to pay death claims. Otherwise the death claims were to be met by assessments of one dollar upon each member but were not to exceed two thousand dollars. At the end of six years, the Elmira society had a membership of about eleven hundred, and ten death claims had been paid. The by-laws of the society were circulated among Patrons all over the country, and furnished a model for the organization of a considerable number of similar societies in other states, usually under the auspices of the state granges. Patrons' mutual aid societies were thus established in Arkansas,[1] Tennessee,[2] Kansas,[3] and Wisconsin,[4] in 1875, in North[5] and South Carolina[6] in 1877, in Maine[7] and New Hampshire[8] in 1878. The Patrons' Benevolent Aid Society of Wisconsin had a membership of about eleven hundred in 1880; but this began to decrease soon after and it went out of existence about 1890. As a general rule, Grange life insurance does not appear to have been as successful as fire insurance. It worked all right for a few years; but soon the death rate began to increase and then the membership generally decreased.[9]

---

[1] Arkansas State Grange, *Proceedings*, v. 23 (1877).

[2] Tennessee State Grange, *Proceedings*, ii. 55 (1875).

[3] Kansas State Grange, *Proceedings*, iii (1875).

[4] Wisconsin State Grange, *Proceedings*, iv–xvi (1876–88); Patrons' Benevolent Aid Society (Wisconsin), *Annual Circular with Articles of Incorporation and By-Laws*, 1878; Lea, *Grange Movement in Wisconsin* (Ms.), 16–18.

[5] North Carolina State Grange, *Proceedings*, iii, iv (1876, 1877).

[6] " Essays Read before the South Carolina State Grange," in South Carolina State Agricultural and Mechanical Society, *Transactions*, 1877, pp. 24–27.

[7] Maine State Grange, *Proceedings*, vi. 29, 32, 39 (1880).

[8] New Hampshire State Grange, *Proceedings*, i–iii, v, vii (1875–80).

[9] A curious insurance scheme made its appearance in Alabama. The Grangers' Life and Health Insurance Company of the United States was organized by private parties at Mobile in 1875 and agreed to give the state grange twenty-five per cent of the first premium on all policies obtained through the influence of the order. Alabama State Grange, *Proceedings*, iii. 5, 36 (1875).

Reasons for Failure

On the whole, in spite of occasional remarkable successes, it can be said that this attempt of the American farmer to regain his economic independence by taking upon himself the business of the middleman, the capitalist, the manufacturer, and the banker, through coöperative organization, was a failure. Necessarily many of the causes for this failure have been suggested in the foregoing sketch but it will be well to summarize them here.

Perhaps the most fundamental cause was the incompatibility between the coöperative method of business and rural life and conditions as they existed in America. Coöperation implies a working together, a reliance on one another, a patience and foresight, which were wanting in the character of the independent, self-reliant, aggressive, and suspicious American farmer. Living on isolated farms, and lacking business experience, the Grangers found themselves at a decided disadvantage when their enterprises came into competition with those run by shrewd, experienced men of business who had no other occupations to distract their attention. Too often, moreover, there was a lamentable lack of foresight. The very ones who had been loudest in denunciation of monopoly prices and foremost in the establishment of coöperative enterprises would allow themselves to be led astray by the temporary low prices of competitors and thus help to bring about the destruction of the institution which had caused the low prices. They were unwilling to forego immediate and temporary gain for ultimate advantage.

Another important factor in the failure was the unsuitability of many of the undertakings to the coöperative system. That was especially true of the manufacturing enterprises, for it should be noted that these were not true examples of productive coöperation as the phrase is understood in England. There the workmen are the coöperators and furnish the capital for the enterprises, but in these schemes the coöperators were either the consumers of the finished product or the producers of the raw material. The Patrons could buy patents and get their machines manufactured cheaply; but they could not prevent their alert competitors from getting control of improvements which threw their machines out of the market, and they lacked the necessary capital to withstand the intense competition to which they were subjected by combinations of regular manufacturers. The system of selling without agents also placed the Grange machines at a disadvantage. If a machine failed to work properly or if the farmer did not know how to run it, there was no one for him to call upon for adjustment of the machine or for instruction. These were services which had been performed by the local agents under the old system of selling. As a consequence, the Grange machines sometimes got the reputation of being unsatisfactory when all that was needed was a little adjustment or instruction to the operator.

The farmers might have had some chance of success if they had gone into business operations on a small scale at the start, as did the " Rochdale Pioneers " in England, and gradually expanded the enterprises as their experience increased. But a few early successes, together with the marvelous growth of the Grange, turned their heads and they rushed pell-mell into all sorts of business schemes without considering where the capital and business ability to carry them out were to come from. The incomes of the state and national granges furnished capital for many of the schemes, and these incomes were large in the early years; but they came principally from dispensations for new granges and could not by any possibility continue at the same rate. The different schemes, moreover, were generally so interwoven one with another, that a disaster to one involved the failure of all the others and the collapse of the whole house of cards.

If the Grangers were not willing to let their business plans develop gradually while they were gaining experience, it would seem as if they might at least have availed themselves of the experience of coöperators elsewhere. Many of them, of course, had never heard of the English coöperators, but even those who had were inclined to believe that their own home-made theories were better than any principles which had been worked out in England. As a consequence, they fell into many pitfalls which the English coöperators had learned to avoid. Even when the leaders of the Grange attempted to introduce the true principles of coöperation they met with considerable opposition, and the old enterprises generally retained their original form to the end. The coöperative undertakings which were begun after 1875 had the advantage, however, not only of the experience of the English coöperators as promulgated in the rules of the National Grange but also of the disastrous experience of their predecessors, and, as has been seen, they were moderately successful. In this connection it might be noted that the laws of many of the states made the organization of coöperative associations in strict accord with the Rochdale plan an impossibility.[1] Had this difficulty appeared in the early years when the Granger movement was a political force, the desired laws would probably have been quickly enacted; but as it was the articles of association had to be modified to conform to the laws, and this was a partial cause of the failure of some of these enterprises.

Finally, the poverty of the farmers and the prevalence of the credit system stood in the way of the success of Grange coöperation. A certain amount of ready money was necessary, not only to provide capital for the stores and agencies, but to enable the farmers to take advantage of the opportunities they offered, and ready money was far from plentiful with the farmers at this time. The substitution of cash payment for the credit system was one of the great objects of the Grange and the business operations under its auspices were generally conducted on a cash basis. The change from a credit system to cash payments can be accomplished only gradually and many farmers who were compelled to go to the regular merchants when they wanted credit felt under obligations to trade with them when they had cash. On the other hand, the giving of credit was a factor in the ruin of some of the coöperative enterprises.[2] When competition became strong, the teaching of the Grange was sometimes forgotten and credit extended. Once started in this direction,

---

[1] Warner, in Johns Hopkins University, *Studies*, vi. 372–374, 389.
[2] *Ibid.* 374–377, 382.

it was easy to continue until a considerable portion of the all too scanty capital was tied up in outstanding claims. A manager, moreover, cannot be expected to be as careful about such things as a proprietor, and in some cases losses were experienced from "bad debts." On the whole it seems to be true that the cash basis is the only safe one for coöperative enterprises.

RESULTS

The results of Grange coöperation can be divided into two classes, the temporary and the permanent. The temporary results are so obvious that they need only to be mentioned. In the first place, the coöperative phase of the movement was one of the principal causes of the rapid growth of the Grange from 1873 to 1875; and, conversely, its failure to meet expectations was one of the principal causes of the rapid decline of the order in the succeeding years. There can be no doubt that hope of pecuniary profit was the motive factor in inducing large numbers of farmers to join the Grange, and when their extravagant expectations failed to be realized, most of them ceased to pay dues. Secondly, it is perfectly clear that a very considerable amount of money was saved to farmers as a result of the business enterprises of the order. Even those who were not members of the Grange or who never patronized a Grange store or agency were benefited by the general reduction of prices which was brought about by this new competitive force. What the total amount of this saving was, it is impossible even to estimate, but it certainly was vastly greater than the losses sustained as a result of occasional failures or misplaced confidence.

The permanent results of Grange coöperation are not quite so tangible. On the whole, it seems to have taught a salutary lesson to both farmers and merchants. The farmers learned that the despised middlemen rendered some very important services in the industrial organization and that if they were going to dispense with these middlemen they must be prepared to render the same services. The merchants and manufacturers, on the other hand, discovered that the farmers were not entirely helpless and that it was not wise to burden them with excessive charges, even when the lack of competition made it possible to do so. As a result, lower prices, smaller profits, and more cordial relations seem to have prevailed for some time after the collapse of the Granger movement. But the farmers as well as the merchants had discovered that they were no longer helpless: they had learned the power of organization and could keep it in reserve even if they did not use it; they had also learned the advantage of direct trade and purchases in large quantities, and, as a result, the business of mail order houses has grown steadily from that day to this.

Again, Grange coöperation undoubtedly helped to break up the credit system, and thus in another way tended to make the farmers independent of the local merchants. The insistence of the Grange on cash purchases caused the farmers to make an effort to free themselves from the bonds of the credit system, and the very savings effected through the Grange agencies made it possible for them to continue to buy for cash even after the agencies had disappeared.

As a result of their connection with the coöperative enterprises of the Grange, a considerable number of farmers received a business training which might be of use to them in many ways. In particular, it gave them a very great advantage in their future dealings with merchants and commission men. Added to this general business training was an increased knowledge of the principles and possibilities of coöperation, as a result not only of the occasional successes but of the failures as well. These things paved the way, in some parts of the country at least, for successful and enduring coöperation not only among farmers, but also among workingmen. On the whole, although the Grangers did not succeed in revolutionizing business as they set out to do, nevertheless, a great deal of good both temporary and permanent resulted from their attempts at business coöperation.

CHAPTER VIII

SOCIAL AND EDUCATIONAL FEATURES

THE founders of the order of Patrons of Husbandry believed that they were establishing an institution, the primary purposes of which should be the promotion of social intercourse and the spread of knowledge among the farmers of the country. For a time these purposes seemed to be overshadowed by the desire to secure cheap transportation and the enthusiasm for business coöperation, but they were present, nevertheless, and the permanence of these features of the movement, or rather, the permanence of the order where these features have been uppermost, has demonstrated the wisdom of the founders. That there was a real need of such an institution is almost self-evident. The lonely and monotonous life, the lack of opportunity for social contact and exchange of ideas, and as a result, the provincialism of the average western farmer and his family of the period can better be imagined than described.[1] Farms were so large that the nearest neighbor was generally at least half a mile away; cities were few and far between; and the crossroads villages, even when accessible, offered no better amusement than lounging in a grocery store or saloon. Rural free delivery of mail, rural telephones, and interurban electric lines were things of the future, and if a book or paper did make its way into the farmer's home it was apt to be about as valuable and interesting as a last year's almanac. Worst of all, this lack of social intercourse often led to a distaste for it and the farmers refused to avail themselves of the opportunities which were offered. Here was where the business plans and the railroad agitation were of service; many a farmer, who cared nothing for the social and educational advantages of the Grange, joined in the hopes of obtaining pecuniary profit, but once in, these features had a chance to exert their influence upon him and in time perhaps to draw him out of his shell.

[1] See Martin, *Grange Movement*, 450–453, 459.

The Grange as a Social Force

The social opportunities of the order came primarily in connection with the regular monthly, semi-monthly, or sometimes weekly meetings of the local granges. Here the farmers, with their wives, and sons and daughters of at least fourteen and sixteen years respectively, met in secret conclave to perform the work of a pleasing and appropriate ritual;[1] a literary and musical[2] program usually followed and then there was opportunity for games and general conversation. The ritual of the order provided for a monthly " Feast of Pomona " but the women generally saw to it that refreshments of some sort were served at the other sessions as well. These meetings were held at first in the country school houses, village halls, or even in the houses of the members; but many granges throughout the country built grange halls, especially equipped for their needs. Generally the meetings were held in the evening; but sometimes they began in the afternoon, and then there was, of course, an enlarged opportunity for social intercourse.[3]

In addition to the regular meetings of the subordinate granges, Patrons' picnics or festivals were of frequent occurrence in many neighborhoods. On these occasions the members of three or four neighboring granges would usually join together; repair to some convenient grove; and spend the day in getting acquainted, discussing matters of local or general interest, playing games, listening to speeches and music, usually furnished by members of the order, and consuming the good things brought in the lunch baskets.[4] Independence Day was commonly chosen as an occasion for these picnics, and in 1874 the farmers' picnics

[1] See Aiken, *The Grange*, 16–18.

[2] A Grange song-book was compiled by Miss Carrie Hall, niece of Secretary Kelley, as early as 1872. The National Grange purchased the copyright of this for one thousand dollars and issued a revised edition in 1874. Large numbers of these song-books were sold to subordinate granges throughout the country. Kelley, *Patrons of Husbandry*, 405; National Grange, *Proceedings*, viii. 33.

[3] Kelley, *Patrons of Husbandry*, 249; Martin, *Grange Movement*, 453–458.

[4] Kelley, *Patrons of Husbandry*, 334; Martin, *Grange Movement*, 457, 461, 466; Ellis, in *Ohio Farmer*, c. 495, ci. 12, cv. 18, 399 (1901–04); Massachusetts State Grange, *Proceedings*, v. 8 (1877); *Prairie Farmer*, 1873–75, *passim*.

and celebrations were so numerous that the day was known as the " Farmers' Fourth of July." Farmers' clubs as well as granges joined in these amusements, in the parts of the country where they existed.[1] The social influence of such gatherings as these could not help but spread; acquaintances would be formed which would ripen into friendships and bring about much more frequent intercourse between farm and farm.

The influence of women in the order and of the order upon the position of women are subjects which are much dwelt upon by Grange writers. It seems to be a fact that the Grange was the first secret order to admit women to full and equal membership. If there was any inequality, indeed, it was in favor of the women, for part of the offices were reserved especially for them, while the remainder were open equally to both sexes. Probably in a majority of local granges the lecturer, who had charge of the programs, was a woman. In the state and national granges, too, the presence of women was insured by the rule which made each delegation consist of the master of the local or state grange, as the case might be, and his wife. Without this feature of the order many of the social advantages would have been impossible. That the example and teaching of the Grange was an influence in causing many farmers to look upon their wives more as companions and less as household drudges is also quite possible. Undoubtedly the order offered to women, even more than to men, an opportunity for broader service and the cultivation of the social graces.[2]

The social service of the Grange, however, was not confined to local matters. If it brought about more sympathetic and friendly relations between individuals of the same neighborhood, it also helped to bring about a better understanding between the people of different sections of the country. The state grange meetings brought together men and women from all parts of a state, with differing ideas and interests, while in the National

---

[1] Kelley, *Patrons of Husbandry*, 338, 390–393; *Prairie Farmer* and *Chicago Tribune*, July, 1874, *passim*.

[2] Kelley, *Patrons of Husbandry*, 423; Martin, *Grange Movement*, 453, 456; State grange proceedings: Indiana, iv. 32; Maryland, i. 12; Michigan, iii. 56, 73; Missouri, iii. 22.

Grange the market gardener and horticulturist of the eastern states, the tobacco and cotton planters of the South, the corn grower of the Middle West, and the wheat raiser of the farther West met and exchanged ideas. These meetings occurred only once a year; but they sometimes lasted ten or twelve days, and the members were the chosen leaders of the agriculturists in their respective states. Here men who had recently been in Confederate armies met men who had fought to save the Union. They met now, not as enemies but as brothers in a great fraternal order with the common purpose of uplifting the American farmer. What better institution could be devised for the eradication of sectional prejudice ?

At the close of the seventh session of the National Grange in St. Louis, in February, 1874, an incident occurred which is illustrative of this influence. Worthy Master Wardlaw of the state grange of Florida delivered an address in which he alluded to the fact that at the Democratic convention of 1860 in Charleston it had fallen to his lot to pronounce a eulogy upon ex-Governor Robinson of Vermont, a member who had suddenly been stricken with death. Wardlaw then added that if the representative of the Grange in Vermont were present he would like to clasp hands with him in token of good will and amity. E. P. Colton, the master of the Vermont State Grange, stepped forward and the two clasped hands amidst prolonged and enthusiastic cheering.[1] The next session of the National Grange, in February, 1875, was held in Charleston and was probably the first national convention of importance held in the southern states since the war. The good will and hospitality exhibited by the southern Patrons on this occasion must have been a revelation to many of the northern delegates.[2] When churches refused to reunite, the Grange was probably one of the most

---

[1] National Grange, *Proceedings*, viii. 112 (February, 1875); *Rural Carolinian*, v. 370 (April, 1874); Ellis, in *Ohio Farmer*, c. 391 (November 21, 1901).

[2] National Grange, *Proceedings*, viii. 109–126, especially 121–122, ix. 203. A Grange committee in Illinois is said to have invited Jefferson Davis to deliver an address at a local fair. *Nation*, xxi. 109 (August 19, 1875). On this general subject, see also Kelley, *Patrons of Husbandry*, 378; National Grange, *Proceedings*, x. 19 (1876).

influential factors in assuaging the sectional bitterness left by
the war.

CHARITABLE WORK OF THE ORDER

As is the case with most fraternal orders, the Grange undertook to assist its members in cases of special affliction. Opportunities for the application of this principle on a rather large
scale occurred in 1874 and 1875, at the time when the order was
at the height of prosperity. In April, 1874, the Mississippi
River overflowed its banks and brought disaster and suffering
to a considerable number of farmers living in Louisiana and
Alabama. Many of these farmers were Patrons and appeals
were at once made for assistance to the masters of the state
granges and through them to the order at large. The executive
committee of the National Grange sent one thousand dollars
of its funds to the master of the Louisiana State Grange to be
used as he might deem best. Later the committee expended
about three thousand dollars in purchasing flour and bacon in
the West, which were distributed to the suffering Patrons through
the masters of their state granges.[1] In addition large amounts
of money were collected from the different state and local granges,
and from individual Patrons in all parts of the country, to relieve
the suffering in this section. There is no way of arriving at the
total amount of these contributions but they were as high as
five thousand dollars from some states and are said to have been
received from every state but one in which the order existed.[2]

During the preceding year the grasshopper plague made its
appearance in the states west of the Mississippi River and its
return during the summer of 1874 caused a great deal of destitu-
tion. Again the appeal went up to the National Grange to make
appropriations from its overflowing treasury, and again the
response was generous. The executive committee sent about
eleven thousand dollars to the masters of state granges in Iowa,
Minnesota, Dakota, Kansas, and Nebraska to be used in relieving

[1] National Grange, *Proceedings*, viii. 31, 136 (February, 1875).

[2] *Prairie Farmer*, xlv. 203 (June 27, 1874); Ellis, in *Ohio Farmer*, ci. 78 (January
23, 1902); State grange proceedings: Missouri, iii. 14 (1874); North Carolina,
ii. 10, 18 (1875); Ohio, ii. 6, 9, 21 (1875); Vermont, i–iii. 14 (1874).

the wants of suffering Patrons. When the National Grange met in February, 1875, these expenditures were approved, and further appropriations made of five hundred dollars to Arkansas, and three thousand dollars to the state grange of Kansas to enable it to pay its dues to the National Grange. Provision was also made for the executive committee to act as a standing committee on relief, and during the following year it made additional appropriations to Dakota, Arkansas, Missouri, Tennessee, Colorado, and Iowa, which brought the total amount for the year up to ten thousand dollars. During 1876 the state grange of South Carolina received a donation of one thousand dollars to aid sufferers from a prolonged drought in that state. Two hundred and sixty-five dollars were also appropriated for Minnesota, and a special loan of thirty-five thousand dollars to the Nebraska State Grange was made a donation, on account of continued distress in those states.[1]

As in the case of the sufferers from the Mississippi floods, large amounts of money were collected throughout the different states to relieve the sufferers from the grasshopper scourge. Some state granges made specific appropriations and others arranged for committees to collect money from local granges and individual Patrons. In many states over a thousand dollars were thus raised and the contributions from Ohio amounted to $8,783. As a general rule this money seems to have been sent to the masters of the state granges in the affected states and then distributed or expended in the purchase of provisions and seed by relief committees in the respective counties. The Patrons in those parts of Iowa and Missouri which were not afflicted by the grasshoppers seem to have been especially active in the collection of money and supplies for their suffering brethren.[2]

The charitable work of the Patrons of Husbandry was not confined to spectacular cases of disaster affecting whole com-

[1] National Grange, *Proceedings*, viii. 31, 69, 71, 73–75, 98, 101, 136, ix. 19, 187, 196, x. 17, 109, 112, 136 (1875–76).

[2] *Prairie Farmer*, xlv. 411 (December 26, 1874); Ellis, in *Ohio Farmer*, ci. 78 (January 23, 1902); State grange proceedings: Kansas, iii (1875); Iowa, iv, v (1873, 1874); Michigan, ii, iii (1874, 1875); Missouri, iv (1875); Nebraska, iv (1874); New York, ii (1875); Ohio, ii, iii (1875, 1876); Vermont, i–iii (1872–74).

munities. The precepts of the order were also applied to cases of individual need. It appears to have been no uncommon occurrence for the members of a subordinate grange to get together and harvest a crop for a sick brother or to rebuild a Patron's house after it had been damaged by fire or tornado.[1] The constitution of the National Grange, as adopted in 1873, made it the duty of Patrons to visit and render needful assistance to sick brothers and sisters and in some states standing committees of relief were appointed for that purpose.[2] In New York arrangements were made for Patrons to help each other in the recovery of strayed or stolen property.[3]

In still another way the order of Patrons of Husbandry attempted to help its members when in trouble. This was by encouraging, and in some cases providing specific machinery for, the arbitration of disputes between members of the order. The object was, of course, to save the Patrons concerned the expense of litigation in the regular courts and to prevent, if possible, the neighborhood feuds which are apt to result from trivial disagreements. No information has been found as to how far this feature was put in practice; but it was recommended by state granges as far apart as Vermont and Iowa.[4]

EDUCATIONAL ACTIVITIES

The educational work of the order, as well as the social feature, came largely in connection with the meetings of the local granges. Each of these granges was a literary society in which the members might train themselves in public speaking and parliamentary practice. It was the duty of one of the officers, known as the lecturer, to prepare a program for each meeting, and these programs might be and undoubtedly often were instructive to both

[1] *Prairie Farmer*, xlv. 100, 339 (March 28, October 24, 1874); State grange proceedings: Alabama, ii. 8; Missouri, iii. 16; New York, ii. 59.

[2] National Grange, *Proceedings*, vi. 16 (1873); Vermont State Grange, *Proceedings*, i–iii. 53; Virginia State Grange, *Proceedings*, 7, 28.

[3] New York State Grange, *Proceedings*, iii. 32–40, 59 (1876).

[4] *Prairie Farmer*, xlv. 123 (1874); Carr, *Patrons of Husbandry*, 123; National Grange, *Proceedings*, vii. 57 (1874); State grange proceedings: Iowa, iv (1873); Michigan, ii (1874); New Hampshire, iii (1876); Vermont, i–iii (1872–74).

participants and listeners.[1] Sometimes the state granges came to the assistance of the local granges in this matter. For example, the executive committee of the Iowa State Grange in 1874 prepared a series of questions for discussion in each of the local granges. These included, as main questions; the desirability of coöperation in business, the benefits secured by the order of Patrons of Husbandry, and the control of transportation companies by law; with subdivisions of each question.[2] Such discussions could not help but be stimulating even though conclusions were sometimes reached which were at variance with orthodox political economy. When funds were available it was quite common for the masters and lecturers and sometimes other officers of the state granges to spend a considerable part of their time visiting local granges throughout the state, encouraging them to continue in the work, lecturing to them on the dignity of farming as an occupation or sometimes on more practical agricultural subjects, and spreading information generally.[3] Similar services were also performed at times by the officers of the National Grange; and in 1875 the national executive committee adopted the plan of suggesting programs and subjects for discussion to the subordinate granges.[4]

The educational advantages to those who went as delegates to meetings of state and national granges are obvious. The traveling expenses were always paid out of the grange treasuries

[1] New Hampshire State Grange, *Proceedings*, vii (1880); Martin, *Grange Movement*, 460; M. Whitehead in New Jersey Bureau of Statistics, *Reports*, ix. 347–349 (1886). Here is a typical Grange program:

" The Patrons of Grange 435 met Saturday night to confer the fourth degree upon a new member. The lady members had prepared a fine table filled with the many blessings bestowed upon us by Our Heavenly Father. It was our harvest feast and we appreciated it very much. After the table was cleared, Sister Hupp read an essay upon Butter Making, and a speech was made by a brother from Hazel Wood Grange. The Worthy Master made a few appropriate remarks, and Brother Henry Bull read an appropriate piece. The question for the next debate will be ‘ Can anything be made by feeding, to hogs, corn worth fifty cents per bushel, when hogs sell for five cents per pound?’ " *Prairie Farmer*, xlv. 371 (1874).

[2] *Prairie Farmer*, xlv. 347 (October 31, 1874). See also National Grange, *Proceedings*, xiii. 25 (1879).

[3] *Ibid*. xi. 38, xiv. 42 (1878, 1881); Carr, *Patrons of Husbandry*, 180.

[4] National Grange, *Proceedings*, ix. 23, 141 (November, 1875).

and thus many farmers were enabled to take trips which would have been impossible for them otherwise. On these occasions, they not only saw something of the world but experienced the liberalizing influence of rubbing shoulders with men from different parts of the state or country. And when they returned they were expected to give an account of their experiences to the home grange, thus passing the influence along to every Patron.

All the leaders of the order from the National Grange down were insistent that members should be encouraged to read. Large numbers of tracts, folders, and leaflets of a more or less educational character were distributed by the National Grange, as well as handbooks, guides, and manuals of parliamentary practice.[1] A considerable number of the more flourishing granges established libraries of their own [2] and it was quite common for a grange to subscribe for four or five leading agricultural papers, which would be passed around among the members.[3] The habit of reading was stimulated in another way — the discussions in the grange aroused the interest of the farmer in all sorts of topics, agricultural, economic, and even political, and he soon discovered that if he were going to take part in or profit by these discussions he must cultivate the acquaintance of books and papers. As a result the sale of books and more especially the circulation of papers is said to have increased very considerably in some neighborhoods.[4] One

[1] *Ibid.* viii. 33, x. 20 (February, 1875, 1876); Martin, *Grange Movement*, 462; Aiken, *The Grange*, 10.

[2] Kelley, *Patrons of Husbandry*, 249; National Grange, *Proceedings*, x. 20, 36, xvi. 46 (1876, 1882); Ohio State Grange, *Proceedings*, i, iii (1874, 1876); Aiken, *The Grange*, 10.

[3] *Rural Carolinian*, iv. 493 (June, 1873); Martin, *Grange Movement*, 468.

[4] National Grange, *Proceedings*, vii. 7, xii. 100 (1873, 1878); Alabama State Grange, *Proceedings*, iii. 14 (1875); Ohio State Grange, *Proceedings*, iii. 66–69 (1876); Martin, *Grange Movement*, 470; Whitehead, in New Jersey Bureau of Statistics, *Reports*, ix. 348 (1886). The number of agricultural journals increased in the United States during the decade 1870–80 from 93 with an aggregate circulation of 770, 752 copies to 173 with an aggregate of 1,022,771 copies. S. N. D. North, " The Newspaper and Periodical Press," in *United States Census*, 1880, viii. 121. Farmers and members of their families were also stimulated to write for the papers. For example, the *Prairie Farmer* offered prizes for essays on such subjects

postmaster reported that " there are now thirty newspapers taken at this office, whilst there was but one taken before the establishment of the Grange in this vicinity." [1]

Part of this increased circulation was undoubtedly due to the appearance of a new sort of agricultural papers which strove to serve as organs of the " farmers' movement." These papers, while not entirely neglecting topics of practical agriculture, devoted a large amount of space to such subjects as railway regulation, coöperation, and the new Independent parties. News of the doings of granges and farmers' clubs also held a prominent place in their columns. The *Prairie Farmer*, of Chicago, one of the oldest and most extensively read of the agricultural papers of the West, quickly adopted this policy, and in January, 1873, a department headed " Patrons of Husbandry " made its appearance, to be followed shortly after by a department for the clubs and the State Farmers' Association. The *Chicago Tribune*, also, though by no means an agricultural paper, reported the doings of the farmers' organizations at length and appeared to be in sympathy with their aims. In August, 1873, however, a number of men connected with the Illinois State Farmers' Association established in Chicago a weekly paper under the name of the *Industrial Age*, and this purported to be the particular organ of the movement. All these papers and a number of others transcended the limits of any one state in their interest and circulation, but there were also a large number of local Granger or industrial papers which sprang into existence at this time throughout the Middle West. Either with or without the endorsement of some branch of the Patrons of Husbandry, they essayed to print news of interest to members of the order and of the farmers' clubs, and generally supported the Independent parties in politics. When the Granger movement died down in this region during the later seventies most

as " The Grange; How Best to Conduct it." *Prairie Farmer*, xlvi. 35, 43, 51 (January 3, February 6, 13, 1875). The amount of correspondence from farmers in the *Prairie Farmer* and other papers was very much greater in 1874 than in 1870.

[1] Aiken, *The Grange*, 10.

of these papers went out of existence or became organs of the Greenback party.[1]

While this first wave of enthusiasm was subsiding, another class of Grange papers began to make its appearance in all parts of the country. The leaders of the order wanted to get into closer touch with the membership, partly perhaps with the idea of checking the decline, and the best and cheapest way in which this could be done was through the press. As a result official Grange organs were established in nearly every state in which the order existed. Sometimes the officers of the state grange themselves edited and published a monthly paper, or bulletin, as it was generally called, but more frequently some established agricultural paper was chosen and an agreement made whereby the paper was recognized as an official organ of the order in return for the publication of such Grange matter as might be furnished to it. In addition, a number of other Grange papers were established as private enterprises, built up a large circulation among the members by printing Grange news, and in the course of time generally succeeded in securing the recognition of state or local granges as official organs. There can be no doubt but that such papers as the *Dirigo Rural* of Maine, the *American Grange Bulletin* of Cincinnati, *The Grange Visitor* of Michigan, the *Patron of Husbandry* of Mississippi and the *Californian Patron*, exerted a wholesome influence upon the social and intellectual conditions of the farmers as well as helped to stay the decline of the Grange.[2]

At the ninth session of the National Grange in November, 1875, resolutions were introduced calling for the establishment of an organ under the direction of the National Grange. The proposition did not meet with favor at the time; but by the next session in November, 1876, the national treasury had reached such a low stage that it seemed necessary to adopt some cheap means of communication or give up altogether the attempt to

---

[1] On the Granger and Anti-Monopoly papers of Illinois, see Franklin W. Scott, *Newspapers and Periodicals of Illinois* (*Illinois Historical Collections*, vi), pp. c–ci.

[2] National Grange, *Proceedings*, x. 87, xiii. 25, 37, xiv. 130, xv. 38, 39, 42, xvi. 26–29, 35, 41, 44 (1876–82). See bibliography below, pp. 321–329.

keep in touch with the subordinate granges. It was probably hoped, also, that a national organ would help to check the alarming decline in the membership. Various plans for an organ were brought forward at this session; and though none of them appear to have received the definite approval of the Grange, the executive committee got out the first number of the *Grange Record* in April, 1877. During the first year this paper was issued as a monthly in editions of about fifteen thousand copies. Only five hundred of these were paid for by subscribers, the remainder being sent gratuitously to state, county, and subordinate granges.[1]

THE GRANGE AND THE SCHOOLS

The educational activities of the Grange were not confined to the improvement of its members, for the order, from the first, took a decided interest in the schools, and especially in the country schools and the agricultural colleges. With regard to the former, the attitude of the order was one of encouragement and support. As a general rule, better teachers, better textbooks and the introduction of practical agricultural subjects into the curricula were called for. Thus a committee on education of the Maine State Grange favored uniform text-books, better teachers, and the teaching of the elements of agricultural chemistry in the public schools, while the North Carolina State Grange adopted a resolution calling for instruction in a variety of subjects " necessary to the intelligent regulation and management of the farm . . . and the household." [2] During the latter part of the decade the National Grange began to take an active interest in the subject of agricultural education, and resolutions advising Patrons to endeavor to have the study of the elementary principles of agriculture introduced into the public schools were adopted in 1878 and 1879. In 1880 the committee on

---

[1] National Grange, *Proceedings*, ix. 55, x. 86, xi. 40 (1875–77).

[2] See *Ibid.* xiii. 25, 37, 85, 99, 111, 112, xiv. 79, xvi. 43 (1879–82); Martin, *Grange Movement*, 470; State grange proceedings: Maine, vi. 29–32 (1879); North Carolina, iii. 28 (1876); New Hampshire, vii (1880). See also Carr, *Patrons of Husbandry*, 200.

education reported that gratifying progress had been made in this direction.[1]

In the southern states, where the local schools were very inadequate, steps were taken by some of the granges to increase their number. The North Carolina State Grange recommended that the subordinate granges of the state interest themselves in the establishment of good local schools and make appropriations for their support. When practicable, it was suggested that primary and even high schools be established in connection with county and local granges.[2] Grange schools, established by the local branches of the order, existed in parts of Alabama, North Carolina, Louisiana, and perhaps in some of the other southern states.[3] In Michigan, also, it was reported in 1879 that there were seven grange schools in active operation in one county, parts of the Grange halls being used for school rooms.[4] Another step in this direction was the establishment of primary granges for the entertainment and instruction of the children of Patrons. This was tried in California with considerable success and was recommended by the secretary of the National Grange in 1877.[5]

During the seventies the various agricultural and mechanical colleges and state universities, which profited by the land grants made by Congress in 1862 for the encouragement of education in agriculture and the mechanic arts, were just getting on their feet. But few students in agriculture presented themselves at these institutions as a rule and so the funds were used for the support of other departments. Some of the farmers were inclined to complain of this and to demand that college farms be established for more practical work in agriculture and that manual labor on the farms be required of the students. Where separate agricultural and mechanical colleges were established, there seems to have been less difficulty; but where the work along

---

[1] National Grange, *Proceedings*, xii. 99, xiii. 113, xiv. 52, 63, 129 (1878–80).

[2] North Carolina State Grange, *Proceedings*, ii. 22, iii. 28, iv. 30 (1875–77).

[3] National Grange, *Proceedings*, xvi. 38 (1882); Randall, in Johns Hopkins University, *Studies*, vi. 505.

[4] National Grange, *Proceedings*, xiii. 36 (1879).

[5] *Ibid*. xi. 42 (1877).

these lines was given in departments of more general institutions, there was often complaint that the result was " a literary kite with an agricultural tail." [1] The Patrons of Husbandry interested themselves in this subject in a number of states. In California, a committee of the state grange investigated the state university in 1873 and reported a neglect of agricultural instruction and mismanagement of funds; [2] and in Ohio a similar investigation was made in 1877 into the workings of the Agricultural and Mechanical College at Columbus, which has since become Ohio State University. [3]

The National Grange in its " Declaration of Purposes" adopted in 1874, asserted: " We especially advocate for our agricultural and industrial colleges that practical agriculture, domestic science, and all the arts which adorn the home, be taught in their courses of study." [4] In 1876 a resolution was adopted declaring " that the agricultural colleges ought to be under the exclusive control of the farmers of the country, and that . . . these colleges ought to be, as far as possible, separate and distinct schools." The following year the committee on education of the National Grange presented a report concerning agricultural colleges in fourteen states, approving some but condemning others because no practical work in agriculture was done or because the agricultural were subordinated to the literary departments. [5] Just how much direct influence all this agitation had upon the colleges concerned is difficult to say; but at least it spread a knowledge of the opportunities in existence for agricultural education and was perhaps a factor in bringing about the great increase in the number of students seeking instruction along these lines. When the demand for better facilities and more attention to the work

[1] Carr, *Patrons of Husbandry*, 376.

[2] *Ibid.* 150, 179, 184–200, 376–381. See W. C. Jones, *Illustrated History of the University of California*, 110, 288–300; University of California, *Reports to the President from the Colleges of Agriculture and the Mechanic Arts*, 1877, pp. 3–11.

[3] Ohio State Grange, *Proceedings*, i, iii–v (1874–78); Ellis, in *Ohio Farmer*, cv. 139 (February 6, 1904); National Grange, *Proceedings*, xi. 129 (1877).

[4] National Grange, *Proceedings*, vii. 58 (1874).

[5] *Ibid.* x. 106–108, xi. 73, 129–132 (1876–77). See also Carr, *Patrons of Husbandry*, ch. xxvi.

in agriculture came from actual or prospective students it seems to have been met in most cases.

THE ADVANCEMENT OF AGRICULTURE

A large part of the educational activity of the Grange related to technical agriculture and here it was on a ground which had been cultivated in part by previous institutions — agricultural papers, boards of agriculture, farmers' clubs, and county or state fairs. The Grange did not seek to supplant any of these institutions but rather to encourage and supplement them. The grange meeting naturally gave opportunity for informal exchanges of experience between practical farmers; the ones who had been most successful in certain lines were able, and generally willing, to explain their methods to less successful brethren; and thus each was able to profit by the experience of his neighbor. In large numbers of granges, more formal methods of agricultural education were undertaken. A grange in South Carolina arranged for each member to take a record of the kinds and quantities of fertilizers used and the results obtained; other granges offered prizes for the best specimen of a certain product or the highest yield on an acre; and in nearly every grange formal papers were read on technical agricultural subjects. The women, likewise, held discussions, made reports, and read papers on various topics of household economy.[1]

The holding of agricultural fairs was especially encouraged by the order and in many instances they took place under its auspices. Thus a local grange in Mississippi held a fair as early as 1872 at which agricultural products and agricultural machinery were exhibited,[2] and a successful state grange fair was held in Alabama in 1875.[3] Fairs were established under the auspices

[1] National Grange, *Proceedings*, xiii. 25, 101 (1879); North Carolina State Grange, *Proceedings*, ii. 19–22, iii. 16, 30–32, 35, iv. 11–16, 23–26 (1875–77); New Hampshire State Grange, *Proceedings*, vii (1880); *American Farmer*, vii. 147 (April, 1878); Martin, *Grange Movement*, 468; Shaw, in Johns Hopkins University, *Studies*, vi. 335. See also above, p. 286, note 1.

[2] *Prairie Farmer*, xliii. 308 (September 28, 1872).

[3] Alabama State Grange, *Proceedings*, ii. 9, 12, 14, 19, iii. 18, 38 (1874, 1875). Mr. T. M. Owen, Carrollton, Alabama, has a copy of the *Programme and Schedule of Premiums* of the Alabama State Grange Fair of 1875.

of state and local granges in other parts of the country, especially in New England, and where they previously existed under the control of other organizations, the granges gave them hearty support and tried to make them something more than mere horse-racing exhibitions and collections of side-shows.[1] In many granges also, and especially in those which owned their own halls, attempts were made to form permanent museums composed of specimens of farm products and other objects of interest. A "National Farmers' Museum" was projected by the National Grange in 1875, and a nucleus of specimens was collected in Louisville.[2] It was thought at that time that permanent headquarters of the National Grange would be established at Louisville and so there would be an opportunity for the preservation of such a collection. In a short time, however, the National Grange resumed its migratory habits and nothing further was heard of the "National Farmers' Museum."

One great desideratum of the farmers of the United States has always been a complete and reliable system of crop reports. Farmers believe that if they have at their disposal information relative to the amounts, conditions, and probabilities of the different crops in all parts of the country they can decide more intelligently what proportion of each crop it is desirable for them to grow, and what prices they should receive for their productions. The bureau of agriculture of the United States government was making some efforts in the direction of the collection and dissemination of agricultural statistics, but its reports are said to have been unreliable and slow in coming out. When the order of Patrons of Husbandry was spreading rapidly all over the country, it seemed to many that it might furnish a most excellent medium for the collection of such statistics.[3] Several of the state granges, especially in the southern states, early

[1] National Grange, *Proceedings*, xvi. 38 (1882).

[2] *Ibid*. viii. 105, ix. 42, 48, 146–149 (February, November, 1875).

[3] On this subject in general, see state grange proceedings: Alabama, ii. 33; Iowa, vi. 51; Michigan, i. 37, iii. 16, 94; Mississippi, v. 29; Missouri, iii. 47, 66–70; iv. 60, 114; New York, ii. 46, iii. 18; North Carolina, iii. 31; Ohio, i. 9, ii. 16; Tennessee, ii. 26; Virginia, i. 23.

undertook this work: special committees were appointed in the local granges to report monthly on the condition of crops and stock in their respective vicinities; and these reports were sent to the secretaries of the state granges who compiled them into general state reports.[1]   Calls for a national crop report to be compiled through the Grange soon began to come from the West;[2] and at its seventh session, in February, 1874, the National Grange authorized the executive committee to establish " a system of statistical crop reports."

The committee deliberated upon the subject and finally decided to issue blanks to and call for reports directly from subordinate granges, thus ignoring the state granges entirely. A force of clerks was engaged in Washington and work was begun in March, 1874.   Circulars and blanks were sent out to from sixteen thousand to twenty-two thousand subordinate granges at intervals of two months throughout the summer; but in no case were returns received from more than one-fifth of the granges, and the vast majority of these were said to be incomplete, unsatisfactory, and " accompanied by lengthy epistles, containing advice, complaints, suggestions, encouragement and caustic criticism."   In spite of the neglect of the great majority of the granges to make these reports, the returns which were received came from all parts of the country, and the consolidated reports are said to have been of considerable value.   The work was very expensive, however, and was not continued by the National Grange after the eighth session in February, 1875.[3] After this experiment was given up, state granges in all parts of the country again took up the work of collecting crop reports, but none of them appear to have had any considerable degree of success.   If the order had continued to flourish as it did for a few years, it is quite possible that a workable method of collecting crop statistics through it might have been developed in

---

[1] Alabama State Grange, *Proceedings*, ii. 33 (1874); Mississippi State Grange, *By-laws*, 1872, p. 11.

[2] Iowa State Grange, *Proceedings*, iv. 82 (1873).

[3] National Grange, *Proceedings*, vii. 31, viii. 26–29 (1874–75); *Western Rural*, xiii. 236 (July 24, 1875); Martin, *Grange Movement*, 463; Carr, *Patrons of Husbandry*, 122; Aiken, *The Grange*, 13.

time. As it was, this phase of the movement is of interest principally as illustrating the aspirations and enthusiasm of the leaders.

The Grange in the South seems to have been especially interested in projects for the advancement of the agricultural interests of that section. It was generally believed that the cotton planters of the South would experience greater prosperity if they could be induced to devote less energy to the production of the staple and more to the growth of breadstuffs. During 1874 and 1875 there was a concerted movement in this direction in which the Grange had a part. At the St. Louis session of the National Grange in February, 1874, the representatives of North and South Carolina, Georgia, Florida, Alabama, Mississippi, Tennessee, Arkansas, and Louisiana got together and drew up a "Memorial to the Cotton States." [1] This memorial, which received the sanction of the National Grange, presented strongly to the Patrons of Husbandry in the cotton-growing sections of the country the desirability of limiting the size of the cotton crop and producing their foodstuffs at home. It was hoped that by these means large sums annually expended for supplies might be saved, and, at the same time, depression of the cotton market avoided. Similar recommendations were made by several of the state granges and by a "Cotton States Convention" which was held at Atlanta in 1874, and it was reported that in Georgia the planters were substituting wheat for cotton in many cases.[2] On the whole, however, it does not seem probable that these efforts had any considerable effect, for there is always a temptation to the individual planter to increase the size of his own crop when he believes that the total crop is going to be decreased and the price enhanced. They are of interest, nevertheless, as illustrating the activities of the order in the South, and also as one of a long series of attempts to restrict by artificial means the production of southern staples — attempts which began in Virginia and Maryland in the seventeenth century

---

[1] National Grange, *Proceedings*, viii. 60–63 (1874).

[2] Alabama State Grange, *Proceedings*, ii (1874); North Carolina State Grange, *Proceedings*, iii. 32 (1876); *Rural Carolinian*, v. 255 (February, 1874).

with colonial laws placing restrictions upon the planting of tobacco.[1]

Another way in which southern granges proposed to advance the agricultural interests of the South was by encouraging immigration. Nearly every state grange in the South and many of the local granges undertook some scheme in this direction.[2] For example, the state grange of Alabama in 1874 had a pamphlet prepared containing information furnished by the subordinate granges with regard to the resources of each county. In several of the counties of Arkansas, the granges appointed joint committees to collect and publish information designed to attract immigrants.[3] A grange in Mobile County, Alabama, issued a pamphlet in German, setting forth to immigrants of that nationality the desirability of settling in southern Alabama.[4] Nor was interest in this subject confined entirely to the South, for the state grange of Iowa resolved in 1873 " that the immigration of skilled farm laborers should be encouraged, and we hail gladly all proper arrangements that foster this enterprise." [5]

MISCELLANEOUS INFLUENCES AND ACTIVITIES

As a result of the sudden prominence attained by the Grange in the middle of the decade of the seventies, all sorts of movements and " reforms " sought its support and alliance. About 1873 a new wave of temperance agitation got under way in western New York and Ohio. This movement, which ultimately led to the organization of the Women's Christian Temperance Union, seems to have been social rather than political

[1] C. M. Andrews, *Colonial Self-Government*, 213.

[2] State grange proceedings: Alabama, ii. 6, 12, 14, 17, 26, iii. 21, 28; Arkansas, v. 6, 18; Louisiana, iii. 19; Maryland, i. 9, 13; Mississippi, v. 6–9; North Carolina, ii. 21, iii. 29, iv. 17; Virginia, i. 33, 35.

[3] *Wisconsin Statesman*, August 21, 1875, p. 3.

[4] This pamphlet is entitled: *Mobile County, eine passende Heimath für den deutschen Farmer. Bericht über die Einwanderung nach Süd-Alabama besonders der deutschen Farmer des Westens, vorgelegt in der Gulf City Grange no. 68, Patrons of Husbandry, nach einem in der am 25. Juni 1874 abgehaltenen Versammlung gefassten Beschlusse.* See also a pamphlet prepared by a Grange committee entitled: *History, Description and Resources of Darlington County, State of South Carolina*, 1874. Copies of both of these pamphlets are in the Library of Congress.

[5] Iowa State Grange, *Proceedings*, iv (1873).

in character, and was carried on principally by bands of women who invaded or camped in front of saloons and by praying and singing or other demonstrations endeavored to persuade the proprietors to give up the business.[1] The influence of the order of Patrons of Husbandry was from the first strongly on the side of temperance: the title of " Bacchus " originally proposed for one of the officers was quickly changed to the more prosaic " lecturer "; temperate habits were a necessary qualification for admission to the order; and lessons in temperance were inculcated by the ritual.[2] It is not strange therefore that attempts were made to get the Grange and the temperance movement to work in harmony for the promotion of the cause.

Temperance resolutions of various sorts were adopted by state and local granges in all parts of the country, and even by the National Grange, while the Illinois State Grange went so far as to condemn the use of tobacco;[3] but it was in Ohio that the closest connection was made between the Grange and the temperance movement. At the time of the first regular session of the Ohio State Grange at Xenia, in February, 1874, the women of that place were conducting a characteristic crusade against the local saloons. Finally the proprietor of the " Shades of Death " was moved to invite the crusaders to pour out his liquor; they in turn invited the state grange to accompany them; and the grange accepted the invitation by a unanimous vote. The procession was formed and marched to the resort, the liquor was poured out, and the master of the state grange made a temperance speech to the multitude from an emptied whiskey barrel. Later the state grange adopted resolutions indorsing and pledging support to the temperance work and it is said to have maintained this position steadily thereafter.[4]

---

[1] E. B. Andrews, *The Last Quarter Century*, ii. ch. xxii.

[2] Kelley, *Patrons of Husbandry*, 54; Martin, *Grange Movement*, 466; Whitehead, in New Jersey Bureau of Statistics, *Reports*, ix. 348 (1886).

[3] National Grange, *Proceedings*, xii. 105 (1878); Texas State Grange, *Minutes*, 14 (1872–74); State grange proceedings: Illinois, iv. 34, 44 (1875); Michigan, i. 33 (1874); Vermont, i–iii. 18 (1872–74).

[4] Ohio State Grange, *Proceedings*, i. 23 (1874); Ellis, in *Ohio Farmer*, c. 368 (November 14, 1901).

In the constitution which was adopted by the National Grange at its sixth session, in January, 1873, one section provided that " Any member found guilty of wanton cruelty to animals shall be expelled from the order." Later in the same session a resolution was adopted expressing the intention of the order to coöperate with the Society for the Prevention of Cruelty to Animals in carrying out the humane principles of that association. Kindness to animals thus became one of the lessons of the order and was occasionally emphasized by resolutions of state and local granges.[1] Other lessons said to have been inculcated by the ritual and otherwise are orderliness, industry, thrift, and economy. The order was declared to be the uncompromising foe of carelessness and disorder, idleness and vice. That greater attention to the care of farm machinery, the condition of the farm and house, and even to the dress and general appearance of the members themselves, was often the result of the establishment of a grange in a community, has been claimed and is probably true.[2]

The subject of women's suffrage naturally attracted the attention of the first order to admit women to full and equal membership; but in this particular, at least, the Grange showed itself to be conservative, and resolutions favoring it were generally frowned down when they made their appearance in the national and state granges.[3] In 1875 a " Woman's Dress Reform Movement " caught the attention of the National Grange for a time. " Sister " Garretson of Iowa addressed the Grange in advocacy of the movement and the subject was " referred to a special committee consisting of all the sisters entitled to vote in the body." The committee does not appear to have made a report, and nothing further was heard of this movement.[4]

At the eighth session of the National Grange in February, 1875, the Washington National Monument Association appealed

[1] National Grange, *Proceedings*, vi. 27 (1873); Virginia State Grange, *Proceedings*, i. 7, 28 (December, 1873).

[2] Mississippi State Grange, *Proceedings*, v (1875); Martin, *Grange Movement*, 465; Aiken, *The Grange*, 10.

[3] National Grange, *Proceedings*, x. 94, 96, 121, 169–171 (1876). See also above, p. 121.

[4] National Grange, *Proceedings*, ix. 53 (November, 1875).

to it for assistance in raising funds to complete the monument before the centennial year. A resolution was introduced for the appropriation of five hundred dollars to the fund; but this was rejected, and another resolution adopted recommending state and subordinate granges to make subscriptions or to endeavor to raise money among their members. Twenty-five thousand letters of appeal furnished by the monument association were circulated by the officers of the National Grange, and a considerable number of subscriptions were received in response.[1]

Another Grange activity of some interest was the Patrons' encampment at the Centennial Exposition in Philadelphia in 1876. As early as February, 1874, the master of the National Grange was instructed to appoint a committee " to devise a scheme whereby the Patrons of Husbandry can be fully represented at such exposition." Shortly after this a " Patrons' Centennial Encampment Association " was organized by members of the order in Pennsylvania, and received the approval of the National Grange. This association erected a temporary hotel with accommodations for about four thousand at a railway station three miles from the exposition grounds, where Patrons were taken care of at very moderate prices. The accommodations of the hotel were open to the general public, but it served as headquarters for Patrons attending the fair. An attempt was also made to have the National Grange designate July 4, 1876, as a date for a special Patrons' celebration at the exposition, but this project does not appear to have been carried out.[2]

Taking it all together, the fraternal, social, and educational side of the Grange movement bulks large. At the time it did not attract a great deal of attention, partly because it was overshadowed in the public mind and, it must be admitted, in the minds of many of the participants, by other phases of the movement, partly also because its work was of the sort which would naturally be carried on quietly and without attracting much

---

[1] National Grange, *Proceedings*, viii. 101, ix. 125 (February, November, 1875).

[2] *Ibid.* vii. 46, ix. 53, 166 (1874, November, 1875); *American Agriculturist*, xxxv. 87 (August, 1876).

attention from the outside world. Even in the sections of the country where the order of Patrons of Husbandry quickly died out the influence of its work in this direction persisted: habits of social intercourse and intellectual activity had been formed; and other organizations, local or general, arose to continue the work. But in New England, in New York and Pennsylvania, in Ohio and Michigan, and in Oregon, the Grange suffered no serious depression, or quickly regained its membership, and by emphasizing the social and educational features it has done and is still doing a great work in improving the conditions of rural life.

CHAPTER IX

CONCLUSION

THE SIGNIFICANCE OF THE MOVEMENT

IF the Granger movement had been a mere episode in American history, it would still have been worthy of investigation because it exhibits the conditions, opinions, and desires, which prevailed among large numbers of American farmers during the seventies, and because it actually played a considerable part in the history of the decade. Many, however, of these conditions, opinions, and desires, which were first brought into prominence by the Granger movement, have remained active forces in American history to the present day.

The Granger movement was, primarily, a movement for agricultural organization, for the advancement of the welfare of farmers in every possible way — socially, intellectually, politically, economically — by concerted effort. It was, moreover, the first attempt at agricultural organization on a large scale, but it was far from being the last, and the ideas and ideals, if not the direct influence, of the Patrons of Husbandry can be traced in every one of the later organizations. In some parts of the country, and particularly in the East, the Grange itself, as has been seen, continued and still continues to serve as the principal agency for united effort among farmers. In the West and South, however, where the Grange flourished most vigorously in the early seventies, and where its most striking manifestations appeared, other organizations arose and assumed the leadership in this more general farmers' movement.

The first of these organizations to become really national in scope was the Farmers' Alliance, which spread all over the South and West in the later eighties. Numerous state and local orders, however, made their appearance in many parts of the country somewhat earlier.[1] About 1874 or 1875 local

[1] On the Farmers' Alliance and its various component parts, see N. A. Dunning, *The Farmers' Alliance History and Agricultural Digest;* W. S. Morgan, *History of*

bodies which were known as farmers' alliances were established in New York, in Kansas, and in Texas. These movements in the first two states came to naught, but in Texas the local alliances spread slowly during the later seventies, county alliances were organized, and in 1879 the " Grand State Alliance of Texas " was formed. The similarities between this organization and the Patrons of Husbandry are striking. Each was a secret order restricted to farmers; each admitted women to full membership; each labored to improve the social and intellectual condition of the farmers; each was professedly non-political and non-partisan but attempted to exert an influence upon legislation; and each engaged in schemes for coöperation in the purchase of supplies and the sale of products. The direct influence of the Grange upon this Texas Farmers' Alliance is clearly visible in the " Declaration of Purposes " adopted by the latter in 1880.[1] This document endorsed the motto, " In things essential, Unity, and in all things Charity " and stated the purposes of the Alliance to be, " to develop a better state, mentally, morally, socially, and financially . . . to constantly strive to secure entire harmony and good will among all mankind and brotherly love among ourselves; to suppress personal, local, sectional, and national prejudices, all unhealthy rivalry and all selfish ambition." A comparison of the two shows this document to be but a crude paraphrase of parts of the " Declaration of Purposes " adopted by the National Grange in 1874.[2]

During the first half of the decade of the eighties two agricultural orders similar to the Alliance of Texas arose in Arkansas,

the Wheel and Alliance; H. R. Chamberlain, The Farmers' Alliance; C. S. Walker, " The Farmers' Alliance," in Andover Review, xiv. 127–140 (August, 1890); H. R. Chamberlain, " Farmers' Alliance and Other Political Parties," in Chautauquan, xiii. 338–342 (June, 1891); W. A. Peffer, " The Farmers' Defensive Movement," in Forum, viii. 464–473 (December, 1889); W. Gladden, " The Embattled Farmers," in Forum, x. 315–322 (November, 1890); J. T. Morgan, " The Danger of the Farmers' Alliance," in Forum, xii. 399–409 (November, 1891); E. M. Drew, " The Present Farmers' Movement," in Political Science Quarterly, vi. 282–310 (June, 1891); K. L. Butterfield, " Farmers' Social Organizations," in Bailey, Cyclopedia of American Agriculture, iv. 295.

[1] Dunning, Farmers' Alliance History, 28.

[2] See above, p. 64.

— the Agricultural Wheel, and the Brothers of Freedom, — and about the same time a Farmers' Union made its appearance in Louisiana. The purposes and characteristics of these various orders were so nearly alike that little difficulty was experienced in merging them in a single organization. In 1885 the Brothers of Freedom were consolidated with the Wheel making a total of over a thousand local branches under the jurisdiction of the State Wheel of Arkansas; in 1887 the Alliance of Texas and the Union of Louisiana joined to form the National Farmers' Alliance and Coöperative Union of America; and in 1889 this National Farmers' Alliance merged with a National Wheel, which had developed from the Arkansas Wheel, and took the name of the " Farmers' and Laborers' Union of America." This last title does not appear to have been used very extensively and the order was generally spoken of from this time on as the National Farmers' Alliance and Industrial Union. Meanwhile this movement had been spreading from the Southwest, where it originated, until at the session of the National Alliance in St. Louis in December, 1889, delegates were present from every southern state except West Virginia, and also from Indiana, Kansas, and Nebraska. At the next session at Ocala, Florida, in 1890, the National Colored Farmers' Alliance, and the Farmers' Mutual Benefit Association, which had a considerable membership in Indiana and Illinois, were absorbed, and a total membership of between three and four million was then claimed for the order. It will be noticed that the course of development of the Alliance was somewhat different from that of the order of Patrons of Husbandry, which started out as a national organization and then established the local and state granges; but all the main features of the Alliance and its component parts, prior to 1890, were strikingly similar to those which had been developed by the Grange in the preceding decade. About 1890, however, the order was drawn into the maelstrom of party politics and from that time on its decline was as rapid as that of the Grange had been.

While this new phase of the farmers' movement was developing in the South, another agricultural organization with a very similar name made its appearance in the Northwest. In April, 1880, a farmers' club or alliance was organized in Chicago under the auspices of Milton George, editor of the *Western Rural*. This "Cook County Alliance No. 1" proceeded to issue dispensations for the establishment of other alliances in the states of the Northwest and in October, 1880, a convention "representing Granges, Farmers' Clubs and Alliances" was held in Chicago to organize a National Farmers' Alliance of the United States.[1] This organization, which is generally spoken of as the Northwestern Alliance to distinguish it from the Southern Alliance, spread rapidly throughout the Northwest, and in 1882 eight state and two thousand local alliances with a membership of over one hundred thousand were claimed. This order was very loosely organized, had no secret features, and was from the beginning openly political in character. Its platforms or resolutions bear a strong resemblance to those adopted by the various Independent parties which arose in connection with the Granger movement. In 1881, for example, resolutions were adopted in favor of government regulation of railroads, prohibition of free passes, reduction of salaries of public officials, restriction of patent rights, and the more equitable adjustment of taxes including an income tax.[2]

Attempts were made at various times to unite the two national alliances and in some states consolidations were effected; but the Northwestern Alliance maintained its separate organization and claimed a membership of three or four hundred thousand, mainly in Iowa, Nebraska, and Minnesota, during the later eighties. This order, like its southern namesake, declined rapidly during the nineties, probably as a result of political developments. A similar fate befell numerous other agricultural orders, such as the Patrons of Industry, which was modeled largely on the Grange and operated in Michigan, New York, Ohio, Indiana, and Wisconsin in the later eighties;[3] and the

[1] On the Northwestern Alliance, see *Western Rural*, publisher, *Rules of Order and . . . History of the Farmers' Alliance Movement;* Dunning, *Farmers' Alliance History*, 225; Butterfield, in Bailey, *Cyclopedia of American Agriculture*, 295.

[2] *Western Rural*, publisher, *Farmers' Alliance Movement*, 14.

[3] Butterfield, in Bailey, *Cyclopedia of American Agriculture*, 295.

National Farmers' League which was established in Massachusetts in 1889, primarily for the purpose of securing a law regulating the sale of oleomargerine.[1] As one organization or one group of organizations declined, however, others arose to take their places and the farmers' movement went on. By 1890 the Grange had recovered sufficiently from the disasters of its early career to begin a reconquest of its old fields; more or less independent farmers' clubs have continued to flourish in many parts of the West; and today the American Society of Equity, with purposes similar to those of the Grange, though perhaps more openly political, is enrolling large numbers of farmers in its ranks.

The influence of the Granger movement as an example of organization was not confined to the agricultural class. When the order of Patrons of Husbandry was at the height of prosperity an attempt was made to combine the workingmen of the country into a similar secret society adapted to their purposes. The order of Sovereigns of Industry, of which the very name betrays an imitation, was founded by William H. Earle in Massachusetts in 1874.[2] Like the Grange this order was composed of subordinate, state, and national councils and the preamble of the constitution adopted by the National Council at its session in Philadelphia in 1875 declared its purpose to be to elevate and improve the condition of the laboring classes of every calling. It further expressed an intention of presenting an " organized resistance to the organized encroachments of the monopolies and other evils of the existing industrial and commercial system." The hand of fellowship was extended to kindred organizations and " especially to the Patrons of Husbandry, whose colossal growth and power already command that consideration so justly due to the great basic industry of agriculture."[3]

---

[1] Butterfield, in Bailey, *Cyclopedia of American Agriculture*, 295; Chamberlain, *Farmers' Alliance*, ch. vii.

[2] Earle was intimate with Dudley W. Adams, master of the National Grange from 1873 to 1875. He admitted that his inspiration came from the Patrons of Husbandry. Bemis, in Johns Hopkins University, *Studies*, vi. 37. On the Sovereigns of Industry, see *ibid.* 37–52; R. T. Ely, *The Labor Movement*, 174–177.

[3] Sovereigns of Industry, *Constitution . . . revised and adopted . . . 1875.*

Trades unions and labor organizations of various sorts had existed in the United States for some time, but this seems to have been the first attempt on a large scale to unite workingmen of all occupations in a single order to advance the welfare of the laboring class as a whole.[1] For a few years the Sovereigns of Industry flourished vigorously and councils were established in all of the New England and Middle States, in all of the states of the old Northwest except Indiana, and in Kentucky, Maryland, and the District of Columbia. About five hundred councils in all appear to have been established with a total membership of nearly forty thousand. Over half of the membership, however, was in Massachusetts and Connecticut. The principal activity of this order was in the direction of distributive coöperation,[2] and large numbers of stores were organized on the Rochdale plan in New England. Some of these were very successful for a few years; but the Springfield store, which was the largest, was dissolved in 1879, and the order collapsed in the following year.

Another labor organization of a somewhat similar character was the order of the Knights of Labor.[3] This was founded in Philadelphia in 1869, but did not spread to any considerable extent until the latter part of the next decade. In 1878 the name of the order was first made public and from that time on it grew rapidly and became the first great national organization of workingmen in America. While it is probable that the Grange exerted no direct influence on the Knights of Labor, still the declarations of the two orders exhibit a similarity of purpose. The preamble adopted by the Knights declared their general aims to be:

[1] The *American Agriculturist*, xxxiii. 47 (February, 1874) mentions the order of "Patrons of Industry" as a weak imitation of the Patrons of Husbandry, for workingmen, with headquarters in New York. This is, of course, not to be confused with the order of "Patrons of Industry" which was organized in Michigan about 1887 as an agricultural order.

[2] At the request of the Ohio Council of the Sovereigns of Industry, the Ohio State Grange ordered its agent to coöperate with the Sovereigns in the purchase of supplies. Ohio State Grange, *Proceedings*, iii (1876).

[3] T. V. Powderly, *Thirty Years of Labor;* Ely, *Labor Movement*, 75–88; *An Historical Paper Showing the Aims and Objects of the Knights of Labor* (leaflet in University of Illinois library).

To secure for the workers the full enjoyment of the wealth they create; sufficient leisure in which to develop their intellectual, moral, and social faculties; all of the benefits, recreation, and pleasure of association; in a word, to enable them to share in the gains and honors of advancing civilization.[1]

In order to secure these results various demands were made upon the state and national governments, among which were the reservation of public lands for actual settlers; the issue of legal-tender money " direct to the people, without the intervention of banks ' ; government ownership of railroads; postal savings banks; and a graduated income tax. It is said that in the later eighties large numbers of farmers joined the Knights of Labor in parts of the South and West. In some states friendly relations were established between the Knights and the different farmers' organizations; while the National Assembly of the Knights of Labor and the National Farmers' Alliance and Industrial Union subscribed to a joint platform in St. Louis in 1889.[2]

The Granger movement, broadly viewed, was more than a movement for class organization and its influence can be traced in other directions. It was a movement to subject railroad corporations to public control and the permanent influence of its work in this direction has already been indicated. It was also a movement for independence in politics, for a preference for men and measures over parties, and even, when necessary, for the organization of third parties. Politically, as otherwise, the movement transcended the organization from which came its name and even the agricultural class; but it was, nevertheless, distinctly a movement, not of leaders, but of the masses. The political organizations of the Grangers soon passed away; but the idea persisted that the people could break away from the old political parties, which were still dividing on bygone issues, and could force new issues to the front in spite of the opposition of conservative political leaders.

In a few instances, as has been seen, it is possible to trace a direct connection between the Independent parties of the Granger

[1] Ely, *Labor Movement*, 86.
[2] *Ibid.* 83; Dunning, *Farmers' Alliance History*, 122, 154.

period and the Greenback party, but the main issues of the
Independent parties were " reform " and railroad regulation,
while the Greenbackers demanded " reform " and fiat money.
The Peoples' or Populist party, however, seems to have been
the heir of both of these. The origin of the Populist party is to
be found in the St. Louis platform adopted by the Farmers'
Alliance and the Knights of Labor in 1889.[1] This platform
demanded the issue of legal tender treasury notes on a *per capita*
basis; laws to prevent speculation in agricultural and mechanical
productions; free coinage of silver; reservation of public lands
for actual settlers; tariff reform and reduction of taxation; and
finally government ownership of railroads. With this platform
and, in the South, with a proposition for government warehouses
or sub-treasuries where the farmer could store his produce as
security for loans at nominal interest, the alliances went into
politics in 1890 and won notable victories in a number of southern
and western states.

In 1892 the Populist party became the political representative
of the alliances, as the Independent parties had been the political
representatives of the Granger movement. The Alliance platform was elaborated and planks added favoring postal savings
banks, the old parties were denounced for agreeing to ignore
such issues as " capitalists, corporations, national banks, rings,
trusts, watered stock, the demonetization of silver, and the
oppressions of the usurers " ; and again victories were won by
the third party, though in many cases by means of fusion with
the weaker of the old parties. By 1896 the free silver plank
had risen to first place among the demands of the Populists;
and in that year this radical political movement, which came
from the West and the South, got control of the organization
of the Democratic party.[2]

The political and economic propositions of the Grangers,
the Alliance, and the Populists, were generally ridiculed by

[1] Dunning, *Farmers' Alliance History*, 122. On the Populist party, see also
F. L. McVey, *The Populist Movement;* J. A. Woodburn, *Political Parties and Party
Problems in the United States*, 110–117; Chamberlain, *Farmers' Alliance*, ch. v;
D. L. Dewey, *National Problems*, 244–246.

[2] Cf. Woodburn, *Political Parties*, ch. viii.

the conservative elements at the time, and some of them, like the sub-treasury plan, were probably quite unsound. Others, however, have remained constantly before the American people and in the course of time have become respectable, at least. Thus the necessity for the regulation of railroads by the government, which was the principal political plank of the Grangers, is now a generally accepted proposition; a postal savings bank law has recently been enacted by Congress; an amendment to the constitution to authorize the income tax has just received the approval of the states; anti-trust laws are being enacted by Congress and the state legislatures; and the reduction and revision of the tariff is expected to be the principal work of Congress at its next session. The " farmers' movement " has been merged in a general "reform" or "progressive" movement which transcends class and party lines; and a new political party, which assumes to be the special representative of this movement, has jumped to second place at its first appearance.

What, then is the significance of all this ? What does it mean that the Grangers, the Sovereigns of Industry, the Greenbackers, the Farmers' Alliances, the Knights of Labor, the Populists, the Bryan Democrats, the La Follette Republicans, and now the Roosevelt Progressives have all denounced capitalists, corporations, monopolies, and special interests and have endeavored to devise ways by which their power might be curbed ? What does it mean that practically every one of these agricultural and labor organizations has attempted schemes of distributive or productive coöperation in the hope of making its members more independent of these same capitalists, these same monopolies ? Does it not mean that with the close of the Civil War American history entered upon a new phase in which the dominant feature has been a struggle of the people, or of parts of them at different times, to preserve the political and economic democracy which they believed to be endangered if not actually destroyed by the rising power and influence of great accumulations and combinations of wealth ?

Prior to about 1870 American history appears to have had two distinguishing and characteristic features to which nearly everything else can be related. In the first place it was the history of the occupation of a continent by a civilized people; and, secondly, it was the history of a struggle between two incompatible social and economic systems established in the two great sections of the country. One of these features passed into the background with the Civil War and reconstruction, the other with the practical disappearance a few years later of free land suitable to the purposes of the individual pioneer. Before the Civil War there had been no great accumulations and combinations of wealth; but the industrial stimulus of the war, the development of the corporate idea, and the great advance in the applied sciences brought such accumulations and combinations rapidly to the front, while the disappearance of the frontier closed a door of opportunity which had previously been open to the oppressed and discontented. The result was a tendency toward protective and coöperative organization along class lines, of which the labor movement is one aspect, and the farmers' movement another. The Grangers organized to fight this " greater capitalism " wherever it made its appearance. They saw it in the great railroad corporations of the country, and they strove to subject them to public control; they saw it in politics, and they organized independent parties to oust it; they saw it in great industrial establishments and their agents, the middlemen, and they established coöperative enterprises in the endeavor to restore their economic independence. The Greenbackers and the Populists believed that the stronghold of this greater capitalism was in the monetary system of the country, and they proposed to break its power by the issue of fiat money. Thus in one form or another the struggle has been carried on by agricultural organizations, by labor unions, and by political parties or factions within political parties until it seems to have culminated in a nation-wide movement for political, social, and economic reform.

If this interpretation be correct, then the Granger movement deserves a prominent place in American history. The decade of the seventies was the period of transition: it witnessed the last stages of reconstruction and the disappearance of the frontier, which mark the passing of the old; and it witnessed the Granger movement which marks the opening of the new period of American history.

BIBLIOGRAPHY

BIBLIOGRAPHY

THE material for the study of the Granger movement is voluminous and widely scattered and much of it is of a fugitive sort and difficult to locate; much of it also is to be found in the files of agricultural and Grange papers, and such files are far from common. For convenience in locating material, the libraries in which the more uncommon items are to be found have been indicated by means of the following symbols: L.C., Library of Congress, Washington; D.A., Library of the Department of Agriculture, Washington; B.P., Boston Public Library; H.C., Harvard College Library, Cambridge; W.H., Wisconsin Historical Society Library, Madison; U.W., University of Wisconsin Library, Madison; C.H., Chicago Historical Society Library; J.C., John Crerar Library, Chicago; U.I., University of Illinois Library, Urbana.

PUBLIC DOCUMENTS

FEDERAL

Senate and *House Journals.* The official record of the activities of Congress.

Congressional Globe. Contains the proceedings and debates in Congress in full to 1873.

Congressional Record. Superseded the *Globe* in 1873.

Reports of Committees. These are printed for each house of each Congress. The principal reports on the railroad question are listed separately under " Railroads," below.

Supreme Court Reports. Contain the decisions of the Granger cases.

Richardson, James D. *Messages and Papers of the Presidents, 1789–1897.* Washington, 1898. 10 vols. Contain President Grant's allusions to the railway question and to political conditions in the West.

United States Census. The eighth, ninth, and tenth censuses, 1860, 1870, and 1880, contain pertinent material, especially the volumes on agriculture.

Commissioner of Agriculture. *Reports,* 1862–88. Washington, 1863–89. These reports contain some valuable material for the study of agricultural conditions during the period.

Interstate Commerce Commission. *Annual Reports,* 1887+. Washington, 1887+. These contain material which is helpful for an understanding of the transportation conditions in the earlier period.

Industrial Commission. *Report*. Washington, 1900–02. 19 vols. Deals mainly with a later period; but parts of the report throw light also on the earlier conditions in agriculture, transportation, and the grain elevator business.

STATE

The official publications of the several states are listed in Richard R. Bowker, *State Publications* (New York, 1899–1908. 1 vol. in 4 parts), and it will be unnecessary to do more here than to indicate the classes of documents in which material on the subject is found. The *Index of Economic Material in the Documents of the States*, now being published by the Carnegie Institution is useful in locating material in the *Journals* and *Collected Documents*. Volumes are out for Maine, New Hampshire, Vermont, Massachusetts, Rhode Island, New York, Delaware, Ohio, Illinois, Kentucky, and California.

Senate and *House* or *Assembly Journals*. The official sources for the legislative history of the Granger laws. They frequently contain also the messages of the governors and reports of committees which deal with the railroad question.

Collected Documents. Under various titles, as *Reports, Executive documents, Legislative documents*, etc., each state publishes a set of collected documents. They contain reports of committees, governors' messages, and special communications on the railroad question.

Session Laws. Under various titles, as *Laws, Public Laws, General Laws*, etc., each state publishes the acts of a general nature enacted at each session of the legislature. These are, therefore, the official sources for the Granger laws.

Revised Statutes. Some of the Granger acts can be found in the various compilations or codes of laws published by the states from time to time. The *Revised Statutes of Illinois* for 1874 contain the Illinois railroad law of 1873 which was omitted from the *Public Laws* of that year. These railroad laws can sometimes be found in the reports of railroad commissions or in special collections.

Supreme Court Reports. Those of Illinois, Minnesota, and Wisconsin contain decisions of Granger cases.

State Railroad Commissions. *Reports*. These are the most valuable sources for the workings of the Granger railroad laws and the litigation over them. The most pertinent are: Illinois, 1871+; Wisconsin, 1874+; Minnesota, 1871+; Iowa, 1878+; Missouri, 1875+; California, 1878+; Michigan, 1872+; Massachusetts, 1870+.

State Boards of Agriculture or Agricultural Societies. *Proceedings, Transactions*, or *Reports*. These frequently contain material which throws light upon the agricultural situation. In some cases, as Wisconsin, they contain proceedings of agricultural conventions.

State Labor Bureaus. *Reports*. Occasionally contain material on the coöperative phase of the Granger movement. Some of this is listed below under "Coöperation."

Legislative Manuals or *Bluebooks.* Annual or biennial publications containing the constitutions, rosters of state officers and legislators, election statistics, etc.

Thorpe, Francis N., editor. *The Federal and State Constitutions.* Washington, 1909. 7 vols.

Debates and Proceedings of the Constitutional Convention of the State of Illinois, convened at the City of Springfield, Tuesday, December 13, 1869. Springfield, 1870. 2 vols.

Journal of the Constitutional Convention of the State of Illinois, convened at Springfield, December 13, 1869. Springfield, 1870. This and the preceding item are essential to an understanding of the origin of the railway and warehouse provisions of the Illinois constitution of 1870.

DOCUMENTS OF AGRICULTURAL ORGANIZATIONS

NATIONAL

Commons, John R. and Andrews, John B. *Labor Movement, 1860-80.* Cleveland, 1911. 2 vols. This collection forms volumes ix and x of the *Documentary History of American Industrial Society,* which has been prepared under the auspices of the American Bureau of Industrial Research. About one hundred pages of the second volume are devoted to documents of farmers' organizations, part of which were selected by the writer when collecting material for the present work. They are taken from Periam, *The Groundswell;* Kelley, *Patrons of Husbandry;* and National Grange, *Proceedings,* vi–xiii (1873–79). The book appeared too late to permit references to be made to it, but many of the resolutions of the National Grange and other documents alluded to in the text can be found in it conveniently. The volume contains documents of the Knights of Labor also and the introduction to the two volumes is suggestive.

National Grange, *Journal of Proceedings.* 1873+. L.C., W.H., U.W., D.A. The published proceedings begin with the sixth session, January, 1873, and continue to the present time. There has been one session every year and in 1875 there were two, one in February and one in November. These proceedings, together with the state grange proceedings, form the principal body of material on the order of Patrons of Husbandry. Kelley, *Patrons of Husbandry,* supplies the place of the proceedings for the sessions prior to 1873. In 1880 a committee was appointed to compile and publish the proceedings of these early sessions, but nothing ever appeared. (National Grange, *Proceedings,* xiv. 113, 119.) Secretary Kelley stated that a mass of letters which he had preserved while secretary was sent to the paper mill by his successor. Smith, *Wisconsin Granger Movement* (Ms.), 17. See also National Grange, *Proceedings,* xiv. 45, 96.

National Grange. *Constitution.* Six different editions, published 1871–76, in W.H.; edition of 1874, in L.C.

National Grange. *Bryan Fund Publication, no. 4,* n. p., n. d. W.H. Thomas B. Bryan of Chicago contributed fifty dollars in 1870 to pay for the publication of tracts advertising the order, and Kelley gave them the above title. Kelley, *Patrons of Husbandry*, 270, 278–280.

National Grange. *Dedication of Grange Halls, adopted by the National Grange, 1875.* Louisville, 1875. W. H. Illustrates the fraternal side of the order.

National Grange. *Digest of the Laws and Enactments of the National Grange to March 1, 1877 . . . issued by authority of the National Grange.* Louisville, 1877. 140 pp. W.H., L.C. Contents: articles of incorporation of the National Grange by the state legislature of Kentucky, 1876; declaration of purposes; outline of organization; constitution and by-laws; rules and suggestions relative to coöperative stores; plan for district granges; parliamentary guide; formula for public installation of officers; formula for dedication of grange halls; funeral ceremony; and digest of laws, decisions, etc.

National Grange. *Manual of Subordinate Granges of the Patrons of Husbandry, adopted and issued by the National Grange.* 3d ed. Washington, 1871. 64 pp. L.C. 4th ed. Washington, 1872. 70 pp. L.C., W.H. 5th ed. Philadelphia, 1874. 72 pp. W.H.

National Grange. *Origin of the Grange*, n. p., n. d. A leaflet published about 1899.

National Grange. *The Patrons' Parliamentary Guide.* Washington, 1874. 16 pp. L.C., W.H.

National Grange. *Secretary's Reports* or *Monthly Bulletins*. W.H. Under various titles, occasional lists of officials of state granges, with statistics of the number of granges in each state were published during 1874 and 1875.

Degree of the Golden Sheaf. *Circulars.* W.H. See above, p. 110, note 1.

National Agricultural Congress. *Proceedings.* i and v (1872, 1876) in L.C.; v in D.A.

National Agricultural Convention. *Proceedings.* 1872. Washington, 1872. 84 pp. (42 Congress, 2 session, *Senate Miscellaneous Documents*, no. 164).

National Agricultural Association. *Proceedings at Organization, December, 1879.* D.A.

Proceedings of a Convention of Agriculturists held at the Department of Agriculture, January 23–29, 1883. (United States, Department of Agriculture, *Special Report*, no. 2, miscellaneous series.)

STATE

No collection of state grange proceedings which is anywhere nearly complete is known to exist. The collection in W.H. is probably the most extensive. The proceedings vary in fulness, in some cases containing but a bare record of business transacted and in others containing speeches and reports of committees in full. Possibly the most valuable parts of them are the numerous resolutions or sets of resolutions which were almost invariably adopted at each session of each state grange. Documents which have to do solely with the business features of the order are listed under Coöperation. The arrangement is alphabetical by states.

Alabama State Grange. *Proceedings.* ii and iii (1874–75) in W.H.

Alabama State Grange. *Alabama State Grange Fair, Selma, Alabama, to commence Tuesday, October 27 [26], 1875 and continue five days. Programme and schedule of premiums etc.* Selma, Alabama, 1875. Copy in library of T. M. Owen, Carrollton, Alabama.

Gulf City Grange, no. 68, Mobile, Alabama. *Mobile County, eine passende Heimath für den deutschen Farmer. Bericht über die Einwanderung nach Süd-Alabama Besonders der deutschen Farmer des Westens, vorgelegt in der Gulf City Grange no. 68, Patrons of Husbandry, nach einem in der am 25. Juni 1874 abgehaltenen Versammlung gefassten Beschlusse.* St. Louis, 1874. 16 pp. L.C.

Arkansas State Grange. *Proceedings.* v (1877) in W.H. J. P. L. Russ of El Paso, Arkansas, is reported to have a complete file. Arkansas Historical Society, *Publications,* i. 224.

California State Grange. *Organization . . . at Napa City, July 15, 1873.* San Francisco, 1873. The proceedings of the first and second annual meetings, October, 1873, and October, 1874, are given quite fully in Carr, *Patrons of Husbandry.*

Illinois State Grange. *Proceedings.* The secretary of the Wisconsin State Grange has iii–v (1874–76); iv and v are in U.I.; and iv is in W.H.

Illinois State Grange. *By-laws, 1875.* Sterling, Illinois, 1876. W.H.

Illinois State Farmers' Association. *Proceedings.* ii (December, 1873) is in L.C.; iii (January, 1875) and v (1877) are in U.I.; and v is also in D.A.

Indiana State Grange. *Proceedings.* A summary of the proceedings at the organization of the state grange, February, 1872, and at sessions November, 1872, and November, 1873, has been published in the appendix to the proceedings of the thirty-sixth annual session, and also as a leaflet. iv (1874) and viii+(1877+) are in W. H.

Iowa State Grange. *Proceedings.* iv–vi (1873–75) are in W. H.

Kansas State Grange. *Proceedings.* iii (1875) is in W. H.

Kansas State Grange. *Constitution and By-laws.* Lawrence [1875 ?]. W.H.

Kentucky State Grange. *Constitution and By-laws, 1874.* Lexington, Ky., 1875. W. H.

Louisiana State Grange. *Proceedings.* iii (1875) is in W.H.

Louisiana State Grange. *Memorial of the Patrons of Husbandry, of the State of Louisiana, to the Forty-third Congress of the United States of America, asking the government to facilitate the navigation of the Mississippi River, by building the Fort St. Philip canal, and until its building can be accomplished, to control the towing of vessels across the bar.* New Orleans, 1873. 4 pp. L.C.

Maine State Grange. *Proceedings.* Proceedings at organization and i and ii (1874–76), all in one pamphlet, are in W.H.; vi (1880) is in D.A.

Maryland State Grange. *Proceedings.* i (1874) and special session (December, 1875) are in W.H.

Maryland State Grange. *Constitution, 1874.* W.H.

Maryland State Grange. *By-laws, 1875.* Baltimore, 1875. W.H. All records and papers of the state grange were consumed by fire in 1878. *American Farmer,* February, 1878, p. 74.

Massachusetts State Grange.   *Proceedings.*   v (1877) is in D.A.

Massachusetts State Grange.   *Quarterly Bulletin.*   Issue for January, 1876, is in W.H.

Michigan State Grange.   *Proceedings.*   ii and iii (January, December, 1875) are in W.H.; vi (1878), viii (1880) in D.A.   The secretary of the state grange has an office file of the proceedings.

Michigan State Grange.   *Blank form for articles of association of Michigan granges under act of the Michigan legislature " to incorporate State and Subordinate Granges," April 8, 1875.*   W.H.

Michigan State Grange.   *Blank form for subordinate grange charter.*   W.H.

Minnesota State Grange.   *Constitution, February, 1873.*   Lake City, Minnesota, 1873.   W.H.

Mississippi State Grange.   *Proceedings.*   v (1875) is in W.H.

Mississippi State Grange.   *By-laws.*   2d ed. (1872).   W.H.

Missouri State Grange.   *Proceedings.*   iii and iv (1874–75), also master's address from v (1876), are in W.H.

Missouri State Grange.   *Constitution and By-laws, 1873.*   Kansas City, 1783.   *Ibid., October, 1874.*   St. Louis, 1874.   W.H.

Montana Territorial Grange.   *Proceedings.*   i (1875) is in W.H.

Nebraska State Grange.   *Proceedings.*   iv (1874) is in W.H.

Nebraska State Grange.   *Constitution, 1873.*   Lincoln, 1874.   W.H.

New Hampshire State Grange.   *Proceedings.*   Proceedings at organization and i and ii (1873–75), in one pamphlet, iii (1876), vii (1880) are in W.H.; iii+ (1876+) in D.A.

New Hampshire State Grange.   *By-laws, 1876.*   Claremont, N. H., 1877.   W.H.

New York State Grange.   *Proceedings.*   ii and iii (1875–76) are in W.H.   The secretary of the state grange has a complete file in his office.

North Carolina State Grange.   *Proceedings.*   ii–iv (1875–77) are in W.H.

Ohio State Grange.   *Proceedings.*   i–iii (1874–76) are in W.H.; vi (1879) is in L.C.

Ohio State Grange.   *Patrons' Song Book; for use in the grange; containing a choice collection of original and selected gems, compiled and published under the auspices of the Ohio State Grange.*   Cincinnati, 1877.   55 pp.   Rev. ed., Cincinnati, 1879.   W.H.

Oregon State Grange.   *Proceedings.*   iii (1876) is in W.H.

Pennsylvania State Grange.   *Proceedings.*   The secretary of the state grange has a complete file in his office.

South Carolina State Grange.   *Proceedings.*   iv (1876) is in W.H.   A manuscript *Minute-book* in the office of the secretary of the state grange contains a complete record of the proceedings.   The South Carolina State Agricultural and Mechanical Society, *Transactions* for 1877 and 1881 (Columbia) contain state grange proceedings.

South Carolina State Grange.   *By-laws.*   Charleston, 1873.   W.H.

History, Description and Resources of Darlington County, State of South Carolina.   Charleston, 1874.   29 pp.   L.C.   Prepared by the committee on immigration of a convention of granges of Darlington County.

Tennessee State Grange.   *Proceedings.*   ii (1875) is in W.H.

Texas State Grange. *Proceedings*. *Minutes* of sessions from organization, October, 1872, to April, 1874, and i (August, 1874) are in W.H.

Texas State Grange. *Constitution, 1874*. Waco, Texas, 1874. W.H.

Vermont State Grange. *Proceedings*. Proceedings at organization, July, 1872, and i–iii (1872–74), in one pamphlet, and iv (1875) are in W.H.

Virginia State Grange. *Proceedings*. *Minutes*, i (December, 1873) and called session (April, 1874), in one pamphlet, are in W.H.

Wisconsin State Grange. *Proceedings*. ii+ (1874+) in W.H.

Wisconsin State Grange. *Grange List of Patrons of Husbandry, of the State of Wisconsin, for the year 1874*. Neenah, 1874. 11 pp. W.H. Lists 505 granges; also gives the names of thirty-nine deputies and county purchasing agents. *The Prairie Farmer*, xlvi. 186 (June 12, 1875) states that the practice of publishing these lists of subordinate granges was to be abandoned and that Illinois and Wisconsin would not publish that year.

Wisconsin State Grange. *Constitution and By-laws . . . together with forms for subordinate granges and county councils*. Oshkosh, 1874. 30 pp. Copy in W.H. bound with the *Proceedings*.

Rock County (Wisconsin) Pomona Grange. *Constitution, By-laws, list of officers and members and time of meeting of Rock County Pomona Grange, no. 5, of Wisconsin*. Janesville, Wisconsin, 1877. 26 pp. W.H.

Fond du Lac County (Wisconsin) Pomona Grange, *Constitution and By-laws*. Fond du Lac, 1877. W.H.

NEWSPAPERS

Next to the state grange proceedings, the Grange and other agricultural papers are the most valuable sources for the study of the movement in particular states or localities. The following list contains the principal agricultural papers published during the period and all papers which are known to have had any special connection with the movement. It is hoped that the publication of this list may lead to the location and preservation of files of some of these papers. The dates given are years during which the paper is known to have been issued and not necessarily the dates of establishment and discontinuance. The arrangement is alphabetical by states and the following abbreviations are used: d., daily; s.-w., semi-weekly; w., weekly; s.-m., semi-monthly; m., monthly.

Rural Alabamian, Mobile, Alabama, m., 1872–73. Complete file for 1872–73 in D.A.

Arkansas Grange, Little Rock, m., 1873–77. Established in 1873 as the official organ of the order in the state.

Weekly Grange, Little Rock, Arkansas, w., 1875–77.

California Farmer, San Francisco, w., 1855–80.

California Granger, San José, 1874. Consolidated with the *Pacific Rural Press*, January, 1875.

California Patron, San Francisco, m., s.-m., 1875–80. Established in May, 1875 and published under the control of the executive committee of the state grange. File, May, 1876–June, 1878, in W.H.

Pacific Rural Press, San Francisco, w., 1870–date.

Sacramento Valley Agriculturist, Sacramento, California, w., 1873–79.   Established in 1873; "devoted to agriculture, horticulture, and Grange interests of California."

Semi-Tropical Farmer, Los Angeles, California, w., 1875–76.   Established in 1875 by a member of the Grange and printed Grange news extensively.

Colorado Grange, Greeley, m., 1876.   Published by the master and secretary of the state grange under the authority of the executive committee.

Florida Agriculturist, De Land, w., 1874–80.

Florida Patron, m., 1874.   Edited by W. H. Wilson, lecturer of the state grange, on his farm near Wellborn.

Grange Bulletin, Wellborn, Florida, m., 1876.   Published by W. H. Wilson. Probably a successor of the *Florida Patron*.

Georgia Grange, Atlanta, w., 1874–76.   Claimed to be the official organ of "the Patrons of Husbandry, the Direct Trade Union, the State Agricultural Society and the Department of Agriculture" and to be read by every farmer in Georgia and many in the adjoining states.   Absorbed by the *Southern Cultivator*.

Rural Southerner and Plantation, Atlanta, Georgia, w., 1868–76.   In 1876 it claimed to represent "the interests of farmers, Patrons of Husbandry, the Direct Trade Union" etc., and to have a circulation of six thousand. File for 1870 in D.A.

Southern Cultivator, Athens, Atlanta, and Augusta, Georgia, m., 1843–date. File, April, 1868–December, 1881, in D.A.

Southern Farmer and Home, Macon, Georgia, m., 1869–73.   File, December, 1869–October, 1873, in D.A.

Southern Planter and Grange, Atlanta, Georgia, w., 1873–80.   Circulation over three thousand in 1879.   File, 1873–80 in L.C.

Anti-Monopolist, Bloomington, Illinois, 1873–74.   Merged with the *McLean County Anti-Monopolist* of Saybrook, January, 1874.

Anti-Monopolist, Hillsboro, Illinois, 1874.

Anti-Monopolist, Salem, Illinois, 1873.

Anti-Monopolist, Woodstock, Illinois, 1873.

Appeal, Bloomington, Illinois, w., 1875.   Supported the Independent movement.

Chicago Tribune, d. and w., 1847–date.   Under the editorship of Horace White the *Tribune* supported the Grangers in their struggle for railroad regulation, but it changed hands in the fall of 1874.   It is an important source of information on the Granger movement in all the western states. Complete files for the decade of the seventies in the Tribune office; C.H.; Chicago Public Library; Newberry Library, Chicago; and nearly complete files in W.H., Boston Athenæum, and the library of the American Antiquarian Society, Worcester, Massachusetts.

Christian County Farmers' Journal, Taylorville, Illinois, w., March, 1875–1907.   Established in March, 1875, as the *Independent*.   Name changed, January, 1876.   Organ of the Granger and Greenback element of the county.

Farmers' Advocate, Bement, Illinois, 1873–75.

Farmers' Advocate, Marion, Illinois, 1873–74.

Farmers' Advocate, Monticello, Illinois, 1874.

Farmers' Union, Lawrenceville, Illinois, 1873–74. **Supported the Granger** movement.

Granger, St. Anne, Illinois, 1873–74.

Illinois Granger, Macomb, Illinois, w., 1873–76. Name changed to *Independent* in 1876. Supported the Greenback party.

Independent, Kewanee, Illinois, w., 1871–95. Supported the Independent party movement.

Independent Reformer, Springfield, Illinois, 1874. A campaign paper in the interests of the Independent party. Circulated gratuitously in the fall of 1874.

Industrial Age, Chicago, w., 1873–77. Established in August, 1873, as the organ of the farmers' movement. Later Greenback in tone. *The Prairie Farmer*, xliv. 289, 292 (September 13, 1873), said it was supposed to be backed by the McCormick Reaper Company. Circulation reported as five thousand in 1876. File from beginning to February, 1877, in W.H.; file for 1876 in U.I.

Industrial Press, Galena, Illinois, w., February, 1874–84. Supported the Independent party movement.

Liberal Reformer, Morris, Illinois, w., 1872–79. Supported the Independent party movement.

McLean County Anti-Monopolist, Saybrook and Bloomington, Illinois, 1874–75.

National Crop Reporter, Jacksonville, 1873. See same title, Jackson, Tennessee.

New Era, Woodstock, Illinois, w., 1873–80. A Grange and later a Greenback paper.

Northern Granger, St. Charles, Illinois, w., 1873–74.

Ogle County Granger, Oregon, Illinois, w., 1873–75.

People's Paper, Chicago, 1873. A Grange paper edited by Edward N. Fuller. Only two numbers, July 26, and August 16, 1873, appear to have been published. The paper was then merged in the *Industrial Age*. Copies of both numbers are in C.H.

Prairie Farmer, Chicago, w., 1843–date. Early favorable to the Patrons of Husbandry and established a Grange department in December, 1873. Later another department was added for the clubs and the State Farmers' Association. Favored railroad regulation and looked with approval upon the Independent party movements. Claimed a circulation of twenty thousand in 1876. Files: nearly complete in U.I.; 1869–75 in B.P.; 1875–76 in C.H.; May–December, 1873, in W.H.

Spirit of the Grange, Bloomington, Illinois, w., 1876. Vol. i. no. 7 (August 3, 1876) owned by the McLean County Historical Society.

State Grange News, Freeport, Illinois, 1877. Published by J. M. Chambers, the secretary of the state grange.

Western Agriculturist (*and Live Stock Journal*), Quincy, Illinois, m., 1868–date. Files: February–December, 1874, 1878–1900, in D.A.; 1875–79 in Chicago Public Library; 1877–88 in U.I.

Western Farmer, Dixon, Illinois, m., 1868–82. Established as *Rock River Farmer*. The *Industrial Age* in 1873 accused it of " working for monopoly masters." Partial file, 1875–77, in C.H.

Western Rural, Chicago, w., 1863–90. Claimed a circulation of twenty-five thousand in 1876. Took the lead in organizing the Northwestern Alliance in 1880 and served as its organ. Files: 1868–70, 1875–94 in C.H.; May–December, 1875, in W.H.

Workingman's Advocate (and Anti-Monopolist), Chicago, w., 1864–79. " Official organ of the labor union, and devoted to the interests of the producing classes."

Grange, Terre Haute, Indiana, 1875.

Hoosier Patron and Lady Granger, Indianapolis, w., 1874–76. Official organ of the state grange. Claimed a circulation of sixty-five hundred in 1876.

Indiana Farmer, Indianapolis, w., 1845–date.

Indiana Granger, Muncie, Indiana, 1874.

Indianapolis Sun, w., 1873–79. Supported the Independent and Greenback parties. Claimed a circulation of nineteen thousand in 1876.

Jay County Granger, Portland, Indiana, w., 1871–79.

National Crop Reporter, Indianapolis. See same title, Jackson, Tennessee.

Western Granger and Home Journal, Lafayette, Indiana, w., 1871–79. " Devoted to the interests of the Grange, farm and fireside." Claimed a circulation of fifteen hundred in 1876.

Des Moines Leader, Iowa, d. and w., 1874–76. Supported the Anti-Monopoly party.

Iowa Homestead and Western Farm Journal, Des Moines, Iowa, w., 1855–date.

Patrons' Helper, Des Moines, Iowa, w., 1874–76.

Waukon Standard, Waukon, Iowa, w., 1868–96. " Has done us good service, both in favoring and opposing the movement." Kelley, *Patrons of Husbandry*, 212.

Western Stock Journal and Farmer, Cedar Rapids, Iowa, m., 1872–80.

Farmers' Advocate, Salina, Kansas, w., 1875–76.

Kansas Farmer, Topeka, w., 1863–80. Established at Leavenworth, moved to Topeka. Edited by J. K. Hudson, author of a *Patrons' Handbook* and prominent in Grange work. Claimed a circulation of over six thousand in 1876.

Kansas Patron and Farmer, Olathe, w., 1878–96. Official paper of the state grange after 1881.

Patrons' Gleaner, Emporia, Kansas.

Spirit of Kansas, Lawrence, Kansas, w., 1872–80. An agricultural paper. Supported the Granger movement.

Standard of Reform, Lawrence, Kansas, d. and w., 1870–79. " The acknowledged state organ of the opposition [Independent] party."

Vox Populi, Lawrence (?), Kansas, 1873–74. Edited by Henry Bronson of the Douglas County Farmers' Union, author of a pamphlet on *Farmers' Unions and Tax Reform*. Reported as " down and out " early in 1874.

Farmers' Home Journal, Lexington and Louisville, Kentucky, w., 1865–date.

Grange Record, Louisville, Kentucky, April, 1877 + (?). Published by order of the National Grange under the supervision of the executive committee. See above, p. 289. Vol. i. no. 1, is in W.H.

Home and Farm, Louisville, Kentucky, s.-m., 1876–80. File, April, 1879–December, 1880, in B.P.

National Granger, Louisville, Kentucky, w., 1875–76. In 1876, claimed to be the leading Grange paper with the hearty support of the order and a circulation of over five thousand, but sold out before the close of the year to the *Southern Agriculturist*.

Patrons' Bulletin, Georgetown, Kentucky, m., 1875–77. "The only official organ of the State Grange." Published by the executive committee and one copy sent to each grange to be read in meetings. Confidential. File, November, 1875–August, 1877 in W.H.

Southern Agriculturist, Louisville, Kentucky, 1870–79.

(Farmers' Vindicator and) Coöperative News, New Orleans, w., 1875–79. Had the approval of the state grange.

Louisiana Sugar Bowl, New Iberia, w., 1870–79. Organ of the sugar planters.

Our Home Journal and Rural Southland, New Orleans, w., 1865–79. Official organ of the state grange in 1875. Claimed a circulation of over seven thousand in 1876.

Son of the Soil, New Orleans, w., 1875–76. "Devoted to the farm and grange interests of the South." Claimed a circulation of over four thousand in 1876.

Southwestern Granger, New Orleans, w., 1876. Claimed to be "generally endorsed by the Grange fraternity," and to have a circulation of over two thousand.

Dirigo Rural, Bangor, Maine, w., 1874–82. A strong Grange paper. Circulation about two thousand.

Maine Farmer, Augusta, 1833–date.

American Farmer, Baltimore, Maryland, m., 1866–81. Published Grange items. Files: 1869, 1872–81 in D.A.; 1876–81, incomplete, in W.H.

Maryland Farmer, Baltimore, m., 1864–96. Published many Grange items. File, 1869–96 in D.A.

Our Fireside, Baltimore, 1877. Assumed to be an organ of the state grange.

American Cultivator, Boston, Massachusetts, w., 1839–date.

Massachusetts Ploughman, w., Boston, 1841–96. Supported the Patrons of Husbandry as early as 1871.

New England Farmer, Boston, w., 1848–date. File, 1866–76 in American Antiquarian Society library, Worcester, Massachusetts.

New England Homestead, Springfield, Massachusetts, w., 1868–date.

Northborough Farmer, Northborough, Massachusetts, w., 1873–80.

Grange Standard, Detroit, Michigan, s.-m., 1876.

Grange Visitor, Schoolcraft, Michigan., m., 1875–76. Issued by the executive committee of the state grange.

Michigan Farmer and State Journal of Agriculture, Detroit, 1867–date.

New Era and Grange Index, Owosso, Michigan, w., 1874–76. Absorbed the *Northern Granger*, of Lansing in 1874.

Northern Granger and Farmers' Advocate, Lansing, Michigan, 1874.

Anti-Monopolist, St. Paul, Minnesota, w., 1874–79. Published by Ignatius Donnelly, who took the lead in the Anti-Monopoly party movement in Minnesota.

Farmers' Union, Minneapolis, w., 1867–80. Favorable to the Grange. Files: 1869–70 in B.P.; 1873 in W.H.

Grange Advance, Red Wing, Minnesota, w., s.-w., 1873–79.

Minnesota Monthly, St. Paul, m., 1869. Edited by D. A. Robertson, who helped Kelley to get the Grange started in the state. File, 1869 in D.A.

Sauk Rapids Sentinel, Sauk Rapids, Minnesota, w., 1868–80. The editor was a friend of Secretary Kelley and the paper served as an organ of the order in the early days.

Canton Mail (Grange), Canton, Mississippi, w., 1865–79. Listed as a Grange paper in 1875.

Farmer's Vindicator, Jackson, Mississippi, 1873–75. Edited by E. G. Wall, a Grange leader in the state.

Patron of Husbandry, Columbus, Mississippi, w., 1873–80. About the most prominent Grange paper in the South.

Coleman's Rural World, St. Louis, Missouri, w., 1848–date. The oldest and most prominent agricultural paper in the Southwest. Early came to the support of the Grange. Files: 1871 in B.P.; 1882–85, incomplete, in W.H.

Grange Correspondent and Dry-Goods Reporter, St. Louis, 1875. Established in August, 1875, by a Grange purchasing agent who got into trouble by printing statements derogatory to some of the officers of the state grange. See National Grange, *Proceedings*, xi. 111 (1877).

Grange Monitor, Missouri, 1874.

Journal of Agriculture and Farmer, St. Louis, w., 1866–96.

Midland Farmer, St. Louis, m., 1871–80.

Missouri Farmer, Boonville, Missouri, 1874–75. Consolidated with the *Journal of Agriculture* of St. Louis, in 1875.

Missouri Granger, Macon, Missouri, w., 1875–76.

Monthly Talk, St. Louis, m., 1875–76. Issued by the executive committee of the state grange.

National Granger, St. Louis, w., 1874.

Patron of Husbandry, Savannah, Missouri, w., 1875–76.

Rocky Mountain Husbandman, White Sulphur Springs, Montana, w., 1875–80.

Center-Union Agriculturist, Omaha, Nebraska, w., 1869–79.

Farmers' Blade, Nebraska, 1874.

Grange Review, Salem, Nebraska, 1875.

Granger, Brownville, Nebraska, w., 1876.

Nebraska Patron, 1874.

Rural Nebraska, Omaha, Nebraska, m., 1868–80.

Mirror and Farmer, Manchester, New Hampshire, w., 1851–date. Published Grange news and announcements. Files: 1859–72, March 23, 1878, in B.P.; 1868–72 in American Antiquarian Society library at Worcester, Massachusetts.

Portsmouth Weekly, Portsmouth, New Hampshire, w., 1877–80. Organ of the state grange in 1880.

New Jersey Granger, Vineland, New Jersey, w., 1874. The *Vineland Independent* adopted this name in 1874.

American Agriculturist, New York City, m., 1842–date. Had probably the largest circulation of any agricultural paper in the country, about fifty thousand. Contained some Grange material. Files: complete to 1900 in D.A.; 1856–94 in B.P.

American Rural Home, Rochester, New York, w., 1870–80.

Chautauqua Farmer, Forestville, New York, w., 1869–80.

Cultivator and Country Gentlemen, Albany, New York, w., 1831–date. Contained a few Grange items but did not become enthusiastic over the order. Files: 1866–79 in D.A., 1869–75 in W.H.

Farmers' Journal, Carthage, New York, w., 1875–76.

Grangers' Prices Current, later *Patrons' Gazette*, New York City, m., 1875. A " Grange Commercial Paper," apparently published in the interests of a mail order firm.

Husbandman, Elmira, New York, w., 1874–80. Edited by the secretary of the state grange.

Moore's Rural New Yorker, Rochester and New York City, w., 1850–date. Contained considerable information on the Granger movement especially after 1873. File, 1856–63, 1869–79 in D.A.

Nation, New York City, w., 1865–date. Denounced the Granger movement vigorously.

National Agriculturist and Working Farmer, New York City, m., 1848–80.

National Record, Dansville, New York, 1876. " To present crop statistics for Patrons only and from Patrons."

New York Tribune, d., w., and s.-w., 1841–date. The *Tribune* took a great interest in the farmers' movement and sent a special correspondent to the West to report on it. Files of the daily are quite common; the semi-weekly, 1861–79, is in U.I.

Scythe, New York City, 1873–74. Its purpose was " to mow down monopoly and extortion," but the *Industrial Age* said it cut the fingers of all who touched it.

Carolina Farmer, Wilmington, North Carolina, m., 1868–79.

Southern Home, Charlotte, North Carolina, w., 1870–79. Had the approval of the state grange.

(American) Grange Bulletin, Cincinnati, Ohio, w., 1875–date. Had a circulation of about three thousand in 1879. Is one of the few Grange papers which have survived to the present day. Files: 1895–1900 in D.A.; 1900–02, containing historical articles on the Grange by J. J. Woodman and others, in W.H.

American Patron, Findlay, Ohio, w., 1875–76. Claimed to be "the leading grange and agricultural paper," and to have a circulation of eight thousand in 1876. The editor was a Patron.

Grange Visitor and Farmers' Monthly Magazine, Springfield, Ohio, m., 1875–79.

Harvest Home, Mt. Washington, Ohio, 1875.

Live Patron, Springfield, Ohio, w., 1877–80.

Ohio (Practical) Farmer, Cleveland, w., 1852–date.

Patrons' Advance, Batavia, Ohio, 1875–76.

Union and Patron, Urbana, Ohio, w., 1875. Probably a name adopted by the *Urbana Union* in 1875 and changed the next year to *Union and Democrat*.

Eugene City Guard, Eugene City, Oregon, 1867–79. Supported the Granger movement and the Independent party.

Oregon Cultivator, Albany, w., 1876.

Oregon Granger, Albany, 1875.

Willamette Farmer, Salem, Oregon, w., 1868–80.

Farmers' Friend, Mechanicsburg, Pennsylvania, 1874–80. Edited by the secretary of the state grange. Claimed to have a circulation of thirteen thousand and to be the official organ of the Patrons of New Jersey, Pennsylvania, Delaware, Maryland, and West Virginia.

National Farmer and Horticulture Register, Philadelphia, Pennsylvania, 1870–71. Used by Secretary Kelley to advertise the Grange in 1871.

Practical Farmer, Philadelphia, Pennsylvania, 1855–date.

Rock Hill Grange, Rock Hill, South Carolina, w., 1875–76.

Rural Carolinian, Charleston and Cokesbury, m., 1869–77. Edited by D. H. Jacques and later by D. Wyatt Aiken, both prominent Grange leaders. One of the first southern papers to take up the Patrons of Husbandry and valuable for following the Granger movement in the South. File, October, 1869–September, 1871, October, 1872–September, 1874 in D.A.

American Farmers' Advocate, Jackson, Tennessee, 1872–73. "Devoted to the interests of the National Agricultural Congress and the order of Patrons of Husbandry." File, 1872–73 in B.P.

Grange Journal, Humboldt, Tennessee, w., 1876.

(Living Age and) Grange Outlook, Knoxville, Tennessee, w., 1874–76. Claimed a large circulation in Tennessee, Virginia, Kentucky, Louisiana, and North Carolina.

National Crop Reporter, Jackson, Tennessee, 1873. An anti-Grange and anti-secret society paper. Moved to Jacksonville, Illinois, and then to Indianapolis.

Patron of Husbandry, Memphis, Tennessee, w., 1874–79.

Rural Sun, Nashville, Tennessee, w., 1872–79.

Southern Farmer, Memphis, Tennessee, w., 1876. Ran a Grange department.

Southern Husbandman, Nashville, Tennessee, m., 1877–79. Organ of the state grange.

Southern Granger, Memphis, Tennessee, s.-m., 1875–76.

(East) Texas Patron, Crockett, Texas, w., 1875–79.

Examiner (and Patron), Waco, Texas, w., 1868–79.

Grange Reporter, Tyler, Texas, w., 1876.

Valley Farmer, Windsor, Vermont, w., 1873–80.

Vermont Record and Farmer, Brattleboro, w., 1862–80. File, 1870–73 in B.P.

Southern Planter and Farmer, Richmond, Virginia, m., 1841–date. Ran a Grange department. Files: 1869–71, 1883 in D.A.; 1875–76 scattered numbers and 1877–80 in W.H.

Virginia Granger, Portsmouth, w., 1879–80.

Virginia Patron, Richmond, w., 1875–78.

Adams County Press, Friendship, Wisconsin, w., 1861–date. Edited by the master of the state grange and official organ of the order in 1871–72. File, 1865–date in W.H.

Bulletin of the Executive Committee of the State Grange of Wisconsin, Patrons of Husbandry, Madison, Oshkosh, and Neenah, m., s.-m., 1875–85. Edited at first by J. H. Osborn, master of the state grange and chairman of the railroad commission, afterwards by the secretary of the state grange. Became semi-monthly in 1880. After 1880 it was a general agricultural paper containing much besides Grange matter. Absorbed by the *Western Farmer* of Madison in 1885. File, 1875–81, and scattered numbers 1881–84, in W.H.

Oshkosh Times, Oshkosh, Wisconsin, w., 1867–date. Was practically an organ of the Grange for several years. File, 1873–83 in W.H.

Western Farmer, Madison, Wisconsin (1), w., 1868–75. Merged in *Western Rural* of Chicago, 1875. File, 1869, 1871–74 in W.H.

Western Farmer, Madison, Wisconsin (2), w., 1882–91. Absorbed the *Grange Bulletin* in 1885 and was the organ of the order, 1885–86. File, 1882–90 in W.H.

Western Journal of Agriculture, Milwaukee, s.-m., 1873–74. Started in the fall of 1873 by Dr. O. W. Wright, one of the leaders of the Peoples' Reform party. Subscription list turned over to the *Industrial Age* of Chicago in January, 1874.

Wisconsin Granger, Madison, w., 1873–75.

Wisconsin Post, Shawano, w., 1872–74. A German paper supporting the Peoples' Reform party. File, 1873–74 in W.H.

Wisconsin Statesman, Madison, w., 1875–76. Successor to the *Wisconsin Granger*. Published Grange news and supported the Peoples' Reform party. Democratic in national politics. In December, 1873, the editor stated that it did not have sufficient patronage to support it but that he would continue to publish it for his own amusement. File, July, 1875–October, 1876 in W.H.

GENERAL AND MISCELLANEOUS MATERIAL

GENERAL

Andrews, Elisha B. *The History of the Last Quarter-Century in the United States, 1870–95.* New York, 1896. 2 vols. Popular and sketchy. Characterizes the Granger movement briefly in a chapter on "Agrarian and Labor Movements in the Seventies" and brings out its connection with the Kearneyite agitation in California.

Appleton's Annual Cyclopedia and Register of Important Events, 1861 +. New York, 1862 +. Prior to 1875 the title reads, *American Annual*

Cyclopedia. Articles: "Patrons of Husbandry," "Illinois," and "Iowa" in the volume for 1873 contain documentary material. There are also convenient summaries of politics and legislation under the different states in each volume of the period.

Bailey, L. H., editor. *Cyclopedia of American Agriculture; a Popular Survey of Agricultural Conditions, Practices, and Ideals in the United States and Canada.* New York, 1907–09. 4 vols. The first volume contains a useful survey of agricultural conditions in the various sections. The last volume, entitled "Farm and Community," is especially pertinent. It contains chapters on "Business Organization in Agriculture," "Social and Service Association," and "Education by Means of Agriculture," which summarize and interpret many phases of the Granger movement.

Bemis, Edward W. "The Discontent of the Farmer," in *Journal of Political Economy*, i. 193–213 (March, 1893). Examines the causes for the failure of farming to increase in profit and attractiveness as rapidly as city occupations.

Bogart, Ernest L. *The Economic History of The United States.* New York, 1910 (copyright, 1907). 522 pp. (*Longmans' Commercial Text-Books.*) A convenient summary of economic conditions and developments.

Bolles, Albert S. *Industrial History of the United States, from the Earliest Settlements to the Present Time.* Norwich, Connecticut, 1879. 936 pp. Contains an inaccurate general account of the Granger movement.

Bryce, James. *The American Commonwealth.* New York, 1888, and later editions. 2 vols. Gives a clear insight into American political conditions since the war. The Granger railroad legislation is treated briefly but fairly.

Butterfield, Kenyon L. *Chapters in Rural Progress.* Chicago, 1908. 251 pp. The chapter on the Grange is a revision of his article in the *Forum*. The other chapters are suggestive on the condition and needs of the farmer.

Cloud, D. C. *Monopolies and the People.* Davenport, Iowa, 1873. 514 pp. A radical exposition of economic and political abuses of monopoly. The book is dedicated to the Patrons of Husbandry.

Coman, Katharine. *The Industrial History of the United States, for high schools and colleges.* New York, 1905. xviii, 343, xxiv pp. Contains a succinct statement of the causes and course of the Granger movement. Also useful for the economic background.

"Condition of Agriculture in the Cotton States," in Commissioner of Agriculture, *Reports*, 1874, pp. 215–238. Gives an insight into the causes of agricultural depression and discontent in the South.

Cooper, Thomas V., and Fenton, Hector T. *American Politics (non-partisan) from the beginning to date; embodying a history of all the political parties, with their views and records on all important questions. Great speeches on all great issues; the text of all existing political laws.* Boston, 1882 and later editions. 1097 pp. Contains a brief account of the Granger movement and the Granger railway legislation of Illinois.

Dodge, John R. " The Discontent of the Farmer," in *Century*, xxi. 447–456 (January, 1892). A discussion of the complaints of the farmers and the causes of discontent both general and local. Sympathetic but optimistic in tone.

Dun, Finlay. *American Farming and Food.* London, 1881. 477 pp. Throws light on agricultural conditions.

Dunning, W. A. *Reconstruction, Political and Economic, 1865–1877.* New York, 1907. 378 pp. (*American Nation*, xxii.) Touches the Granger movement only incidentally, but is useful for the political and economic background.

Elliot, J. R. *American Farms; their Condition and Future.* New York, 1890. 262 pp. An inquiry into the causes of the lack of prosperity in rural districts and an examination of the proposed remedies.

Ely, Richard T. *The Labor Movement in America.* New York, 1886. xvi. 399 pp. Treats the Patrons of Husbandry and Sovereigns of Industry incidentally in the chapter on " Coöperation." The Knights of Labor are treated more at length.

Emerick, C. F. " An Analysis of the Agricultural Discontent in the United States," in *Political Science Quarterly*, xi. 433–463, 601–639, xii. 93–127 (September, December, 1896, March, 1897). A thorough-going and scientific analysis of the agricultural situation in the nineties, throwing light also upon previous conditions. Among the proposed remedies for the ills of the farmers, reform in taxation and thrift are approved. A useful bibliography is appended.

Fite, Emerson D. *Social and Industrial Conditions in the North during the Civil War.* New York, 1910. 318 pp. Furnishes a background for the Granger movement.

Greathouse, Charles H. *Historical Sketch of the United States Department of Agriculture.* Washington, 1898. 74 pp. (United States Department of Agriculture, Division of Publications, *Bulletins*, no. 3.) Recognizes the influence of the Grange in securing the creation of the agricultural department.

Hammond, Matthew B. *The Cotton Industry; an Essay in American Economic History.* New York, 1897. 382 pp. Throws light on the economic condition of the southern cotton planters during the period.

Hammond, Matthew B. " The Southern Farmer and the Cotton Question," in *Political Science Quarterly*, xii. 450–475 (September, 1897). Deals with the effects of the war, the credit system, and the over-production of cotton upon the southern farmers.

Hart, Albert B. " The Disposition of our Public Lands," in *Quarterly Journal of Economics*, i. 176 (January, 1887). Helpful for an understanding of the causes of the great agricultural expansion following the Civil War.

Lloyd, Henry D. *Wealth against Commonwealth.* New York, 1894. 563 pp. A radical and unsystematic work dealing with monopolies, trusts, railroad abuses, corruption in politics, etc.

McPherson, Edward. *Political History of the United States during the Period of Reconstruction.* 2d ed., Washington, 1875. *A Handbook of Politics.*

Washington, 1872–80. 5 vols. The *Political History* covers the period 1866–70 and the *Handbook*, the decade 1870–80. They contain national and state platforms, laws, election statistics, etc.

McVey, Frank L. "The Populist Movement," in American Economic Association, *Economic Studies*, i. no. 3, pp. 131–209. (London, 1896.) A superficial treatment. Contains a bibliography.

Moody, William G. *Land and Labor in the United States.* New York, 1883. 360 pp. Some features of the agricultural situation such as the influence of machinery on agriculture and the "bonanza" farms are treated.

New Englander (pseudonym). "The Farmers' Grievance," in *Nation*, xvii. 112 (August 14, 1873). Sees the causes of the farmers' evils in the tariff and the too rapid extension of agriculture resulting in over-production.

New York Tribune Almanac and Political Register. New York, 1838+. Useful for party platforms and election statistics.

Otken, Charles H. *The Ills of the South; or Related Causes Hostile to the General Prosperity of the Southern People.* New York, 1894. xii, 277 pp.

Peffer, William A. *The Farmer's Side; his Troubles and their Remedy.* New York, 1891. 275 pp. Peffer was a Populist leader and the book discusses agricultural conditions. Free silver is the remedy proposed.

Peters, Alfred H. "The Depreciation of Farming Land," in *Quarterly Journal of Economics*, iv. 18–33 (October, 1889). Among the causes of agricultural depression are included heavy and unequal taxation, railway abuses, social disadvantages, etc.

Peto, Sir Samuel M. *The Resources and Prospects of America, ascertained during a Visit to the States in the Autumn of 1865.* London and New York, 1866. xv. 428 pp. Peto was a member of Parliament. The sections on agriculture and the South throw light on the causes of rural discontent.

Porter, Robert P., and others. *The West, from the Census of 1880.* Chicago, 1882. 630 pp. Presents agricultural and other statistics from the census in convenient form.

Quaintance, H. W. "The Influence of Farm Machinery on Production and Labor," in American Economic Association, *Publications*, series 3, v. no. 4, pp. 731–904 (February, 1904). Throws light on the causes of agricultural expansion following the Civil War.

Rhodes, James F. *History of the United States from the Compromise of 1850.* New York, 1892–1906. 7 vols. Touches upon the Granger movement only incidentally, but furnishes a political background.

Sargent, C. S. "Agricultural Depression," in *Garden and Farm*, ix. 391–392 (September 30, 1896). Finds the cause of agricultural depression in over-production due to the homestead act, the development of machinery, improved technique, etc.

Spahr, Charles B. *An Essay on the Present Distribution of Wealth in the United States.* New York, 1896. 184 pp. High and unequally distributed taxes and extortionate and discriminating railway charges are dwelt upon as causes of the concentration of wealth.

Sparks, Edwin E. *National Development, 1877-1885.* New York, 1907. 378 pp. (*American Nation,* xxiii.) The three or four pages on the Granger legislation and the Granger cases contain a number of inaccuracies.

Stahl, John M. *The Real Farmer, especially how he has voted on the "repudiation of the public debt," fiat-greenback, free coinage of silver and Populism.* Quincy, Illinois, [ca. 1908]. 110 pp. U.I. Stahl, who is editor of the *Illinois Farmer* and has been prominent in the efforts of the National Farmers' Congress to obtain legislation believed to be in the interest of farmers, attempts to prove that these radical movements originated among and received their support from the workingmen of the cities rather than the farmers. He over-emphasises the part played by the Knights of Labor in the origin of the Populist party and minimizes the part of the Farmers' Alliance.

Tobey, Edward S. *The Industry of the South: its Immediate Organization Indispensable to the Financial Security of the Country.* Boston, 1865. 15 pp. J.C. Portrays the agricultural situation in the South at the close of the war.

Trowbridge, John T. *The South: a Description of the Present State of the Country — its Agriculture — Railroads — Business and Finances.* Hartford, 1866. xiii, 590 pp. Observations made on a long tour through the South.

Veblen, Thorstein B. "The Price of Wheat since 1867," in *Journal of Political Economy,* i. 68–103 (December, 1892). A detailed discussion, with charts, of the fluctuations in wheat prices and their causes.

Wells, David A. "Rational Principles of Taxation," in *Journal of Social Science,* vi. 120–133 (1874). Brings out the inequalities of taxation.

West, Max. "The Distribution of Property Taxes between City and Country," in *Political Science Quarterly,* xiv. 305–324, 470–499 (June, September, 1899). A careful study leading to the conclusion that, as a general rule, farmers are relatively overtaxed.

Woodburn, James A. *Political Parties and Party Problems in the United States.* New York, 1903. 314 pp. The chapter on recent party history is suggestive as to the influence of farmers' organizations and agricultural unrest upon political conditions since the Civil War.

LOCAL

"Does Farming in New England Pay?" in *United States Commissioner of Agriculture, Reports,* 1874, pp. 187–214. Throws light on agricultural conditions in New England and answers the question in the affirmative, if the farming is "conducted with skill and enterprise, combined with the use of sufficient capital."

Scharf, John T. *History of Delaware, 1609–1888.* Philadelphia, 1888. 2 vols. Contains an account of the development of the order of Patrons of Husbandry in Delaware.

Bennett, Fremont O. *Politics and Politicians of Chicago, Cook County, and Illinois.* Chicago, 1886. 612 pp. L.C., W.H. Touches upon the political aspects of the Granger movement in Illinois.

Davidson, Alexander, and Stuvé, Bernard. *Complete History of Illinois from 1873 to 1884.* Springfield, Illinois, 1884. 1040 pp. Treats the Granger railway legislation and the political aspects of the Granger movement in the state.

Moses, John. *Illinois, Historical and Statistical* . . . 2d ed., rev., Chicago, 1895. 2 vols. The second volume contains a superficial account of the Independent party movement and Granger legislation in Illinois.

Campbell, Henry C., editor. *Wisconsin in Three Centuries, 1634–1905.* New York, 1906. 4 vols. Several chapters in the last volume touch upon the political or railroad aspects of the Granger movement.

Hibbard, B. H. *The History of Agriculture in Dane County, Wisconsin.* Madison, Wisconsin, 1904. (University of Wisconsin, *Bulletins*, Economics and Political Science Series, i. no. 2, pp. 67–214.) Illuminating on the causes of agricultural depression in the Middle West.

Matteson, Clark S. *The History of Wisconsin from Prehistoric Periods.* Milwaukee, 1893. 587 pp. Treats superficially the political and railroad aspects of the Granger movement in Wisconsin.

Peck, George W., editor. *Wisconsin; comprising Sketches of Counties, Towns, Events, Institutions, and Persons, arranged in Cyclopedic Form.* Madison, Wisconsin, 1906. 417 pp. Articles on " The Granger Movement," and " The Potter Law " treat the subject in the conventional manner.

Thompson, John G. *The Rise and Decline of the Wheat Growing Industry in Wisconsin.* Madison, Wisconsin, 1909. 250 pp. (University of Wisconsin, *Bulletins*, Economics and Political Science Series, v. no. 3.) Throws light on agricultural conditions and the causes of rural antagonism to railroads.

Tuttle, Charles R. *An Illustrated History of the State of Wisconsin.* Boston, 1875. 800 pp. L. C., W. H., J. C. Treats the political aspects of the Granger movement in the state.

Folwell, William W. *Minnesota, the North Star State.* Boston, 1908. 382 pp. Contains an impartial and accurate but necessarily brief, account of the Granger movement for railroad regulation in Minnesota.

Kirk, Thomas H. *Illustrated History of Minnesota; a Handbook for Citizens and General Readers.* St. Paul, 1887. 299 pp. W.H. Treats briefly the political and railroad phases of the Granger movement in Minnesota.

Neill, Edward D. *The History of Minnesota: from the Earliest French Explorations to the Present Time.* 4th ed. 928 pp. L.C., W.H. This edition covers the Granger period of Minnesota history briefly.

Gue, Benjamin F. *History of Iowa from the Earliest Times to the Beginning of the Twentieth Century.* New York, 1903. 4 vols. Treats the Granger movement in the state briefly.

Tuttle, Charles R., and Durrie, Daniel S. *An Illustrated History of the State of Iowa* . . . *including a Cyclopedia of Legislation.* Chicago, 1876. 732 pp. L.C., W.H. Covers the Granger period of Iowa history.

Boyle, J. E. *The Financial History of Kansas.* Madison, Wisconsin, 1908. 178 pp. (University of Wisconsin, *Bulletins*, Economics and Political

Science Series, v. no. 1.) Discusses the attitude of the Grangers toward taxation in Kansas.

History of the State of Kansas . . . illustrated. Chicago, Andreas, 1883. 1616 pp. Treats the political phase of the Granger movement in Kansas.

Wilder, Daniel W. *The Annals of Kansas.* Topeka, Kansas, 1875. 691 pp. Contains information upon the political aspects of the Granger movement in Kansas.

Bentley, Arthur F. *The Condition of the Western Farmer as Illustrated by the Economic History of a Nebraska Township.* Baltimore, 1893. 92 pp. (Johns Hopkins University, *Studies,* ii. nos. 7, 8.) Throws light on the agricultural situation in the West.

Collins, Lewis, and Collins, R. H. *Collins' Historical Sketches of Kentucky.* Covington, Kentucky, 1882. 2 vols. L.C. This edition treats of the order of Patrons of Husbandry in the state.

Fleming, Walter L. *Civil War and Reconstruction in Alabama.* New York, 1905. xxiii, 815 pp. The political, social and economic conditions prevailing during the reconstruction period are brought out with a wealth of illustration.

Garner, James W. *Reconstruction in Mississippi.* New York, 1901. xiii, 422 pp. Portrays political and economic conditions in Mississippi during the period.

Wooten, Dudley G., editor. *A Comprehensive History of Texas, 1685–1897.* Dallas, 1898. 2 vols. Touches upon the Grange and states that it was reported to have exerted an influence on the constitutional convention of 1876 in favor of measures of economy.

Bancroft, Hubert H. *History of California.* San Francisco, 1884–90. 7 vols. (in his *Works,* xviii–xxiv). The development of agriculture, the Granger movement, railroad legislation, and the constitutional convention of 1878 are dealt with in the last volume.

Davis, Winfield J. *History of Political Conventions in California, 1849–92.* Sacramento, 1893. 711 pp. (California State Library, *Publications,* no. 1.)

Hittell, Theodore H. *History of California.* San Francisco, 1885–97. 4 vols. The Granger period is covered in the last volume.

ORGANIZATION

GENERAL

Aiken, D. W. *The Grange: its Origin, Progress, and Educational Purposes.* Washington, 1883. 18 pp. (United States Department of Agriculture, *Special Report,* no. 55.) This is a paper " read before a convention called by the Commissioner of Agriculture January 23, 1883, to consider the subject of agricultural education." It is also published in the proceedings of the convention. Aiken was a member of the executive committee of the National Grange in 1874 and 1875. The paper is especially useful on the educational work of the order.

Allen, Emory A., editor. *Labor and Capital; containing an account of the various organizations of farmers, planters, and mechanics, for mutual improvement and protection against monopoly.* Cincinnati, 1891. 518 pp. L. C. Contains chapters on the Grange by John Trimble, one of the "founders" and later secretary of the National Grange, Mortimer Whitehead, lecturer of the National Grange, and Colonel Hiram Hawkins, master of the Alabama State Grange. Other chapters deal with the later organizations of farmers.

Ashby, N. B. *The Riddle of the Sphinx. A discussion of the economic questions relating to agriculture, land, transportation, money, taxation, and cost of interchange: a consideration of possible remedies for existing inequalities, and an outline of the position of agriculture in the industrial world; with a comprehensive history of the leading farm organizations, their constitutions and by-laws.* Des Moines, 1890. 474 pp. L.C.

Bricktop (pseudonym of George C. Small). *Joining the Grangers; or trying to be a Patron of Husbandry.* New York, 1873. 64 pp. L.C. A comical account of the experiences of a politician among the Grangers.

Bronson, Henry. *Farmers' Unions and Tax Reform.* Jackson, Tennessee, 1873. 56 pp. W.H. Bronson was a member of the Douglas County, Kansas, Farmers' Union.

Butterfield, K. L. "Farmers' Social Organizations," in L. H. Bailey, *Cyclopedia of American Agriculture,* iv. 289–297 (New York, 1909). An excellent summary of the movement for rural organization. The period, 1870–92, is treated under the head of "The Farmers' Movement." The Grange, the Alliance, and minor organizations are outlined and the significance of the movement well brought out.

Butterfield, K. L. "The Grange," in *Forum,* xxxi, 231–242 (April, 1901). An exposition of the order, its aims and achievements, with the emphasis on the social and educational side.

Chamberlain, H. R. "Farmers' Alliance and other Political Parties," in *Chautauquan,* xiii. 338–342 (June, 1891). Sketches the career of the organization and discusses its influence on the political situation.

Chamberlain, H. R. *The Farmers' Alliance; what it aims to accomplish.* New York, 1891. 91 pp. Chamberlain was a reporter on the *New York Sun.* The book gives a succinct account of the origin and the growth of the Alliance, with platforms and other documents. Also treats of other organizations, especially the "Citizens' Alliance."

Coulter, John L. "Organization among the Farmers of the United States," in *Yale Review,* xviii. 273–298 (November, 1909). Based largely on Periam's *Groundswell.*

Cramer, J.A. *The Patrons' Pocket Companion.* Cincinnati,1875. 257 pp. L.C.

Darrow, J. W. *Origin and Early History of the Order of Patrons of Husbandry in the United States.* Chatham, New York, 1904. 56 pp. Based mainly on Kelley's work, with a chapter on "Achievements" in which the author claims everything from the interstate commerce act to the Sherman anti-trust law for the order.

Drew, Frank M. "The Present Farmers' Movement," in *Political Science Quarterly,* vi. 282–310 (June, 1891). Describes the various organizations, including the Grange, states their demands, and summarizes the results achieved.

Dunning, N. A., editor. *The Farmers' Alliance History and Agricultural Digest.* Washington, 1891. 742 pp. Contains much padding, but also a great deal of information about the alliances and other farmers' organizations, their origins, careers, and purposes.

Everitt, James A. *The American Society of Equity and its Need in our Country.* [1906 ?]. 15 pp. U. I. An address by the founder and president of the order at its annual session in St. Louis, October, 1906.

Everitt, James A. *The Third Power, Farmers to the Front.* Indianapolis, 1903. 275 pp. Deals with the American Society of Equity.

Geeslin, A. W., editor. *Exposition of the Grange.* Chicago, 1875. 96 pp. L.C.

Gladden, Washington. " The Embattled Farmers," in *Forum*, x. 315–322 (November, 1890). An account of the causes and objects of the Farmers' Alliance movement, with an estimate of its probable results.

Gracchus Americanus (pseudonym of T. S. Goodwin). *The Grange: a Study in the Science of Society.* New York, 1874. Copy in the Brooklyn Mercantile Library.

The Grangers, or Patrons of Husbandry; their textbook; including the complete secret work, with the illustrations of the signs of all the degrees. New York, [1875]. L.C., J.C.

" Granges and Farmers' Clubs in America," in *Cornhill*, xxviii. 556–567 (November, 1873). An inaccurate general account of the order and its manifestations in politics, and of railroad regulation in Illinois.

Grosh, Aaron B. *Mentor in the Granges and Homes of Patrons of Husbandry, designed to explain the Origin, Aims, and Government of the Order.* New York, 1876. 478 pp. L.C.

Gustin, M. E. *An Expose of the Grangers; containing the opening and closing ceremonies of a Grangers' lodge; the ceremonies of initiation, and the eight degrees of the order; being an accurate description of one of the greatest monopolies of the age.* Dayton, Ohio, 1875. 130 pp. A copy of this curious pamphlet was picked up by the writer in a second-hand book store. The first part purports to give the secret work of the Grange and this is followed by " Dr. J. Gustin's experience, confession, and burlesque on the Patrons of Husbandry."

Hall, Carrie A. *Songs for the Grange, set to music and dedicated to the order of Patrons of Husbandry in the United States.* New York, 1872. W.H.

An Historical Paper, showing the aims and objects of the order of Knights of Labor, as promulgated by the founder in 1869 — its growth and success caused by appealing to reason and not to passion. 4 pp. [1897 ?]. U.I.

Howland, Marie. " The Patrons of Husbandry," in *Lippincott's*, xii. 338–342 (September, 1873). A general account of the order for English readers. Deals particularly with the coöperative and social features.

Hudson, J. K. *The Patrons' Handbook; for the use and benefit of the order of the Patrons of Husbandry.* Topeka, Kansas, 1874. W.H. Hudson was editor of the *Kansas Farmer*. The book contains a large amount of material, partly documentary, relative to the Grange in Kansas, with some on the order in general.

Kelley, O. H. " Early Struggles of the Grange," in *American Grange Bulletin*, xxxiv. no. 9 (September 1, 1904). This is an address which was read at a Grange Chautauqua on August 20, 1904.

Kelley, O. H. " Grange History; Personal Reminiscences and Gossip of the Early Days," in *American Grange Bulletin*, xxxv. nos. 5–9 (1905). W. H.

Kelley, O. H. *Origin and Progress of the Order of Patrons of Husbandry in the United States; a History from 1866 to 1873.* Philadelphia, 1875. 441 pp. U. W., W. H., U. I. A detailed account of the inception and development of the order, with a large number of letters and other documents. Invaluable for the early history of the Grange.

List of Agricultural Societies and Farmers' Clubs . . . on the Books of the Department of Agriculture, July 4, 1876. Washington, 1876. 63 pp. (United States Department of Agriculture, *Reports*, no. 12.) Similar lists were issued for 1870 and 1872.

Martin, E. W. (pseudonym of J. D. McCabe). *History of the Grange Movement; or the Farmers' War against Monopolies; being a full and authentic account of the struggles of the American farmers against the extortions of the railroad companies; with a history of the rise and progress of the Order of Patrons of Husbandry, its objects, present condition and prospects; to which is added sketches of the leading Grangers.* Chicago, 1874. 544 pp. U.I., W.H. This work, which was gotten out at the height of the movement to be sold at subscription, is especially useful for giving an insight into the Grangers' point of view. Naturally, it is prejudiced, unreliable, and carelessly put together.

Messer, Alpha. *The Grange: its Advantages; what it has accomplished; what it hopes to accomplish; Organization of Granges; Declaration of Purposes.* Washington, 1895. 40 pp. L.C., W.H. Messer was lecturer of the National Grange and got out several editions of this pamphlet during the nineties. It is partly historical. In some editions, the title is *Benefits of the Grange*.

Morgan, John T. " The Danger of the Farmers' Alliance," in *Forum*, xii. 399–409 (November, 1891). Sympathizes with the farmers in their efforts to curb the power of monopoly, but fears that the movement is being discredited by intruders who hope to exploit their vagaries and their personal politics.

Morgan, W. S. *History of the Wheel and Alliance, and the impending Revolution.* St. Louis, 1891. 776 pp. W. H., J. C.

New York Tribune, publisher. *The Farmers' War: Letter from the Western States; the Rise, Progress, and Purpose of the Farmers' Granges.* (*New York Tribune Extra*, no. 13.) The writer has been unable to find this pamphlet but has seen several references to it. It was probably published early in 1874, and was all out of print by September, 1874.

Peffer, W. A. " The Farmers' Alliance," in *Cosmopolitan*, x. 694 (1885). Peffer was the editor of an agricultural paper and one of the leaders of the alliance movement in Kansas.

Peffer, W. A. " The Farmers' Defensive Movement," in *Forum*, viii. 463–473 (December, 1889). Sees the origin of the movement in the operations of " railroads, middlemen, and banks." Describes the Grange, the alliances, and other farmers' organizations.

Periam, Jonathan. *The Groundswell; a History of the Origin, Aims, and Progress of the Farmers' Movement: embracing an authentic account of farmers' clubs, granges, etc.; a full discussion of the transportation question and other grievances; and a history of industrial education in the United States, together with sketches of the lives of prominent leaders.* Cincinnati and Chicago, 1874. 576 pp. W.H., U.I. Like Martin's *Grange Movement*, this book was designed to be sold by subscription to farmers. It aims to present the farmers' side of the various questions and contains considerable documentary material, especially with reference to the movement in Illinois.

Pierson, Charles W. " The Rise of the Granger Movement," and " The Outcome of the Granger Movement," in *Popular Science Monthly*, xxxii. 199–208, 368–373 (December, 1887, January, 1888). The first article deals mainly with the railroad side of the movement and the second with coöperation. They are popular and unreliable.

Powderly, T. V. *Thirty Years of Labor, 1859–1889; in which the history of the attempts to form organizations of workingmen for the discussion of political, social, and economic questions is traced: the National Labor Union of 1866; the Industrial Brotherhood of 1874; and the order of the Knights of Labor of America and the World. . . .* Columbus, Ohio, 1890. 693 pp. U.I. Powderly was " Grand Master Workman " of the Knights of Labor for many years.

Root, George F., and Smith, Mrs. S. M. *The Trumpet of Reform; a collection of songs, hymns, charts, and set pieces for the grange, the club, and all industrial and reform organizations.* Cincinnati and Chicago, 1874. W.H.

Smedley, A. B. *Manual of Jurisprudence and Coöperation of the Patrons of Husbandry.* Des Moines, 1875. xvi, 200 pp. L.C. Smedley was a prominent Iowa Granger.

Smedley, A. B. *The Principles and Aims of the Patrons of Husbandry; their Origin, Rapid Growth, and General Statistics.* Burlington, Iowa, 1874. 44 pp. L.C.

Smith, Stephe. *Grains for the Grangers; discussing the Farmers' Movement for the Emancipation of White Slaves from the Power of Monopoly.* W.H.

Sovereigns of Industry. *Constitution of the Order . . . revised and adopted at the annual session of the National Council held at Philadelphia, Pennsylvania . . . 1875.* Worcester, Massachusetts, 1875. U.I.

Swalm, Mrs. Pauline. " The Granges of the Patrons of Husbandry," in *Old and New*, vii. 96–100 (1873). A brief and quite inaccurate account of the order.

Trimble, John. *An Address before the Patrons' Reunion at the Ohio State Fair, Columbus, Ohio, Thursday, September 5th, 1895.* Washington, 1895. 16 pp. U.I. Treats of the value of the order, especially along social and educational lines.

Walker, C. S. " The Farmers' Alliance," in *Andover Review*, xiv. 127–140 (August, 1890). A discussion of the agricultural situation is followed by a sympathetic exposition of the Alliance and its purposes.

Walker, C. S. " The Farmers' Movement," in *Annals of the American Academy*, iv. 790–798 (March, 1894). Treats the general farmers' movement under headings of organization, education, coöperation, political action. Suggestive also on agricultural conditions.

Wells, John G. *The Grange illustrated; or Patrons' Handbook, in the interests of the Order of Patrons of Husbandry; embracing the origin and history of the Order, constitutions, by-laws . . . together with valuable suggestions for farmers' every day wants.* New York, 1874. 184, 55, 48 pp. L.C., U.I.

Western Rural, publisher. *Rules of Order and Rallying Song-book; also History of the Farmers' Alliance movement, which began in 1880.* Chicago, 1882. U.I. Contains an account of the Northwestern alliance, which was the special protegé of the *Western Rural*. The songs included such titles as " Alliance Rallying Song " and " Justice and Freedom for the Farmers."

Whitehead, Mortimer. " The Grange in Politics," in *American Journal of Politics*, i. 113–123 (August, 1892). The author was lecturer of the National Grange.

Whitehead, Mortimer. " The Patrons of Husbandry," in New Jersey Bureau of Statistics of Labor and Industries, *Reports*, 333–350 (1886). General and sketchy account of the order and its work.

Whitehead, Mortimer. *A Silver Jubilee; Twenty-fifth Anniversary of the Organization of the First Farmers' Grange in the world; Fredonia, Chautauqua Co., N. Y., April 20 and 21, 1893.* Washington, 1893. 44 pp. U.I. Contains considerable material on the early history of the order, including an address by O. H. Kelley.

Woodman, J. J. " Early History and Reminiscences of the National Grange, Patrons of Husbandry," in *American Grange Bulletin*, xxx. no. 21, to xxxii. no. 3 (1900–02). Based mainly on the *Proceedings*, but contains some personal reminiscences.

LOCAL

The Connecticut Granges, edited by a committee of the Connecticut State Grange. New Haven, 1900. W.H. The Grange did not flourish in Connecticut until after 1880, so the book has to do mainly with the later aspects of the order. It opens with an account of the origin of the order, written by O. H. Kelley, which supplements his *Patrons of Husbandry* in one or two points.

Ellis, S. H. " Early History of the Grange in Ohio," in *Ohio Farmer*, c–cv (1900–04). Ellis was the most prominent man in Grange work in Ohio in the early years, being master of the state grange for several years. He makes use of the published proceedings and other documentary material.

Paine, A. E. *The Granger Movement in Illinois.* Urbana, Illinois, 1904. 53 pp. (University of Illinois, *Studies*, i. no. 8.) A useful but not very thorough study of the movement in a single state.

Butterfield, Kenyon L. "Recent Grange Work in Michigan," in *Outlook*, lx. 176–179 (September 17, 1898). Illustrates the influence of the order on state legislation and describes certain charitable and coöperative enterprises. The early career of the order is briefly sketched by way of introduction.

Lea, Charles W. *The Grange Movement in Wisconsin.* (University of Wisconsin, Ms. thesis, 1897.) U.W. Based largely upon a study of local papers.

Maynard, Myra Edith. *History of the Order of Patrons of Husbandry in Wisconsin up to 1875.* (University of Wisconsin, Ms. thesis, 1895.) U.W.

Smith, R. E. *Wisconsin Granger Movement.* (University of Wisconsin, Ms. thesis, 1895.) U.W. Goes into detail on the first few years of the order in the state. The bibliography mentions a series of letters, dated 1870–72, relating to early Grange history in Wisconsin in possession of S. C. Carr of Milton Junction, Wisconsin, also letters in possession of the author.

Carr, Ezra. *The Patrons of Husbandry on the Pacific Coast: being a complete history of the origin, condition, and progress of agriculture in different parts of the world; of the origin and the growth of the order of Patrons, with a general and special Grange directory, and full list of charter members of the subordinate granges of California; also, of the foes of the farmers, or monopolies of land, water, transportation and education; of a protective tariff, currency and banking.* San Francisco, 1875. 461 pp. U.W., W.H. Carr had been professor of agriculture in the University of California, but was removed in 1874. He was prominent in Grange circles. The book is an unscholarly hodge-podge, but illustrates the Grangers' point of view, and gives much documentary material on the movement in California.

History of the Grange in Canada, by a member of the Dominion Grange. Toronto, 1876. Pamphlet. H.C.

RAILROADS

GENERAL

The number of books dealing with the relations between railroads and the state is very large and most of them contain some reference to the Granger movement. No attempt is here made to list all such works, and many additional titles can be found in a bibliography compiled by the Bureau of Railway Economics and entitled: *Railway Economics; a Collective Catalogue of Books in Fourteen American Libraries* (Chicago, 1912. 446 pp.).

Adams, Alton D. "Reasonable Rates," in *Journal of Political Economy*, xii. 79–97 (December, 1903). Deals with the Granger cases and the later decisions of the Supreme Court which have swept away the power of the state to fix conclusive rates.

Adams, Charles F., Jr. *An Address, delivered at Oshkosh, Wis., Sept. 3, 1875.* " *Which will quickest solve the railroad question: force bills or public opinion ?* " n. p., n. d. 20 pp. H.C.

Adams, Charles F., Jr. " The Granger Movement," in *North American Review*, cxx. 394–424 (April, 1875). Probably the most widely known article on the railroad phase of the Granger movement. Mr. Adams looked upon the movement as a thing of the past and assumed to treat it " in a spirit of critical justice." Though he admitted that there were adequate causes for the movement in the abuses of railway management and that much good would probably result from it, still he made assumptions as to the character and effects of the Granger legislation which are not well founded.

Adams, Charles F., Jr. *Railroads; their Origin and Problems.* New York, 1878. 216 pp. A classic book on the subject. The abuses in railway organization and management are clearly set forth and it is admitted that the Granger movement was perhaps necessary for the purpose of bringing about a better understanding of the obligations of railway corporations to the public.

Adams, Charles F., Jr. " The State and the Railroads," in *Atlantic*, xxxvii. 360–371, 691–699, xxxviii. 72–85 (1876). The first article deals with the problem abroad, the others bring out the events which result from unrestrained competition and advocate consolidation as the remedy.

Adams, Henry C. "The Farmer and Railway Legislation," in *Century*, xxi. 780–783 (March, 1892). A statement of reasons why the farmer is especially affected by the railway problem and of the abuses in railway management, followed by an account of railway legislation in effect in 1892.

American Cheap Transportation Association. *National Convention . . . held at Washington, D. C., January 14th, 1874.* Troy, New York, 1874. 99 pp. U.I. Contains proceedings and numerous addresses, including those of Messrs. Flagg and Allen of Illinois.

American Board of Transportation and Commerce. *Report of the committee on railroad transportation . . . at the third annual convention of that body, held in Chicago, December 18th, 1875.* 15 pp. U.I. This was merely the American Cheap Transportation Association under another name. The committee was composed of five delegates from New York, Iowa, Kentucky, Illinois, and Indiana. The Iowa and Illinois representatives were A. B. Smedley and S. R. Moore, both of whom were prominent in the farmers' movement in their respective states.

Atkinson, Edward. *The Railroad and the Farmer, nos. one and two, and The Standard of Adequate Railroad Service.* New York, 1883. 56 pp. L.C., U.I. An argument against government control.

Atlantic Monthly. Editorials: " Railway Despotism," xxxi. 380–384 (March, 1875). " Report of the Erie Investigating Committee," xxxii. 124–128 (July, 1873). " Granges against the Railroads," xxxii. 508–512 (October, 1873). " Railway Stock and Stockholders," xxxii. 764–768 (December, 1873). These editorials bring out clearly a number of abuses in railway management; but the position is taken that it was the stockholders and not the western farmers who were injured. The cause of the farmers' movement is seen in a " glut in the grain market."

Cary, J. W. *The Organization and History of the Chicago, Milwaukee and St. Paul Railway Company.* Milwaukee, 1873. 392 pp. J.C. Cary was general counsel for the company in the early days, and his book throws a strong light on early methods of railway financiering.

Clark, Frederick C. " State Railroad Commissions, and how they may be made effective," in American Economic Association, *Publications*, vi. no. 6, pp. 473–583 (November, 1891). The Granger agitation is said to be " the real beginning of an enlightened public opinion on the railroad question." The work of the Illinois commission is treated at some length.

Coleman, John A. " The Fight of a Man with a Railroad," and " My Railroad Fight in and out of Court," in *Atlantic*, xxx. 641–653, xxxi. 610–618 (December, 1872, May, 1873). Illustrates what Charles Francis Adams, Jr., termed " bad manners " on the part of railway employees and officials.

Cook, William W. *The Corporation Problem.* New York, 1893. 262 pp. Sets forth the abuses in railway management and the dangers to be feared from the increased power of corporations. Cook was a New York lawyer and had written a treatise on corporation law.

[Cullom Committee.] *Report of the Select Committee on Interstate Commerce.* Washington, 1886. 2 vols. (49 Congress, 1 session, *Senate Reports*, no. 46.) The report contains a useful summary of state railway legislation, and some of the testimony in the second volume relates to the Granger legislation.

Davis, C. W. " The Farmer, the Investor, and the Railway," in *Arena*, iii. 291–313 (February, 1891). Discusses railway profits and discriminations and favors government control.

Detrick, Charles R. " The Effects of the Granger Acts," in *Journal of Political Economy*, xi. 237–256 (March, 1903). A careful statistical study. See above, p. 235.

Dunbar, William H. " State Regulation of Prices and Rates," in *Quarterly Journal of Economics*, xi. 305–332 (April, 1895). Discusses the Granger cases and later decisions along the same line.

Edsall, James K. " The Granger Cases and the Police Power," in American Bar Association, *Reports*, x. 288–316 (1887). Bases the right of the state to regulate railroads upon the inherent power of every government to protect its citizens; in other words, upon the police power. Edsall was attorney-general of Illinois at the time the Granger cases were being tried in that state.

Fink, Albert. *Cost of Railroad Transportation; Railroad Accounts and Government Regulation of Railroad Tariffs.* Louisville, 1875. 48 pp. L.C., W.H. An argument against government control of railroad rates by the president of the Louisville and Nashville Railway Company.

Grosvenor, W. M. " The Communist and the Railway," in *International Review*, iv. 585–599 (September, 1877). Calls the Granger legislation communistic and assigns it as the principal cause of the panic of 1873.

Grosvenor, W. M. " The Railroads and the Farms," in *Atlantic*, xxxii. 591–610 (November, 1873). A discussion of the relation of railroad rates to land values. The *pro rata* idea is condemned, and the blame for high local rates placed upon the tariff on iron.

Hadley, Arthur T. *Railroad Transportation, its History and its Laws.* New York, 1885. 269 pp. Accepts fully the railroad claims as to the effects of the Granger legislation. See above, p. 234, note 1.

Hadley, Arthur T. " The Railway in its Business Relations," in *The American Railway, its Construction, Development and Appliances*, 344–369 (New York, 1889). Contains an exaggerated statement of the disastrous effects of the Granger laws.

Haines, Henry S. *The Railroads and the State.* 1879. Pamphlet. W.H. Opposed to government regulation of railroad rates.

Haney, L. H. *A Congressional History of Railways in the United States, 1850–1887.* Madison, Wisconsin, 1910. 335 pp. (University of Wisconsin, *Bulletins*, Economics and Political Science Series, vi. no. 1.) A detailed study of the railway question in Congress. Contains a chapter on " Congress and the Granger Movement " but this period is also partially treated in other chapters. The arrangement is somewhat confusing.

Hanson, Burton. *Unfair Railway Agitation.* [Chicago, 1905.] 52 pp. U.I. See above, p. 235, note 4.

Hassler, Charles W. *Railroad Rings.* New York, 1876. Pamphlet. H.C. A paper read before the American Social Science Association, September 8, 1876.

Hendrick, Frank. *Railway Control by Commissions.* New York, 1900. 161 pp. The Granger laws are condemned and the conventional view of their disastrous effects is set forth. The supervisory commission of the Massachusetts type is preferred to the Granger commissions.

[Hepburn Committee.] *Proceedings of the special Committee on Railroads appointed under Resolution of the Assembly to investigate alleged abuses in the management of railroads chartered by the state of New York.* New York, 1789. 5 vols. Throws a flood of light on the abuses in railway management.

House Committee on Roads and Canals. *Regulation and Control of Railroads.* Washington, 1868. 20 pp. (40 Congress, 2 session, *House Reports*, no. 57, serial no. 1352.) This was the first report ever made to Congress on the subject.

Hudson, James F. *The Railways and the Republic.* New York, 1889. 532 pp. A strong indictment of the railroads.

James, Edmund J. " The Agitation for the Federal Regulation of Railways," in American Economic Association, *Publications*, ii. no. 3, pp. 344–395 (July, 1887). An account of the early abuses in railway management is followed by a sketch of the activity of Congress in the direction of railway regulation.

Johnson, Emory R. *American Railway Transportation.* 2d ed., rev., New York, 1908. 434 pp. One of the best books on the subject. Contains a brief but accurate and unprejudiced account of the Granger movement for railway regulation.

Kupka, P. F. *Die Verkehrsmittel in den Vereinigten Staaten von Nord-Amerika.* Leipzig, 1883. x, 413 pp. Contains an account of the Granger movement and the railway legislation of Illinois.

La Follette, Robert M. *Railway Regulation, State and Interstate.* Chicago, 1905. 115 pp. See above, p. 235, note 4.

Langstroth, Charles S., and Stilz, Wilson. *Railway Coöperation.* Philadelphia, 1899. xv, 210 pp. The Granger legislation is treated in the second part by Mr. Stilz with the conventional view of its disastrous effects.

Larrabee, William. *The Railway Question; a Historical and Practical Treatise on Railroads, and Remedies for their Abuses.* 11th ed., Chicago, 1906 (copyright, 1893). 488 pp. Larrabee was a member of the Iowa legislature during the Granger legislation in that state. The book is unscientific; but it makes clear the evils complained of, and throws light on the legislation of Iowa.

McLean, Simon J. " State Regulation of Railways in the United States," in *Economic Journal*, 349–369 (September, 1900). A useful summary, containing a succinct and fairly accurate account of the Granger legislation.

May, Charles S. *The Farmers' Movement; an address delivered at the St. Clair County Fair at Port Huron, Michigan, Thursday, October 14, 1874.* Kalamazoo, Michigan, 1875. 4 pp. W.H. Deals principally with the railroad question and takes exception to the statements by C. F. Adams, Jr., in " The Granger Movement," which appeared in the *North American Review* of the preceding April.

Meyer, B. H. *Railway Legislation in the United States.* New York, 1903. 329 pp. Discusses the Granger movement incidentally as one of the events leading up to the interstate commerce act.

Meyer, Hugo R. *Government Regulation of Railway Rates.* New York, 1905. xxvii, 486 pp. Opposed to government regulation. Treats the Granger agitation as one of the " growing pains of progress."

The Nation. Editorial and miscellaneous articles.

" The ' Farmers' Clubs ' and the Railroads," xvi. 249 (April 10, 1873).

" Transportation and the Tariff," xvi. 296 (May 1, 1873).

" The Latest Reform Movement," xvi. 329 (May 15, 1873).

" The Causes of the Farmers' Discontent," xvi. 381 (June 5, 1873).

" The ' Grangers ' and the Judges," xvi. 397 (June 12, 1873).

" The Latest Device for Fixing Rates of Transportation," xvii. 36 (July 17, 1873).

" Another Aspect of the Farmers' Movement," xvii. 68 (July 31, 1873).

" Agricultural Exposition of Corporate Law," xvii. 140 (August 28, 1873).

" The Next Descent upon the Treasury," xvii. 156 (September 4, 1873).

" A Few Words to Railroad Moralists," xvii. 220 (October 2, 1873).

" The Watered-Stock Hallucination," xvii. 237 (October 9, 1873).

" The Railroad Mystery," xvii. 285 (October 30, 1873).

" The Farmers' Future," xviii. 55 (January 22, 1874).

" Congress and the Railways," xviii. 87 (February 5, 1874).

" Railroad Evolution," xviii. 120 (February 19, 1874).

" The Cheap Transportation Report," xviii. 294 (May 7, 1874).

" Corporations and Monopolies," xviii. 359 (June 4, 1874).

" The Granger Method of Reform," xix. 36 (July 16, 1874).

" The Right to Confiscate," xix. 199 (September 24, 1874).

" Potter and His Law," xix. 231 (October 8, 1874).

" The Farmers and the Supreme Court," xx. 53 (January 28, 1875).

" The Farmer as a ' Mediaeval Baron,' " xxi. 145 (September 2, 1875).

" A General Regulation Act," xxi. 384 (December 16, 1875).

" The Granger Collapse," xxii. 57 (January 27, 1876).

" The Last Railroad Grievance," xxii. 189 (March 23, 1876).

" The Granger Decisions," xxiv. 143 (March 8, 1877).

" The Granger Theory applied to the Grangers," xxvii. 37 (July 18, 1878).

" The Farm Change in Politics," lii. 453 (June 4, 1891).

These articles together with the briefer paragraph editorials scattered through the *Nation* are largely responsible for the long prevalent idea of the Granger movement as a dishonest attempt of the western farmers to confiscate railroad property by securing control of the legislatures and the courts.

Railroad Companies. *Annual Reports to the Stockholders.* Some of these contain discussions of the Granger legislation from the railroad standpoint. The most significant are: Chicago, Burlington, and Quincy, 1874, 1876; Chicago and Northwestern, 1874–76; Chicago, Milwaukee, and St. Paul, 1874, 1875.

Ringwalt, John L. *Development of Transportation Systems in the United States.* Philadelphia, 1888. 398 pp. The Granger legislation is treated at some length and the abuses in railway construction and management are brought out; but the laws themselves are looked upon as attempts " to compel railways to render services for inadequate compensation."

Sanborn, J. B. *Congressional Grants of Land in Aid of Railways.* Madison, Wisconsin, 1899. 130 pp. (University of Wisconsin, *Bulletins*, Economics, Political Science, and History Series, ii. no. 3.) The standard work on the subject. Useful for an understanding of the railway situation during the Granger period.

Seligman, Edwin R. A. " Railway Tariffs and the Interstate Commerce Law," in *Political Science Quarterly*, ii. 222–264, 369–413 (June, September, 1887). The Granger movement is discussed as one of the origins of the commission system of government control. The conclusions that " the Granger movement was economically as unwise as it was politically important and successful " and that " the compulsory commissions were an avowed failure," are stronger statements than the facts would seem to warrant.

Senate Committee on Commerce. *Rates of Freight on Railroads.* Washington, 1873. 20 pp. (42 Congress, 3 session, *Senate Reports*, no. 462, serial no. 1550.)

Seymour, Charles. " A Western View of Interstate Transportation," in *Atlantic*, xxx. 345–351 (September, 1872). Maintained that transportation rates were too high and favored the construction of canals.

Smalley, Harrison S. " Railway Rate Control in its Legal Aspects," in American Economic Association, *Publications*, series 3, vii. no. 2, pp. 327–473 (1905). The Granger cases are discussed at some length.

Stanwood, E. " Farmers and Railroads," in *Old and New*, vii. 335–342 (September, 1873). A general consideration of railway abuses and their effect on the farmer.

Stickney, Albert B. *The Railway Problem*, St. Paul, 1891. 249 pp. The author was president of the Chicago and Great Western Railway Company; but his book is a tremendous indictment of railway management, and sustains many of the charges of the farmers as well as the justice of the Granger legislation.

Stickney, Albert B. *State Control of Trade and Commerce by National or State Authority*. New York, 1897. xiv, 202 pp. Discusses the Granger cases as establishing the right of the state to control public employment.

Thompson, J. Q. *The Farmers' Fight against the Railroads; an Impartial View of the Merits of the Quarrel; Facts and Figures for the Calm Consideration of Honest Men*. Indianapolis, 1874. 16 pp. L.C.

Van Oss, Steven F. *American Railroads as Investments; a Handbook for Investors in American Railway Securities*. New York, 1893. 815 pp. Railway abuses and the Granger legislation are summarized. The treatment is fair in spite of some inaccuracies.

Wells, David A. " How will the United States Supreme Court Decide the Granger Railroad Cases ? " in *Nation*, xix. 282–284 (October 29, 1874). Relying upon the Dartmouth decision and the fourteenth amendment to the constitution, Mr. Wells expected the decision to be adverse to the laws.

Wharton, Francis. " Retrospective Legislation and Grangerism," in *International Review*, iii. 50–63 (January, 1876). A judicial discussion leading to the conclusion that the Granger laws were invalid.

[Windom Committee.] *Report of the Select Committee on Transportation Routes to the Seaboard*. Washington, 1874. 2 vols. (43 Congress, 1 session, *Senate Reports*, no. 307.) The second volume, " Testimony," contains statements of W. C. Flagg, President of the Illinois State Farmers' Association and Samuel P. Tufts, both representing the Northwestern Farmers' Convention which met at Chicago, October 22–23, 1873. The entire proceedings of this convention are also incorporated in the volume. On the report proper see above, pp. 220–222.

Yesterday and Today; a History of the Chicago and Northwestern Railway Company. Chicago, 1905. 124 pp. Contains extracts from the annual reports relative to the Granger legislation.

LOCAL

Gordon, J. H. *Illinois Railway Legislation and Commission Control since 1870*. Urbana, 1904. 81 pp. (University of Illinois, *Studies*, i. no. 6.) Valuable, but does not exhaust the material.

Newton, Fred E. *Railway Legislation in Illinois from 1828 to 1870*. (University of Illinois, Ms. theses, 1901.) U.I.

Adams, Edward F. "The Wisconsin Method of Railway Reform," and "The Granger Morality," in *Nation*, xix. 121, 234–236 (August 20, October 8, 1874). Mr. Adams defends the Wisconsin "Reformers" whom the *Nation* had charged with dishonesty. He also gives an account of the way in which the Potter law was passed.

Carpenter, Matthew H. *Speech on the Power of the Legislature to Govern Corporations.* 1874. Pamphlet. W.H. Senator Carpenter early affirmed the right of a state to regulate railroads.

Cary, John W. *Brief in the Case of the State of Wisconsin vs. Chicago, Milwaukee, and St. Paul Railway Company.* n. p., [1874]. 40 pp. W. H. This was one of the Granger cases. Cary was counsel for the railroad company.

Flower, Frank A. *Life of Matthew Hale Carpenter.* Madison, Wisconsin, 1883. 584 pp. L.C., W.H. Brings out the connection of Senator Carpenter with railroad legislation and litigation in Wisconsin.

A Granger (pseudonym). "Good and Bad Grangers," in *Nation*, xx. 241 (April 8, 1875). Reply to the letter of F. R. Leland on the "Second Stage of Wisconsin Railroad Legislation." Denies that the order of Patrons of Husbandry was responsible for the legislation.

Howe, James H. *Statement in behalf of the Chicago and Northwestern Railroad Company relative to Assembly Bill no. 260, relating to Railroad Tariffs.* Chicago, 1870. Pamphlet. W.H. Argument against a bill pending in the Wisconsin legislature.

Hoyt, John W. "Second Stage of Wisconsin Railroad Legislation," in *Nation*, xx. 275 (April 22, 1875). Hoyt was a member of the railroad commission of Wisconsin. This is a reply to charges made by F. R. Leland of Lacrosse in a letter published under the same heading in an earlier number of the *Nation*.

Keep, Albert, and Mitchell, Alexander. *Memorial of the Chicago and Northwestern and the Chicago, Milwaukee, and St. Paul Railway Companies to the Senate and Assembly of the State of Wisconsin.* 1875. Pamphlet. W.H. An appeal for relief from the Potter law.

Lawrence, C. B., and Cook, B. C. *Brief in the Case of the State of Wisconsin vs. Chicago and Northwestern Railway Company.* Chicago, [1874]. 4 pp. W.H.

Leland, F. R. "The Second Stage of Wisconsin Railroad Legislation," in *Nation*, xx. 189, 313 (March 18, May 6, 1875). The first letter purports to be an account of the way in which the Grangers controlled the legislature of 1875 and prevented any just amendment of the Potter law; the second is a rejoinder to a reply by Commissioner Hoyt of Wisconsin to the first.

Orton, H. S. *Brief in the Case of the State of Wisconsin ex rel. Attorney-General vs. the Chicago and Northwestern Railway Company.* n. p., [1874]. 42 pp. W.H.

Pope, Carl C., and another. *Railroads are Private Property and Subject to Legislative Control.* Lacrosse, Wisconsin, 1869. Pamphlet. W.H. A reprint of newspaper correspondence discussing the legal character of railroads.

Smith and Lamb. *Brief in the Case of State of Wisconsin vs. the Chicago and Northwestern Railway Company.* n. p., [1874]. 29 pp. W.H. The injunction case.

The Wisconsin Railroad Law: Letter of Hon. Alex. Mitchell, Pres't C. M. & St. P. R'y; Letter of Albert Keep, President C. & N.-W. Railway; Opinion of Honorable B. R. Curtis; Opinion of Honorable Wm. M. Evarts. n. p., [1874]. Pamphlet. W.H. One of the documents used in the campaign for the repeal of the Potter law.

Wisconsin Granger (pseudonym). " The Grange and the Potter Law," in *International Review*, iii. 665–673 (September, 1876). A reply to a previous article by Francis Wharton in the same review. Throws light on the Granger legislation in Wisconsin.

Saby, Rasmus S. *Railroad Legislation in Minnesota, 1849 to 1875.* St. Paul, 1912. 188 pp. A University of Pennsylvania thesis reprinted from Minnesota Historical Society, *Collections*, xv. Besides an exhaustive account of the Granger railway legislation in Minnesota, the work contains a treatment of the beginnings of the order of Patrons of Husbandry and a useful bibliography. It did not come to hand until the present work was in press.

Aldrich, Charles R. " Repeal of the Granger Law in Iowa," in *Iowa Journal of History and Politics*, iii. 256–270 (April, 1905). An account of the way in which the Illinois Central Railway Company created sentiment in favor of the repeal of the Iowa law. Aldrich acted as agent of the company in this connection.

Dey, Peter A. "Railroad Legislation in Iowa," in *Iowa Historical Record*, ix. 555 (October, 1893). Dey was railroad commissioner in Iowa after the Granger period. He did not believe in the Granger method of regulation.

Dixon, Frank H. *State Railroad Control, with a History of its Development in Iowa.* New York, 1896. 251 pp. The treatment of the Granger period is brief and unsatisfactory.

Allen, Thomas. *The Railroad Problem*, 1875. Pamphlet. W.H. Denounces the attempt of Missouri to regulate railroad rates.

Dixon, Frank H. " Railroad Control in Nebraska," in *Political Science Quarterly*, xiii. 617–647 (December, 1898). The Granger period and the constitution of 1875 are briefly treated.

Warner, Amos G. " Railroad Problems in a Western State," in *Political Science Quarterly*, vi (March, 1891). A clear statement of the railway abuses and attempts at regulation in Nebraska.

Alexander, E. P. *Reply to Circular No. 19 of the Railroad Commission of Alabama.* Louisville, 1881. 20 pp. L.C., W.H. Denounces the attempt of Alabama to regulate railway charges.

COÖPERATION

Adams, Herbert B., editor. *History of Coöperation in the United States.* Baltimore, 1888. 540 pp. (Johns Hopkins University, *Studies*, vi.) This is itself a coöperative work; but it is by no means an adequate history of the subject. The various parts are also listed separately.

Bemis, Edward W. *Coöperation in New England.* Baltimore, 1888. (Johns Hopkins University, *Studies*, vi. nos. 1–2, pp. 11–134.) Contains a brief account of Grange coöperation in New England, mainly, however, of the period since 1880.

Catalogue of Prices at which Goods will be Sold to Patrons of Husbandry by Elrich and Company, Managers of the Business-Sales Department of the Patrons' Gazette. New York, 1875. (Supplement to the *Patrons' Gazette*, ii. no. 12.) W.H.

Coulter, John L. *Coöperation among Farmers, the Keystone of Rural Prosperity.* New York, Sturgis & Walton, 1911, vii, 281 pp. Deals mainly with the present, but contains a few references to the Granger attempts at coöperation.

Dunn County (Wisconsin) Council, Patrons of Husbandry. *Constitution and By-laws of the Coöperative Council of Dunn County Patrons of Husbandry.* Neenah, Wisconsin, 1875. Pamphlet. W.H.

Flower, Frank A. " Coöperation in the United States and Coöperation in Wisconsin," in Wisconsin Bureau of Labor and Industrial Statistics, *Reports*, ii. parts iii–iv. 117–237 (1876).

Foster, Florence J. " The Grange and the Coöperative Enterprises in New England," in *Annals of the American Academy*, iv. 798–805 (March, 1894). Very general on coöperative stores, agencies, and insurance.

Hill, W. H. *Revised and Consolidated Confidential Price List and Grange Book of References of the Ohio State Grange, Patrons of Husbandry; compiled and published by Authority of the State Executive Committee.* Sharonville, Ohio, 1876. W.H. Hill conducted the business agency of the Ohio State Grange.

Kentucky State Grange. *Circular Letter No. 1, January 19, 1876.* W.H. Relates to coöperative plans.

Leavitt, Samuel. *Township Coöperation; the Legitimate Fruit of the Protectionist Theory; also the History of American Socialism; Two Lectures delivered before the New York Liberal Club.* Pamphlet. W.H. Contains a section entitled " The Great Farmers' League," which deals with Grange coöperation in Iowa.

Morsell, James N., publisher. *The Grangers' Friend; a Business Guide to Baltimore, comprising a Descriptive List of the most Reliable and Fair Dealing Mercantile Houses in the City.* Baltimore, 1875. 112 pp. L.C.

National Grange. *Rules for Patrons' Coöperative Associations of the Order of Patrons of Husbandry, and Directions for Organizing such Associations; recommended by the National Grange, November, 1875.* Louisville, Kentucky, 1876. W.H.

Nieuwland, E. J. *The Grangers' Glucose Company; a very Safe and most Profitable Investment for Farmers.* New York, 1874. Circular. W.H. Capital, one hundred and fifty thousand dollars in shares of fifty, one hundred, five hundred, and a thousand dollars; dividends, forty-six per cent.

Nieuwland, E. J. *High Interest Monopoly and its Remedies; dedicated to Patrons of Husbandry.* New York, 1874. Folder. W.H. A prospectus for a " Granger's mortgage bank " in New York.

Patrons' Aid Society of Elmira, New York. *By-laws . . . adopted December 24, 1874.* Elmira, New York, 1875. *By-laws . . . as amended March 16, 1876.* Elmira, New York, 1876. *Sixth Annual Report.* Elmira, New York, 1881. W.H.

Patrons' Benevolent Aid Society of Wisconsin, *Annual Circular with Articles of Incorporation and By-laws.* Madison, 1878. 16 pp. W.H.

Patrons' New York Business Directory; a List of Leading Business Houses and Manufacturers in New York City, to be filed for Reference in each Grange Room in the United States and Canada. New York, [1876 ?]. W.H. No indication is given of the authority by which this directory was issued.

Randall, Daniel R. *Coöperation in Maryland and the South.* Baltimore, 1888. (Johns Hopkins University, *Studies*, vi. nos. 11–12, pp. 483–528). The section on "Distributive Coöperation" contains a good account of Grange coöperation in Texas.

St. Louis (Missouri) Grange Coöperative Store. *Constitution.* Pamphlet. W.H.

Shaw, Albert. *Coöperation in the Northwest.* Baltimore, 1888. (Johns Hopkins University, *Studies*, vi. nos. 4–6, pp. 193–360.) Contains a few pages on the origin, character, and significance of the Granger movement, which are suggestive. Also treats briefly of Grange coöperation in Wisconsin and Iowa.

Warner, Amos G. *Three Phases of Coöperation in the West.* Baltimore, 1888. (Johns Hopkins University, *Studies*, vi. nos. 7–8, pp. 361–440.) Also in American Economic Association, *Publications*, ii. no. 1, pp. 1–119 (1888). The first part, entitled "Coöperation among Farmers," deals almost entirely with Grange coöperation in Ohio, Indiana, Michigan, Illinois, Kansas, and Nebraska. The discussion of causes of failure and residual benefits is suggestive.

Winnebago County (Wisconsin) Council, Patrons of Husbandry. *Trading card* (issued to J. H. Osborn), April 11, 1874. W.H. Illustrates one form of coöperation practised by the Granges in the neighborhood of Oshkosh, Wisconsin.

Winnebago County (Wisconsin) Industrial and Provident Society. *Application for shares.* W.H.

Winnebago County (Wisconsin) Industrial and Provident Society. *Articles of Association.* Oshkosh, 1878. Pamphlet. W.H. This was a Grange coöperative organization in Oshkosh.

Wright, J. W. A. *Address on Rochdale and Grange Coöperation and other Grange Topics.* [1877 ?] Pamphlet. W.H.

Wright, J. W. A. *Coöperation; Europe and the Grange.* 1876. Pamphlet. W.H. An address delivered at the Patrons' centennial encampment at Philadelphia in 1876. Wright had been in Europe as agent of the National Grange.

INDEX

INDEX

Abbot, J. C., organizes granges, 54, 62.

Aberdeen (Miss.), grange organized, 51.

Absentee ownership of railroads, 13.

Ackley, Chicago, Milwaukee, and St. Paul Railroad Company v., 211.

Adams, A. D., " Reasonable Rates," 341.

Adams, C. F., Jr., books and articles on railroads, 342.

Adams, D. W., secretary Waukon (Ia.) Grange, 47; master Iowa State Grange, 50; master National Grange, 58; revokes dispensation Boston Grange, 62; advocates railroad regulation, 224; influence on Sovereigns of Industry, 306 note 2.

Adams, E. F., *Wisconsin Method of Railway Reform*, 348.

Adams, H. B., ed., *Coöperation in the United States*, 349.

Adams, H. C., " The Farmer and Railway Legislation," 342.

Adams County (Wis.), granges organized, 50.

Adams County Press (Friendship, Wis.), 329.

Agricultural and Mechanical College of Ohio, 292.

Agricultural clubs, *see* Farmers' clubs.

Agricultural colleges, land grants, 26; attitude of National Grange, 292. *See also* Agricultural education.

Agricultural Congress, organized, 78.

Agricultural discontent, 3; in East, 5; in prairie states, 7; bibliography, 331–333.

Agricultural education, gifts by Congress misapplied, 37; advocated by Grange, 64, 104, 292.

Agricultural fairs, encouraged by Grange, 293.

Agricultural organization, arguments for,

39; before the Civil War, 40; bibliography, 317–321, 335–341. *See also* Farmers' Alliance, Farmers' clubs, Patrons of Husbandry.

Agricultural population, proportion of granges to, 58 ff.

Agricultural press, 38; supports Grange, 44, 46, 49, 52; increased circulation, 287.

Agricultural products, statistics (1866–80), 28–34.

Agricultural Wheel, 304; bibliography, 338.

Agriculture, relative status, 3; in East, 4; in South, 5–7; in upper Mississippi Valley, 7; in Far West, 8; effect of panic of 1873, 20; inflation following Civil War, 24–31; technical advance, 27; proportion of population engaged in, 35; efforts of Grange to advance, 293–297.

Aiken, D. W., Grange deputy, 55; officer National Grange, 58, 256; pushes department of agriculture bill, 118; editor *Rural Carolinian*, 328; *The Grange*, 335.

Alabama, railroad regulation, 202, 203; flood sufferers, 283; bibliography, 319, 321, 335, 349.

Alabama Patrons of Husbandry, first granges, 56; statistics, 58 ff.; growth, 59; influence on legislation, 108; business agency, 253; coöperative stores, 265; insurance, 273 note 9; schools, 291; encourage immigration, 297.

Alabama State Grange, organized, 63; influences legislation, 108; advocates return of cotton tax, 117; establishes agencies, 253.

Aldrich, C. R., " Repeal of the Granger Law in Iowa," 349.

Women's Christian Temperance Union, 297.

Wood, Judge (Ill.), decision in railroad case, 140.

Woodburn, J. A., *Political Parties*, 333.

Woodman, J. J., "Early History and Reminiscences of the National Grange," 340.

Wooten, D. G., ed., *Texas*, 335.

Workingman's Advocate (and Anti-Monopolist) (Chicago), 324.

Workingmen, influence of Granger movement on organization, 306–308.

Workingmen's party (Calif.), organized, 99; influence in constitutional convention, 198.

Wright, Dr. O. W., comments on Potter law, 183 note 1; editor *Western Journal of Agriculture*, 329.

Wright, J. W. A., author of "Declaration of Purposes of the National Grange," 64; *Rochdale and Grange Coöperation*, 351; *Coöperation; Europe and the Grange*, 351.

Xenia (O.), state grange session, 121, 298.

Yesterday and Today; History of the Northwestern Railway, 347.

Ypsilanti (Mich.), grange agency, 248.